Family Law
IN JAMAICA

Family Law
IN JAMAICA

Fara Brown

The Caribbean Law
PUBLISHING COMPANY

First published in Jamaica, 2018 by
The Caribbean Law Publishing Company
an imprint of Ian Randle Publishers

16 Herb McKenley Drive
Box 686
Kingston 6
www.ianrandlepublishers.com

© Fara Brown
ISBN: 978-976-8167-91-0

National Library of Jamaica Cataloguing-In-Publication Data

Brown, Fara
    Family law in Jamaica / Fara Brown

    p. ; cm
Bibliography : p.
ISBN 978-976-8167-91-0 (pbk)

1. Domestic relations – Jamaica
2. Marriage law
3. Parent and child (Law)
I. Title

346.015   dc 23

Cover and Publication Design
by The Caribbean Law Publishing Company
Printed in the United States of America

For Dennis
1949–2014

Contents

Table of Cases

Table of Statutes

Acknowledgements

My sincere thanks to a whole host of legal and non-legal people who wittingly and sometimes unwittingly stimulated, challenged and encouraged me in the course of writing this book:

Stephen Vasciannie who made it happen.

Eileen Boxhill who gave me the benefit of her extraordinary and extensive knowledge and went out of her way despite numerous commitments and personal challenges to give shape and meaning to the text.

Tracy Robinson who at the initiation and conclusion of my writing provided invaluable and incisive advice and comments.

Lynette Joseph-Brown who was always available with a realistic, workable perspective as each development arose. Dennis would be so proud of us.

Then there was: Saverna Chambers, Sherry-Ann McGregor, Marjorie Shaw, Beverley Bryan, Marlyn Delisser, Janet Daley Powell of the Supreme Court Library and Debbie Ann Lynch Witter.

A special mention to Dorcas White, Senior Tutor Emerita of the Norman Manley Law School, for getting me over the last hump and telling me to 'Get it to the publishers and let it go!'

Of course it would be remiss of me not to express my gratitude to the Principal, staff and students of the Norman Manley Law School; and Christine Randle who believed in my vision and waited patiently for it to come into being.

Finally to my mother, Lena Bell who at 92 has made it clear that her only remaining life's wish is to hold my book in her hands: Here it is.

Fara Brown
September 2018

Introduction

    Those engaged in the study and practice of family law in Jamaica occupy all tiers of legal knowledge and understanding, from the secondary school students doing 'CAPE' or 'A' levels who ponder entering the legal profession to the seasoned judge or practitioner who is faced with a novel point law that must be researched.

    The first experience I had with practising family law in the Caribbean was when I worked at the Kingston Legal Aid Clinic in Jamaica. Working there was a steep learning curve that involved daily attendance in court to obtain decrees in undefended divorce cases. I relied heavily on my skills as an advocate which had been honed in the criminal courts and picked up a thing or two by overhearing conversations between other attorneys that often sounded vaguely familiar to what I had learnt when reading for my LLB in London. As with most courts around the world, much of the day-to-day family hearings that take place at both court tiers proceed with little or no reference to case law because the system assumes certain knowledge, which need not be restated.

    At the Norman Manley Law School (NMLS) Legal Aid Clinic, once again doing divorce cases, I was happy to find myself so closely aligned to the classroom and seized the invitation to teach a tutorial in family practice and procedure. For any practitioner, the most valuable way of developing knowledge of the law – other than the time-honoured method of sitting in court – is to teach. All of the associate tutors at the NMLS who either practise or preside in court will attest that teaching law provides such rigorous exposure that it will usually have a telling impact on the way you carry out your professional duties. At NMLS, as a regional institution, students from five or six other Caribbean countries will be in attendance in any given year and, as such, teachers at the school are expected to have (or at least acquire) some knowledge of the law and procedure in these other jurisdictions. This comparative context within which Caribbean academic lawyers must thrive is exceptional. It is a reflection of the way that legal professional training was established in the Caribbean and is still seen at the undergraduate level in the University of the West Indies.

While I was teaching at the law school, I also began to tutor students who were reading for the London External LLB and, taught English family law to those students. This gave me another perspective on how family law in Jamaica had come to be what it is today.

There have been many papers, articles, dissertations, and reports on different aspects of Jamaican family law. We, as a profession, whether practitioners, judges, teachers, or as students, have a fair amount to say about the law, but the discipline required to capture the law in the form of a book frequently eludes us. I fully understand why. This endeavour has not been an overnight escapade, but I firmly believe that to seriously make a contribution to developing the legal system we must bite the bullet and do the best. I do not profess to have produced the definitive tome on family law in Jamaica; many will find something in the book with which to vehemently disagree or to dismiss outright, but it remains my fervent wish that some may find it enlightening.

Some fundamental and possibly controversial matters of methodology have to be addressed, for example: What is the role of 'foreign' law in a book whose professed emphasis is on the local law of Jamaica?

More than five decades after Jamaica became independent, there is no doubt that Commonwealth Caribbean Jurisprudence is well established. Indeed, the creation and exemplary operation of the Caribbean Court of Justice lays to rest any lingering doubts in that regard. So to what extent do laws and decisions of the court in other Caribbean jurisdictions have a place for consideration in this text?

One thing that must be considered when addressing this, is that no matter how litigious the people of one Caribbean island or another may consider themselves to be, the population usually does not have the capacity to generate the breadth of legal questions for the courts to rule on, to the extent that a comprehensive body of case law will be formed. So, from a practical standpoint, we must rely on each other, and since we have similar laws and similar societal contexts, it makes sense to be receptive to the persuasive nature of rulings from Jamaica's closest Commonwealth neighbours.

That said, this is not a comparative work and as such a balance has to be struck between substantively Jamaican content and a book on Commonwealth Caribbean family law. In any event, Karen Nunez Tesheira's book, *Commonwealth Caribbean Family Law, Husband, Wife and Cohabitant*, more than adequately covers that niche, and will no doubt be followed by an equally comprehensive coverage of the law in relation to children. On the other hand, I have tried to use case law and the laws themselves from other Caribbean countries only as a means of putting Jamaican law in context, and in some instances to allude to an alternative approach, but no more than that. Some may believe that further exploration is needed to explain, for example, why the law differs in Jamaica and in Antigua and Barbuda. My response is that having considered the matter carefully, I felt that such an approach was stretching the bounds of my mandate, and I take responsibility for that decision.

In some instances, the law in Jamaica, that is the governing statute, contains provisions that have been heavily influenced by legislation from another Commonwealth jurisdiction: Australia, New Zealand, or even Saskatchewan, in Canada. Those concerned with law reform, including the various committees and policy groups tend to be extremely meticulous in examining and ultimately recommending specific statutory formulations. In this way, the law, even if originating elsewhere, becomes very much our own. Sometimes I have made reference to such origins, often for the purpose of showing that

Jamaica is not alone in embracing a particular concept, without, I hope, veering off into a comparative exercise.

Then there is the question of English law. There is no doubt that to all intents and purposes Jamaica stands alone and is forging its own destiny, notwithstanding the fact that the Queen of England remains head of state. The courts, Parliament, the administration of justice, the judiciary, and law teachers – all are aware, mindful, and even diligent in the application of a vision of the law that has at its core the notion of independent nationhood.

However, the everyday reality in Jamaican courts is that English cases are cited liberally, and the courts continue to give due (some might say undue) respect to them. This arises from the unique place that the English common law holds in the judicial system. Inevitably, its significance will diminish over time, but given the objects of this book, I have had to strike a balance between aspiration and realism.

Increasingly, the courts will, if so directed, place as much weight on cases from New Zealand, Australia, or Canada, but it would be misleading not to recognize the unique place that English case law still has in legal reasoning and rulings. What approach then, is a text such as this to take? It can be argued that the role of this book is to take us further along the independence road and therefore further away from the era of colonial rule and mother country. To some this would mean a 'radical' stance where one starts with the Jamaican law at all times and in all circumstances.

I have taken a more moderate approach, first because I find the historical development of the law interesting and second because I believe that sometimes where the law is coming from (which in a lot of instances goes further back than the Constitution) can assist in grasping the scope and understanding of intent of the law. This understanding may also prevent us from going down the wrong road in blissful ignorance of the fact that something has been tried before and worse yet, not able to decipher the reasons for the previous lack of success. Too many non-lawyers (and some lawyers) sometimes from a position of considerable power and influence, advance some quite startling legal positions, which are primarily due to a yawning gap in their understanding of the law and its purpose – the gap in their knowledge is not usually what the law is, but how the law came to be what it is.

This, in many ways, is as much a question of ideology as of methodology, and I am highly sympathetic to the radical position: In the chapter on matrimonial property, for example, the need to deal with constructive and resulting trusts as they arose out of Married Women's Property Act applications is a mere stepping stone to what I most wanted to talk about: the Property (Rights of Spouses) Act (PROSA). Ultimately, a balancing act is being performed in each chapter as to what I thought was the best format, and that turned on my own perception of the usefulness of this book to the reader.

This brings me to another conundrum which arose in the course of writing: if my reader may be at the academic stage of legal learning, or the vocational stage of legal training, or the professional stage of legal practice, how do I ensure that there is something for everyone? Striking that kind of balance does not necessarily mean that all constituents get the same share (as any politician will tell you!), but my aim is that the readership, no matter what the stage of their legal exploration, should feel that they have got something worthwhile out of this work. The practice and procedure section in each chapter is brief for some areas such as Children and the State – and could almost be another book in other areas, such as in the chapter on divorce. This perceived inconsistency is an occupational hazard with which I am prepared to live, because in a publishing landscape, local family law material, outside of articles, is sparse. Therefore, the irresistible priority must be to attempt to reach as many as possible in a format that provides something for everyone. I hope that the reader can make allowance for this approach.

On the matter of case citation, I have generally tried to adhere to the standardized neutral system now used in Jamaica. (See Practice

Directions No 1 of 2010, No 1 of 2012 and No 1 of 2014.) Firstly the year when the judgment is delivered followed by the 'JM' signifying the country immediately followed by SC or CA indicating the court and then a number which is the number of the judgment. Jamaican Supreme Court decisions prior to 2012 and Court of Appeal decisions prior to 2010 do not have a neutral citation. They are properly cited by claim, name, and date of delivery. I have modified slightly to put the case name first, so name, claim, (including year), and date of delivery. Cases from other Caribbean countries are cited by the Carilaw citation, that is, the name, the initials of the country, followed by the year that the decision is given, then the court, then the page number.

Whilst I have tried to put forward an accurate account of the law, it is unashamedly, my own view. From my standpoint, we must not shirk responsibility for our views and opinions which admittedly, may have no more intrinsic value than helping to spur the ongoing debate as to what the law is, who we are as a people, and how the law should reflect that. It is my fervent wish that others will accompany me on this journey.

The other guideline to which I have clung throughout the creation of this work is that for the ideas contained in a book to be accessible, they must be understandable. The desire to express oneself precisely can easily obscure clarity. Nevertheless, I hope that the reader will be prepared to deliberate carefully and through some level of engagement be rewarded with some insight.

To me, this book is a gateway through which the reader may pass en route to further exploration. I hope it conveys that family law is interesting and that this area of the law provides a backdrop to observe the development of our society and our growth as a nation. I hope that it will stimulate readers' minds and provide much food for thought.

Fara Brown, July 2018.

1. Marriage

INTRODUCTION

Marriage in Jamaica, as in many countries, is an institution which is driven by a desire for social respectability and an opportunity to make a fashion statement. There is also a major religious imperative which lies behind the motivation to get married in Jamaica. The first motivator – social respectability – at least makes reference to marriage as an ongoing relationship that alters the lifestyle of the parties who enter into it. The second motivator, on the other hand, has nothing to do with the nature of the subsequent relationship and is focused entirely on the ritual of the ceremony; in short, it is not so much a marriage, it is much more a wedding. The third motivator acknowledges the power and influence of the church, which remains even in the second decade of the twenty-first century. The push to get young people who are about to become sexually active into the state of wedlock is far-reaching. Among any group of people in the workplace or any other social grouping, some will be prepared to quietly admit that they got married because of pressure from the church. Sometimes, such marriages end in divorce, but often the parties persevere and a stable family unit will emerge.

Another interesting observation of prevailing attitudes to marriage in Jamaica and indeed other Caribbean islands is that, unlike the Western notion of starting out with nothing and building life together, many people want to have certain economic and familial markers in place before getting married. This, undoubtedly, is a longstanding position that will be examined in the next section.

> ...many slave women had their first child with one man and the rest of their children several years later with another man with whom they settled for the rest of their lives.[1]

> You see, in them days, man and woman married when them old, so nega man wedding was far and few between....[2]

There are many possible reasons for this marriage in later life practice. It may hark back to the material difficulties of entertaining the possibility of marriage during slavery and afterwards. It may also be due to other factors.[3] In any event, it exemplifies the cultural differences in the approach to and role of marriage in the Caribbean as opposed to Western societies.

HISTORICAL OVERVIEW: MARRIAGE IN JAMAICA

'The voluntary union for life of one man to one woman to the exclusion of all others' as a description of marriage,[4] has over time diminished in relevance and is less definitive of the marital

---

1. See Henrice Altink, 'To Wed or not to Wed? The Struggle to Define Afro-Jamaican Relationships, 1834–1838' *Journal of Social History* 38, no. 1 (2004).
2. From Mindie Lazarus-Black, *Legitimate Acts and Illegal Encounters: Law and Society in Antigua and Barbuda* (Washington: Smithsonian Institution Press, 1994).
3. See Keith Patchett, 'Some Aspects of Marriage and Divorce in the West Indies (1959) 1 CLQ 632.
4. *Hyde v Hyde* (1866) LR 1 P & D 130, specifically referring to marriage according to English law.

relationship, especially in the country from which this statement emerged – England. However, in many ways and for many reasons, it was never applicable to the Caribbean in general and Jamaica in particular.[5] Marriage came to the majority of the population long after our sensibilities had been battered by the rigours of plantation life, which not only discouraged but actively prohibited the kind of stable and enduring relationship that marriage is supposed to exemplify:

> Slave marriages differed from those of free persons: they were never contracts in the same sense of the term, they did not allow men to legally pass their name, status, or property to their children; and they did not provide a route for social mobility.[6]

And in any event: 'Not only could one of the partners abandon the marriage, a planter could also at any time separate a married couple by selling one of the partners'.[7]

This last statement assumed that the parties were living together, which, in fact, for many reasons, was often not the case:

> The planter's practice of separating couples when in debt partly explains why between 30 and 50 per cent of all Jamaican slave couples did not co-reside…Many slave men preferred a partner who lived on another estate so that they would not have to witness their daily abuse….[8]

Even for those in charge, the unchecked accessibility of slave owners and others to female slaves constantly undermined the notion of excluding all others:

> Scholars furthermore agree upon the omni-presence of the threat of sexual abuse in slave women's lives. Sexual abuse could take various forms, ranging from bribing slave women into having sex to outright rape.[9]

---

5. For an interesting discourse on how marriage laws were tied up with emancipation, see Altink, 'To Wed or Not to Wed?'
6. Lazarus-Black, 'Legitimate Acts and Illegal Encounters.'
7. Altink, 'To Wed or Not to Wed?', 2.
8. Ibid., 5.
9. Ibid., 6.

The succeeding system of Apprenticeship may have made things worse as it was not only planters and their white employees who sexually abused female apprentices but also men who were appointed to administer the Apprenticeship System.[10]

Despite the destructive intervention of slavery on African family life, in some respects, there were enduring patterns of marital association. In addition, some slaves were married by Anglican priests, but such marriage required paying an onerous fee and gaining permission from slave owners. Often, the latter was extremely difficult to obtain. Therefore, the enslaved were usually married by non-conformist missionaries. Originally, such marriages were the subject of considerable debate and were not recognized, but the authorities gradually relented in the post-emancipation era, as it became more expedient to bring these unions into the legal framework. The Dissenters' Marriage Act of 1840 required that for full legal recognition these marriages had to be registered, and in the immediate years of the law being passed, many marriages which had already taken place were recognized by reference to church records.

A principle subsequently embraced by the law was that marriage should be supported as it encouraged civilized habits in the population. The stumbling block, however, was that apart from the question of recognition, the practical difficulties of maintaining any semblance of ordinary marital relations during slavery and post slavery under the Apprenticeship System, acted as a major deterrent. Therefore, the freedom to form voluntary, lasting, and stable bonds was often exercised outside of the formality of marriage.

According to Jemmott:[11]

> In spite of optimistic missionary pronouncements about the increase of marriages in the immediate post-slavery years, by the mid-1840s it was evident that for a variety of reasons, the majority of blacks were intent on organizing their families in

---

10. Ibid., 12.
11. Jenny M. Jemmott, *Ties That Bind: The Black Family in Post-Slavery Jamaica, 1834–1882* (Kingston: University of the West Indies Press, 2015), 170.

unions external to the married state. These reasons included the expense entailed in the ceremony, a desire not to be tied to one person and an expressed preference for "faithful concubinage".

Stipendiary magistrate Hall Pringle, for example, reported from Vere that although "a prodigious number of black people got married in 1838, 1839 and 1840...since that period marriages in this country district among the lower classes become more and more uncommon".

This was a common approach across the Caribbean, as Christine Barrow[12] points out:

Lower class family patterns were not a function of slave status or of economic conditions of the slave and post-emancipation periods. When the abolition of slavery removed legal distinctions on the basis of race and colour, there was no rush to marry among the ex-slaves despite pressure from missionaries and priests. Neither, it would appear, was there any reduction in "outside" unions and the "outside children".

In short, the early Marriage Laws,[13] despite the professed objective of encouraging marriage, did not have that effect on the majority of the population.

Furthermore, the fact that prior to 1879, there was no statutory divorce, created an air of finality around marriage, and this was something that many were not prepared to entertain. Concepts of marriage based on a West African model where it may not be recognized until the first child is born, or when the marriage presents are paid for or where there may be what might be seen as a trial marriage'[14] persisted among ex-slaves, but could readily be interpreted as something else by the authorities.[15] Furthermore, slaves and ex-slaves had their own practices for terminating a

12. Christine Barrow, *Family in the Caribbean: Themes and Perspectives* (Kingston: Ian Randle Publishers, 1996), 180, extracted by Leighton Jackson in 'Family Law and Domestic Violence in the Eastern Caribbean: Judicial and Legislative Reform,' 2002.
13. The Marriage Law was passed in 1879.
14. For Ashanti-Fanti African religions, see Mbiti, *Ties That Bind*.
15. According to Edith Clarke, *Systematic Study of Family Systems in Jamaica* (1957): 'in the parishes of St. Catherine and coastal St. Thomas, consensual cohabitations are prevalent and often lifelong, while marriage is statistically marginal'.

relationship which closely resembled certain African rituals and, as such, made non-marital relationships a preferable option. Many of these perceptions and practices have been handed down through the generations.[16] What this led to was a pattern of what Henrice Altink calls 'sequential monogamy', where 'they did not spend their adult life in one but several successive relationships.'[17]

The Royal Commission in 1938 referred to promiscuity and the 'disorganization' of family life in Jamaica and called for 'an organized campaign against the social, moral, and economic evils of promiscuity.'[18] In 1945–46, the governor's wife, Lady Huggins, attempted to launch a 'Mass Marriage Movement' ostensibly to overcome the problem of marriage costs, but really to 'normalize' family life on the island.[19]

Over the years, marriage has fluctuated in popularity. In 2002, there were 8.82 marriages per 1,000 persons and although dipping slightly in 2004 to 8.23, the rate rose again significantly to 9.81. However, since 2008 when the rate was 8.29, there has been a steady decline to a point where in 2013, it had fallen to 6.94. Over this period, the actual numbers of marriages fell from 23,070 in 2002 to 18,835 in 2013. There is every reason to expect from the trends that the number of marriages taking place annually will continue to decline:[20]

> From my observation, less Jamaicans are choosing to get married now than in former times. The society has become more secular, and secularism doesn't promote marriage as the ideal union…There is less inclination to bureaucracy and greater attraction to responding instinctively to physical passion.[21]

16. It was not unusual for people to marry after they had had several children and the relationship had withstood the rigours of early life in the absence of material comforts.
17. Altink, 'To Wed or Not to Wed?'
18. Report of West India Royal Commission (Moyne Report) 1938. Reprinted Kingston: Ian Randle Publishers [2011].
19. By 1946, the marriage rate was lifted from 4.44 per 1,000 to 5.82 per 1,000, but by 1951 it had fallen to its former level and the movement ended in 1955.
20. Statistical Institute of Jamaica (STATIN), *Demographic Statistics: Marriages and Divorces*
21. Reverend Stevenson Samuels, 'Marriages Down Divorces Up – RGD, STATIN,' *Sunday Observer*, January 24 2016.

As the law gives greater recognition to non-marital unions, fewer people may find it necessary to establish family units in marriage. However, it is perhaps too early to draw any reliable conclusions on the effects this will have on marriage rates until sufficient time has elapsed and empirical studies have been conducted.

Today, marriage in Jamaica is generally considered to be a desirable attainment of status. It is aspired to as a safe haven from the perilous waters of single life, which is entirely consistent with the sentiments behind the definition in *Hyde v Hyde*.[22] The reality does not usually live up to that expectation, though. The notion of the man being the head of the household as expressed by the church often precedes an abusive scenario in which male dominance is entrenched. The idea that rape within marriage is impossible is still widely held. Marital infidelity is viewed differently by gender either worthy of a badge of honour or a painful but almost inescapable reality. As a result, marriage may offer much less of a haven from the vicissitudes of life than people think. Indeed, it may, in fact, be a veritable minefield. Finally, it should be remembered that the combination of greater financial independence for women and easier divorce have reduced the applicability of the *Hyde v Hyde* definition of marriage to little more than an ideal.

THE LAW: THE MARRIAGE ACT

Turning to the law, the problem of clandestine marriages and the need to rein in the prevalence of common law marriages in England, which informed the passage of Lord Hardwicke's Act[23] (as the grandfather of all Marriage Acts in England and the Caribbean) were not the kind of issues with which Jamaica was preoccupied.[24] On the contrary, in small societies, it is difficult to hide a marriage

---

22. 'The voluntary union for life of one man to one woman to the exclusion of all others'.
23. This act was passed in 1753.
24. Historically, marriage can be seen as an instrument of social engineering in a post-slavery society.

ceremony, and in any event, in the Caribbean the ritual[25] is every bit as important as the legal requirements, if not even more so. This is very much in keeping with Jamaican ancestry, so rarely do people have 'a simple wedding'. Indeed, the whole point of the ceremony is to show and tell the immediate community and the world that the parties have changed their status. So, Jamaica inherited a law which is not premised on its own circumstances, but notwithstanding has served the country quite well regardless of the route by which it came. Nevertheless, as the society grows and changes and as Jamaicans acknowledge their place in the international community, the need for review cannot be ignored.

The Marriage Act

The Marriage Act is set up as a facilitative piece of legislation in that it creates a framework within which marriage can occur and be legally recognized. The content of the Marriage Act in Jamaica is shared with most of its English-speaking Caribbean neighbours and is divided into six main sections:

1. Void Marriages
2. Marriage Officers
3. Pre-Ceremony Requirements
4. The Ceremony
5. Post Ceremony Requirements
6. Criminal Penalties

This type of legislation is designed to facilitate and guide the process of marriage along lines which conform to the standards set by Parliament. Therefore, the overall intention of the legislation is to uphold the institution of marriage by allowing marriages to be entered into legitimately, and thereby creating a valid marriage, rather than rigorous punishment and consequent invalidation for

---

25.   This is in keeping with the concept of marriage as taking place between families rather than a union of two people.

inadvertently falling short of the statutory requirements.[26] So, the format of the law is to set out what cannot be a valid marriage, then go through the lawful requirements, and conclude with certain criminal sanctions, which are directed primarily at officials to ensure that duties are carried out properly rather than the parties who may unwittingly fail to conform to the statutory requirements.

Marriages which are Void under the Marriage Act

In this section, it is only those nullity grounds contained in the Marriage Act which will be mentioned. There are additional grounds in section 4 of the Matrimonial Causes Act (MCA), and all the grounds upon which a marriage can be held void will be examined in greater detail in the chapter on nullity.

A marriage will be void according to the Marriage Act if:

1. there is a disregard of certain formalities (section 3(1));
2. either of the parties is under age (section 3(2));
3. the parties are within the prohibited degrees of consanguinity of affinity (section 3(3)); and
4. there is a failure to comply with the formalities in the case of Marriage in *articulo mortis* (section 37).

Void grounds under the Marriage Act fall into two categories – those which are premised on capacity, that is sections 3(2) and (3), and those which set the minimum standards in terms of required formalities for a valid marriage, sections 3(1)(a) and (b) and section 37.[27]

Disregard of Certain Formalities

Section 3 of the Act refers to three main instances of a marriage being a nullity. The first is where there is a wilful disregard of the specified formalities. Thus, section 3 reads:

26. For example, *Da Silva v Da Silva* 28 WIR 357.
27. For an account of the historical origins of void and voidable marriages, see 'Void and Voidable Marriages, 27 MLR 385.

1. If both parties to a marriage knowingly and wilfully acquiesce in the solemnization of the marriage ceremony between them –

    a. by or before a person not being a Marriage Officer; or

    b. otherwise than in the presence of two witnesses besides the Marriage Officer solemnizing or witnessing and registering the marriage, the marriage shall be void.

The requirement for the marriage to be conducted by a marriage officer is fundamental to the act. The act creates the post of marriage officer, sets out the duties of such a post, and prescribes the penalties for failing to carry out those duties or for encroachment by others. As such, the marriage officer is the central figure with regard to the formalities of marriage. This issue is considered further under nullity.

It is only where there is a deliberate disregard of the formalities set out in section 3(1)(a) and (b) by both parties that the marriage will be void. If one party knows (and is essentially fooling the other) then the marriage will be valid, that is, the view of the 'innocent' party will prevail, and the 'guilty' party will not be able to 'pull the rug from under the feet' of the other at a point of their own choosing. Also, in cases where either of these formalities has not been complied with out of ignorance or mistake, the marriage will still be valid. This construction ensures little incentive for the parties to enter into the realm of non-compliance, and that the criminal sanctions which are available to be used against those who disregard the requirements do not override the ultimate objective of the legislation, which is to facilitate marriages.[28] Under section 62 of the Act, a person who impersonates a marriage officer is guilty of a misdemeanour.

General Non-Compliance of the Marriage Requirements

Section 4 of the Marriage Act makes it clear that the disregard of the numerous 'requirements' which indicate how a marriage should be formalized will not by itself render the marriage void. It is only where the marriage flouts the terms of section 3 or section 37 that it will be void.

---

28.   For a useful review of the relevant cases in this area under English law, see *MA v JA* [2012] EWHC 2219. Further consideration under Nullity.

Section 4 reads:

> Except as aforesaid, and except as in section 37 provided with respect to marriages under that section, no marriage otherwise lawful which has been actually solemnized shall be declared void on the ground that any of the conditions of this Act directed to be observed have not been duly observed.

This represents a codification of the common law position as Dr Lushington stated in *Catterall v Sweetman:*[29]

> From this examination I draw two conclusions: first, so far as my research extends, it appears that there never has been a decision that any words in a statute as to marriage though prohibitory and negative, have been held to infer a nullity, unless that nullity was declared in the act. Second, that, viewing the successive Marriage Acts, it appears that prohibitory words, without a declaration of nullity, were not considered by the Legislature as creating a nullity, and that this is a legislative interpretation of acts relative to marriage.

For example, in the case of *Da Silva v Da Silva*, the marriage was solemnized outside of the prescribed hours, but was nevertheless held to be valid. This case relied on some of the older English cases,[30] and demonstrated that the presumption of marriage can play a role in resolving these issues.

This does not, however, allow parties to ignore the stipulations of the Act because in practice it is almost impossible to conduct a marriage without fulfilling certain requirements which are important, but not included in section 3.[31] As a result, many requirements are virtually unavoidable without employing an elaborate scheme of deception, if only because it would not generally be possible to get a marriage officer to act without those requirements having been met. Furthermore, the creation of criminal offences to rein in marriage officers who might take a cavalier approach to their responsibilities or to the stipulated process is a useful fall back to encourage compliance.

29.   (1845) 163 ER 1047.
30.   *Campbell v Corley* (1856) 28 LTOS 109, and *Wing v Taylor* (1856) 28 LTOS as well as *Catterall v Sweetman.*
31.   Such as having a licence.

Minimum Age – section 3(2)

A person who is under the age of 16 is incapable of contracting a valid marriage. Section 3(2) states: 'A marriage solemnized between persons either of whom is under the age of sixteen years shall be void'.

Unlike subsection (1) which relates to formalities, this stipulation is absolute. There is no question that arises as to the knowledge or state of mind of the parties. The issue is one of capacity.

The provision as to the legal age of marriage is often linked to the legal age of consent and is the subject of constant debate.[32] The deepening of child care and protection principles in both law and policy seem to almost dictate that the age of majority is 18. This came about by way of the Law Reform (Age of Majority) Act[33] and has been reinforced in recent Jamaican legislation.[34] This means that the minimum age of marriage is increasingly being viewed as inconsistent with the dominant norm. The rationale behind this viewpoint is that the place for a child up to the age of majority is in an institution of learning, not a marital bed. This position also does not attach significance to the graduated acquisition of status as currently reflected in the act by the need for parental consent between the ages of 16 and 18; see section 24. While it is right that, with greater educational opportunities, marriage is generally being postponed as a matter of choice, there are those[35] who believe that it is necessary for this position to be reinforced by statute. However, if according to section 8 of the Law Reform (Age of Majority) Act, there are some decisions that a person may make before turning 18, why should they not be allowed to marry?

To set Jamaica in its regional context, the marriage laws across the Caribbean, in this regard, are by no means uniform. In Antigua

---

32.   However, the age of consent used to be 14, and therefore, can be lower than the age of marriage.
33.   1979, but which itself recognizes a younger age for certain activities, see section 8.
34.   The Child Care and Protection Act 2004.
35.   See representations to Parliament by the Children's Advocate, 2014.

and Barbuda, the Marriage Act stipulates a minimum age for marriage of 15, and in Belize the minimum age of 16 was raised from 14 in 2005. The justification for the variance in the countries with indigenous communities [36] was that their culture and traditions should be respected. This was also the case on religious grounds for Hindus and Muslims in Trinidad and Tobago and Guyana; however, with further assimilation, this is increasingly being adjusted to a national norm.[37] In countries such as Guyana, a low age of marriage [38] is sometimes used as a means of escaping criminal prosecution, as well as covering the shame of teenage pregnancy and thereby preserving family reputation and status within a community. In any event, the overall trend is to increase the age of marriage as is similarly the case with the age of consent, but while these two maturation markers often coincide, they are not inextricably linked.

Prohibited Degrees – section 3(3)

If the parties to a marriage are so closely related as to fall within the prohibited degrees of consanguinity or affinity 'according to the law of England from time to time in force,' then the marriage will be void; see section 3(3) of the Marriage Act. The wording of the provision is exceptional in that it hinges the Jamaican law to what has been decided in the legislature or the courts of another jurisdiction. This may have been acceptable prior to independence, but it seems to be highly anomalous now. In particular, the law in England has not only developed some way in this regard, with legislation allowing 'step' relations to marry in certain circumstances,[39] but this has been taken further by cases from the United Kingdom (UK) decided in the European Court of Human Rights.[40] These developments also highlight that the law of England has incorporated the law of the European Union in the form of the Human Rights Act and recognizes

36. For example, Mayan and Kalinago in Belize and Dominica, respectively.
37. Miscellaneous Provisions (Marriage) Act 2017 in Trinidad and Tobago.
38. It is 14 for females, 16 for males.
39. Marriage (Prohibited Degrees of Relationship) Act 1986.
40. *B and L v The United Kingdom* [2005] ECHR 584.

the European Court of Human Rights as its highest court. That all these developments which have taken place so far away can affect the content of the domestic law of Jamaica is not a satisfactory situation, and should be addressed promptly.[41] To compound the issue, there are some instances where, rather than relying on the automatic application of the law in England, the Jamaican legislature has taken it upon itself to supplement the process by passing its own enactments.[42]

This format is to be compared with that employed in the Belizean Marriage Act, for example, where the prohibited degrees are set out in a schedule to the Act,[43] and in St Kitts and Nevis where there is a separate act dealing with this issue.[44]

Affinity

'A husband is of affinity to his wife's kindred, and a wife of affinity to her husband's kindred; but the kindred of the husband are not of affinity to the kindred of his wife'.[45]

Simply put, persons are essentially related by affinity where they are related by marriage, generally in-laws and step-relations.

The legal rules in relation to affinity as distinct from consanguinity are subject to the cultural norms of the particular society as well as other factors.[46] The size of the population and its density are important issues. It is an area which should be the subject of occasional legislative review in order to keep abreast of current migratory patterns and the changes in the structure of the family in the Caribbean.[47]

---

41. At the time of writing, the legal position post Brexit is impossible to predict.
42. Marriage (Deceased Wife's Sister or Brother's Widow) Act.
43. First Schedule, part 1 of the Marriage Act, Belize.
44. Marriage (Prohibited Degrees of Relationship) Act.
45. William Rayden and J. Jackson. *Law and Practice in Divorce and Family Matters.* 15th Ed. (London Butterworth & Co. Publishers Ltd, 1988).
46. Marriage (Deceased Wife's Sister or Brother's Widow) Act.
47. For an Australian perspective on this topic, see H.A. Finlay, 'Farewell to Affinity and the Calculus of Kinship,' *University of Tasmania Law Review* 16 (1975).

Consanguinity

Persons who are within the prohibited degrees of consanguinity are related by blood. The reason for the prohibition against marriage between those who are within the prohibited degrees of consanguinity is that the offspring of such unions are likely to have a concentration of negative traits, which are found in the gene pool, and as a result, may exhibit congenital weaknesses whether physical, mental, or both.

The prohibited degrees are considered further under nullity.

Marriages in Articulo Mortis

Section 37 of the act sets out the required formalities for a marriage in anticipation of death. Section 37 reads:

> It shall be lawful for a Marriage Officer to solemnize a marriage without any certificate of notice or banns in the following special case, that is to say, where the marriage is between two persons one of whom is in articulo mortis.
>
> No such marriage shall be solemnized unless both parties are able to signify their consent thereto in the presence of two witnesses.
>
> No such marriage shall be solemnized where either of the parties is under twenty-one years of age, not being a widower or widow, unless the person whose consent is required is present and gives his or her consent verbally.
>
> A marriage so solemnized shall be specially registered.
>
> The Register shall contain the particulars and be in the form indicated in Schedule M.
>
> No marriage solemnized under the provisions of this section shall be valid unless the foregoing conditions are observed.

The effect of this provision is that unless all the formalities set out under this section are carried out, then the marriage will not be legally recognized

As stated above, these provisions under the Marriage Act, whereby marriages will be void in the circumstances set out must be read in conjunction with section 4 of the Matrimonial Causes

Act. This section, as well as incorporating these grounds, contains additional grounds upon which a marriage will be void. The grounds mentioned above are considered in further detail in the chapter on nullity.

Marriage Officers

Sections 5 to 15 of the Marriage Act establish the position of marriage officer and make the post of civil registrar to be that of an ex officio marriage officer. The minister[48] can appoint civil registrars as he sees fit, and such ministers of religion as maybe entitled to appointment under the provisions of the act to be marriage officers.[49] A minister of religion who seeks to become a marriage officer must 'name or describe the place of public worship in which he so acts, or place of public worship of the congregation over which he has such local superintendence.' This creates a strong allegiance between the position of marriage officer and the church. Historically, there is a distinction to be made between the recognition of an officiating officer in English marriage acts, where the position was entirely controlled by the Anglican Church followed by concessions being made for other religions to perform marital rites and the position in Jamaica (and the Caribbean as a whole) where the power to marry vests primarily in the marriage officer who may or may not be of any religious persuasion.[50]

For those who do not wish to have a religious ceremony, a civil registrar can solemnize the marriage. In fact, the civil registrar is first bestowed with the title of marriage officer and then 'such ministers of religion as may be entitled to appointment under the provisions of the Act....'

The Act sets out the duties of the marriage officer before, during, and after the ceremony. It begins with the issue of the certificate or licence, then publicizing the intended marriage, performance

---

48. Minister of National Security.
49. Section 5.
50. For an interesting discourse on this, see Eileen Boxhill, 'Developments in Family Law since Emancipation,' *West Indian Law Journal* 9, no. 2 (1985): 9.

of the ceremony, and subsequent registration. The creation of the authority, which is the marriage officer, is the cornerstone to the regulation of marriages under the Act, because it is the marriage officer who bears responsibility for the compliance with all these formalities.

From section 55 onwards, a number of criminal offences are created to address malpractice by marriage officers and also to protect the office from infringement by others. It is important that the penalties which are applicable where a criminal offence is committed by a marriage officer remain commensurate with the recognized gravity of the responsibilities of the office. At present, most of the criminal penalties are in keeping with this proposition, but with respect to the high penalties which are stipulated – one million dollars and imprisonment for up to seven years – it is important that such an approach carries over into the courts that are dealing with these matters.

Pre-Ceremony Requirements

Under the Marriage Act,[51] marriages are solemnized under the authority of either a marriage officer's certificate, a civil registrar's certificate, a minister's licence, or a licence issued by a justice, clerk of the court, or any person appointed by the minister. There are a number pre-conditions to the issuing of a licence or certificate.

1. Residence – Ordinarily, the parties are supposed to have been resident in a parish for at least 15 days.[52] The issue of a 'special' licence for persons who have not been in the jurisdiction for long enough to fulfil that requirement is a frequent occurrence by virtue of wedding tourism.

2. Publication – Whether the marriage is to be conducted by a marriage officer or civil registrar, there must be publication of the intended marriage. Under the civil registrar procedure,

---

51.   Section 16.
52.   Section 17.

the particulars are recorded in the Marriage Notice Book, which 'shall be open at all reasonable times to any person desiring to inspect it.'[53] A public notice is also to be 'put up in a conspicuous and accessible place on the door or outer wall of his office'.[54] Where a religious ceremony is to take place, there must be a publication of banns which is made in an audible manner during the public divine service, whether it be a Saturday or a Sunday, in the morning or if not in the evening service. A notice must also be affixed to the outside of the principal door of the place of public worship at which the banns are published for seven clear days.[55]

3. Parental Consent – The minimum age of marriage is 16, and persons who have reached the age of 18 can marry without consent. However, between the ages of 16 and 18 years, consent from a parent or a person who stands in loco parentis is required.[56] Where there is a requirement for consent, if it is not forthcoming, there is provision for an application to be made to a judge of the Supreme Court, who 'shall decide upon the same in a summary way.'[57] Where the marriage has taken place without the required consent, unless there is some other reason why the marriage is void, it is valid.[58] In such circumstances, the attorney general may apply to the Supreme Court to declare a forfeiture of all interest in any property acquired by the 'other party', and to secure the property for the benefit of the underage party and any children of the union.[59]

---

53. Ibid.
54. Section 18.
55. Ibid.
56. Section 24.
57. Ibid.
58. *Bess v Bess* (1986) 39 WIR 59, *R v Birmingham* (Inhabitants) 1828 8 B&C 29, see also Marriage Act, section 4.
59. Section 18.

4. Objections – If someone wishes to object to a marriage taking place, they must do so in accordance with section 25 of the act or else the official is entitled to disregard it. The marriage officer or civil registrar may suspend the issue of the certificate or licence in order to consider the matter and decide as he sees fit. Where a legal impediment is disclosed, the matter is to be referred to a judge of the Supreme Court to be decided upon. There are penalties for frivolous and vexatious objections, and the adjustment to the fine has kept pace with inflation and can still be considered punitive.[60]

The certificate or licence is valid for a period of three months, during which time the marriage should be solemnized. If it does not take place, a fresh authorization will have to be obtained.[61] Where a marriage officer 'destroys, injures, falsifies or conceals any notice or certificate', an offence is committed under section 64 for which a penalty of up to two years imprisonment can be imposed. Whoever tampers with a marriage register with intent to obstruct or defeat the course of justice is liable to imprisonment for up to seven years.[62]

The Ceremony

The parties to a marriage are given considerable latitude in terms of the 'form and ceremony' of the solemnization.[63] There are, however, certain provisos: The marriage is to take place between the hours of 6:00 a.m. and 8:00 p.m. in the presence of a marriage officer and two witnesses, with open doors. The certificate or licence is to be delivered to the marriage officer before the ceremony, and there should be no lawful impediment.[64] At some point, whether just before or during the ceremony, but in the presence of the marriage officer and the witnesses, certain statements as set out in

---

60. Last amendment 2011.
61. Section 26.
62. Section 61.
63. Section 27.
64. Ibid.

the act must be made.[65] For the avoidance of doubt, parties may be married by a civil registrar or marriage officer, and the ceremony may take part in any form of religious service. This ensures that where the minister of a certain religion is not a marriage officer, the parties can nevertheless marry according to the rites and practices of their faith.[66] Impersonating a marriage officer is a misdemeanour offence,[67] but performing a marriage ceremony without being duly qualified or knowledgeable about matters that would make the marriage void or unlawful carries a penalty of up to seven years imprisonment.[68] However, the more serious offences are reserved for anyone who goes through a ceremony of marriage, knowing that it is void or impersonating another, or marries under a false name with intent to deceive the other party. In such cases, upon conviction, that person may be imprisoned for up to 10 years.[69]

Post-Ceremony Requirements

After the marriage has been solemnized, the marriage officer should register the marriage in the Marriage Register Book and give a certified copy of the marriage certificate to one of the parties (usually the wife) and 'deliver or cause to be delivered the duplicate copy of the marriage certificate to the Registrar-General'.[70] The marriage certificate is the primary means by which a marriage is proven and as such is an important document. Failure to comply with the post-ceremony requirements is an offence under section 56 of the Act, and this includes the failure to retain the Marriage Register Book for inspection or to 'lose or injure, or allow (it) to be injured, whilst in his keeping'. The penalty for commission of this offence is a sum up to one million dollars. Interestingly, under section 34 of the Act, if the marriage has not been registered or the

---

65. Ibid.
66. Section 28.
67. Section 62.
68. Section 68.
69. Sections 66 and 67.
70. Sections 31 and 32.

register has been lost or destroyed, an application can be made to a resident magistrate for an order that the marriage be registered.

The Role of Criminal Offences under the Marriage Act

The act imposes express and extensive duties on marriage officers with regard to the conduct and registration of marriages, and in default, a criminal offence is committed.[71] Sections 56, and sections 61–69 create further offences in respect of marriage officers and others who act in a way that is contrary to the provisions of the statute. It is only in sections 65, 66, 67, and 69 that civilians, be they a party to a marriage or someone else, may become criminally liable. When viewed in the context of the entire Act, it becomes clear that the purpose of criminalizing certain actions that undermine the stipulated marriage process is deterrence. Section 4 of the Act shows that Parliament does not intend that the courts be quick to invalidate a marriage. This would lead to instability and uncertainty. Criminal offences, therefore, have an important role to play in curbing any inclination to abuse the process, and if properly applied with realistic sanctions, they work hand-in-hand with the fundamental penalty of non-recognition, which should be maintained as a last resort. Essentially, these criminal offences are subordinate to the penalty that carries the greatest weight under the Marriage Act, namely that the marriage is not legally recognized, that is, void under section 3.

OTHER MARRIAGE ACTS

The Hindu Marriage Act

Persons of the Hindu faith are permitted to marry by way of a Hindu ceremony under the Hindu Marriage Act. The act creates the same structure as with the Marriage Act whereby it is the marriage officer who is the authorized person to conduct marriages under the Act. In this instance, any priest of the Hindu religion may apply to

---

71.   See Section 55.

be licensed as a marriage officer.[72] The requisites of a valid Hindu marriage are set out in section 7, and these provisions essentially blend certain requirements of the Marriage Act into the framework of a marriage being conducted according to Hindu law. For example, the prohibited degrees of consanguinity and affinity are those 'according to Hindu law relating to marriage'.[73] In deference to the general act, the free consent of the parties is a requirement, and polygamous marriages or marriages between direct descendants are not permitted. Similarly, the minimum age of marriage is 16, which is consistent with the terms of the Marriage Act. Parental consent, as a requirement, extends beyond the general act to 21 for men and 18 for women.[74] In this regard, where the consent of the parents is not forthcoming, the power of the minister to grant consent is devolved to 'a person being a member of the Hindu community to investigate the circumstances of the intended marriage'.[75] A Hindu marriage may lawfully be conducted without any formality required by the Marriage Act and still be recognized. Hindu marriages that took place prior to the passing of the Act are recognized and can be registered under the Act.[76] The children of any Hindu marriage that has been registered are deemed to be legitimate.[77] The Hindu Marriage Act, like the general act, creates certain criminal offences, and these are in connection with the responsibilities of the marriage officer.[78]

The Muslim Marriage Act

The Muslim Marriage Act is structured in much the same way as the Hindu Marriage Act. There are certain prerequisites for the marriage to be recognized under this Act.[79] The minimum age of

---

72. Section 6.
73. Section 7(c).
74. Section 8(1).
75. Section 8(4).
76. Section 11(1).
77. Section 13.
78. Sections 3(4), 18, and 19.
79. Section 6.

marriage is 16 years, and there is a prohibition on polygamous marriages and marriages to direct descendants and other close relatives.[80] Interestingly, anyone of the Muslim faith may be appointed a marriage officer for the purposes of this act.[81] Both the Muslim Marriage Act and the Hindu Marriage Act require that all applications, certificates, and entries in the Register Book be in the English language.[82] A civil registrar is required to keep a list of Hindu marriage officers and Muslim marriage officers.[83]

In practice, parties of the Muslim or Hindu faith may exercise the option of being married by a civil registrar under the general Marriage Act, and then go through a form of religious ceremony later.

From a historical perspective, marriage laws initially recognized only those marriages conducted by an Anglican priest, and subsequently accepted those in which a non-conformist minister officiated. Legal provision for civil ceremonies and the variations in these acts to accommodate the religious principles attaching marriage in the Indian communities came later and were seen as a concession on the part of the authorities to those who were brought to Jamaica as indentured labourers. It was eventually accepted that to encourage the settlement of these people it was important to assimilate the marriage protocols which they practised.

CONSORTIUM: THE LEGAL CONSEQUENCES OF MARRIAGE

The essence of the word 'consortium' is partnership, communion, being in the company of; but the application of this term to married persons does not have its origins in the level of equality that is initially suggested. In fact, the legal status of the parties from a historical standpoint was that there was a complete subordination

80. Section 7.
81. Section 3.
82. Section 17.
83. Section 5.

of the woman who was effectively swallowed up in the identity of the man:

> [The] very being or legal existence of the woman is suspended during the marriage, or at least is incorporated and consolidated into that of the husband: under whose wing, protection, and cover she performs everything.[84]

The emphasis in this quotation should really be on the wife's 'performance of everything', because it is the loss of these services to the husband that is at the heart of the legal recognition of this peculiar relationship.

In *Best v Samuel Fox & Co. Ltd.*[85] per Lord Goddard:

> The action which the law gives to the husband for loss of consortium is founded on the proprietary right which from ancient times it was considered the husband had in his wife. It was, in fact, based on the same ground as gave a master a right to sue for an injury to his servant if the latter was thereby unable to perform his duties.

So, the notion of being united as one was a historical illusion which masked the reality of a quasi-master and servant relationship between wife and husband. In the case of *Best*, the husband was injured as a result of the negligence and breach of statutory duty of the respondents. The wife claimed against the respondents for interference with her right to consortium on the grounds of the husband's resultant sexual incapacity. Despite the fact that this was recognized as a claim that vested in the husband, in an effort to bring some equality to the situation it was argued in *Best* that such actions for loss of consortium could also be brought by the wife.[86] This was, however, rejected by their Lordships who described this right of the husband as 'anomalous' and 'illogical' and therefore unworthy of extension.

---

84. Herbert Broom, Edward A. Hadley, William Wait, and William Blackstone, *Commentaries on the Laws of England Book* (Albany, New York: John D. Parsons Jr., 1875), quoted in Stephen M. Cretney, Judith M. Masson, and Rebecca Bailey-Harris, *Principles of Family Law*, 7th ed. (London: Sweet & Maxwell Ltd, 2002).
85. [1952] 2 All ER 394.
86. See also the case of *Lynch v Knight* (1861) 9 HL Cas. 577.

It nevertheless remains the case that the relationship of husband and wife is still viewed as 'special' in light of legal decisions made over the centuries. Many of these cases, if subject to judicial consideration in modern times, would undoubtedly be decided differently, but that illusive notion of consortium as between husband and wife endures as a basis of how we decide if the essential characteristics of marriage are present.

What then does this 'bundle of rights, which stem from common home and common life' consist of? It includes:

a. Mutual right to cohabit – This was considered in the case of *Nanda v Nanda*[87] in the context of a decree for restitution of conjugal rights and an ensuing application for an injunction, and was severely curtailed.

2. Right to husband's name – This is a matter of custom and convention rather than law.

3. Mutual right to normal sexual intercourse – This, however, is not to be enforced by restraining the wife by force and keeping her in confinement.[88] It is this right that has become the most contentious in recent times in respect of the offence of marital rape (see below).

4. Duty to consummate the marriage – It is this right that from a religious standpoint represents the central tenet and purpose of marriage, and provides the premise for the formerly voidable nullity grounds of lack of consummation whether by virtue of wilful refusal or incapacity. Non-consummation by agreement has moved from being unenforceable by reason of being contrary to public policy,[89] through being permissible in certain circumstances,[90] to being considered a matter of personal choice for the parties with which the law has little concern.[91]

87. [1967] 3 All ER 401.
88. *R v Jackson* [1891] 1 QB 671.
89. *Brodie v Brodie* [1917] P 271.
90. 'Companionate marriage' per *Morgan v Morgan* [1959] P 92.
91. In Jamaica non-consummation grounds has been abolished by the repeal of the Divorce Act.

5. Mutual protection – The criminal law extends the principle of self-defence to acting in protection of a spouse.

6. Marital confidence – *Argyll v Argyll*.[92] In relation to married couples and third parties, see *Douglas v Hello! Ltd (No.1)*.[93]

7. Special status regarding criminal evidence and prosecutions – A number of common law distinctions exist between ordinary criminal parties and those who are married to each other from the standpoint of the law of evidence. In particular, their competence and compellability to give evidence against each other has been a source of frustration for the courts when dealing with domestic violence and other criminal complaints. Some jurisdictions have made inroads into this area by way of statutory intervention, and it may be that Jamaica will follow suit at an appropriate time. *Mawji v R*[94] looks at the question of restrictions on the charging of parties who are married for conspiracy.

8. Immigration and domicile – Marriage has been used for a long time as a means of gaining immigration rights consequent upon the change of status. The challenge for the court has been to restrict this avenue of gaining entry while at the same time not undermining the sanctity of marriage. The courts were at one time prepared to invalidate the marriage when it was clear that its main purpose was to facilitate migration.[95] However, eventually,[96] there was a reassertion of the traditional position as was decided in the case of *Swift v Kelly*.[97] The law has turned towards increasingly more intricate immigration laws (in the UK and Australia) to address these matters rather than undermining the nature and function of marriage as a social regulator.

---

92. [1965] 1 All ER 611. For an interesting discussion on this case, see 'The Argyll Charade,' *The Journal*, 1/7/99.
93. [2005] EWCA 595.
94. [1957] AC 126.
95. *Marriage of Deniz* (1977) 7 Fam LN 3.
96. *Marriage of Otway* (1986) 11 Fam LR 99.
97. (1835) 12 ER 648.

All of these 'rights' as seen in the cases referred to, have been modified by progressive judicial reasoning, and it becomes clear that the application of the rights has changed with the development of society. As Lord Halsbury LC put it in the late nineteenth century:

> I confess that some of the propositions which have been referred to in the argument are such as I should be reluctant to suppose ever to have been the law of England. More than a century ago it was boldly contended that slavery existed in England; but, if any were to set up such a contention now, it would be regarded as ridiculous. In the same way, such quaint and absurd dicta as are to be found in the books as to the right of a husband over his wife in respect of personal chastisement are not, I think, now capable of being cited as authorities in a court of justice in this or any civilized country.[98]

These modifications have also taken place by the use of statute,[99] but perhaps the one that remains most contentious in Jamaica is the right to sexual intercourse. The extent to which a wife's consent to sexual intercourse is irrevocable and in what circumstances it might reasonably be considered to have been revoked has followed the common law in England without variance up until the case of *R v R*.[100] However, that decision of the House of Lords in England raised questions about how the ruling would apply in Jamaica, and in the absence of any statutory provisions, whether it was, in fact, appropriate for the courts to be bound by such a ruling. The Sexual Offences Act 2009[101] now sets out the offence of marital rape for the purposes of the Jamaican criminal law and represents an attempt by the Jamaican legislators to set the position at common law within the Jamaican context. Nevertheless, the issue continues to be controversial, and has been raised at the parliamentary level in the course of hearings by the review committee.[102]

---

98.   *R v Jackson* [1891] 1 QB 678.
99.   For example, see section 23(4) of the Sexual Offences Act and section 34(1)(a) of the Matrimonial Causes Act.
100. [1991] 4 All ER 481.
101. Section 5.
102. *Gleaner*, October 16, 2014.

PROCEDURAL ASPECTS OF THE MARRIAGE ACT

Where matters concerning the prerequisites to a marriage such as parental consent and lawful impediments arise, the Marriage Act prescribes that an application may be made to a judge of the Supreme Court who should deal with the matter 'in a summary way'. This implies that the application would be made by a fixed date claim form and if time is of the essence, by dispensing with the ordinary timelines as to service by way of an ex parte application. It is doubtful that the proceedings would come within part 76 of the Civil Procedure Rules (CPR), because it appears that applications under the Marriage Act do not come within the meaning of 'matrimonial proceedings',[103] nor do they come within the meaning of 'matrimonial cause'.[104]

In keeping with Rule 8(8) of the CPR, a fixed date claim form must be accompanied by an affidavit in support, setting out the nature of the claim. In the case of parental consent, the application being under section 24 of the act would be made by either party to the intended marriage. Where the question to be resolved is whether there is a lawful impediment to the marriage, the matter is 'referred' by the marriage officer.[105]

An application to secure the property of a person under the age of 18 who has married without parental consent is made by way of attorney general's reference for a declaration of forfeiture.[106]

The applications so far discussed are made in the Supreme Court.

The application for an order that a marriage be registered where the marriage officer has failed to do so is made under section 34 in the Parish Court. The application would be by way of a summons on information, and it is likely that such an application would be heard in chambers.

---

103.   As set out in rule 76(2).
104.   As expressed in the Matrimonial Causes Act, section 2.
105.   Section 25(b) Marriage Act.
106.   Section 24 Marriage Act.

THE WAY FORWARD

Like many countries, the institution of marriage is alive and well in Jamaica, but is under attack from an increasing divorce rate and a drop in the number of marriages taking place each year. While the State continues to support marriage, it is recognized that it cannot do so by ignoring the families that are formed without a marriage taking place, particularly where children are involved. There are those in society who view the legislation that recognizes cohabitation for five years as a spousal relationship as undermining the institution of marriage. On the other hand, to do otherwise would be viewed by many as flying in the face of social reality. It remains the case that the large majority of children are born out of wedlock,[107] and the position is unlikely to change as Jamaica and the wider Caribbean are further influenced by the trend in Western countries away from marriage.

In this scenario, the provisions of the Marriage Act have increasingly less impact on people's lives. However, the question of whether the minimum age of marriage, should be linked with the age of consent and whether both of these age qualifications should be aligned with the age of majority is a matter of some intricacy, and requires careful consideration. Furthermore, it is a source of concern both from within and outside our borders.[108]

The recognition of the status of marriage occurs at a constitutional level by way of section 18 of the Charter of Fundamental Rights and Freedoms (Constitutional Amendment) Act 2011. However, it is clear from its wording that the biggest concern was limiting the definition of marriage to 'one man and one woman'.

Legal challenges are being mounted in relation to the buggery law in some Caribbean countries, and this will inevitably lead to questioning the constitutional status of marriage. These matters

---

107.   Over 80 per cent according to the Census 2011.
108.   Development goals and the implementation of legislation on access to education, age of consent, child trafficking, rights of the child, etc.

have not yet been presented in the Jamaican courts although questions about discrimination have.[109]

Legal scholars have highlighted that the way in which legal rights are exercised within the family still hinges significantly on whether or not there is a marriage. There have been calls for the reorganization of the concept of family, not based on marriage, and also for greater clarity, without which there remains uncertainty.

The Marriage Act remains the hallmark legislation in respect of the solemnization of marriages and the paraphernalia of requirements that surround the process. For this reason, it is important that the penal sections in the Act which protect the institution of marriage from interference and abuse are robust and forthright. It is equally important that where breaches or omissions occur, that these matters are vigorously prosecuted, and since responsibility lies with the director of public prosecutions,[110] that office has to ensure that the law is upheld.

109. *Tomlinson v The Attorney General of Jamaica* [2016] JMSC Civ 119.
110. Section 57.

2. Nullity

INTRODUCTION

Mr and Mrs James came into the lawyer's office together. They held hands with each other; they looked into each other's eyes, and were obviously very much in love. Their instructions: to terminate their marriage.

Mr James had been married before. He and the first Mrs James lived quite happily together until she went abroad to work. The lengthy periods of separation took their toll on the marriage, and they grew apart. One day, Mrs James called Mr James and told him that the marriage was over, and he would be getting the divorce papers in the mail. Sure enough, in a few weeks' time Mr James received several documents which indicated that his wife was divorcing him. Mr James carried on with his life and a few months later met the second Mrs James to be. There followed a whirlwind romance, and by the time Mr James popped the question he was confident that his first marriage had ended. Mr James married the second Mrs James and settled down to another round of marital bliss. It was in the course of travelling abroad (to the country where the first Mrs James still resided) that he discovered that at the time of his second marriage the proceedings instituted by the first Mrs James had not yet been completed. Upon further enquiry, Mr James found out that the second marriage and the divorce took place within a matter of weeks. Unfortunately, for Mr James it was the marriage that had come first, not the divorce. Mr James wanted to know if there was any chance of his second marriage being valid from the point that the divorce had been granted. If it was not, then he wanted to terminate the marriage so that he could marry his wife properly.

A GENERAL OVERVIEW

Prior to the introduction of divorce proceedings by statute in 1879, the only feasible way for most people to bring a marriage to an end was by annulment.[1] This in itself was a complicated process governed by canon law that deterred all but the most determined and resourceful. Nullity is an area of law which emerged when marriage was under the control of the church, and as such many of the grounds upon which a marriage can be annulled originate from the reasoning of the church as to the role and purpose of marriage in the religious sense. The heart of the matter is that the church, and hence the law, recognized that some defects in the marriage where of such a fundamental nature that it could not be said that there was a true marriage. Even though divorce proceedings have completely eclipsed nullity as the accepted means of terminating

---

1.   It was possible to bring a private bill to the legislature for an enactment terminating a marriage, but this was an option only for those with the resources to take such a step.

a marriage in modern times, statutory provisions concerning the validity of marriage and the circumstances in which the marriage may be declared null and void may at times be invoked by way of nullity proceedings in the court.

Where one or in some cases more than one ground of nullity is established by the court, the result is that the marriage will be annulled or, in other words, declared void. Historically, the result of annulment could be devastating: children became illegitimate at the stroke of a pen, and drastic changes in inheritance rights could occur. The courts, therefore, took a strict approach to annulment:

According to Dr Lushington in *Catterall v Sweetman:*[2]

> …it must always be remembered that a marriage is essentially distinguished from every other species of contract whether of legislative or judicial determination…that not only is all presumption in favour of the validity and against the nullity of a marriage, but it is so on principle; that a legislative enactment to annul a marriage de facto is a penal enactment, not only penal to the parties, but highly penal to the innocent offspring and therefore to be construed according to the acknowledged rule most strictly.

The impact of nullity and the hardship that it could bring have been mitigated in many areas by successive instances of legislative intervention,[3] but some of the vagaries still remain and go for the most part unnoticed.[4]

As was recognized in *Catterall*, nullity is an area of law where the concept of marriage as a contract is pronounced, and much of the terminology rests on constructions derived from the law of contract. So Caribbean jurisdictions, in adopting the English law, recognized two premises upon which a marriage may be annulled:

1. Where the marriage is void.

2. Where the marriage is voidable.

The grounds that were originally deemed to make the marriage

2.   (1845) 63 ER 1047.
3.   Legitimation Act, section 6(1), Divorce Law, section 9.
4.   Nullity procedure is slightly different from that of dissolution.

void have rested on circumstances which existed prior to the marriage and could be viewed as a failure to qualify or incapacity, such as being within the prohibited degrees, sexual incapacity. Voidable grounds on the other hand, often related to circumstances which arose subsequent to the marriage such as a wilful refusal to consummate, or exposing the party to venereal disease. There are some grounds[5] which have over time moved by statutory intervention from one category to the other, that is, from void to voidable and vice versa, according to policy considerations.[6]

Void vs Voidable

Before considering the particular grounds of nullity, the question arises, what is the difference between void and voidable marriages? Although voidable marriages are no longer recognized in Jamaican law,[7] an appreciation of the concept is helpful in a general understanding of the area, and to the extent that the vestiges of voidable grounds may still lurk in certain aspects of the procedure,[8] it should not be ignored.

If a marriage is void it is viewed in law as never having come into existence, that is, it is 'void ab initio'. Historically, this meant that not only was there no marriage, but that the relationships which arose out of the marriage and any consequences which would ordinarily flow from it would not be recognized. This could have serious repercussions in many respects. Children born within the marriage would lose their legitimacy, and this, in turn, would affect their right to maintenance and inheritance. Importantly, the special provisions for division of matrimonial property under the Married Woman's

---

5. For example, non-consummation, mental disorder, and lack of consent.
6. Under the Matrimonial Causes Act (MCA), section 4, lack of consent became a void ground, when previously under the Divorce Act (as is still the case in England) it was a voidable ground. However, according to D. Tolstoy, in 'Void and Voidable Marriages,' *Modern Law Review* 27, no. 4:385, prior to the Reformation, this was a void ground.
7. See MCA, section 4.
8. Voidable grounds may provide a case for an application under section 8(2) of the MCA.

Property Act would not apply since there was no longer a 'married woman' for the purposes of the proceedings. Legal measures to mitigate the devastating effect of annulment were enacted, either by extending the definition of 'marriage' in specific circumstances to include a void marriage,[9] or broadening the class of persons entitled to benefit, for example, in inheritance under the Status of Children Act.

To summerize, in cases where the marriage is void:

i.   The marriage never came into existence, 'and can be treated by both parties to it as never having taken place'.[10]

ii. Any interested party may approach the court for a declaration in such terms. The interest may stem from a right to inherit under a will, recognition of which is dependent on the status of the marriage or whether a child is born in or out of wedlock. See *In re Park*[11] and *Re Estate of Princess Nina Aga Khan (Dec'd) orse Nina Dyer.*[12]

iii. A marriage may be declared void after the death of either or both of the parties to the marriage.[13]

By comparison, a marriage which is voidable:

i.   is a valid subsisting marriage until a court of competent jurisdiction has granted a decree of nullity;

ii. can only be annulled by the parties to the marriage; and

iii. can only be annulled while both parties are alive.

Section 4 of the Matrimonial Causes Act (MCA), along with the repeal of the Divorce Act by the same statute, had the effect of leaving no voidable grounds for nullity under Jamaican law. As a

---

9.   Maintenance Act, Property (Rights of Spouses) Act (PROSA), and earlier the Legitimation Act.
10.   *De Renville v De Renville* [1948] P 100.
11.   [1953] 2 All ER 1411.
12.   19 WIR 102.
13.   Therefore, a void marriage can be annulled by petition (*inter partes*) or by declaration (third parties).

matter of law, this means that where circumstances which previously fell into the category of voidable grounds exist, nullity is no longer available as a remedy. In these cases, there is no alternative but to terminate the marriage by dissolution: to obtain a divorce. This makes sense from the standpoint of the law because from the characteristics listed above, voidable marriages are virtually indistinguishable from valid marriages, so why should they not both be terminated by dissolution?

There remains, however, a certain resistance from religious quarters in the society because theologically the distinction between a marriage which is voidable for non-consummation, for example, and a valid marriage is of great importance. The way in which such a marriage is terminated determines if, and the manner in which, the parties may remarry in accordance with the particular religious rites. To lump such marriages into one category (valid) and prescribe one method of termination, that is, dissolution will, in some instances, close the door to remarriage where the religion does not countenance divorce. However, this is becoming less significant to the bulk of the population, and those who cling to these ideals must consider what is most important: remarriage if necessary outside of their church, or remaining in a dead marriage out of refusal to accept the prescribed methodology of the law.[14]

The 'Non-Marriage'

As a matter of public policy, the law generally leans in favour of recognizing a marriage, but, at the same, has to balance this principle with the need to guard against marriage being used for ulterior motives.[15] While the Marriage Act provides an elaborate process for contracting or entering into a marriage and demands that these rules be followed, it is balanced by limiting the circumstances in which the marriage will be void to a few important breaches.[16]

---

14. For example, by law, if the marriage is unconsummated it should now be terminated by dissolution not nullity.
15. Immigration, citizenship, or taking advantage of the vulnerable.
16. Section 3.

However, before considering whether or not the marriage is subject to annulment by reason of nullity, the question arises as to whether there are some circumstances in which a marriage has taken place that simply do not conform to the ceremony of marriage as we understand it and, therefore, cannot be legitimately described as a marriage. This has been termed in other jurisdictions a 'non-marriage.'[17]

Where, for example, the marriage does not breach any of the formalities in section 3 of the Marriage Act, but in every other respect is virtually unrecognizable, or is repugnant to the dignity and solemnity which we expect to underpin these proceedings, what is the court to do? This presumes, of course, that there is a challenge to its legitimacy, or an opportunity presents itself for the court to enter into these deliberations, which may not be the case at all. Also, certain English cases,[18] which recognize a situation where there is a 'non-marriage', not by reason of it being void or voidable, but simply (or perhaps not so simply), because the ceremony did not have the essential hallmarks necessary for it to be recognized, may provide some guidance. So for us in the Caribbean region, is there a notion of a marriage ceremony that is in accordance with Caribbean laws or Caribbean presumptions of what a marriage should be? Furthermore, to what extent are Jamaican marriage laws a reflection of this concept, even if there is such a thing as marriage according to Caribbean precepts at all? There are two factors which make it unlikely that this area will be of anything more than academic interest in Jamaica and the wider Caribbean: One, locally, there is no extensive system of state benefits where entitlement rests on establishing that the parties were married.[19] Two, ancillary relief in marriage is almost equally accessible to parties to a void marriage as well as to common law spouses.[20]

---

17.   *R v Bham* [1966] 1 QB 159.
18.   See Ibid., and *R v Ali Mohamed* (1943) unreported, quoted in *Bham*.
19.   See *Chief Adjudication Officer v Bath* 2000 1 FLR 8, *Abassi v Abassi* 2006 EWCA 355 and *Brown v Milwood* 2006 EWHC 642.
20.   See Maintenance Act and PROSA.

Nevertheless, there may be circumstances where marriage is being used systematically for some advantage, the attainment of citizenship, for example, that the authorities may seek to frame the process within a context where even if the marriage is recognized, it will not convey certain status if certain disqualifications are evident.[21] This is a different (and perhaps preferable) approach to the problem of addressing the purpose for which the marriage was contracted without having to call into question the status or validity of the marriage.

NULLITY GROUNDS: THE LAW

The grounds upon which a marriage can be terminated by nullity proceedings are contained in the MCA. They are:[22]

i. One of the parties was married to someone else at the time of the marriage – section 4(1)(a).

ii. The marriage is void under the Marriage Act or any other legal provisions – section 4(1)(b).

iii. Lack of consent by reason of

   a. duress or fraud;

   b. mistake as to identity or the nature of the ceremony;

   c. mental incapacity – section 4(1)(c).

iv. The parties were of the same sex – section 4(1)(d).

   a. One of the parties is married to someone else at the time of the marriage: Bigamy

Section 4(1)(a) Bigamy

Section 4(1)(a) states that a marriage will be void if: 'one of the parties to the marriage had a husband or wife living at the time of the marriage'.

---

21. See Jamaican Nationality Act, section 5A.
22. Section 4.

A valid marriage to another person, in respect of either party at the time of their marriage to each other, will render their marriage void. The ground in nullity is to be distinguished from the criminal offence of bigamy which requires mens rea or guilty knowledge.[23] In nullity, it matters not that the parties were ignorant, careless, or acted inadvertently, the second marriage will be void by the fact of the pre-existing marriage. Furthermore, the subsequent termination of the first marriage will not validate the second (void) marriage. In small island jurisdictions where there is a high incidence of migration, the tendency to act in anticipation of the termination of a marriage, particularly when the divorce is being pursued in another country, is strong. This may not become apparent until further steps are being taken in reliance on the marriage such as travel abroad or inheritance.[24] The situation which is outlined at the beginning of this chapter is far from unusual.

Section 4(1)(b) Void under the Provisions of the Marriage Act

Under the Marriage Acts of all the Commonwealth Caribbean jurisdictions including Jamaica, certain provisions refer to circumstances in which a marriage will not be recognized and will therefore be void. These provisions are important because they reinforce the parliamentary intention behind the legislation that marriages should be conducted within a certain framework. The mischief behind the wording is that without imposing too much stricture in the form of absolute compliance with all the provisions, there must be a level of conformity at least to certain basic tenets. In Jamaica, these provisions are found in section 3 of the Marriage Act.[25]

---

23.   For recent cases, see *Daily Observer*, February 12, 2015 and March 9, 2015.
24.   See *McCarthy and Another v McCarthy* (1966) 9 WIR 443; children of bigamous marriage held not to qualify for share in estate.
25.   These grounds are also discussed in the chapter on marriage.

i.   *Formalities*

Section 3(1) of the Marriage Act refers to the essential formalities which if both parties knowingly and wilfully disregard, then the marriage will be void.

> If both the parties to a marriage knowingly and wilfully acquiesce in the solemnization of the marriage ceremony between them –
>
> By or before a person not being a Marriage Officer, or
>
> Otherwise than in the presence of two witnesses besides the Marriage Officer solemnizing or witnessing and registering the marriage,
>
> The marriage shall be void.

These provisions are incorporated into the MCA under section 4(1)(b).

Whilst the Marriage Act sets out an array of stipulations pertaining to marriage, it is the requirement that the marriage be conducted in the presence of a marriage officer and two witnesses which are singled out as going to the root of validity. In each Caribbean jurisdiction, the requirements that are highlighted as essential in this regard may vary.[26]

This section generally relies on the knowledge of the parties to determine the validity of the marriage, that is, whether or not the marriage takes place with or without a marriage officer.

However, in the case of *Thompson v Thompson*,[27] it was argued that the absence of the marriage officer as matter of fact was what defeated validity rather than the knowledge of the parties. When section 3 is construed in this way, 'knowingly and wilfully' refers to going through the ceremony rather than to the defect itself, and leads to the position where the fact of absence of a marriage officer will render the marriage void regardless of whether any of the parties are aware. This can be justified on the basis that the need for the ceremony to be conducted by a marriage officer is intended by

---

26.   Antigua and Barbuda, Marriage Act, section 62. Also Belize, Marriage Act, section 58.

27.   BS 1994 SC 5, this was preceded by *Perkins v Perkins* BB 1984 HC 26 (Barbados).

Parliament as sacrosanct, and that the possibility of a valid marriage being contracted without a marriage officer opposes that intention and renders the Act absurd. Indeed, this interpretation was applied to the original Marriage Act of 1753 in England in a number of cases; however, it was soon realized that such an interpretation could lead to unfortunate results and when the issue came to be considered under later acts, the court reconsidered its position; see *Wright v Elwood*.[28] The requirement for a marriage officer was therefore seen as a condition which was contingent on the circumstances, including the knowledge of the parties.[29] So, in the situation where the person officiating was not a marriage officer, the presumption of marriage, or the innocence of one or both of the parties, or the limitations of their knowledge, could be employed to preserve the validity of the marriage. Certainly, it can be argued that it is equally absurd that the ignorance of the parties could be exploited by an unscrupulous imposter and render the marriage void despite their best intentions, as it is to say that the requirement for such an important official as a marriage officer should be conditional on the knowledge of the parties. The balance that has to be struck is between the importance of the marriage officer as an officiating component in contracting a lawful marriage and the need certainty in the parties as to the status of their marriage. The judge in *Thompson* expressed the need for the question to be considered by a higher court in order to bring proper resolution to the issue.

The pre-condition that 'both parties knowingly and wilfully acquiesce' supports the policy position that marriages will generally be recognized and not easily overturned,[30] although in many jurisdictions this has been changed to 'either party'.

The reference to have at least two witnesses present suggests that secret or clandestine marriages will not be tolerated. Whereas a marriage need not be a massive public spectacle, it is not to be

---

28.   (1837) 163 ER 231.
29.   *Dormer v Williams* (1838) 1 Curt 870.
30.   For an exception to this viewpoint, see *Thompson v Thompson*.

so private that it excludes all but the participants. The witnesses, therefore, are a hallmark of the balance between respecting the privacy of the parties, but at the same time ensuring that there are 'onlookers'. Witnesses also become important in terms of proving a marriage when the records of the marriage have been lost, damaged, or destroyed.[31]

The reasoning behind the approach that knowledge is required is that otherwise an inadvertent breach could bring the validity of the marriage into question. If it is too easy to fall between the cracks such as by ignorance or inadvertence, people will be deterred from entering into marriage because it could be invalidated at a stroke and therefore the importance of marriage would be significantly undermined. Therefore, in Jamaica, it is only if the parties set out deliberately to thwart the legal requirements in these vital respects as set out in the Marriage Act, that the marriage will be void. It appears that the only circumstances in which a failure to comply with all the formalities as stipulated will result in the marriage being void is under section 37 of the Marriage Act where a marriage in contemplation of death is being contracted.

ii. Minimum Age

Section 3(2) of the Marriage Act states:

'A marriage solemnized between persons either of whom is under the age of sixteen shall be void.'

As a provision under the Marriage Act, this provision comes into the MCA by way of section 4(1)(b).

This provision, like bigamy, does not depend on any knowledge or intention of the parties; being under age 16 is sufficient to make the marriage void. This provision has changed over time in accordance with societal norms and, at this time, the debate continues as to whether or not the current age is or should be consistent with legal

---

31.   They can provide or be relied on as evidence of the marriage without the court having to resort to the presumption of marriage. This was mentioned in the case of *Douglas v Hello!* (No. 1) [2005] EWCA 595.

age limits in other pieces of legislation, for example, the Child Care and Protection Act, the Children (Guardianship and Custody) Act, and the Maintenance Act. There is considerable support for increasing the minimum age for marriage (and along with it, the age of consent) to 18. In the context of the discussion on marriage, it is important to take into account the requirement for parental consent between 16 and 18[32] and the effect that changing the minimum age of marriage would have on these and other provisions. The Law Reform (Age of Majority) Act brings the age of majority down from 21, and that act also recognizes the common law 'mature minor' rule whereby certain decisions as to medical and other treatment can be made by a young person of age 16.[33] So the premise that there should be a singular age of majority from which all rights flow could be viewed as naïve and is certainly unsupported by statute.

iii. *Prohibited Degrees of Consanguinity and Affinity*

Section 3(3) of the Marriage Act states:

'If the parties to any marriage are within the prohibited degrees of consanguinity or affinity according to the law of England from time to time in force, the marriage shall be void.'

This provision comes into the MCA at section 4(1)(b).

The prohibited degrees of consanguinity and affinity are restrictions which the law places on marriage between people who are related by blood (consanguinity) or by marriage (affinity). In both cases, the thinking behind the restrictions is that such marriages undermine the stability of the family. In the case of consanguinity, inter-marriage between persons who are blood relatives causes a concentration of the negative traits in the genes of the children produced in such a marriage. These children then face a greater risk of being afflicted by physical or mental deformities. This ground also does not depend on the knowledge or intention of the parties, and rests entirely on the fact of being within the prohibited degrees that will make the marriage void.

32.   Marriage Act, section 24.
33.   Section 8, also Status of Children Act, section 12.

The prohibitive degrees are traditionally a wider class than those relationships that are deemed to be incestuous. So that only sexual relations with direct relatives are criminalized[34] and therefore, in some situations where it may not be permissible for the parties to marry, there is no offence of incest committed if the parties merely cohabit or engage in sexual relations. This was the case with uncle/niece or aunt/nephew liaisons, and became a matter of grave concern for Parliament when considering the Sexual Offences Bill. As a result, in Jamaica, Parliament has addressed this by including uncle/niece and aunt/nephew relationships within the definition of incest as set out in sections 7(1) and (2) of the Sexual Offences Act.

What then are the prohibited degrees of marriage in Jamaica? The list of forbidden marriages in England was first set out in *The Book of Common Prayer* in 1560 and remained unchanged until the beginning of the twentieth century. From then until now, the law has been governed primarily by the Prohibited Degrees of Relationship Act 1949, to which there have been a succession of amendments that are extensive and highly complex.[35]

Inroads have been made in relation to *affines*, so that the Marriage (Deceased Wife's Sister) Act, as in other jurisdictions, allows for marriage between persons related by marriage by virtue of the death of the person who linked them. Laws as to marriage between persons who have a connection by marriage have always been a question of social and religious custom.[36] In some societies,[37] not only is marriage between in-laws permitted, but in the case where a man has died, it is expected that his brother will then become responsible for the family and marry his widow.

While there is no legal prohibition to a marriage between first cousins, the dominant social mindset in the Caribbean is to

34. For a male: grandmother, mother, sister, daughter, or granddaughter.
35. A comprehensive list may be found in F.M. Lancaster, *Genetic and Quantitative Aspects of Genealogy*, under Forbidden Marriage Laws of the United Kingdom, tables 22–32.
36. Australia, under section 23B of the Marriage Act, places no restriction on marriage between persons related by marriage.
37. Examples are seen in Somalia, Cameroon, and Kurdistan.

regard such unions with a certain amount of disapproval or even repugnance. Nevertheless, Jamaica, like many countries is not a homogenous society.[38] Among some racial sub-groups, this is not viewed as exceptional. However, the general resistance to such unions leads to a change in attitudes and the virtual elimination of marriage between close relatives. As such, there is little need for legislative intervention in this area.

In larger Western societies, the ease of divorce has led to successive and separate monogamous unions as a common occurrence. In such circumstances, as people move into the next marriage, they also may move away from members of the last marriage. There may be little or no contact between persons who are, in fact, in-laws or step relatives. Such persons would never have lived together within the same family setting and in such a situation the notion of being someone's step-parent or child (and the consequent destabilization of the family unit by such a marriage) is entirely artificial.[39] In smaller countries such as Jamaica, the likelihood of people who are related by marriage not knowing each other is lessened. However, island migration patterns counteract that position and make it possible for step-relatives to meet as adults and possibly wish to marry. This has yet to be addressed in the form of legislation, and will continue to be viewed as unworthy of Parliament's attention until such time as the courts are presented with the issue. Of course, that so many family arrangements exist in the form of common law unions to which these provisions do not apply is another reason why these questions will often not arise.

The real legal issue on this topic, is that this section encapsulates the prohibitive degrees for marriage in Jamaica within 'the law of England from time to time in force'. As well as being somewhat incongruous, this leads to a state of uncertainty which should not exist in the law.

---

38.   Jamaica's motto 'Out of many one people' bears testimony to this.
39.   See *B v L* [2005] ECHR 584.

Sound constitutional reasons exist for preserving existing laws when a country moves from a colonial regime to independence. The reception of English law into the law of the colonial state is itself a matter of considerable complexity.[40] Then, at the time of transformation, this legal impostition in itself becomes a matter for the constitution of the new state.[41] Then, going forward, it will be a matter for the new independent legislature whether to keep the old law unchanged or introduce new provisions, as and when required. Ultimately, it will be a matter for the courts, if called upon, to interpret and decipher the validity and status of the law which may be dependent on the route which it took to become incorporated into the legal system. The process by which the law transitions from one legal system, in this case a colonial system, into the legal system of an independent sovereign state has been the subject of much debate.[42] It is a central issue in the area of Commonwealth Caribbean constitutional law,[43] but it may suffice to say for these purposes, that the common law of England with certain exceptions is applicable in Jamaica.[44]

The phrase 'the law of England from time to time in force' specifically separates this area from the changes made by the local legislature. So even though local legislation has been enacted,[45] it can at least be argued that it has little effect. The law of England, in this area, is governed by the Prohibited Degrees of Relationship Act 1949 and its subsequent amendments. Furthermore, the Jamaican

---

40. See Rose-Marie Belle Antoine, *Commonwealth Caribbean Law and Legal Systems*, 2nd ed. (London: Routledge-Cavendish, 2008).
41. Saving Clauses.
42. Indeed, some have argued that the process is fundamentally flawed, see Ralph Carnegie, 'The Approach of Independence for the Associated States: A Constitutional Law Perspective,' 4 *Bulletin of Eastern Caribbean Affairs* 8 (1971).
43. See Keith Patchett, 'English Law in the West Indies: A Conference Report' (1963) 12 ICLQ 922; Dorcas White, 'Patterns of Law Making in the West Indies,' UWI Faculty of Law Library; and Leighton Jackson, 'Fi We Law,' in *Transitions in Caribbean Law: Law-making, Constitutionalism and the Convergence of National and International Law*, ed. David Berry and Tracy Robinson (Kingston: The Caribbean Law Publishing Company, 2013).
44. Raphael Codlin, *Historical Foundations of Jamaican Law* (Kingston: Canoe Press, 2003).
45. Marriage (Deceased Wife's Sister or Brother's Widow) Act.

Interpretation Act seems to direct that this act be received into Jamaican law.[46] The legislation as currently worded not only has the effect of hitching the law in Jamaica to the law in England but also to the developments of the law in England, and is thereby taking the country on a journey without good reason. There have been a number of legislative changes [47] in England that have been ignored in Jamaica, but are by this provision, an integral part of local law. The impact of the UK Human Rights Act and its link to the European Court of Human Rights further compounds the problem. Currently, even the status of the law in the UK is uncertain by virtue of the decision to leave the European Union.

Other Caribbean countries have removed this formulation, some simply set out the prohibited degrees as a schedule to the legislation,[48] some simply recite it within the section;[49] in any event, this is something which should be rectified by legislators.[50] Whether enacting legislation [51] in this area has the effect of 'unhitching' Jamaican law, is far from clear, but might be a suitable argument to advance as a preliminary step to jolting Parliament into a legislative response.

Section 4(1)(c) Lack of Consent

Section 4(1)(c) of the MCA states that a marriage shall be void if:

> In the case of marriages celebrated on or after the commencement of this Act the consent of either of the parties to the marriage was not a valid consent because-
>
> It was obtained by duress or fraud; or
>
> One party was mistaken as to the identity of the other party or as to the nature of the ceremony performed; or
>
> One party was mentally incapable of understanding the nature and effect of the marriage ceremony at the time of the marriage;

46. Section 41.
47. For example, the Marriages (Prohibited Degrees of Relationship) Act 1986.
48. Belize.
49. St Kitts and Nevis.
50. See article 12 of the Convention for the Protection of Human Rights and Fundamental Freedoms.
51. Marriage (Deceased Wife's Sister or Brother's Widow) Act.

Marriage is a binding contract. The absence of the element of agreement removes the foundation of marriage as a consensual arrangement. The question of forced marriages, which amounts to a serious attack on the principle of voluntariness in marriage, has challenged the authorities in other countries with an increase in the number of immigrants from the Indian subcontinent and has brought the status of arranged marriages under close scrutiny,[52] but this is not a significant issue in Jamaica. There have been instances where the question for the courts has been: can a promise to marry be enforced?[53] However, the issue of consent at the time of the ceremony is rarely an explicit source of contention.[54] As such, Jamaican common law, in this area, is largely based on cases from outside of the Commonwealth Caribbean.

i. Duress or Fraud

For duress to be established, fear must override free will. This is seen in cases such as *Scott v Sebright*,[55] *Hirani*,[56] and *Szechter*.[57] This issue was also raised, unsuccessfully, in the Barbadian case of *Small v Small*.[58] The question for the court to decide in each case is, whether the person's will was so overborne as to negate consent and how an assessment of this question should be made, whether subjectively as in *Hirani* or objectively as in *Buckland*.[59] Also, in both instances, the question arises as to what circumstances can be relied on to establish the matter one way or the other. For example, is the threat of being reported to the police for a criminal offence

---

52. Forced Marriage (Civil Protection) Act 2007, UK.
53. *Alfred Maragh v James Williams and Edith Williams, Rachel Williams v Leonard Maragh* [1970] 12 JLR 253.
54. For a rare exception, see the Barbadian case of *Small v Small* BB 1990 HC 33. In this case, duress was raised as a subsidiary point to the main issue of mental capacity.
55. (1886) 12 PD 21.
56. (1983) 4 FLR 232.
57. [1970] 3 All ER 905.
58. BB 1990 HC 33.
59. [1967] 2 All ER 300.

sufficient[60] or does it have to be an immediate threat to life, limb or liberty; or is it simply carrying out one's parents' wishes?[61] There was, in the past, in some quarters of Jamaican society, a tradition that the bride should display some measure of reluctance and some of us may have witnessed ceremonies where the bride has entered with a flood of tears. This is usually put down to being overcome with emotion, and the question of whether or not consent, in a legal sense, was being freely given would not enter into the minds of the congregation even for one moment.

Fraud

In Jamaica, questions such as what is fraud in this context have been raised. Many believe that if it turns out that the person married only to secure a right to travel or if they did not disclose that they had children, for example, that this can give rise to a claim for annulment on the grounds of fraud.[62] The rationale depends on the discovery of certain 'facts' after the marriage which, if they had been known to the other party prior to the marriage, would have deterred the complainant (or so they now say) from entering into the marriage, in short, a 'deal-breaker'. On the other hand, it is difficult to see why Jamaican courts should depart from the decisions in England and Australia on the same point.[63] These decisions make it clear that unless the fraud is in relation to the identity of the party, or the nature of the ceremony, fraudulent deceptive representations will not vitiate consent; see *Swift v Kelly*.[64] There are a series of Australian cases that show the course of judicial thinking on the question of fraud: In *Deniz*,[65] Frederico J was sympathetic to the notion that fraud should vitiate consent and therefore render the marriage void, which he did in that case. The facts in that case

---

60. *Buckland,* defilement.
61. *Singh v Singh* [1971] P 226.
62. 'A Fraudulent Marriage', *Daily Observer*, November 16, 2009.
63. In the case of *Perkins v Perkins*, the court in Barbados relied on *Deniz*, but it is unclear whether a court today would uphold the decision.
64. (1835) 2 Knapp 257.
65. (1977) 7 Fam LR 3.

were that a woman was tricked into marriage by a man who falsely represented that he loved her when his real intention was to obtain permanent residence. However, in the case of *Suria*,[66] the court decided otherwise. Eventually in the case of *Osman and Mourrali*,[67] Nygh J rejected the contention that false representations or a mistake as to a certain state of affairs could result in the marriage being annulled. He relied on another case, *Otway*[68] and the English case of *Puttick v AG*.[69] In *Otway*, the presiding judge stated: 'In my view, whatever the means of fraud may be, it has so far not been extended in English law to include fraudulent misrepresentations....'

In Jamaica, there have been several cases where a party to a marriage has alleged that certain facts were revealed after the marriage, which, had they been known previously, the marriage would not have taken place. It is an attractive proposition that if deceitful assertions were made and the other party relying on them entered into the marriage, then consent is negated. However, a careful examination of the cases does not support this view. At first glance, it would appear to be instinctively repugnant that a person who is deliberately misled as to the true intentions of the other party should find that the marriage is nevertheless valid. However, the difficulty for the courts is that such allegations are all too easy to fabricate after the event, whether unilaterally or by both the parties in collusion with each other. Such a permissive interpretation would have the practical effect of opening the floodgates to anyone who with hindsight questions the wisdom of their decision to marry. The institution of marriage with all its sanctity would be severely undermined by such an approach. The question which therefore remains is if, as is currently stipulated in Jamaican legislation, fraud is a separate head from mistake, what does it mean? In some Caribbean jurisdictions, following the amendments to the English

---

66. (1977) 3 Fam LR 11.
67. (1989) 13 Fam LR 444.
68. (1986) 11 Fam LR 99.
69. [1980] Fam 1.

legislation, the word fraud has been completely omitted. This would make seeing how case law has developed. This has not yet been considered in Jamaica.

The fact that lack of consent is a ground upon which the marriage will be held void in Jamaica as opposed to being voidable as it is in most Caribbean countries coincides with the abolition of voidable grounds in this country. However, this is the nullity ground which is considered to be so important that if the state opts to recognize only void grounds then it is retained even if it was previously a voidable ground as it remains in several other Caribbean jurisdictions.

ii.   *Mistake*
– 'as to the identity of the other party'

It is a legal requirement for a party to know who they are marrying for a marriage to be considered valid, and if a mistake occurs as to the identity of the other party the necessary consent will be vitiated. In the case of *Allerdyce v Mitchell*,[70] the 'wife' believed that she was marrying a member of a well-known family, and this was held to be a mistake of identity as opposed to a mistake of the name. Similarly, in the case of *Militante v Ogunwomoju*,[71] the marriage was annulled because the petitioner believed she was marrying Richard Ogunwomoju , in fact, she was marrying Anthony Osimen, an illegal immigrant. The legal requirement is that the mistake should be a mistake of identity and not of attributes, but in many of these cases the line between identity and attributes seems blurred. In *C v C*,[72] although the 'wife' believed that she was marrying a famous boxer, the error was determined as a mistake as to attributes and therefore the marriage was held to be valid. This was on the basis that she intended to marry the man who was present at the ceremony and therefore the name of the person was immaterial to her decision. It is hard to distinguish this case from the situation in *Militante*, which

---

70.   (1869) 6 WW & A'B. 45.
71.   [1993] 2 FCR 355.
72.   [1942] NZLR 356.

appears to have been decided on grounds of sympathy rather than law. The ruling in *Militante* may have been no more than a subtle means of thwarting illegal immigration by marriage. However, 'sham' or 'business' marriages, in the absence of fear or duress, can be upheld as valid.[73] Certainly, in Jamaica, marriages contracted in the belief that a party will apply for the other to migrate are far from uncommon and perhaps in keeping with this latter view, are usually terminated by way of dissolution rather than nullity.

– 'as to the nature of the ceremony'

A mistake as to the nature of the ceremony is self-explanatory. If a party whether through ignorance, naiveté, or lack of cultural or religious awareness does not know that they are going through a ceremony of marriage, their consent is invalid. In *Hall v Hall*,[74] a woman had a marriage annulled for mistake as she thought that marriage could only be conducted in church and therefore that the ceremony in a registrar's office was simply to register her name.

iii. *Mental Incapacity*

Section 4 of the MCA states that where there is incapacity in understanding the nature and effect of the ceremony the marriage will be void. Generally, in the law of nullity there are two types of grounds dealing with the mental state of the parties. The first ground is that either party is incapable of understanding the nature of the ceremony and its consequences, which we find at section 4(1)(c)(iii) of the MCA. The second type of mental incapacity ground, which is not used in Jamaica, is having a specified mental disorder, which we find in other Caribbean jurisdictions such as Montserrat[75] and also Belize (which uses both). The ground as expressed in Jamaica, like duress, fraud, or mistake is treated as a sub-heading of lack of consent and will make the marriage void. To establish this ground,

---

73.   See *Silver v Silver* [1958] 1 WLR 259.
74.   *Hall v Hall* (1908) 24 TLR 756. See also *Mehta v Mehta* [1945] 2 All ER 690.
75.   Section 16(1)(b) MCA.

careful scrutiny of the party's mental capacity in relation to his or her ability to understand the nature of marriage is required. The cases[76] reflect a balancing act between construing the responsibilities of marriage as sufficiently onerous to disqualify the mentally vulnerable, and thereby protect them from abuse, whilst preserving the essence of simplicity which allows everyone else to qualify. The issue has been compounded by a line of argument that instead of protecting the mentally vulnerable from being taken advantage of in marriage, such a person should be seen as having a right to family life which includes the right to marry[77] just like anyone else. The Convention on the Rights of Persons with Disabilities, at Article 23(1)(a) states: 'The right of all persons with disabilities who are of marriageable age to marry and to found a family on the basis of free and full consent of the intending spouses is recognized'.

Arguably, the question of whether 'free and full consent' is consistent with the case law would be an interesting topic for debate.

This has been further refined under the Convention on the Elimination of All Forms of Discrimination Against Women (CEDAW).[78] According to developing positions on mental competence, the fact that the particular marriage may fall outside the bounds of societal norms is not sufficient to justify the person being deprived of the right to enter into family relations.[79]

Section 4(1)(d) 'parties of the same sex'

The definition of marriage as enunciated in *Hyde v Hyde* has been under attack from many directions. (Few people now regard the stipulation 'for life' as being anything other than a fanciful ideal). In recent times, the assault on this proposition has been centred on

---

76. *In the Estate of Park* [1954] P 112, and *Hill v Hill* [1959] 1 All ER 281, *In re B* (a minor) [1988] AC 199.
77. Article 16, Universal Declaration of Human Rights; Article 23, International Covenant on Civil and Political Rights.
78. Article 16, The Convention on the Elimination of all forms of Discrimination Against Women, 1979.
79. 'Mental Health Aspects of Women's Reproductive Health, A Global Review of the Literature'; WHO, 2009.

the union being between 'one man and one woman'. While most people have a ready grasp of what this means, it is important to consider a number of aspects of this proposition in order to have an understanding of the law on the matter.

Under English law, which has become the law in Jamaica, a distinction is made between sex and gender. Sex is determined at birth and is a medical determination of physiological characteristics. Once recorded on the birth certificate, the law does not permit a change.[80] This was confirmed in the case of *Corbett v Corbett*.[81] Although this is a case which was decided in England after Jamaica had become independent, if called upon, it is likely that the Jamaican courts would attach considerable weight to it even though the law in England has, by virtue of the Human Rights Act,[82] somewhat moved on from this position.

In *Bellinger v Bellinger*,[83] while upholding the fixed position as expressed in *Corbett*, it was conceded by the House of Lords, that the statutory provision which gave rise to this interpretation was incompatible with articles 8 and 12 of the European Convention on Human Rights (ECHR). This ruling, then, provided the gateway for parliamentary intervention in what became the Gender Recognition Act 2004.

The challenges to legally recognize gender rather than sex have not yet crystallized in the Caribbean,[84] but it will be, as seen elsewhere, an area which encompasses constitutional law, human rights law, as well as family law and possibly criminal law considerations.

For the time being, it is sufficient to proceed by recognizing that the parties being of the same sex makes a marriage void in most Commonwealth Caribbean jurisdictions, including Jamaica. The differing positions of Antigua and Barbuda, and St Kitts and

---

80. Compared with the position in France as exemplified by the decision in *B v France* [1992] ECHR 40.
81. [1971] P 83.
82. 1998.
83. [2001] 2 FLR 1048.
84. Although the constitutionality of certain same sex activities has.

Nevis provide an interesting comparison. Both countries repealed the legislation which included grounds for nullity and replaced it with the Divorce Act. In Antigua and Barbuda, there has been no legislation that retrieves these provisions, and therefore it provides no reference in their statutory provisions to the stipulation that the parties to a marriage be respectively male and female.

By comparison, in 2005, St Kitts and Nevis adopted the Antiguan Divorce Act, but subsequently amended the act to insert certain voidable grounds, including lack of consent that has been re-constructed and adapted from the former MCA.[85] In this way, the voidable ground of lack of consent has been extended to include the parties not being respectively male and female. This is of significance in two respects: the change in phraseology from 'of the same sex' to the gender terms 'male and female' and the re-categorization of this ground from void to voidable.

The operative time for establishing whether this ground is established as with most void grounds is at the time of the marriage. Therefore, no accommodation is made for any subsequent change in status whether by way of medical procedure or otherwise.[86]

Conclusion

The law and the general understanding of nullity in society is at variance. For example, contrary to the layman's perception, the non-consummation of a marriage does not affect its validity according to Jamaican law. Prior to the passing of the MCA in 1989, there were certain voidable grounds for annulment based on non-consummation, but even then simply not consummating a marriage was never sufficient.[87] As the law now stands, the previous grounds of wilful refusal to consummate and failure to consummate due to incapacity are no longer applicable; the grounds for nullity being specifically restricted to section 4 of the MCA.

85. Section 12A.
86. Compare with the Gender Recognition legislation in the UK.
87. *Treasure v Treasure* (1978) 16 JLR 163.

PRACTICE AND PROCEDURE IN NULLITY

Under Jamaican law, the only grounds that are appropriate for nullity proceedings are where the marriage is void. However, a marriage that is void is 'void ab initio', in other words, there is no marriage at all. This, then, raises the issue of the need to annul a marriage that is void. Why enter into legal proceedings when both parties could simply go their separate ways. The logic of this position is not to be faulted, but there are practical reasons why it is generally prudent to take steps to have a void marriage legally declared as such.

1. The termination of a void marriage is, in many instances, a gateway to obtaining ancillary relief whether it is maintenance for the spouse[88] or children, custody, or for division of matrimonial property.[89]

2. Until such time as there is a judgment as to the nullity of the marriage, the public records will show that the marriage has taken place and there will be no basis for looking behind its presumed validity.

So while it is perfectly permissible to walk away from such a marriage without going through the inconvenience and expense of legal proceedings, there may be equally inconvenient and expensive repercussions for doing so.

The rules of practice and procedure in relation to nullity are to be found in part 76 of the civil procedure rules (CPR) concerning matrimonial proceedings: rule 76.1(b).

Commencement of Nullity Proceedings
Petition or Fixed Date Claim Form

By rule 76.4(1): 'Proceedings...for nullity of marriage...must be commenced by petition...in form no...MP2....' The contents of the petition are dictated by rule 76.4(3).

---

88.   See Section 23, MCA.
89.   See Section 13, PROSA.

Form MP2 assumes that the petitioner will be a party to the marriage rather than a third party. As mentioned earlier, where the marriage is void, it is open to challenge by third parties: see *In re Park*. As such, the form prescribed in the rules may not be appropriate in those circumstances. A distinction can be made between seeking to have a marriage annulled on the ground that it is void as opposed to seeking a declaration that the marriage is void.[90] Certainly, within the context of matrimonial proceedings, rule 76.4(15) as presently drafted does not envisage an alternative to the petition in proceedings for nullity of marriage. It would appear, therefore, that where a party is seeking annulment of the marriage on the grounds that the marriage is void, the action must be commenced by way of petition in accordance with the matrimonial proceedings rules. Where on the other hand, a declaration that the marriage is void is being sought by a third party, possibly for inheritance purposes, it would be permissable to use a fixed date claim form.

The Contents of the Petition for Nullity

The petition for nullity of marriage is, in many respects, similar to the petition for dissolution of marriage. The main difference is to be found in paragraphs 12 and 13 where instead of the grounds and particulars of breakdown of the marriage, the petition for nullity will cite the ground upon which the marriage is void and the particulars relied on to establish that ground.

The petition may include an application for ancillary relief[91] and where the petition discloses that there are relevant children under the age of 18 or dependents under the age of 21 receiving tertiary education, the petition must be accompanied by an affidavit.[92]

That there is no restriction on commencement of an action in the early years as with dissolution of a valid marriage (for obvious

---

90.   This type of application could be made by a third party in the course of probate by way of a fixed date claim or notice of application for court orders.
91.   Rule 76.4(5).
92.   CPR, Form MP5, rule 76.4(7).

reasons) is an important factor in nullity procedure. Also, nullity actions are not 'hampered' by required separation periods, and thus nullity is the only basis in Jamaican law in which a person could marry today and commence proceedings for termination of the marriage tomorrow. This clearly is an exception to considerations to the sanctity of the marriage as legally there is no marriage.

Service, Proceedings in Default, etc.

The procedure for nullity petitions is generally similar to the procedure for dissolution of marriage; however, the default procedure set out in CPR rule 76.12 does not appear to include nullity:

'The petitioner for a decree of dissolution of marriage may proceed to default by filing an application to dispense with a hearing in form No. MP 7 accompanied by affidavit evidence'.

This appears to mean that all nullity proceedings would go by way of case management with the possibility of a hearing in open court whether the case is contested or not. Given the issues of law which may arise and the potential for legal complexity, this could be considered prudent. Unfortunately, rule 76.13 is not explicit in this regard. Certainly, it is understandable that the authorities would wish to provide an opportunity for consideration of the law, whether by way of legal submissions or an oral hearing in nullity matters and, in any event, the number of such cases is so small that they are not likely to encumber the court unduly.

Decree Nisi and Absolute

By CPR rule 76.14(2), the decree nisi for nullity is to be filed by way of form MP9. The same rules applicable to dissolution guide the process of making the decree nisi absolute. Both dissolution and nullity of marriage require a six-week expiration period before applying for a decree absolute.[93] While it is sensible to provide a

---

93.   Rule 76.14(4).

'cooling off period' in the case of dissolution, and that has always been a feature of the procedure in divorce, this would not be necessary in the case of nullity. However, staggering the process in this way may yet serve a purpose in nullity proceedings since the case issues involve more than an irretrievable breakdown and might, in all fairness, require an opportunity for review, which such a delay affords. This may nevertheless be seen as an unnecessary precaution. In addition, the court has the express power to rescind the decree[94] should there be any dishonesty or failure with respect to the procedural requirements.

Nullity and Ancillary Relief

Although in theory a void marriage is non-existent and should not affect or create any legal obligations, the rigours of such a purist approach have been mitigated by statutory intervention.

Maintenance

The MCA gives power to the Supreme Court to make orders for the care and maintenance 'of any relevant child or for the maintenance of any spouse (a)...in any proceedings...for the dissolution or nullity of marriage, before, by or after the final decree'.[95]

Spousal Maintenance

Section 23 of the MCA specifically refers to the provision of ancillary relief, including maintenance, for parties to a void marriage. Therefore, upon the commencement of proceedings for nullity, the court may consider such applications in the same way it does with applications made during proceedings for dissolution.

Applications for maintenance can also be made under the Maintenance Act in the Parish (formerly, Resident Magistrates') Court or the Family Court. In the case of a void marriage where nullity proceedings have not yet commenced, the court is unlikely

---

94.   Rule 76.15.
95.   Section 23(1).

to question the status of the marriage and, in such circumstances, would treat the application in the usual summary way. Even if the matter were raised, it would be open to the court to treat the parties as spouses by virtue of having lived together as man and wife for a period of at least five years, and thereby qualifying for maintenance. It is possible, however, that if the marriage were alleged to be void and the parties had not, in fact, lived together for a period of at least five years in order to qualify under the extended definition, there could be a challenge to entitlement to spousal maintenance.

For the preceding reasons, it may be important for parties to a void marriage who are seeking spousal maintenance to institute nullity proceedings in the high court under the MCA to avoid the possibility of any challenge to entitlement under the Maintenance Act, which is based on the status of the marriage.

Child Maintenance

Under the Maintenance Act, powers of the court to make orders in respect of children who are dependant would apply irrespective of the status of the marriage. In particular, section 8(3)(b) stipulates that a person is a parent within the meaning of the act if that person 'is or was a party to a marriage (including a void marriage)....'

Furthermore, the definition of a relevant child under the MCA includes the child of a void marriage, and the provisions of the Maintenance Act have been incorporated into the MCA.[96] In the case of maintenance being granted pursuant to making custody orders under the Children (Guardianship and Custody) Act,[97] the Act does not consider the marital relationship of the parents. As a result, it is difficult to see how a child could be disentitled to maintenance under any legislation currently in place, simply on the basis of their parents' marriage being void.

---

96.   Section 23(2).
97.   Section 7(3).

Claims under the Property (Rights of Spouses) Act (PROSA)

A claim for division under PROSA must be made by a spouse. The question of whether or not a party to a void marriage is a spouse is not expressly addressed in the legislation, although it is stated that a 'marriage' by definition includes a void marriage.[98] It is open to interpretation whether or not a party to a void marriage is 'single' for the purposes of being able to establish a spousal relationship by cohabitation. Even if it is the case that a party to a void marriage can still rely on that marriage in order to be considered a spouse, the Act does not go so far as to address the question of whether or not interests which vest by virtue of marriage will take effect in the case of a void marriage. This omission may be inadvertent, but it could also be deliberate on the basis that the degree of culpability as to the invalidity of the marriage is a pertinent issue and should remain within the discretion of the court.

THE WAY FORWARD

Nullity is an area which could benefit from the further development of the ideas included in the MCA. The current law recognizes that there is no significant distinction between annulment based on voidable grounds and dissolution of a valid marriage: In both instances, the marriage is valid until terminated, both can only be terminated by the parties themselves and neither can be terminated after the death of one of the parties. The reasoning is that since they are for all practical purposes of the same status, a voidable ground may be considered merely a circumstance that is indicative of irretrievable breakdown. This is the present state of the law, and acting on that premise, should we go further and examine the role of nullity in the framework of marriage in today's society? Should there be a re-examination of the grounds and what the law says, and the implications for Jamaicans? Are voidable grounds in nullity

---

98.   Section 2.

merely an exemption to the restriction on dissolution in the earlier years? If a significant number of people in the population enter into marriage thinking that if it is not consummated then there is no marriage (as many people still do), should pre-marital counselling be more formalized?[99] While not advocating a short law course for prospective marriage partners, it does seem that we have left many segments of society behind as we forge ahead with making and applying the law. While there is a clear relegation of marriage to fit it into the framework of spouse for the purposes of the Maintenance Act and PROSA, under the Maintenance Act in particular, the status of void marriages is unclear. Of course, it can be argued that parties to a void marriage would normally qualify because their relationship will usually fit within the definition of spouse. However, that requires cohabitation for a minimum of five years, so if the parties to a void marriage have lived together for two years, are they entitled to relief? This may be deliberate in order to establish a broader legal regime for the entitlement to maintenance. It can also be seen as realistic, in that the number of claims for maintenance premised on a void marriage are probably few and far between (although this does not justify not addressing it). The matter is clear in relation to claims for children, but with regards to claims for maintenance by the parties to a void marriage, (unless the claim is ancillary to the annulment) or by anyone who lives in a common law union with a party to a void marriage, the position is far from settled.

The fact that comparatively, nullity does not arise very often, should not be a sufficient reason not to have resolved it as clearly as in PROSA. As it is, it will be for the courts to decide if and when the need arises.

There can be no gainsaying the fact that the curtailment of certain specific voidable grounds is laudable. There remain some void grounds which touch and concern the most intimate and personal aspects of marital life. Not only can it be extremely embarrassing,

---

99.   Attempts at altering the format of divorce to incorporate counselling in the UK have been fraught with difficulties.

there is also the potential to use these proceedings to gratuitously malign. For many, it will be far more palatable to wait two years and file for dissolution rather than to adhere to strict legal distinctions and embark on a highly contentious suit in nullity. The accompanying difficulties of evidence and proof are also powerful factors which will deter all but the most robust applicant from seeking a nullity decree under these grounds.

In respect of the nullity grounds under the Marriage Act, the necessary distinction between consanguinity and affinity on the one hand and incest on the other is lost on most who take little more than a cursory glance at the provisions.[100] Similarly, the minimum age of marriage is frequently questioned, on the grounds that we think children should be in school until the age of 18 and not engaged in sexual relations whether 'churched' or otherwise. What impact will this have on the age of consent?[101] In some countries in the Caribbean, people take issue with child marriage,[102] but in Jamaica the occurrence of sexual intercourse below the age of consent and teenage pregnancies do not appear to give rise to considerations of marriage in the vast majority of cases.[103] Can parental consent have a role in the question of marriage, if it is restricted to persons who have attained full adulthood? If it does not, and as the pressure to re-align the age of consent with the age of majority grows, it is likely that parental consent within marriage will be seen as unnecessary. The question of the legal definition of 'child' is a matter that raises issues across the entire landscape of family law, not just in the area of nullity. The need for a comprehensive rationalization exercise is long overdue.

---

100. Although most people seem to have a sense of what is permissible or 'right' in these areas.
101. Periodical parliamentary review of the Sexual Offences Act and the Child Care and Protection Act brings this issue to the fore on a regular basis.
102. Guyana and Trinidad and Tobago.
103. Comparisons between the number of teenage women in reproductive age and the number of teenage brides seem to bear this out. See 'Economic and Social Survey Jamaica and Statistical Institute Reports'.

In light of the medical advances, the current legal position in Jamaica that a person's sex is fixed at birth is likely to make a mockery of the arrangements that people may make in their lives so as to genuinely reflect who they believe themselves to be. Is it likely that in the near future the policymakers of this country will have to address these issues.

3. Divorce

INTRODUCTION

Marcia has had a hard life, but things are looking up. She made a mistake while she was in high school and ended up pregnant at 15, but when she was put out of school, her boyfriend, Dane, looked after her and the baby, Marcus. That was until Dane was shot by the police. His parents didn't want anything to do with Marcia and her mother was ashamed, so she was on her own. She managed to get a job at the local supermarket and harboured secret plans to go back to school and get some subjects. James was the storeroom supervisor, he had an easy, charming way about him, and all the female employees were smitten. Marcia kept away from James, but that seemed to draw him to her and soon they were a couple. They rented a place together, and when it became clear that James accepted Marcus as his own and was ready to settle down, they decided to marry.

After the marriage, they were happy and prospered, they had two children together. James was promoted to store manager, Marcia became the cashier supervisor, and they bought a house and a small car. When the last child went to school, Marcia decided that it was time to resume her studies; she really wanted to be an accountant. James was not happy when Marcia was away from home for two evenings per week, and could not see why she wasn't satisfied with what he provided, but he kept quiet about it.

When James was transferred to another branch, he thought that Marcia would curtail her studies and stay with the children, because he now had to do so much travelling. Instead, she switched to weekend classes and soon they found that they were actually together for no more than a few hours per week and both were very tired. Britney, a young voluptuous cashier at James's supermarket, was very sympathetic when James poured out his problems on their second date. She listened attentively and made it clear that Marcia was, in her opinion, wrong to neglect such a fine man as James.

Six months later, matters came to a head. James and Marcia had been arguing frequently about James staying in the country for one weekend in every month. She suspected infidelity and James had denied it, but it was not until she found incriminating material on his phone, that she became convinced. She moved into her daughter's bedroom that night. For two months James tried to woo Marcia back to the marital bed, but to no avail. Feeling hurt and rejected, he finally moved out of the matrimonial home at the end of the third month and went to live with Britney in the country.

Within four months of James's departure, Marcia has obtained maintenance orders in the Family Court, and is sitting in a lawyer's office. She is developing a deep and meaningful relationship with a male classmate in her accountancy course. They are in their final year, and see the possibility of a glowing future together. She wants a divorce.

One of the most common types of proceedings in family law for any legal practitioner is divorce. Although marriage is viewed favourably as a societal institution, the number of divorces is steadily increasing, and because divorce is a procedure that takes place in the high court, a lawyer is needed. This is the mainstay of family practice, along with the ancillary issues such as maintenance, custody, and property matters that naturally arise when a marriage is brought to an end.

The stigma of divorce in a small society, particularly when fault grounds such as adultery or cruelty needed to be established, may have been a deterrent in the past, especially when every minute and embarrassing detail of a divorce proceeding became subject to public scrutiny. Eventually, the public's access to the details of divorce cases was effectively curtailed by the introduction of legislation,[1] and the proceedings, while still in open court, took on a more dignified tenor. The introduction of divorce based on the sole ground of irretrievable breakdown undoubtedly has made divorce easier to obtain. The procedural changes that make it no longer necessary to attend court have added fuel to the relentless drive for the speedy termination of marriages. In numeric terms, between 2012 and 2015, divorces obtained fell from 2,409 to 1,734.[2] However, consider that easier means of proving divorce does not guarantee an easier divorce. The increasing technicality of the procedural rules may be just one factor contributing to an overall decreasing trend in the number of divorces granted.

THE LAW – A HISTORICAL AND COMPARATIVE OVERVIEW

Divorce was introduced to Jamaica by the Divorce Law of 1879. It was seen as an instrument that would encourage marriage because prior to the Act, once the parties were in it, it was almost impossible to get out of it. Those in informal unions found ways of marking the end of the union in a recognized manner drawing from 'their

---

1.   The Judicial Proceedings (Regulation of Reports) Act 1987.
2.   See Statistical Institute of Jamaica, *Demographic Statistics: Marriages and Divorces.*

cultural tradition' such as division of the cotta.[3] So, essentially, there were (and still are) two independent strands of family life: that which took place under the auspices of formal marriage and that which did not.[4] The 1879 Law allowed for dissolution on the grounds of adultery, cruelty, and desertion, as well as decrees of nullity and judicial separation. This remained the central content of Jamaican divorce laws until the Divorce Act was repealed by the Matrimonial Causes Act (MCA) in 1989.[5] The MCA is the current legislation in this area of the law.

The MCA heralded the country's entry into the uncharted territory of no fault divorce. The act was preceded by the Family Law Committee Report No. 1,[6] which reviewed the law and made extensive recommendations. There were 24 main recommendations which formed the basis of the new divorce policy in Jamaica. The significant recommendations were:

1. Irretrievable breakdown as the sole ground for dissolution.

2. No divorce until at least two years have elapsed from the date of the marriage unless there are exceptional circumstances.

3. Restrictions on the grant of the decree absolute where there are relevant children under the age of 18.

4. Voidable marriages abolished.

5. Judicial separation, damages for adultery, and restitution of conjugal rights, abolished.

6. Domicile of married woman to be determined as if never married.

Barbados was the first Caribbean country to stipulate the sole ground for divorce (or dissolution of marriage as it is strictly defined),

---

3.   Jenny M. Jemmott, *Ties That Bind: The Black Family in Post-Slavery Jamaica, 1834–1882* (Kingston: University of the West Indies Press, 2015), 174.
4.   Sometimes referred to as faithful concubinage.
5.   An amendment to the Divorce Law in 1969, which introduced a ground of five years' separation, was the first tentative step towards 'no fault' divorce.
6.   Chaired by the Hon. Mr Justice Ira Rowe.

as irretrievable breakdown without any specific fault grounds.[7] This was a pioneering approach to the reform of divorce law in the Caribbean, and still most countries have not taken the 'purist' line of Barbados and Jamaica.[8] When compared with the old law with numerous grounds accompanied by long-decided definitions and intricate conditions and exceptions, the legal components of irretrievable breakdown are fairly easily established. In practical terms, matrimonial offences such as adultery, cruelty, or desertion, which were required to be proved against the respondent for a petitioner to succeed in obtaining a decree of dissolution under the old law, were often difficult to establish. Also, the notion of a guilty party who had committed a marital offence which was predicated on the innocence of the other party was itself highly debatable. The advent of a single ground for divorce of irretrievable breakdown, in many ways, represented a more honest and realistic approach to marital breakdown. It encompasses the fact that often the breakdown may be due to the conduct of both parties, and that the breakdown has more to do with the decision not to want to continue with the marriage than the reason(s) which cause one or both parties to arrive at that decision. In other words, the proverbial straw which breaks the back of one marriage may not have the same effect on another, and it doesn't necessarily matter whose straw it is. While this may be recognized in law,[9] a petitioner seeking a divorce is likely to approach the matter from the age-old standpoint of having been wronged by the other party. It is still rare, but entirely permissible legally, for a petitioner to rely on their own indiscretions as a basis for the breakdown of the marriage. The legal factors, as set out in the MCA, to satisfy a court that the marriage has broken down, and ensuring that issues such as the arrangements for any

---

7.   Family Law Act, 1982, section 27.
8.   Most countries such as Belize, Antigua and Barbuda, and St Kitts have a mix of fault grounds and a period of separation. Some such as Anguilla and Trinidad and Tobago use the British formula of irretrievable breakdown based on certain facts.
9.   See *Heron-Muir v Heron-Muir* FD 00144/2004 21/10/2005.

children are suitably addressed, are now the primary concern of the court in the area of divorce. This has shifted attention away from the substantive law towards the procedural requirements that are necessary to pass the matter through the courts and ultimately obtain the desired end, the granting of the decree absolute.

DISSOLUTION OF MARRIAGE – THE STATUTE AND MAIN PRINCIPLES

The Matrimonial Causes Act 1989

It is generally accepted that the drafters relied heavily on the Australian legislation in preparing the Jamaican Matrimonial Causes Act. This view is borne out by reference to the Family Law Committee[10] Report No. 1, which guided and informed Parliament's enactment of a new divorce statute. Barbados took a similar approach, but the Jamaican MCA, coming eight years after the 1981 Family Law Act in Barbados[11] was considerably scaled down from the Barbadian position. Unlike the Barbadian enactment, it sought to restrict itself to matrimonial causes and not venture into broader aspects of family law that have been dealt with in later legislation.[12] This was a reflection of the policy position in Jamaica, that changes should be introduced on a phased basis, rather than by sweeping comprehensive measures.

Matrimonial Cause

The Act confines itself to matrimonial causes and in section 2 the term is defined. With the termination of marriages, the act encompasses dissolution,[13] annulment,[14] and the compound decree of presumption of death and dissolution of marriage.[15] Apart from

---

10. Formed in 1975 under the chairmanship of the Hon. Mr Justice Ira Rowe.
11. Re-enacted in 1985.
12. Maintenance Act and PROSA.
13. Section 5.
14. Section 4.
15. Section 9.

the pronouncement of decrees, there is specific retention of the court's declaratory powers in the validity of a marriage.[16]

The comprehensive approach to dealing with the status and termination of marriages is to be contrasted with later legislation in other Commonwealth jurisdictions such as Antigua and Barbuda[17] and St Kitts and Nevis.[18] The Antiguan Act omitted certain nullity provisions that appeared in their former Matrimonial Causes Act, and the Kittitian legislation was revisited in order to avoid the same pitfall. Both acts, whether deliberately or otherwise, make no reference to dissolution on presumption of death.

The definition of matrimonial cause in the Jamaican MCA also contemplates actions by persons other than the parties to a marriage where the validity of the marriage is in question and, while this occurrence may be infrequent, it is an important safeguard of the interests of third parties such as children and beneficiaries.

The usual ancillary proceedings of custody and maintenance of a child or spouse, as well as injunctive powers under section 10 are specifically included in the definition of matrimonial cause. Of interest is the inclusion of guardianship proceedings within the definition. In societies where guardianship generally arises on death of a parent and where it is the norm for parents in those circumstances to have been married to each other, this is not incongruous. In this jurisdiction, however, guardianship applications often take place outside of that factual context. Its inclusion therefore represents a rigorous anticipation of all possible eventualities, recognizing that the court may, in the course of a custody application, seek to exercise its inherent powers.[19] In any event, the intertwined relationship between custody and guardianship may require the court to take over parental responsibility for the child.[20] With the recognition of such far-reaching powers, it becomes less remote and therefore

16. Section 2 subparagraph (b).
17. Divorce Act 1997.
18. Divorce Act 2005.
19. See Section 23(1).
20. See *B v C and the Office of the Children's Advocate* [2016] JMCA Civ 48.

more reasonable that guardianship is included within the scope of a matrimonial cause. Subsections d, e, and f of the definition of matrimonial cause extend the boundary to proceedings and applications ancillary to proceedings and applications which may themselves be ancillary to those originating proceedings.

This introductory section of the act makes reference to approved marriage counsellors which seems to have been in anticipation of state supervision or support for a conciliation process as a means of saving marriages. This has not materialized in Jamaica, although there is at least one church-based counselling service that has been recognized and is usually relied on by the court.[21] The process of becoming an approved marriage counsellor is set out in the schedule to the MCA, but the court does not usually use this facility, although there are explicit provisions in the Act.[22] By way of contrast, Barbados, which has extensive provisions in support of this kind of intervention and assistance for troubled marriages, used the law to establish social workers and counsellors as an available resource to the court. The principal impediment to a court-based, state-supported counselling service in Jamaica is resources. The cost of not having a developed counselling service is a considerable waste of court time, but greater efforts are being made with the use of mediation to resolve ancillary disputes as an out-of-court alternative.[23] The Supreme Court is also now more inclined to the use the services of the Child Protection and Family Services Agency, formerly Child Development Agency (CDA).

The Jurisdiction of the Court

It is the Supreme Court that has jurisdiction to hear matrimonial causes under the MCA and, therefore, all proceedings for divorce must be commenced in that jurisdiction. This means that even though a parish judge in the Family Court or the Parish Court may

---

21.   Family Life Ministries.
22.   Section 11(2)(c).
23.   This is strongly encouraged by the judges.

adjudicate on certain matters relating to the marriage, such as domestic violence,[24] marital property,[25] custody,[26] or maintenance[27] hearings, the divorce itself can only be dealt with in the high court which, in Jamaica, is called the Supreme Court. Once the divorce proceedings have been commenced,[28] the Supreme Court will itself have jurisdiction to hear applications that are ancillary to the divorce by virtue of section 23. In this way, there is an overlap or straddling of the jurisdictions of the summary courts and the high court to hear these ancillary matters.

Who Can Get a Divorce?

The court, which in all cases under the MCA is the Supreme Court,[29] will exercise its powers to grant relief in respect of divorce proceedings[30] initiated by either one of the parties to the marriage in accordance with section 15 of the Act that sets out the circumstances in which the Jamaican court will have jurisdiction to deal with matrimonial causes. Either of the parties must be:

a. A Jamaican national,

b. Domiciled in Jamaica when the proceedings are commenced, or

c. Resident in Jamaica at the commencement of the proceedings and has been so resident for at least 12 months immediately preceding the date of commencement.

A Jamaican national or a person who is domiciled in Jamaica may petition the court for dissolution of his/her marriage or be the respondent to such proceedings initiated by the other party to the marriage. A person who has been ordinarily resident in

---

24.   Under the Domestic Violence Act.
25.   Under PROSA.
26.   Under the Children (Guardianship and Custody) Act.
27.   Under the Maintenance Act.
28.   Or proceedings under section 10.
29.   MCA, section 3.
30.   This section also applies to nullity and dissolution on presumption of death.

Jamaica for a period of at least 12 months may similarly be a party to proceedings under the act. This is so regardless of whether the marriage took place in Jamaica or elsewhere. When seeking to terminate a marriage under the MCA, it is necessary to establish the jurisdictional basis relied on as set out in section 15(1). A person may become a Jamaican national by different routes:[31] by birth, descent, registration, or by marriage, and, as such, it the petition does not disclose that one or other party was born in Jamaica and the status relied on is nationality, it is possible that the court may seek clarification of the basis upon which it is claimed. By comparison, domicile is a qualification that can be less formally acquired and is grounded on the actions and intentions of the person claiming domicile. Under section 34 of the act, a woman's domicile is no longer affected by her marriage or determined by the domicile of her husband for the purposes of this Act' and, as such, the automatic assumption of her husband's domicile has at least been partially curtailed in Jamaican law. The difficulty that this previously posed was that a woman could be deprived of Jamaican domicile by virtue of the whereabouts and intentions of her husband over which she had no control. Furthermore, neither of the parties is a Jamaican national or domiciled in Jamaica, the court will nevertheless have jurisdiction if either one of them has been resident for at least 12 months. The effect of this is that even where the connection with Jamaica is relatively short and tenuous, the court will have jurisdiction in divorce proceedings under the MCA. This non-restrictive, facilitating approach enables persons to get access to the court in order to organize their affairs and move forward with their lives.

---

31.   Jamaican Nationality Act.

When Can a Divorce Be Obtained: Restriction in 'the Early Years'

A restriction on divorce in the early years is a standard mechanism by which the State reinforces the sanctity of marriage. A marital union is not to be seen as something that you can get into today and get out of tomorrow. Perhaps, with this awareness, people are expected to consider the matter carefully before entering into the estate of marriage. Most people, however, do not become aware of this restriction until it becomes an obstacle to correcting what with hindsight may seem an unfortunate mistake. Section 8 of the act establishes a two-year restriction on the presentation of a petition for dissolution. This means that the court will not entertain a petition unless two years have passed from the date of the marriage, unless there are special circumstances, in which case an application for leave to file a petition within the two years can be made. The justification for this provision is that with the demise of the fault grounds, the ease with which one could obtain a divorce would undermine the sanctity of marriage unless there remained some restriction on divorce in the early years. The church considered this particularly important. By comparison, there are some Caribbean jurisdictions that have no time restriction,[32] and some which have even lengthier restrictions than Jamaica.[33] In Barbados, the question of divorce in the early years and the basis upon which this can be established to the satisfaction of the court was considered in the case of *Nurse v Nurse*.[34]

The court is empowered to grant leave for petitions to be presented before the expiration of two years if the parties have attempted reconciliation with the aid of an approved marriage counsellor and there are special circumstances. The requirement for conciliatory counselling is laudable, but often special circumstances would make

32. Antigua and Barbuda, and St Kitts and Nevis.
33. Belize, Montserrat, and Anguilla.
34. (1985) 38 WIR 59.

counselling redundant. Equally, arguments can be advanced for the redundancy of the 12-month separation requirement in these circumstances if the role of the counsellor is really one of 'certifying' the irretrievable state of the marriage.

What then are the special circumstances that are likely to move the court to grant leave? Some countries[35] add 'exceptional depravity on the part of the respondent',[36] and it may be presumed that such a situation would satisfy the special circumstances requirement. In Jamaica, there has been some discussion as to whether in the absence of defined voidable grounds for nullity, such as non-consummation, those situations could be relied on as special circumstances within the meaning of section 8. This would allow for earlier termination and should not offend the underlying motives of the rule.

The presentation of the petition before two years has elapsed on the grounds of whatever special circumstances are put forward does not affect the requirement to prove that the dissolution of the marriage is premised on 12 months separation. The wording of section 5, namely that it is 'if and only if' there is the required period of separation that the ground is made out seems to preclude presentation of the petition until at least 12 months and a day after the marriage has taken place even if leave to apply within the two years is granted. The wisdom of this outcome has been questioned from the standpoint that if the whole purpose of the provision is to release the parties from the marriage bond because of the special circumstances, then that object is itself defeated by a slavish adherence to the requirements of section 5 as to the substantive ground. The answer to this must be yes, and perhaps it is an unforeseen consequence of a single ground for divorce based on a period of separation. It is also right to conclude that this arrangement puts the parties at a disadvantage compared with people in jurisdictions where grounds for divorce may rest on the fault of one of the parties. For example, if leave could be

35.   Belize, Montserrat, and Anguilla.
36.   This used to be the case in Jamaica. See *Williams v Williams* (1987) 24 JLR 439.

obtained and the petition is to be presented on the grounds of adultery, then the parties could, in theory, get married and apply for an early divorce some months afterward. Could this not be used as a 'quick getaway' in the case of a substantive ground such as irretrievable breakdown? Furthermore, is the line between the basis for leave, if it rests on some sort of depravity on the part of the respondent, and the grounds for divorce somewhat blurred in these circumstances? Clearly, this debate goes beyond the context of the law in Jamaica and shows the interaction of several different motives. Developing the law with reference to provisions in other jurisdictions, balancing the right for people to free themselves from unworkable marriages, and having due respect for the sanctity of marriage and its importance as a mechanism for family stability are a constant concern in most jurisdictions. If the law takes a restrictive approach to early dissolution, are there alternative matrimonial remedies which can provide interim relief?[37] Do we need to have regard to what our Caribbean neighbours are doing, is there such a concept as the Caribbean family, or are we each going our separate ways in answering these questions?

The present formulation in Jamaica on this issue demonstrates a balance between a wide judicial discretion in terms of 'special circumstances' and a fairly (or perhaps unfairly) rigid position regarding easily complied with substantive ground for divorce. Certainly, upon the present construction of the MCA, it is difficult to extend the generous judicial discretion as to special circumstances to include the power to dispense with the requirement for 12 months separation. That would seemingly necessitate legislative intervention.

The Concept of Irretrievable Breakdown

In Jamaica, the sole ground of irretrievable breakdown is set out in section 5 of the Act:

---

37.   In the past, judicial separation would have been useful in this regard.

1. A petition for a decree of dissolution of marriage may be presented to the court by either party to a marriage on the ground that the marriage has broken down irretrievably.

2. Subject to subsection (3), in proceedings for a decree of dissolution of marriage the ground shall be held to have been established, and such decree shall be made, if, and only if, the court is satisfied that the parties separated and thereafter lived separately and apart for a continuous period of not less than 12 months immediately preceding the date of filing of the petition for that decree.

3. A decree of dissolution of marriage shall not be made if the court is satisfied that there is a reasonable likelihood of cohabitation being resumed.

Irretrievable breakdown is the foundation ground for divorce in much of the commonwealth jurisdictions. In England and in many Commonwealth Caribbean countries, the sole ground of irretrievable breakdown has to be evidenced by one of five facts: adultery,[38] behaviour or cruelty,[39] desertion,[40] and additional separation grounds.[41] In this way, the ground for divorce rests on a mixture of circumstances, some of which involve the misbehaviour of one of the parties (fault grounds) and some that simply involve the separation of the parties for a minimum period of time (no fault grounds). Some countries have the same arrangement as in the United Kingdom (UK), and some have varied the general format to suit their own requirements.

Jamaica and Barbados took what is generally described as the Australian model. The convenience of this approach should not be overlooked; it means that the significant legal issues intrinsic to this concept have already been addressed by courts in the UK and Australia, and that body of law is subsumed in the Jamaican

---

38. UK MCA Section 1(2)(a).
39. Ibid., 1(2)(b).
40. Ibid., 1(2)(c).
41. Ibid., 1(2)(d) and (e).

legislation. It also leaves the Caribbean free to refine the stipulations of the law to suit the circumstances of the region and the social and moral outlook. For example, the size of our jurisdictions is a factor that influences our view of separation. In the Caribbean, it is not unusual for parties to a marriage to reside and work in other countries on a semi-permanent basis and to regard the marriage as perfectly viable throughout. It must also be recognized that people the world over will get in and out of marriages as an integral part of the development of their life, not simply as a romantic excursion. Whether the motives behind entering into marriage are of a romantic nature, whether it is wholly arranged (which also features in our societies by virtue of the Indian segments of the population), or whether it is what we euphemistically call a 'business marriage', the Caribbean and, hence, Jamaican approach to marriage may not fit a Western stereotype for one or more of these reasons. As such, when Jamaican judges come to look at the status of the marriage and, in particular, the question of whether or not it should be put asunder, the approach may be different from the judges in other countries whose decisions are nevertheless held to be of persuasive authority.

Closer examination of the Jamaican provisions shows that there are two issues that a court has to decide in divorce cases: (i) whether the separation criterion is satisfied and (ii) whether there is any reasonable likelihood of cohabitation being resumed.[42]

A Period of Separation

In small-island nations, such as Jamaica, a large number of marriages subsist despite extended periods of separation due to migration, usually for economic reasons. Historically, partners might have lived in different parts of the country as the drift to urban areas took place. There were also significant hemispheric developments, such as the construction of the Panama Canal, which caused parties

---

42.　This proposition is to be viewed in the light of cases such as *Benjamin v Benjamin* (1993) 30 JLR 288, where the parties never lived together.

to be separated for many years. This is but one example of physical (rather than legal) separation due to the migration of one spouse for economic reasons and this continues to be a common feature of Caribbean family life. Physical separation is not necessarily an indication of marital breakdown. That there should be physical separation (even under the same roof) combined with a settled intention in the mind of at least one of the parties that the marriage is over, is of vital importance.[43]

The legal definition of separation under the MCA adopted the English and Australian decisions on the point,[44] and in sections 6 and 7, codifies certain principles that are seen in these cases. Paragraph 24.10 of the Family Law Report No. 1 states:

> Our concept of the type of separation necessary for the purposes of our proposals coincides with that of the English Court in *Santos v Santos* and the Australian Full Court in *Pavey v Pavey*. Our recommendations have, therefore, been made on the basis of such a concept.

A continuous period of 12 months during which the parties have lived separately and apart must have elapsed immediately preceding the date of the filing of the petition for the legal requirement of irretrievable breakdown to be made out: see section 5(2).

Separation is defined in section 6 of the Act, which recognizes the decisions like *Pavey*. The reference to the cohabitation as being 'brought to an end by the action of one of the parties', means that separation can be viewed as a form of desertion which is exercisable by either party,[45] instead of the requirement under the traditional ground of desertion that only the deserted party could rely on this ground. There must be something that puts the marriage on a different footing – a recognition by at least one party that the marriage has broken down and, as acknowledged

---

43. *Heron-Muir v Heron-Muir* per Sykes J; also *Nooks v Nooks* (1983) 20 JLR 9.
44. *Santos v Santos* (1972) 2 All ER 246, and in the marriage of *Pavey* (1976) 10 ALR 259; seen in *Heron-Muir, Benjamin*, etc.
45. Per *Heron-Muir*.

in *Heron-Muir*,[46] the Act does not impose any requirement for the would-be-respondent to recognize this action or conduct (which can include words) as indicative of the end of the marriage. This is understandable from a legal standpoint, but in practice it can lead to an inclination to contest the divorce simply because of the summary way in which the respondent may have been discarded. In a small society, a disrespectful or inconsiderate way of ending the marriage is perceived as grievous and can be highly injurious to a person's standing within the community or district in which the parties live, as well as one's general self-esteem. While marriage should not be seen as a cage with the parties locked inside, there is still generally held resistance to the idea of opting out without account. This notion of 'impregnability' manifests itself in the mistaken and still quite widely held belief that a divorce cannot be obtained unless the other person 'signs the paper'. In the past, when cases resting on separation under section 6(2) came before the courts, some judges regarded any provision of household services as inimical to the notion of separation. This seems contrary to the wording of the section, if not to life experience and common sense, but sometimes general disquiet as to the ease of obtaining a divorce can express itself in an overly stringent interpretation of the law in this or any other jurisdiction. Practitioners are, therefore, at pains to advise their clients that from an evidential standpoint, the provision of any household services could be fatal in trying to establish grounds for divorce. In the same vein, it could also be tempting to a reluctant respondent to use any provision of household services as a platform upon which the divorce could be contested. This is not borne out by the decided cases, but continues to be a delicate issue when pleading the circumstances of separation in the petition where the parties remain under the same roof.

Section 7 which explains the meaning of continuity as it applies to separation is also viewed cautiously and interpreted carefully when

---

46.   See also similar reasoning in *Nooks v Nooks*, albeit based on the Divorce Act which preceded the MCA.

pleading the circumstances to be used to establish irretrievable breakdown. Basically, this provision means that:

1. No account will be taken of a period of less than three months resumption of cohabitation and, therefore, such period cannot be included when calculating the required 12-month period of separation.

2. Nevertheless, the effect of a period of resumption of cohabitation of less than three months is that while not breaking the continuity of separation,[47] an equivalent period would have to be added to the length of separation in order to make up a minimum of 12 months.[48]

This seems to suggest that a period in excess of three months, and possibly any two periods of whatever duration, could break continuity. The judge is also given the discretion to find the cohabitation continuous, notwithstanding any interruption, as long as in the opinion of the court the interruption is not substantial. It could, therefore, be possible to argue that notwithstanding a period of reconciliation lasting longer than three months, that by virtue of the fact that the period was punctuated by substantial interruptions, that the period could therefore be overlooked, and would not break the continuity of the separation. Occasional instances of sexual intercourse between the parties do not amount to a resumption of cohabitation.[49]

Likelihood of Cohabitation Being Resumed

The other requirement for a decree to be granted is that there is no reasonable likelihood of cohabitation being resumed.[50] The way

---

47. That is, the starting date of the separation will not change and will continue to run.
48. See *Ingraham v Ingraham* (née Pinder) BS 2004 SC 140, quoted in Karen Tesheira, *Commonwealth Caribbean Family Law: Husband, Wife and Cohabitant* (London: Routledge, 2016), 153.
49. *Ramsay v Ramsay* BB 1987 HC 63, quoted in Tesheira, *Commonwealth Caribbean Family* Law, 153.
50. Section 5(3).

that this section is framed suggests that irretrievable breakdown is not necessarily established unless there is no reasonable liklihood of cohabitation being resumed. Certainly, it is difficult to see, for practical purposes, how, if the marriage has broken down irretrievably, there can be any reasonable likelihood of cohabitation being resumed. It may be that the legislators were concerned that the possibility of interpreting these factors as being alternatives and thereby 'watering down' the sole legal ground was undesirable, and therefore wanted to preclude such an approach.

On the other hand, if there is no requirement for the parties to have cohabited initially, the question of the likelihood of cohabitation being resumed is superfluous.[51] As Harrison, J (Ag) stated, 'Clearly, the Petitioner would have satisfied the requirements of section 5(2). He has stated that there is no hope of them cohabiting in the future.' And further, quoting *Silver v Silver*,[52] 'I can see no social advantage in insisting on the maintenance of a union which has been a mere travesty from the beginning'.

Dissolution on Presumption of Death

There is one further ground upon which a marriage may be dissolved under the MCA of Jamaica. By section 9, where the court is satisfied that there are reasonable grounds for it to be presumed that the respondent is dead, a decree of presumption of death and dissolution of marriage may be granted. The prerequisite for a petition under this section is that there has been seven years of continuous absence of the respondent,[53] and also the subsection goes on to state that the petitioner should not have any reason to believe that the other party is alive during that time. It appears, however, that the test is not entirely subjective. In practice, the decree will not usually be granted unless the petitioner has a sound basis for the belief and, to that end, has contacted all known

51.   *Benjamin v Benjamin.*
52.   [1952] 2 All ER 614.
53.   Section 9(2).

relatives, advertised in newspapers and any other media as required by the court, checked with all places of employment, checked immigration records, etc. What may appear to the layman (and many students) as an attractive and simple option is, in fact, fraught with evidential pitfalls in seeking to achieve a high standard of proof. The court will, as a matter of necessity, set the bar extremely high, and as a result, the petitioner can be put to considerable expense and be required to go to great lengths to establish a presumption of death to the satisfaction of the court. These proceedings are generally understood to be the precursor to administration of the respondent's estate and are therefore a wholly exceptional way of bringing a marriage to an end. It applies in circumstances where death is almost certain, but a body may not have been recovered. In ordinary cases of absence of the respondent for periods in excess of seven years without substantial evidence of the respondent's demise, it is better dealt with by way of a petition under section 5.

CHILDREN AND DIVORCE

The most important issue in divorce proceedings, apart from the dissolution itself, is the arrangements that need to be made for the care and upbringing of the children once the marriage is terminated and the parties have gone their separate ways. The law takes this question so seriously that there is the power to withhold granting the decree absolute where the arrangements for the child do not meet the satisfaction of the judge who is considering the matter.[54] Under the MCA, the court has the power to grant custody and maintenance orders in respect of the relevant children.[55] The court also has the power under the act to place a child under the supervision of a welfare officer although, in general, this power is rarely exercised.[56] The law requires that where there are relevant

54.   Section 27.
55.   Section 23(1).
56.   Section 29 acknowledges the court's power to directly supervise the upbringing of a child; however, even in cases where the custody of children is bitterly contested, the court will not usually make orders pursuant to this section. This

children who are minors or are under the age of 23 and in tertiary education, that a petition be accompanied by an affidavit setting out the proposed arrangements for the care and upbringing of those children.[57] The court will rely on this information to decide whether or not the arrangements are 'satisfactory or are the best that may be devised in the circumstances'.[58] If the arrangements as disclosed do not satisfy the court or are being challenged by the other party, it will be open to either party to apply for the issue to be aired and for orders to be made by the court. Certifying the arrangements can then be revisited after these matters have been decided. Indeed, in the past, if it came to the attention of the court that there were matters pending concerning children, then a judge or master would adjourn the grant of the decree nisi. The powers of the court when dealing with children at the decree nisi stage are now set out in CPR Rule 76 (12)(6).

The Relevant Child

The concept of the relevant child was introduced into Jamaican law by way of the MCA[59] and is significant. The relevant child is defined as:

> A child of both parties to the marriage in question; or
>
> A child of one party to the marriage who has been accepted as one of the family by the other party.
>
> And in paragraphs (a) and (b) of this definition "child" includes adopted child and a child of a void marriage.

The definition of relevant child that is set out in the interpretation section of the act is essentially a statutory amalgamation of the two terms: a child of the marriage and a child of the family. The definition emphasizes the position of the child in relation to the parties and does not include any stipulations as to age. Furthermore, the

---

may be because of limited resources or because the powers under the Child Care and Protection Act have made these provisions redundant.

57.   Rule 76.4(7).
58.   Rule 76.12(4)(a).
59.   See Section 46(2) MCA 1965 (UK), New Zealand, Australia.

definition makes it clear that a party to a marriage need have no biological connection to the child that they become responsible for since that responsibility will come about where they are married to the biological parent and have accepted the child as a child of the family. These factors encompassed in the definition of relevant child give rise to two aspects worthy of closer examination: (i) What is the definition of 'child' under the MCA and (ii) How does a child become a relevant child under the MCA?

What is the definition of 'Child'?

Generally, the definition of child in Jamaican law is set within the context of the area of law that is under consideration and so the relevant statutory provisions will reflect that. Notwithstanding a set age limit, frequently the law will provide extensions and retractions depending on the circumstances.[60] This makes it all the more difficult, in the case of the MCA, where there is no specified age limit within the definition of relevant child, to imply a specific age. Nevertheless, practitioners will often construe the absence of an age limit within the definition of relevant child in the MCA as simply an omission by the legislature.

On the other hand, there are circumstances in which the law categorizes a child, not by age, but by virtue of being a descendant or the progeny of a person. This is seen in the area of succession.[61] So the question arises with regard to the MCA: does the absence of a specified age within the definition of relevant child necessitate the insertion of an implied age (and if so, which), or is it indicative of a broader definition as found in the inheritance laws?

This remains an area of uncertainty for practitioners and judges alike, and, as a result, there is still some variance between which children are included and which children are expected to be included in divorce documents for consideration by the court.[62] It is

---

60.   For an elaboration of this, see chapter 9, 'Children and the State'.
61.   Intestates' Estates and Property Charges Act.
62.   By way of comparison, see *D (JR) v D (JM)* [1970] 3 All ER 893.

generally assumed that Parliament intended what is written in law. So, what then could be the purpose of not having an age limit? There may be circumstances where provision needs to be made for an adult child, for example, a child who is suffering from a 'physical or mental infirmity or disability'.[63] If the definition of relevant child is to be construed with an implied age limit, the Supreme Court would be deprived of the power to make maintenance orders for such a child in the course of divorce proceedings. A precise and literal interpretation of the words of the statute, leads to a broad and inclusive power, which it is suggested is the most desirable outcome in this area of the law.

How Does a Child Become a Relevant Child?

The first category of child who is relevant is 'a child of both parties to the marriage in question'.

There is no reference to when the marriage took place in relation to the birth of the child.[64] So, that the marriage may take place when the child is an adult would mean the child would become a relevant child at that point, even though there will, in all probability, be no legal obligations which flow from that occurrence. This would clearly not be so if the MCA included an age limit in the definition. Interestingly, there is also no reference to any intervening event such as separation, termination of the marriage, or remarriage of the parties when defining a relevant child.[65] Close reading of the definition discloses a measure of ambiguity, in that, '... the marriage in question' could be a marriage which has already been terminated.[66] This makes it possible for a child to be relevant, whether as a child of the marriage, or a child of the family (premised on another marriage) at the same time, by virtue of succeeding family arrangements. In

63. Section 8(1)(b) of the Maintenance Act, incorporated into the MCA by section 23(2).
64. The Legitimation Act.
65. For example, the obligation to maintain a child (unlike the obligation to maintain a spouse) is not affected by the remarriage of the parties.
66. See Section 23(1)(a).

either case such a child could be a dependent to whom there is an obligation to maintain under the Maintenance Act.[67]

Therefore, for a child of both parties to the marriage, the basis upon which they are classified as a relevant child rests on the occurrence of a marriage, and a genetic connection to both of the parties to the marriage. Interestingly, in the recent amendments to the rules, relevant is being interpreted as relevant to the proceedings which in itself is yet to be explained by the courts.[68]

The other main head by which a child may be classified as a relevant child is as 'a child of one party to the marriage who has been accepted as one of the family by the other party'.

The deciding question of whether or not such a child will come within the definition depends on whether or not there is acceptance.

What is Acceptance?

The child who is a relevant child, by virtue of being a child of the marriage, is the child of both parties whether born before or after the date on which the marriage took place. Although the point of reference is the marriage, in actual fact, the parties would have an obligation to maintain such a child or to be granted custody of that child whether or not they were married because they are the biological parents. In contrast, the child who is a relevant child by virtue of being a child of the family must rely on the acceptance of the party who is married to the biological parent.

What then is acceptance so as to bring about this parental responsibility for a child to whom a party has no biological connection? In the case of R v R,[69] it was stated by Park J that 'a child of one party to the marriage could not be held to have been accepted as one of the family by the other party unless it was

---

67. This is consistent with the policy that by whatever statutory means, there should be some adult who has parental responsibility for a child. As a result, depending on the circumstances, the law can create at least four 'parents': two biological, and a spouse of either or both who 'accepts' the child.
68. Paragraph 6 of Petition for Dissolution of Marriage Form.
69. [1968] 2 All ER 608.

established by the evidence, first, that the other party consented either expressly or impliedly to receive the child as one of the family and, secondly, that that consent was given with knowledge of the material facts.'[70] Interestingly, to overcome the strictures of 'acceptance' in the UK, and thereby provide greater protection for the child, there was statutory intervention under certain enactments to replace the term with a child who is 'treated by both parties as a child of the family'.[71] Inevitably, the basis upon which a court will decide that there has been an acceptance of a child will be peculiar to the factual arrangements made within each family. Whereas the second limb of the concept of relevant child rests on the child being a child of the family, it is the acceptance of the child that makes the child a relevant child in such circumstances.

Despite the statutory definition of relevant child, the latest forms published for Petitions seem to restrict the information required in relation to children to the first part of the definition, namely, children of the marriage. This may be an oversight.

THE PRACTICE AND PROCEDURE OF DIVORCE

Usually when a person attends a lawyer's office to discuss a divorce, their mind is already made up, and there is a settled conviction that the marriage has broken down irretrievably. However, there are occasions when things are not so clear. For example, a person may seek advice as to whether or not they could obtain a divorce if and when the decision is made to so to do. A person may not be at the point where they feel that the marriage cannot be saved but simply wish to weigh the options.

While the MCA speaks of the powers of the court to take a number of steps to encourage reconciliation and thereby save the marriage,[72] this can only happen after the proceedings have

---

70.   Matthew Thorpe, Phillip Waller, Mark Everall, Nigel Dyer, Rebecca J. Bailey-Harris, Stephen Trowell, *Rayden and Jackson on Divorce and Family Matters*, 18th ed (London: LexisNexis Butterworths, 2016).
71.   Domestic Proceedings and Magistrates' Courts Act.
72.   Sections 11–14.

been commenced. The general view is that there is a duty on the attorney to satisfy himself that the marriage has irretrievably broken down before filing the matter in court. Indeed, from the standpoint of the law, it may be construed that an important component of establishing the irretrievable part of irretrievable breakdown is that the parties have made the effort to address their problems by receiving counselling. Of course, there may be circumstances when such steps would be redundant, but it is necessary for the parties to understand that, in most instances, some attempt to save the marriage should be made. Depending on the circumstances of the breakdown, the client should be advised to seek counselling and explore available services to address the problems in the marriage, which may not have got to the stage where the only reasonable action to take is dissolution.

In the area of marital breakdown, it has long been appreciated by the courts that despite the protestations made in public, it is not usually a case of black and white, and there will be more grey areas in a marriage than anything else. Parties still 'edit' their instructions to lawyers to paint a picture of their own innocence, and the insightful lawyer should not be at all surprised to be presented with a completely different perspective of the marriage from the other side. In fact, the astute lawyer will seek to convince his client that it may be more advantageous to take a less hostile approach so as to avoid provoking a costly and time-consuming reaction. Impliedly, the law seeks to reduce the gory details of the breakdown to the basic legal requirements of proving that the marriage has broken down irretrievably.

In a competitive professional environment, it is optimistic to expect that these principles (of caution and discretion) will be conscientiously applied, but the danger is that if the parties are pushed into divorce proceedings before they are ready, not only may the action be halted at a later point, but the parties may regard their counsel as not acting in their best interests. Furthermore, if matters are pleaded in a salacious manner, the other side may respond in kind and embarrassment will be caused as a result. Also, where children are involved, it is all the more important to pay attention to this precept.

The informal position in Jamaica is to be contrasted with the elevation of this duty into a procedural requirement in some jurisdictions that a declaration be filed at the time of commencing proceedings to the effect that the attorney has discussed the matter of counselling with the client.[73]

It is also important to consider all aspects of the marriage as a part of the divorce strategy. What of the children, where will they live and how will they be supported? Is there a need for financial support for either of the parties? What is the totality of the matrimonial property? How is it to be divided? Is there a pre-nuptial agreement or can all or any of these issues be settled by way of a post-nuptial or separation agreement? The consideration of these matters before starting the matter in court can be a considerable aid to resolving any potential areas of conflict before they arise and can save a great deal of time and expense.

The Divorce Petition

Divorce procedure is governed by part 76 of the Civil Procedure Rules (CPR).

The petition is one of the few forms of pleadings that have survived the advent of the CPR. While the writ, the summons, and the originating summons have been replaced by other forms, the petition remains largely unchanged. From the time when divorce cases were heard in open court, relying on fault grounds that were eagerly devoured by the public gallery and reported in meticulous detail by the newspapers, to the present day where these proceedings are dealt with as a quasi-administrative process without even the parties present, the format of the petition remains much the same.

---

73.   For example, Belize.

The contents of the petition set out the details of the marriage, including any children and any previous proceedings in court. It will also provide personal details of the parties, such as the date and place of birth and their respective addresses and occupations. Most important will be the fact that the marriage has broken down irretrievably, as well as the circumstances of the breakdown of the marriage. The proceedings are commenced when the petition is presented, which is when it is filed in the Supreme Court registry.[74] As a result of streamlining the procedure, the objective of pleading in the petition is to conform to the rules, and deviation from the general format is discouraged.

The petition will be headed in the format as prescribed by the rules in Form MP1. The names of the parties[75] will be set out and the opening paragraph will set out the details of the marriage. For the marriage to be dissolved, it must be proved that it existed in the first place. This is usually done by production of the marriage certificate in the course of the proceedings. Problems may arise if the marriage certificate has been lost or cannot be located by the Registrar General's Department (RGD). In the former case, it might simply be a matter of applying for another certified copy. If, on the other hand, the certificate cannot be located at the RGD, then an application may be made before a Parish Court judge for a certificate to be issued and registered.[76] This situation usually arises where there has been a failure on the part of the marriage officer to carry out his responsibilities as prescribed by the Marriage Act.[77] The date of the marriage is significant in that it must comply with the stipulations of section 8.

The next section of the petition introduces the parties as well as the court's jurisdiction to entertain a petition for dissolution from either of these parties as set out in section 15 of the MCA which

74.   Rule 76.4(12).
75.   The most recent divorce forms acknowledge the possibility of a wife petitioner who may have retained her former/maiden name during the marriage.
76.   Marriage Act, section 34.
77.   Sections 55 and 56.

must be addressed. As set out in section 15, the court's jurisdiction to hear a petition for dissolution rests on either of the parties being a Jamaican national, or being domiciled in Jamaica, or being resident in Jamaica for at least 12 months before the start of the proceedings.

The parties will usually have lived together as man and wife at one or more locations, whether within or outside of the country. This will provide the platform from which separation will be established.[78] The occupation and current addresses of the parties should also be disclosed to the court in this section of the petition.

The next section of the petition is concerned with children, namely whether there is any relevant child of the marriage. There may be children born outside of the marriage while the marriage is subsisting and, if so, the petition should provide information as to the name, date of birth, and address of any such child. The court also expects that there will be disclosure of the financial resources of the parties if there is any application for ancillary relief that is to be included in the petition.[79] In relation to the children, the petitioner should also state whether or not there is any dispute that he is aware of in relation to whether or not a child is a child of the family, and of course this raises the question of both paternity and acceptance.

The petition must also include the details of any previous court proceedings, whether in relation to the marriage, the children, or any property owned or co-owned by the parties, and the orders that were made by a court pursuant to those proceedings.

In the final paragraphs of the body of the petition, the petitioner must state that the marriage has broken down irretrievably, since this is the sole legal ground upon which the marriage can be dissolved. Furthermore, the circumstances that the petitioner will rely on as evidence of the breakdown of the marriage have to be set out, including the date of separation. The assertion that there is no

---

78.   But see also the case of *Benjamin* (1993) 30 JLR 289 where the parties never lived together.
79.   CPR, Rule 76.4(6).

reasonable likelihood of cohabitation being resumed will conclude the numbered paragraphs of the petition.

The petitioner will then encapsulate the claim by listing the order(s) being sought from the court.

The petition will close with the name and address of the person to be served, that is the respondent, and finally the certificate of truth, followed by the date and signature of the petitioner.

Divorce in the 'Early Years'

The law prescribes that two years should elapse from the date of the marriage before a petition for divorce can be presented to the court, unless a judge permits a shorter time.[80] The earliest point in time that a divorce action can be commenced is therefore when an application for leave to present a petition within two years of the date of the marriage is made. This application is made under section 8 of the act. Prior to the incorporation of matrimonial proceedings in the CPR, these applications were made by fixed date claim form, but rule 76.5(1) stipulates that the application is to be made by notice of application for court orders, that is under part 11 of the CPR. This is consistent with the view that the substantive proceedings being divorce (which is commenced by petition), make the application for leave subsidiary to the main proceedings, and therefore even though they are preliminary to the commencement per se, are nevertheless to be made by form 7. The required contents of the affidavit in support are set out in rule 76.5(2), and the proposed petition is to be exhibited to the affidavit. Service under rule 76.5 and the time for the respondent's reply depart from the rules under part 11, presumably to ensure that the matter is dealt with promptly and with the expediency that such an application deserves. Under rule 76.5(5), the judge who hears the application in chambers is given wide powers to grant appropriate orders.

---

80.   Section 8, the operation of this section and the requirements for the judge's discretion to be exercised are discussed above.

Service

The requirement of service is the cornerstone upon which divorce proceedings rest; therefore, it is vital that the procedural requirements for service on the respondent be complied with. Personal service is mandatory unless the leave of the court is obtained for it to be dispensed with. It is, therefore, still possible to get a divorce where the other party has not been personally served, but it is expected that every effort will be made to bring the action to the attention of the respondent. The documents to be served, when effecting personal service are the petition, the acknowledgement of service form, and where applicable an affidavit accompanying petition. Failure to serve or to serve properly can bring about inconvenient and costly consequences that will be discussed below.

If the precise whereabouts of the respondent is unknown,[81] then service by another method may be permitted with the leave of the court. The usual alternative methods of service in matrimonial proceedings are service on a relative of the respondent, or publication of a notice of proceedings in a newspaper.[82] Matrimonial proceedings having been incorporated into the CPR by way of part 76, and with successive amendments are gradually becoming fully integrated with the procedural methods that are applicable to general civil proceedings, including non-traditional methods of service involving the use of technology. The petitioner himself/herself is not permitted to effect service on the respondent. The affidavit of service is the document that proves to the court that the respondent has been served or given notice of the divorce proceedings. The requisite information that must be included in the affidavit of service is set out in rule 76.7(6). It is a document that needs to be accurate in all respects, because the requirement to serve and hence to prove service to the satisfaction of the court, is applied strictly. Affidavits of service that have been sworn outside of Jamaica must conform to

---

81.   But see *Gatherer v Gatherer* (1967) 10 JLR 187, consequences of failure to disclose full extent of knowledge as to whereabouts of the respondent.
82.   See *Bailey v Bailey* [2015] JMCA App 9.

the attesting rules applicable to documents being sworn to outside of the jurisdiction.[83]

Failure to Serve

If at the time that the court[84] is considering the grant of the decree nisi, it appears that service has not been effected properly or to the satisfaction of the court, the decree may not be granted. Whereas it appears that the court does have a residual discretion to waive the requirement for service under section 30, this is rarely, if ever, exercised. Normally, in the face of incorrect or inadequate service, whereby adequate notice of the proceedings has not been given to the respondent, the court will not grant the decree and will direct that the respondent be served correctly, and following which the court will consider the matter. Re-serving a respondent can itself be a time-consuming and expensive process, particularly if substituted service was employed, or if the respondent has moved. It may be that because of an intervening change in circumstances, a respondent who was previously given the documents can no longer be found. For all these reasons, a vital part of expediting divorce proceedings is to ensure that the respondent is served in accordance with the stipulated requirements at the first opportunity.

It is impossible to guess how many divorces are granted without the knowledge of the respondent. Clearly, in cases where service by an alternative method[85] has been used, there is always the risk that the respondent will remain unaware of the process. This, in itself, is not considered objectionable because a balance of interests requires that the petitioner, having done the best that he can to comply with the procedural requirements, should not then be impeded by the respondent's non-availability. On the other hand, it may come to light that the information as to service that was put forward was untrue and the respondent, though available to be served, was

---

83. Judicature (Supreme Court) Act, section 22.
84. This may be either a judge or a master of the Supreme Court.
85. Formerly substituted service.

deliberately left in ignorance. If the court becomes aware of this after the decree nisi has been granted, but before the final order, then the decree nisi can be rescinded.[86] The difficulty which arises is deciding the appropriate course after the decree absolute has been granted.[87]

Defended and Undefended Divorces

The vast majority of divorces take place at a point when both parties realize that the marriage has broken down irretrievably. Therefore, upon receipt of the petition, most respondents will, while possibly in disagreement with the circumstances that are being relied on, have no objection to the marriage being terminated by the court. Even if they are particularly incensed with the manner in which responsibility for the breakdown has been laid at their door, a prudent attorney will explain that this is not in and of itself a basis for defending the suit. As a result of this, most divorces proceed as undefended cases, and the rules as set out in part 76 of the CPR are an acknowledgement of this trend. The petitioner is no longer required to attend court and the matter will proceed by way of an application to dispense with hearing and, if approved by the judge or master,[88] the decree will be granted by signing the draft which is prepared by the petitioner's attorney.

A divorce is not contested unless a cross petition or answer[89] is filed in court by the respondent. Previously, this would have the effect of putting the matter on the cause list and, as a result, a considerable delay would ensue because the case would be treated like any other contested matter and would be set down for trial in

---

86. Section 19, also see *Stephenson v Stephenson* (1997) 34 JLR 1, citing *Everett v Everett* [1948] 2 All ER 545.
87. See *Boothe v Boothe* 0006/2004 27/11/08 discussed below.
88. A Master of the Supreme Court is now empowered to grant decrees in matrimonial proceedings; see amendment to part 76 of the CPR dated September 10, 2015.
89. *Minott v Minott* (1991) 28 JLR 466. The act contemplates a defence where the parties are not separated or there is separation for less than 12 months and a reasonable likelihood of cohabitation being resumed.

open court. The matter will now be referred by the court to a case management conference (CMC). What is seen in practice is that, in most divorce cases, where an answer is filed, there is disagreement over the reasons for the breakdown of the marriage[90] or there is an ancillary issue which needs to be determined.[91] Unfortunately, there may be occasions when the respondent will enter a defence,[92] or answer simply because this is a means of dragging out the process, or in the erroneous belief that it is possible to prevent the petitioner from leaving the marriage.[93] For all these reasons, an abbreviated hearing in the form of the CMC to assess how the matter is to go forward is a useful exercise. In the unlikely event that the case remains a defended action after the CMC,[94] the matter can be set down for hearing before a judge in open court.

Decree Nisi and Decree Absolute: The Two Stages of Divorce

Historically, the termination of a marriage by dissolution has always been a two-stage process.[95] The court will grant a decree nisi upon being satisfied that the grounds for divorce claimed in the petition are made out. This pronouncement was previously made orally in open court when the judge had heard the evidence in the case, and this would then be followed by the perfection of the order by submitting a written order which would then be signed by the court. After the pronouncement in court, there would then follow a period of six weeks[96] during which the parties could supposedly reflect on the matter and decide if they still want to end the marriage by

---

90. As opposed to the fact that it has broken down.
91. But see *McKenzie v McKenzie* (1978) 16 JLR 364; answer filed admitting allegations in petition, save as to arrangements for the children.
92. Although, strictly speaking, a defence in contesting a claim for dissolution is properly framed in the form of an answer.
93. This may be for religious reasons.
94. The powers of the judge in the CMC, as well as the case law, ensure that this possibility is remote.
95. Now MCA, section 16.
96. In other Caribbean jurisdictions such as Belize, this lapse period is still for as long as six months.

proceeding to the final stage of applying for the decree absolute to be granted. The application for decree nisi is now 'heard' by way of written documents submitted to the court and if the papers are in order, the file will be put before a judge to consider. If the judge or master, relying on the documents, is satisfied, then the draft decree nisi will be signed and dated at which point the order will have been granted. The application for the decree absolute is made in a similar way after the requisite period of six weeks has elapsed.[97] If the application for the decree absolute is not made within 12 months, it will be necessary to explain to the court, by way of affidavit evidence, the reason for the delay. Otherwise, the court might infer that the parties are not genuine in their desire to end the marriage because, for example, they may have reconciled.

Certifying the Arrangements for the Children

The MCA specifically addresses the need to protect the children as a prerequisite to terminating the marriage. It should never be legally permissible to walk away from a marriage without putting in place proper and adequate arrangements for the children, and the Act prioritizes this approach. While it will never be possible to constrain the party who is determined to avoid their parental responsibilities, the law makes it difficult for that to happen. In effect, the court's pronouncement that the marriage has broken down irretrievably is conditional upon the court being satisfied as to the care and upbringing of any relevant child.[98] The result of the court's increasing emphasis on the arrangements for the relevant children is that practitioners are forced to have ancillary questions resolved with greater alacrity, since failure to do so may cause the case to falter at the first rather than the second hurdle. Overall, this procedural development[99] may not be a bad thing because it forces

---

97.   This waiting period can be dispensed with where a judge grants leave for the order to made sooner, rule 76.14(6).
98.   *Sebastian v Sebastian* (supra).
99.   Rule 76 (12)(6), see below.

the parties to address these questions early in the proceedings and, in so doing, to re-direct their energies in a constructive way for the benefit of the relevant children.

The Decree Nisi

Provided that the papers are in order, the registrar will refer the file for consideration by a Judge or master to decide whether or not the decree nisi should be made. This is not a hearing as such because the deliberation will take place in the absence of the parties and their legal representatives. The main considerations in this process are:

i.   Whether or not the legal requirements are made out, that is, that the marriage has broken down irretrievably and there is no reasonable likelihood of cohabitation being resumed.

ii. Whether or not the procedural requirements have been met, in particular that the respondent has been properly served.

iii. Where there are relevant children under the age of 18 or up to the age of 23 in tertiary studies, that the arrangements for those children are the best that can be devised in the circumstances.

Although the court is not required to have regard to iii) according to the Act, a ruling in a case[100] and subsequent amendment to the rules now make it a requirement that the court take the arrangements for the children into account when granting the decree nisi.

In relation to children, when considering granting the decree nisi the judge or master:

a.   Must, if satisfied, certify that having regard to the evidence of the applicant together with any other relevant evidence, the arrangements for the maintenance, care, and upbringing of any relevant children are satisfactory or are the best that may be devised in the circumstances.

---

100.   *Boothe v Boothe* 0006/2004 27/11/08.

b. May make such order as to custody, care, and upbringing of the relevant children as in all the circumstances he deems fit.

c. If not satisfied with the arrangements for the maintenance, care, and upbringing of any relevant children or that the arrangements are not the best that can be devised in the circumstances, must defer consideration of the certification.[101]

It is not clear at this stage whether, in practice, the court will in the case of (c) grant the decree nisi and defer the certification until the absolute stage, or withhold the grant of the decree nisi until the application is renewed with improved and thereby satisfactory arrangements for the children. It would appear, however, that the new format of the affidavit in support of decree absolute allows for postponing of the certification until the court is considering the grant of the absolute.

It is also procedurally possible to apply to the court for a hearing in open court, notwithstanding that the case is undefended and the default procedure would ordinarily be appropriate.[102]

Rescission of the Decree Nisi

The decree nisi may be rescinded when the parties have reconciled.[103] Furthermore, if there has been a miscarriage of justice by reason of fraud, perjury, suppression of evidence, or any other circumstances, the decree can be rescinded (section 19). The problem, however, is that usually the grounds upon which the decree nisi could be rescinded under section 19 are not discovered until the decree nisi has been made absolute. The court once considered that the decree nisi could not be set aside and that the appropriate remedy was appeal.[104] However, the current stance of the court is better reflected in subsequent cases.[105]

---

101. Rule 76.12(6).
102. This would be by way of motion.
103. Section 18.
104. *Loftman v Loftman* (1967)10 JLR 170.
105. *Gatherer v Gatherer* (1967) 10 JLR 187 and *Scott v Scott* (1989) 26 JLR 354.

The Decree Absolute

In most instances, the application for the decree absolute is a mere 'rubber stamp' to the decree nisi previously granted. If the application is made promptly, that is after the requisite six-week hiatus has expired, there may be little or no change in the circumstances of the parties or the children. Given that the legal grounds for dissolution have already been met, which is established by the grant of the decree nisi, the court will be concerned that there has been change of circumstances so as to undermine the legal foundation upon which the nisi decree was premised. The other considerations would be that the respondent has been notified of this final stage if necessary,[106] and that the arrangements for the children are in compliance with the legal stipulations.[107] It is the question of children that is most likely to occupy the court's time, because although it is possible to make further applications in relation to the children after the divorce has been completed,[108] this is the point at which the court has the greatest power to hold the adult parties to account with regard to the obligations that they have in relation to the children.

Restrictions on the Granting of the Decree Absolute

In keeping with the modern divorce legislation worldwide, the MCA in Jamaica places conditions on attaining a decree absolute where there are young children to be cared for. As a matter of policy, it is not desirable to allow the parties to a marriage to exit the union without making adequate provision for those children. The tenor of the court's approach to this question is made clear from the outset by the requirement to provide an outline of the arrangements for children under the age of 18 (or up to the age of 23 if undergoing tertiary education) with the petition.[109] These arrangements, then,

---

106. Having acknowledged service of the petition.
107. *Sebastian v Sebastian* (1993) 30 JLR 149.
108. Section 23 MCA.
109. Rule 76.4(7).

come under scrutiny when the decree nisi is being granted as discussed above. However, it is at the end of the process when the decree absolute is to be made that the importance that Parliament places on provision for the children becomes plain.

Section 27 of the Act states:

> Notwithstanding anything in this Act but subject to subsection (2), the court shall not make absolute a decree for dissolution or nullity of marriage in any proceedings unless it is satisfied as respects every relevant child who is under eighteen that-
>
> Arrangements for his care and upbringing have been made and are satisfactory, or are to the best that can be devised in the circumstances; or
>
> It is impracticable for the party or parties appearing before the court to make such arrangements.
>
> The Court may if it thinks fit proceed without observing the requirements of subsection (1) if –
>
> It appears that there are circumstances making it desirable that the decree should be made absolute or should be made, as the case may be, without delay; and
>
> The Court has obtained a satisfactory undertaking from either or both of the parties to bring the question of the arrangement of the children before the Court within a specified time.

This section allows for the court to override the need for satisfactory arrangements to be in place in exceptional circumstances, but as a matter of practice this exception is rarely, if ever exercised. While the legislators may correctly imagine some emergency in which the conditions in section 27(1) should be ignored, nevertheless, the court is more inclined to regard this provision as a basis upon which litigants may seek to sidestep their obligations and will, therefore, exercise the power to dispense with section 27(1) only in the most extreme circumstances. Indeed, section 27(1)(b) is generally considered to give sufficient latitude to the court to obviate the need to resort to section 27(2). For example, in circumstances where a party to a divorce who is the parent of a relevant child, as defined by section 8(3) of the Maintenance Act 2005, is incapacitated by physical or mental impairment, section 27(2) need not be invoked since section 27(1)(b) may be adequate. The phrase 'appearing before the court' seems to exclude respondents who cannot be found, that is, there is a need to submit to the jurisdiction of the court. This can present problems where a relevant child lives with the respondent abroad and the respondent, for reasons that may or may not be justified, has kept all information about themselves and the child secret. Is the forthright petitioner in such circumstances to be imprisoned in the marriage because he simply does not have the necessary information about the child, or should he employ some other means of circumventing these requirements?

Section 27 does not impose a duty on the parties to maintain their children; it merely sets out a requirement for proper arrangements to be made. As a result, parties may set out arrangements which rely on the support or accommodation of relatives. However, the court has been reluctant to interpret the wording of section 27 as relieving a father of the obligation to maintain his children. Female petitioners are, therefore, expected to make exhaustive efforts to find, and if needs be, get maintenance orders against the respondent father before seeking to rely on other family members. This can be perplexing for the female petitioner who is inclined towards an independent mindset and will proudly declare that she supports her children and cannot be bothered with seeking maintenance from the father. This will also cause consternation among those female petitioners who are in fear of their spouse and have gone to great lengths to avoid their attention. Whereas an independent spirit, commendable as it may be in other circumstances, is not sufficient to escape section 27(1)(a), it may be that impracticability within the meaning of section 27(1)(b) can avail a victim of abuse. The question, therefore, arises as to how far impracticability can be stretched.

Section 27 of the MCA is concerned with the exercise of the court's powers at the stage of making the decree absolute. It was therefore possible, until CPR part 76 was introduced, to obtain a decree nisi where the court had not certified the arrangements in keeping with section 27(1)(a). It was then a question of whether the judge would then direct that custody and/or maintenance of the relevant children should be heard in chambers, or whether it would be left up to the petitioner to ensure that satisfactory arrangements be put in place before applying for the decree absolute. This could be by way of:

a. a chambers application,

b. an application before a Parish Judge, or

c. informal arrangements.

Subsequently, for reasons discussed earlier, it has become the norm to ensure that any issue as to the arrangements for the children be resolved before the application for the decree nisi is made. The latest amendment to part 76 seems to provide for the re-introduction of this option, because it is now permissible to 'defer' consideration of the arrangements at the nisi stage[110] to be considered later when the court decides whether or not the decree nisi should be made absolute.

The provisions of section 27 will usually be met by the court certifying the arrangements for the children as being the best that can be devised in the circumstances.

Rescission of the Decree Absolute

While the law envisages the possibility of rescinding the decree nisi, there is silence in respect of rescinding the decree absolute. This is understandable because it is expected that there must be some finality to proceedings such as this, and it is important for people to be able to get on with their lives without their status being affected at some later date. In *Boothe*, the court examined the question of whether and in what circumstances it would be appropriate to set aside or rescind the decree absolute.

The issue gives rise to two practical considerations:

---

110.   Rule 76.12(6)(c).

i. Lack of service, causing an inability to be heard in the divorce proceedings. At the decree nisi stage, once it has been established that service has not taken place, the court will set aside the decree as stipulated in section 19 of the act since a failure to serve will be viewed as a miscarriage of justice. At the absolute stage, where there has been a breach of the rules, as in *Boothe*, the applicant is entitled as of right, to have the absolute set aside. Even where there are no children, property, or other issues, the primacy of adherence to the rules justifies setting aside the decree. From a practical standpoint, there may be no loss but the loss of the opportunity to be heard. Yet this, combined with the lack of compliance, is difficult to overlook.

ii. Lack of service, causing detriment regarding ancillary applications. Generally, time can be extended if there are limitations of that nature, but there may be adverse procedural consequences, such as having to apply for leave out of time.

    a. Where the application is in respect of children, applications can be made regardless of whether the divorce proceedings are ongoing or have been completed, and therefore this would not, without more, provide a basis for setting aside the decree.

    b. Maintenance of spouse – While a time limit is implied rather than expressly stated,[111] this can be surmounted by an application for leave to extend time. The success of such an application would depend on the totality of circumstances put forward. Therefore the lost opportunity to make such a claim in time may not provide a basis for rescission.

---

111. Section 23 of the MCA speaks of a 'reasonable period', and section 7 may also be of relevance.

c. Property – In *Boothe*,[112] it was argued that the applicant was adversely affected because the time limit for making applications under the Married Women's Property Act had expired. This is no longer applicable under the Property Right of Spouses Act (PROSA) because the court can entertain an application out of time, but from a practical standpoint, it could allow a party to sell, transfer or destroy property without the knowledge of the other party before the powers of the court could be invoked.[113]

Decree Absolute v Divorce Order

As stated before, the termination of a marriage is a two-stage process, that is, the court must first be satisfied that the legal ground for the divorce is made out, in which case a decree nisi will be granted. After this, and some time has elapsed (a minimum of six weeks in Jamaica), the court can then make a final order that puts an end to the marriage, the decree absolute. The incorporation of this 'cooling off' period is, to some extent, a relic of a divorce regime based on fault grounds where the proceedings could progress quickly. In such circumstances, the parties could easily be carried away by the momentum of the lawsuit, which might also be accompanied by a sense of righteous indignation. In this context, a period of reflection is necessary, and this may also be seen as yet another way that the sanctity of marriage is buttressed.

The advent of the single ground for divorce, which is premised on 12 months' separation, considerably lessens the need for a graduated procedure. The parties have ample time to consider their position during the mandatory period of separation. As the law stands, the final decree is only granted upon application which is, in itself a check on the process. In those jurisdictions[114] where

---

112.   0006/2004 27/11 08.
113.   Arguably, rescission of the absolute would not affect such transactions but could be punitive, as well as possibly having the effect of disturbing the validity of subsequent actions, such as marriages.
114.   Antigua and Barbuda, and St Kitts and Nevis, for example.

the divorce order becomes absolute automatically, the burden then switches to the person who wants to stop the process, to intervene, and even then it is only permitted with good cause. In the vast majority of cases, the result is a more efficient way of getting to the end of the suit. In Jamaica, the pitfalls of the two-step process are apparent: unnecessary delay between nisi and absolute, often due to the lethargy of the petitioner or intervening financial commitments that relegate the divorce to the back-burner. Whereas there is sometimes an explanation that concerns the resolution of ancillary matters, where it concerns children, this has now become a matter that generally requires attention at an earlier stage and therefore becomes increasingly less of a reason for not applying for the absolute.

Ancillary Relief

The various forms of ancillary relief are essentially supplementary applications that are attached to the main claim for divorce. Usually, this is for reasons of convenience in settling the issues concerning the family as a whole. An application for ancillary relief in the course of divorce proceedings[115] could, in fact, be made independently of the proceedings for dissolution under some other statutory provision. However, when made under the MCA, these applications are, only permitted in conjunction with proceedings to terminate the marriage. The usual applications for ancillary relief are:

1. Maintenance of Spouse.[116]

2. Maintenance of Children.

3. Custody Care and Education of Children.

Applications for property division,[117] even though not included in MCA, are specified in part 76 of the CPR, relying on *Eldemire* 1990 UKPC 36 and *Goodison* SCCA 95/1994. Applications for the

---

115. Section 23.
116. Sections 20 and 22.
117. See *Gordon v Gordon* [2012] JMCA Civ 51.

protection of matrimonial property are included in the MCA[118] and can, therefore, provide additional safeguards to those which are contained in PROSA.

An application for ancillary relief can generally be made in one of two ways:

a. as an application included in the originating document, that is within the petition or fixed date claim form,[119] or

b. by way of notice of application for court orders.

From a procedural standpoint, pursuant to rule 76.4(15), if the application for ancillary relief is made by fixed date claim form after the main proceedings have been commenced, even though it is not what the rules envisage, rule 76.6(1), the application will not be defeated simply because it should have been made by a notice of application for court orders.

The Time to Make Applications for Ancillary Relief

Applications concerning children should be completed as soon as possible and preferably before an application for the grant of the decree nisi is made. Although the rules now contemplate granting the decree nisi without certification by the judge at that time, it is always prudent to address and resolve these matters as early as possible. While it is right to say that the judge at the time of considering whether to grant the decree nisi has the power to make orders for custody, maintenance, and the upbringing of a relevant child, this may be problematic. Problems can arise because the default process does not provide for representation to be made at the time that it is being considered. As a result, the application may fail for lack of sufficient information, or in anticipation of a response from the other party. Furthermore, the court is generally not inclined to make orders regarding children unless the matter is fully aired or

---

118. Section 26.
119. Where the proceedings are being commenced by way of an application for injunctive relief under section 10.

agreed. For all these reasons, it is preferable to have applications relating to children addressed in chambers, or before the lower court, before applying for the decree nisi, or concurrent with the application by relying on an agreement.

Having looked at how applications may be dealt with during the proceedings, it is necessary to consider how applications may be made after the main proceedings have been completed or ended. In the case of suits that have been completed, there does not appear to be a time limit in bringing ancillary claims. This seems to be entirely reasonable in the case of children, but in the case of a former spouse, the court having been given no guidance on 'late claims' by the CPR, will undoubtedly exercise its discretion. (This is to be compared with the rule in the previous Matrimonial Causes Rules, which has not been included in part 76.)

By contrast, claims after the proceedings have been dismissed are to be dealt with 'forthwith or within a reasonable period after the dismissal', section 23(1)(b). From a procedural perspective, it may be that even though there is no explicit requirement to seek leave, the ambit of the court's discretion is such that if the delay is great, and there is no justification or change in circumstances, then the court might refuse to entertain an application for spousal orders if there is an inordinate delay.

Applications for maintenance of a spouse or children and custody of children can be made before or concurrent with divorce proceedings in the Parish Courts or Family Courts. In such circumstances, the maintenance application will be made under the Maintenance Act, and the custody applications will be made under the Children (Guardianship and Custody) Act. In keeping with general summary procedure, the applications are made by issuing a summons on the back of an information or complaint that is laid before the clerk of courts. The advantages of the summary process are speed and cost, and legal representation is often not necessary. Since the Supreme Court, in processing the divorce will recognize orders from the lower court, this route will often expedite the main suit that otherwise could be bogged down awaiting far-off dates for a hearing in chambers, if the application was made in the high court. Once divorce proceedings have begun, the lower courts often decline jurisdiction, there being no power to transfer these cases as the law currently stands. This is posited on the basis that it is in the interest of justice that all matters pertaining to the family should be dealt with in one place. Well-meaning as that may be, there are at least two reasons why this may not be as beneficial as it would first appear. In the first place, there is a difference between being dealt with in one court and being dealt with by one judge. There are some jurisdictions that seek to ensure that all applications concerning the family are heard by the same judge. The structure of the family court in Trinidad and Tobago lends itself to this approach. In Jamaica, at present, when a family case is heard in the Supreme Court, it goes from one judge to another until a hearing commences. In the meantime, successive judges will make a variety of interim orders and the parties will find themselves on a roller-coaster from one hearing to the next. In such circumstances, it can be seen as advantageous for the lower court to hear the case. Another reason why confining the case to the Supreme Court would not necessarily be an improvement, is because of the need for legal representation in that court. Even with the advent of the CPR, the Supreme Court is difficult to navigate. Many applicants who cannot afford legal representation would be denied the relief they may desperately need because they do not know how to file a notice of application for court orders with a supporting affidavit, and cannot afford a lawyer to do it for them. It remains advantageous to the litigant to have all the current legal options available.

Injunctions and Other Orders under the MCA

The definition of 'matrimonial cause' in section 2 of the Act (which is to be compared with the definition of 'matrimonial proceedings' in part 76 of the CPR) refers at subsection (d) to the ordinary ancillary claims for custody and maintenance of both children and of the parties. Subsection (e) refers to orders under section 10 of the MCA.

Section 10(1)(a), (b), (c) and (e) of the MCA[120] mirrors the general powers of the court under the Domestic Violence Act that are exercised in the Parish Court and specifically in the Family Court.[121] Section 10(2) raises a number of issues as to its effect although, as a matter of practice, this provision is rarely invoked. First of all, it would appear to be anomalous that the law should recognize any 'obligation to perform marital services or render conjugal rights' in light of section 35. If a court can make an order to relieve a party of such an obligation, is that not a tacit endorsement of the obligation and that but for the intervention of the court it is to be honoured? Furthermore, why would a party apply for such an order rather than apply for dissolution? The mischief behind this provision seems to be that there may be circumstances in which a party to a marriage has not been separated long enough to institute divorce proceedings, but may nevertheless need the protection of the court from unwanted and possibly forceful advances from the other party. Indeed, by obtaining such an order, it could then strengthen a later allegation of rape. Even though section 10(2) only arises where the court is considering its powers under section 10(1), it does seem to revive the spectre of fault by referring to obligations and, hence, implying a right of the other party to take action when those obligations are not met. This may well be illusory, but it certainly invites consideration of who may rely on unmet obligations. While it may be intended as a shield to protect a victim, isn't the law as expressed in section 10(2) allowing for the possibility of it being used as a sword?

The court's powers to punish for breach of an injunction by way of contempt are preserved and supplemented with specific powers

---

120. Section 10(1)(d) was repealed by PROSA.
121. See *Toyloy-Wilmott v Wilmott* (1997) 34 JLR 635, for an example of the court making injunctive orders pending proceedings for property division.

in section 10(3)(a)–(d). It would appear, therefore, that a clear distinction is being drawn between the breach of 'an injunction and orders under Section 10' and other ancillary orders obtained in the course of the proceedings. Those orders may be dealt with by way of proceedings for contempt and depending on the nature of the order and the circumstances of non-compliance, may not automatically be deemed to be a contempt of court. Ancillary relief often takes the form of financial orders that are of a different quality from orders for the protection of a party and/or a relevant child. That said, it may be open to argument that an order for custody, for example, although not strictly a protective order, is almost hybrid in nature and that, even though it does not come under section 10, the option of contempt proceedings may arise depending on the facts, particularly in the light of the welfare principle.[122]

Sections 11–14 of the MCA give the court itself powers to direct the parties towards counselling and reconciliation and even to act as a mediator 'with a view to effecting a reconciliation'.[123]

THE LEGAL EFFECTS OF DIVORCE

In the first place, the end of the marriage may have an effect on the status of the parties in terms of applications to the court. The Matrimonial Causes Act, by its very name assumes that a marriage between the parties has taken place. However, it is not the case that once the marriage has come to an end, the Act is no longer available to provide relief. In particular, section 23 of the Act specifically allows for applications to be made 'after the final decree', section 23(1)a. This is particularly pertinent in relation to the relevant children, but with the amendment to section 23 by the Maintenance Act, to include maintenance of a spouse it becomes clear that if the court can order maintenance for a spouse 'after the final decree', then spouse includes ex-spouse. The old MCA rules had included a restriction that applications for spousal maintenance

---

122.   *Adjudah v Lalor* [2016] JMCA Civ 52.
123.   Section 11(2)(b).

had to be brought no later than one month after the date of the decree absolute, and thereafter only with the leave of the court. This provision has been omitted from the rules as expressed in part 76 of the CPR. It is, therefore, concluded that while there may not be an absolute requirement to seek leave to apply for spousal maintenance after the decree absolute has been granted, nevertheless it is reasonable to assume that the court will expect that reasons for the delay in making the claim would be included in an application made after the decree absolute has been granted. Certainly, the greater the amount of time which has elapsed between granting the absolute and making the application, the more closely the court is likely to scrutinize whatever reasons for delay there may be. The fact of delay may not by itself be a ground for dismissing a claim for maintenance, the parties are after all, husband and wife.[124] It may well affect the amount and duration of support.[125] It may also call into question whether there is, in fact, a need, or whether that need is 'reasonable' in the circumstances and therefore whether it can be seen as one which the defendant has an obligation to meet. The court's approach to this will always depend on the particular facts of the case.

Also, the mere grant of a decree absolute does not itself, bring a pre-existing order to an end.[126]

Married Name versus Maiden Name

According to *Cowley v Cowley*,[127] a former wife is entitled to call herself by her married name, by her former name, or by any other name she may acquire by reputation, subject to certain conditions as to the intention and effect of using the name. The mere fact that this right is termed as an entitlement establishes that it is not necessary to use a deed poll as a means of maintaining the current

---

124. This is one of the cardinal distinctions between a marital union and a common law spousal relationship.
125. Section 14(4) (m).
126. *Jarrett v Jarrett* RMMA 5/1999 20/7/00.
127. [1900] P 305 that was affirmed by the House of Lords in [1901] AC 450.

name or reverting to one's former name[128] as is frequently employed in Jamaica.

Effects of Divorce on Matrimonial Property

   i.   Claims under PROSA

   ii.   Wills and Inheritance

   iii.   Joint Tenancies – *Wills v Wills*, etc.

PROSA directs that claims for division of matrimonial property be brought within 12 months of the dissolution of the marriage, or such longer period as the court may allow after hearing the applicant (section 13(2)). In this way, the court's discretion to hear late claims is preserved. The procedural implications of this have been considered extensively by the courts, and are discussed in more detail in chapter 5.

Whereas a subsequent marriage will vitiate a will,[129] divorce does not invalidate a will made during the marriage. As such, it is important that a party to a marriage which has been terminated by divorce review the provisions concerning their estate, particularly where there are mutual wills.

Even if divorce proceedings have just begun, it is important to consider making a fresh will, particularly if there is need to provide for a third party. Conversely, the right to inherit under a will is not affected by divorce unless it is a stipulation in the will. Divorce affects the right to inherit on intestacy by virtue of the Intestates' Estates and Property Charges Act.

Getting a divorce, does not sever a joint tenancy. A divorce may well be a contributing factor in an ongoing state of affairs which will lead the court to conclude that the joint tenancy has been abandoned, (see *Wills v Wills*),[130] but the act of divorce without

---

128.   Whether this is a maiden name or a name otherwise previously acquired is apparently immaterial.

129.   *In the Estate of Park* [1954] P 112.

130.   [2003] All ER 27 and 64 WIR 176.

more, is not likely to be sufficient. This question is considered in greater detail in the chapter on matrimonial property.

THE WAY FORWARD

Divorce proceedings have become mechanized as a result of the changes in the law brought about by the Matrimonial Causes Act. The sole ground of irretrievable breakdown has made it easier to establish grounds for a divorce and may have been responsible for the general upward trend in the numbers of divorces per year until 2013.[131] For some,[132] the numbers tell a story of the way that the society is changing and its views on the nature of the family in Jamaica. For others, it is indicative of how effectively the courts are providing necessary services. It appears that the rate of divorce in Jamaica is far from exceptional and, therefore, the authorities are correct in concentrating on making the process of terminating a marriage as efficient as possible. The court has been sensitive to, what is a fairly constant demand, by trying to make the process more streamlined and with attempts to standardize the forms. The incorporation of matrimonial proceedings into the CPR is, in itself a welcome step which is starting to unfold after several tentative years. CMCs, discovery, and enforcement procedures have had an impact on family proceedings in different ways some of which may not have been previously anticipated. This is generally seen by family practitioners in the legal profession as progressive.

One of the consequences of the standardization is that divorce procedure can look deceptively easy. The layman thinks that all that is to be done is to fill in a few forms, file them with the court and the job is done. Those who work with lawyers or have paralegal training and are familiar with the procedure also look on and may

131. Statistical Institute of Jamaica (STATIN), Demographic Statistics: Marriages and Divorces. The significant drop in the number of divorces granted in 2014 and 2015 may be attributable to administrative adjustments rather than a change in societal trends.
132. Rev. Stephenson Samuels, 'Marriages Down, Divorces Up – RGD, Statin', *Sunday Observer*, January 24, 2016.

be tempted to offer a service of their own. As the authorities press on towards a more user-friendly environment, the many factors such as accessibility for the litigant, predictability, reliability for the practitioner, and the protection of the integrity of the process have to be balanced and weighed against each other.

4. Maintenance

INTRODUCTION

Maisie lived in the country with her four children: Junior whose real name is Claude, named after his father; Susie, Dave, and the baby, Benjie. Their father lives on the other side of the district. He has a small piece of land, but spends more time in the bar than in farming it. He has a visiting relationship with Pansy, which is why Maisie put him out two years ago. Life is hard for Maisie; she had a 'days work' with Mrs Johnson for nearly a year, but the woman's husband was becoming a bit familiar when he dropped her at the bus stop, so she decided to leave before she got into trouble. For the last four months she has been out of work and when she went to the children's father for help, he told her that 'is only if she spend the night she can get a little something to go home with'. The big children have not been to school for the last two weeks because she does not have bus fare or lunch money for them, and Benjie has a bad rash on his legs. In desperation, Maisie dresses the children and sends them off to their father for money. She notes that Junior is getting tall as he strides off wearing the 'name brand' hand-me-down sneakers that Mrs Johnson's son had outgrown. Two hours later, the children return, Susie and Dave are squabbling, Benjie is irritable and crying, and Junior asks for dinner. Maisie enquires of Junior if his father has sent anything, and in doing so notices that Junior is leaning against the wall in his bare feet. Before she can ask, Junior says, "Daddy say 'im neva have a shoes look good so, and since we is de same size, it will serve him betta".

Felicia is ambitious and has a good job. She also has high hopes for her son Joel. She is determined that, unlike his father Marlon from whom she separated three years ago, Joel will fulfil his potential and become a successful professional. Felicia and Marlon left school with a couple of CXCs between them, but unlike Marlon who was comfortable having learnt a trade, Felicia wanted more. As soon as she said she wanted to go back to school, Marlon got her pregnant. That didn't stop her though and she simply left Joel with her mother and carried on studying in the evenings after work. When Felicia got into university, Marlon tried to get her pregnant again, but Felicia was not about to be caught twice. Things went downhill from there, and when Marlon started going to the university campus and then accused her of cheating on him with one of her classmates, she knew it was over. Felicia and Joel now live in a rented apartment, and she has plans to buy her first house soon. She is dating someone who she studied with at university. Joel is in second form at a good high school and is doing well. When they broke up Felicia went to court and got an order for Marlon to maintain Joel, which he does. Regarding educational expenses, Marlon is supposed to buy Joel's school books while Felicia pays for his uniform. Three weeks into the new school year, Felicia gets a call from one of Joel's teachers. He says that Joel is doing well at school, but it is a shame that he has to be sharing his friends textbooks because he does not have any of his own.

HISTORY AND GENERAL OVERVIEW

Maintenance within the family, particularly child maintenance, has always been a vexed question. Historically, there were two separate legal routes by which a woman could obtain maintenance for her children.

In the first place, society was concerned with women who did not have the so-called protection of coverture (marriage) and any children they might have, because unless the man who fathered those children could be brought to account, they would have to be supported out of the public purse. Maintenance laws generally were, and still are, concerned with creating a duty to support children and other members of the family. Initially, 'illegitimacy' and 'bastardy' had different legal meanings, the former being a child of unmarried parents who were living together, and the latter being the child of unmarried parents who did not live together. Since neither scenario, falls within marriage, and with the passage of successive laws, the significance of such a distinction has become negligible. Bastardy laws, as distinct from maintenance laws, gave a woman a way to establish, through the courts, a man's affiliation to her child, as a prelude to being granted maintenance for that child. It can be seen, therefore, that maintenance and bastardy were for a long time, closely linked.

The Maintenance Law of 1869, created an obligation on both parents to support their 'illegitimate' children. This notion of a responsibility that rested on both parents was quite different from the situation where the parents were married. There were successive amendments to the early maintenance laws between 1869 and 1882, and these generally took a highly punitive approach to the failure to maintain. The seeds of a bastardy law were also found in this legislation, but it was not until 1881 that the matter was specifically addressed,[1] as the legislature was reluctant to resolve certain inherent inconsistencies between life and law in a post-slavery society.

---

1. Bastardy Law 1881 is followed by the Bastardy Law Amendment Act 1882.

The other strand of maintenance law pertained to persons who were married. In 1865, a previous Act 'for the punishment of idle and disorderly persons, rogues and vagabonds', was extended. Husbands or fathers who neglected their family obligations could be deemed rogues and vagabonds and thereby subject to custodial sentences.

The Maintenance Act of 1881 amalgamated both strands of the earlier provisions and with periodical amendment defined the law of maintenance in Jamaica until 2005. Even in the latest legislation, many provisions which have their root in earlier maintenance laws, for example, a duty to maintain parents and grandparents are still present.

The Maintenace Act 2005, is the most comprehensive piece of legislation dealing with family maintenance in Jamaica. It replaced the 1881 act of the same name. While there are other acts that give the court powers to make maintenance orders between family members, in most cases, that power is specific to the particular circumstances[2] compared with the general powers under the Maintenance Act. In that respect, the Maintenance Act is overarching and its principles and guidelines reach into the pages of some other pieces of legislation to provide an adequate level of consistency. Nevertheless, as is to be expected with new legislation, some issues have only become apparent after the Act came into force and was applied in the courts. However, it is this Act which provides the most encompassing framework upon which the law of maintenance in Jamaica rests.

The Maintenance Act 2005, in conjunction with the Property (Rights of Spouses) Act (PROSA), represents a new chapter in Jamaican family law. The extension of the definition of 'spouse' as a basis for maintenance gives legal recognition to non-marital relationships to a significant degree. In respect of children, the obligation to maintain has been expanded by extending the definition of parent.

---

2.   Such as custody or domestic violence.

Statutory endorsement of the right to make agreements is another development in the law which features in this legislation.[3] There is also an appreciation of many other options of conveying a benefit under a maintenance order apart from the age-old periodical payments mechanism. In many respects, the Act goes ahead of the current norms and beliefs that are evident in society at this time. The Act educates the Jamaican family about their obligations to each other with respect to maintenance. In the view of some, this is merely a codification of current family norms, whereas for others it would appear that Parliament is setting a standard to be met. As Jamaica comes face to face with the societal norms of our neighbours in the United States, the local legislation forms an important buffer and a timely reminder of what the Jamaican family is about. While the law is keeping pace with the changing social and economic face of the country, there remains a need to protect the vulnerable and disadvantaged.

The reach of the Maintenance laws to provide relief for those most in need is questionable. Some dependents now combine their perceived impoverished status with an astute exercise of the entitlement to maintenance (whether for themselves or for their children), to reap significant material benefits, especially with the aid of a sympathetic court. Others may be less astute. To obtain an order from the court, interaction with 'the system' is inescapable, many of those who are genuinely in dire need are easily frustrated by the procedural hurdles (despite the best intentions of helpful court staff), and may simply retire to a state of abject misery for themselves and their children. Legislation is usually a blunt instrument that works best when applied with other social mechanisms: public education, employment opportunities, and family support in the form of comprehensive health care and housing.

---

3.   While there is reference to agreements in the earlier Children (Guardianship and Custody) Act legislation (ssection 11), the tone is restrictive rather than facilitative.

As previously stated, there are statutory provisions for the court to make maintenance orders are found in many other acts from domestic violence, property division, and even in inheritance laws. This recognizes that the need for this type of family support may arise in many different circumstances. These provisions do not necessarily co-ordinate seamlessly with the main law, and this has much to do with the diverse origins and various situations that the laws seek to address. These other provisions are also examined in this chapter as well as the question of statutory cohesion.

THE MAINTENANCE ACT 2005

The preamble to the Maintenance Act 2005 states that the purpose of the act is to:

> Confer obligations on spouses to maintain each other;
>
> On parents to maintain their children; and
>
> On persons to maintain their parents and grandparents....

The Maintenance Act was brought into force in December 2005 along with PROSA, which had been passed in 2004. These two pieces of legislation share similar terminology in the course of giving recognition to common law unions. They also adopt a similar format in setting out the applicable factors and principles which are to be used when applications are being considered by the court.

The Maintenance Act allows for applications to be made in: 'the Resident Magistrate's Court[4] in the parish in which the person resides, or as the case may be, to the Family Court for a maintenance order....'

This provision grounds the jurisdiction of the court at a summary level. The question of access to the court in situations where financial need may be acute is crucial. It is important that the applicant can seek and obtain relief quickly, without being faced with procedural intricacies and thereby having to obtain legal representation. The broad application of the Maintenance Act to most circumstances

---

4.   Now Parish Court.

further assists accessibility so that whether the parties are married or not, whether making orders for children, or for a spouse, or for children and the spouse, the court is sufficiently empowered.

The exception to the exclusively summary jurisdiction for applications under the Maintenance Act is found in section 3(2). Where the court is hearing an application for the division of property under PROSA, it may also make maintenance orders under the Maintenance Act. An application for division will usually be heard in the High Court, and as such will be heard before a judge in chambers. This is consistent with the definition of 'court' in section 2 of the Maintenance Act. This is the only High Court jurisdiction to make orders directly under the Maintenance Act itself. The courts powers in this instance are to be distinguished from the courts power to make maintenance orders under the Matrimonial Causes Act (MCA), where the applicable principles of the Maintenance Act have been imported into the MCA by amendments to sections 20 and 23.

It is clear from this framework that Parliament is generally encouraging applications for maintenance to be made before parish judges (formerly magistrates) and, both from a legal and practical standpoint, parish judges have an extremely important role in maintenance proceedings generally. This is endorsed by the fact that, unlike in some other Caribbean jurisdictions, there is no monetary limit to the amount of maintenance which a magistrate can award. As a result, an overwhelming number of applications for maintenance are filed in the Family Courts or Parish Courts and these cases are a significant segment of the court list on any day. New cases, variations, and other contingent applications – particularly in respect of enforcement – contribute to an onerous caseload in most of the courts.

Geography and Jurisdiction

Each Parish Court or Family Court operates within the parish in which it is situated. Therefore, the applicant can commence proceedings in the court for the parish in which he or she resides.[5] In many instances, the person against whom orders are being sought is not resident in the same parish as the applicant. It may also be that where a child is the subject of the application, that child may not be a resident in that parish (although this is unusual). In such circumstances, it is open to the court to transfer the matter, if it is more convenient for it to be heard in another parish. This means that there are occasions where a party may have to travel across the island in order to participate in the proceedings.

It may be that the system could benefit from family/child courts, covering perhaps a county, where there could be a concentration of resources in a place where it is relatively convenient for all the parties. This would also allow for improved facilities in terms of an adequate number of courtrooms and judges, suitable holding areas with books, games and study corners under the supervision of properly trained staff, a crèche, specialist support services (psychologists and social workers) and a less intimidating courtroom layout which would allow for children to be questioned with greater convenience.[6]

SPOUSAL MAINTENANCE

Maintenance of a spouse under the Maintenance Act 2005 highlights a number of ways in which the old law has been updated to address the modern day family circumstances in Jamaica.

The old Maintenance Act, in keeping with the common law, provided for a wife's maintenance and was, therefore, restricted to parties who were married to each other.[7] It was a duty of the husband to maintain his wife and not vice versa.[8] Under the 2005 Act, the obligation to maintain between married couples has been

---

5.   Section 3(1).
6.   The Family Court of Trinidad and Tobago is an excellent example of a modern, centralized court.
7.   See Stephen M. Cretney, Judith M. Masson, and Rebecca Bailey-Harris, *Principles of Family Law*, 7th ed. (London: Sweet & Maxwell Ltd, 2002), 73.
8.   *Povey v Povey* [1972] Fam 40.

extended to apply to persons who are cohabiting as long as it is within the circumstances set out in the Act, that is, that they are single and living together as husband and wife for a period of at least five years.[9] So both married and cohabiting parties now come within the definition of spouse under the Act.

Since the definition of spouse brings in cohabitation relationships, the question that immediately arises is: What are the key features of a cohabiting relationship that make the parties spouses in the legal sense? It is a precondition, in Jamaica, that both parties are single.[10] In calculating the time from which the cohabitation starts, it may be that the Jamaican courts would look at cases from elsewhere in the Caribbean that recognize de facto spouses.[11] Cases decided in Barbados such as *Kinch v Clarke*[12] and the recent case of *Smith v Selby*[13] may provide some insight. However, the extended definition of spouse in these jurisdictions is not in all cases *ad idem* with the wording in Jamaica, and this can produce significant distinctions.

This leads to the issue of what are the features of a spousal relationship, because arguably, not every instance of cohabitation between single people of the requisite duration falls within the Act. The UK decision of *Kimber*[14] was largely followed in the case of *Bowles v Taylor*,[15] which set out certain hallmarks of a cohabiting relationship. Many but not all of these features may, in fact, be present in the Jamaican phenomenon of the 'visiting relationship'.[16] The factors recognized in *Bowes v Taylor*[17] are as follows:

1. Living together in the same household.

2. Sharing daily life.

---

9. Section 2.
10. *Murray v Neita* 0176/2006 18/8/2006.
11. Barbados, Guyana, and Trinidad and Tobago.
12. BB 1985 HC 17.
13. [2017] CCJ 13. Discussed in Sherry Ann, McGregor, 'Laws of Eve,' *The Gleaner*, September 11, 2017.
14. [2001] 1 FLR 383.
15. 05/2007, 19/1/ 2009.
16. Domestic Violence Act, section 2.
17. Page 13, paragraph 43.

3. Stability and a degree of permanence in the relationship; that is not a temporary infatuation or passing relationship such as a holiday romance.

4. Finances: the way in which financial matters are handled is an indication of a relationship.

5. A sexual relationship.

6. Children.

7. Intention and motivation.

8. The opinion of the reasonable person with normal perception.

So it may be that the relationship displays some but not all of these characteristics, but it will be for the court to assess the preponderance of evidence and come to a finding in the particular circumstances. It would also appear that there is no hierarchy in such a deliberation, since what is important in one relationship may be of less significance in another.

The Obligation to Maintain a Spouse

The most significant change in the law apart from the inclusion of cohabitation relationships is that the obligation to maintain has also been extended to apply to both spouses. It is not just the husband or male cohabitant that has a duty to maintain their female partner; the obligation to maintain under the Maintenance Act applies to 'each spouse..,' and therefore the law has become gender neutral.

A spouse will have an obligation:

1. Where the other spouse cannot meet the whole or any part of their own needs; and

2. To the extent that he/she has the capacity to provide for the other spouse's unmet needs.

So a spouse does not have an automatic right to maintenance; the entitlement will always be dependent on that person's ability to provide for themselves in the first place. In the case of *Darby v*

Darby,[18] the applicant was found to be earning a sufficient amount to meet her own needs and was therefore not entitled to maintenance from her husband. Similarly, in the case of *Francis v Francis*,[19] the applicant wife was found to be possessed of sufficient means to be able to maintain herself, and although there was a minor property adjustment, her application for maintenance was dismissed.[20]

Even if the person seeking maintenance does have a shortfall between what they are earning or have in the form of assets and what their needs are, the other spouse will only have to maintain him/her if, and to the extent that, they are capable of so doing.

The capacity to maintain refers to the ability of a person to generate an income. This can be affected by a number of factors. These factors relate to the individual, such as physical and mental well-being; to educational, vocational, or professional qualifications; to social and family connections; status; and so on. There are also factors that are outside of the person's immediate control, such as the economic conditions of the country, the area where the person is living, or the demand for persons with the particular skills that the person may have. It is expected that the Jamaican courts will follow the decisions made in other Commonwealth jurisdictions where it has been specifically stated that a person is expected to seek work at a level befitting their qualifications, and to pursue all reasonable options. For example, it is not open to a respondent with advanced technical or academic qualifications to put forward his earnings working part-time as a server in a fast food establishment as representative of his earning capacity.[21] Thus, in assessing earning capacity, the court will expect that if a person is out of work, he will be actively seeking a means of generating income that is

---

18.   053/1998 13/6/07, see also *Sewell v Sewell* [2017] JMSC Civ. 86.
19.   [2013] JMSC Civ 25.
20.   For further consideration of this pre-condition, see *Mitchell v Mitchell* (1995) Fam LR 44.
21.   *Hardy v Hardy* [1981] 2 FLR 321. The problem with this scenario is that it was so extreme, whereas if there had been a slight under capacity it might not have been so starkly apparent.

commensurate with their skills, qualifications, and station in life.[22] That having been said, the effect of the wording 'so far as', seems to limit the obligation to the bounds of a person's capacity. This would mean that if a person does not have the capacity, the obligation is not established. In practice in the Jamaican courts, particularly the family court, a judge will make an order which anticipates that the able-bodied respondent father will go out and make a greater effort to obtain employment, as the obligation is now legally enforceable.

Needs

A spousal maintenance order is for the purpose of meeting the reasonable needs of the applicant. The question of what is a reasonable need will always be relative to the circumstances of the particular couple, and is to be answered by 'having regard to the accustomed standard of living during the marriage or cohabitation.'[23] The court in *Bloomfield*[24] attributed needs to be 'the inescapable expenses of each of the parties including the maintenance of the relevant children'. This line of thinking is set out as a guideline in section 5(2)(d) – that the court must have regard to: 'the spouse's needs, having regard to the accustomed standard of living during the marriage or cohabitation'.

Importantly, needs also explicitly includes 'assisting the spouse to become able to contribute to (their) own support[25] and this is reinforced under section 5(2)(b) and (c), which gives recognition to the fact that many spouses will put their own advancement on hold while they devote themselves to the overall well-being of the family. This tends to be the situation in long relationships, for example, in the case of *Maragh v Maragh*.[26]

---

22.   *Marryshow v Marryshow* (1965) 6 WIR 141.
23.   *Preston v Preston* [1982] 1 All ER 41 and *Gojkovic v Gojkovic* [1990] 1FLR 140.
24.   *Bloomfield v Bloomfield* 048/2002 13/12/04, quoted in Karen Tesheira, *Commonwealth Caribbean Family Law: Husband, Wife and Cohabitant* (London: Routledge, 2016).
25.   Section 5(1)(b).
26.   2343/2005 9/2/09.

In practice, many applicants seek to adjust the standard of living upward when these matters come up for consideration by the court, or as in the case of *Antoine v Antoine* [27] they may seek to hinge the standard of living on what turned out to be an unexpected windfall of fleeting impact. Generally, the court will look at what is being claimed and be able to decide whether or not this is at an appropriate level to the lifestyle of the parties.

The Time to Apply for Spousal Maintenance

Married spouses will have an obligation to maintain each other throughout the marriage whether or not they are separated. While it is unusual for a person who is not separated to apply for maintenance, there is nothing to prevent an application being made and for the court to make the order as long as the legal requirements are made out. The difficulty that arises when the parties are living together is that if there is a comingling of funds, it may be hard to prove the required elements of entitlement. Furthermore, if the parties were separated when the order was made, but subsequently resume cohabitation, this could be a basis for applying for the order to be suspended. [28]

Even though there is no restriction on when married spouses may apply for maintenance, the longer they are separated prior to the application being made, the harder it may be for the applicant to convince the court that he/she is not capable of meeting his or her own needs. In the case of *Krystman v Krystman*, [29] the parties parted in 1949, and the wife made an application for financial relief in response to the husband's petition for dissolution in 1972. The wife's application was dismissed by the Court of Appeal.

By way of contrast, for spouses in cohabiting relationships (that is, outside of marriage), an application for maintenance from the other spouse must be made within 12 months from when the cohabitation

---

27. TT 2009 HC 244.
28. Section 18.
29. [1973] 3 All ER 247.

ends.[30] The court is also charged with seeking to achieve a 'clean break' between the parties when making any orders in these circumstances.[31]

Married spouses can also apply for maintenance on termination of the marriage. This can be done as an ancillary application by way of section 23(1) of the MCA and is discussed later in the chapter.

Types of Orders

a. Periodical Payments

Generally, orders for spousal maintenance are in the form of periodical payments. Periodical payments are described in the Act as: 'an amount (to) be paid periodically whether for an indefinite or limited period, or until the happening of a specified event.'[32]

In practice, spousal maintenance orders are usually for a limited period of time, that is, a specified number of years, unless there are some extenuating circumstances which would justify an extended period or even maintenance for life. The rationale behind the limited duration of spousal maintenance is that it is for the purpose of cushioning the effect of the loss of relying on two incomes, and this begs the question: For how long is a spouse expecting to live as if he or she is still part of a couple, and how long is the other spouse supposed to underwrite this expectation? In circumstances where there was some degree of fault alleged particularly upon the breakdown of the marriage, the court always had the discretion to take that into account,[33] but now in the era of no fault divorce, the question of the place that conduct holds is highly debatable.[34] There is also the question of whether an order for life offends the concept of 'clean break' as set out in section 6(3)(b), although as this

---

30. Section 6(2).
31. Section 6(3)(b).
32. Section 15(1)(a).
33. Section 14(4)(m).
34. In the UK the question of whether wife's maintenance should be a 'meal ticket' for life, continues to rage, see Ronnie Mortimer, 'Spousal Maintenance: A 'meal ticket' for life?' *Solicitor's Journal* 28/2/17.

is currently expressed it may be that this is only applicable to those who became spouses by cohabitation. Ultimately, there may not be a clear cut answer to this other than to say that it will be dependent on the circumstances in every case.

b.   Lump Sum Orders and Property Adjustment

Lump sum orders can be made[35] and can be ordered to be immediately payable or held in trust. This might arise where the lump sum is derived from an interest in property, such as the matrimonial home and that property is still being occupied by one spouse and the children to be sold at a later date. Similar issues arose in the case of *Heywood v Heywood,*[36] and this underscores the linkages between the law of maintenance and division of matrimonial property. In fact, section 15(1)(c) gives the court the power when dealing with a maintenance application, to make a property adjustment order. What would be expected is that this would arise when the court is also being asked to make property orders under PROSA. However, in *Francis,*[37] the court did use the property adjustment as a means of doing justice between the parties, while at the same time dismissing the wife's application for maintenance.

Lump sum orders are a good mechanism for achieving a clean break, so that the parties are then able to move on with their lives without recurrent obligations that are derived from a relationship which has come to an end.

Guidelines in Making Orders

Section 5 of the Maintenance Act sets out the matters to which the court must have regard when making spousal maintenance orders, and these are to be considered along with those set out in section 14(4) which are the general guidelines for all types of orders.[38]

---

35.   Section 15(1)(b).
36.   01471/2005 2/06/05.
37.   [2013] JMSC Civ 25.
38.   Section 4(a).

In respect of section 5(1)(a), the economic burden of child support, in other words, the impact that child support has on the financial position of the parents is to be shared equitably, so that a party does not end up having to use spousal maintenance to maintain the children. It seems that this provision envisages apportionment where necessary. If, for example, one spouse is earning twice as much as the other and their expenses are approximately the same, then the court may be expected to make an apportionment reflecting the greater capacity of that parent in the maintenance order for their child.[39] However, if in the case of that same couple, the spouse who earns more has proportionately greater allowable expenses, it may be that under section 5(1)(a), an adjustment can be made to the spousal maintenance that that spouse would have to pay. Equity in this situation may require a degree of mathematical dexterity which a parish judge has neither the time nor possibly the inclination to apply.

The capacity of the court in this regard requires greater resources than are presently available. What is likely to take place to find a reasonable figure is no more than a cursory assessment of the parties' financial circumstances. Even where the court goes further and orders an enquiry into means, the investigation and hence the quality of the recommendations, is affected by limited resources particularly a very limited number of court social workers. It is not always clear to what extent the application of the factors set out in the law has a bearing on the recommendation contained in the reports provided by social workers and therefore to what extent the court should safely place reliance on them.

With regard to section 5(1)(b), this is an endorsement of the fact that the dependent spouse is not usually expected to remain in his dependent position indefinitely.[40] If it is necessary for that spouse to get assistance from the other spouse to upgrade his skills so be it, but there is also a message to the recipient of the order that efforts must be made to attain financial independence.

39.   In accordance with section 9(1).
40.   See also section 14(4)(f).

Section 5(2) contains an extensive list of relevant factors for the court in determining the amount and duration of any order it is considering making. This list is in addition to the factors listed in section 14(4) which have general applicability to all obligations under the Act.

It appears, therefore, that even where there is an obligation, the effect of section 5 is that the court may make no order, or an order *de minimis*, if the circumstances call for it. 'Child support' in the ordinary sense is likely to have a wider definition than 'maintenance order for a child'. The distinction between the two will allow the court to adjust spousal maintenance in order to offset the de facto burden of child support which may not for one reason or another, be legally enforceable or readily quantifiable.[41]

Most of the factors listed in section 5(2) and section 14(4) are examples of non-financial contributions and establish that they have an effect not only on property issues but also on matters of maintenance. The list also specifically acknowledges orders or proposed orders under PROSA. This should now give the court significant powers in assessing assets and underscores the court's powers to set off maintenance obligations against property interests.[42] In particular, section 5(2)(h) may encourage the court to overcome a general reluctance to make secured payment orders.

The trend towards recognition of the value of work in the home and the care of children in the family is referred to in section 5(2)(f) and (g), where from the standpoint of maintenance, it is acknowledged that this will have an effect on a party's ability to earn and should therefore be taken into account.[43] With respect to section 5(2)(i), there is an understandable reticence in the legislation to intervene in contractual arrangements between a spouse and a third party so as not to jeopardize privity of the contract. As a result, the court may

---

41. An example would be the cost of supporting a child over 18 who is in full-time studies but for whom there had been no order made prior to the child reaching 18.

42. *Heywood v Heywood* 01471/2005 2/6/05, this in turn facilitates lump sum orders, and hence a clean break.

43. See Marriage of *Nixon* [1992] FLC 92 (Aust.).

not be empowered to take or reserve money which is the subject of such instruments as pensions and insurance policies. (This required a separate statute in the UK.)[44] This view has been borne out by the *Ministry of Finanace v Winsome Bennett* [2018] JMCA Civ 9 and importantly the Pensions (Public Service) Act 2017. However, by taking it into account,[45] the court can direct an equivalent amount to be paid to the dependent spouse under the maintenance order.

It is not unusual for one party to work and thereby facilitate the further studies of the other party, clearly with the expectation that both will benefit from the increased earning capacity that will result. This situation is set out as a relevant factor at section 14(4)(i). In the Australian case of *Tye v Tye*,[46] a young wife did exactly that, 'only to be deprived of the fruits thereof' when the marriage broke down shortly after.

When making a spousal maintenance order, the court is to consider the factors set out in section 14(4), these will be examined later in the chapter. However, like section 5, section 14(4) gives the court a wide general discretion to consider 'any other circumstances which in the opinion of the court, the justice of the case requires to be taken into account.'[47] While this provision may be useful in some respects, it is unfortunate that the discretion was not grounded in a framework which would minimize the possibility of inappropriate or extraneous matters having a bearing on the court's deliberation. It is also likely that the Court of Appeal would be reluctant to interfere with a decision of a judge at first instance, where it rests on that tribunal's assessment of what the justice of the case requires.[48] The question of conduct is not specifically referred to as a factor to be taken into account and it would appear that the conduct of either of the parties could find its way into the deliberations by way of this clause. Whereas the adultery of the wife would not be considered

44.   Welfare Reform and Pensions Reform Act 1999.
45.   Offsetting.
46.   (No. 2) [1976] FLC 90.
47.   Section 4(b).
48.   *Valentine v Valentine* (1992) 29 JLR 35.

to be an absolute bar to maintenance as it was in the previous legislation,[49] it would be open to the court to look at it within the context of the relationship under section 4(b) and section 14(4)(l) and (m).

Duration of Spousal Maintenance Orders

Where the order for periodic payments is set for a particular time, then at the expiration of that time, the order will come to an end. Such an order will not be affected by the procedural granting of a decree absolute ending the marriage.[50] Nevertheless, it is equally permissible for the court to have the order last until the occurrence of a particular event, such as the applicant's remarriage or the attainment of certain qualifications. Particularly in the case of persons who become spouses by way of cohabitation the court is directed to 'as far as practicable, make such orders as will finally determine the financial relationship of the parties and avoid further proceedings between them.'[51] This suggests that the principle of 'clean break' is prominent in such cases and it is quite possible that the court may be more inclined to make a lump sum order rather than periodical payments in this situation.[52]

Section 7(1) of the Maintenance Act states: 'A person shall not be liable to maintain another person under section 6 if the other person marries someone else or is cohabiting with someone else.'

This provision clearly sets out the limitations in relation to a class of spouse that was not previously covered by the law. In relation to married or formerly married spouses this will simply be a ground relied on in an application for discharge of the order.

The death of the recipient spouse will also bring an end to the order. The death of the paying spouse will also bring the order to an end, but there are provisions in the law to alleviate the situation.

---

49. Section 12 Maintenance Act 1881, see *Samuels v Samuels* (1992) 29 JLR 44.
50. *Jarrett v Jarrett* RMCA 05/1999 20/7/2000.
51. Section 6(2)(b).
52. *Parker v Parker* (1993) 16 Fam LR 863 (Aust.).

In the first place, if the order was secured in accordance with section 20(1)(a) of the Matrimonial Causes Act, the recipient could seek continuation of the payments by liquidation of the asset to which the order was secured, if necessary. This is an option which would only have been available to married spouses or former spouses by marriage using the MCA.

In general, section 6 of the Inheritance (Provision for Family and Dependants) Act allows any person listed in section 4 to apply for payment out of the deceased's estate in respect of maintenance. This Act includes the power to make orders for a person who was cohabiting with the deceased for a period of at least five years.[53] However, if the parties were spouses by cohabitation, and an order for maintenance had been made after the cohabitation ended, then it might not be possible to extend the maintenance beyond death under these provisions, because the Act states that the minimum five-year period must be 'immediately preceding the date of the deceased's death'.

Under section 18 of the Maintenance Act, the court has wide powers to vary an order, and therefore that would include the power to extend the date of an order. The circumstances in which the court may be prepared to lengthen an order will vary from case to case, but generally it is to be expected that such powers would be exercised sparingly.

CHILD MAINTENANCE

Historically, maintenance of children has developed through two distinct strands of the law. The Maintenance Act of 2005 is a fusion of those strands. The provisions for children born out of wedlock expressed in the bastardy laws are still in some respects evident in the present law.[54] The provisions for children born of a marriage have remained consistent except for the wife now having a joint,

---

53. Section 4(1)(e).
54. Prenatal and birth expenses.

rather than a secondary, obligation with her husband to maintain their children.

The Obligation to Maintain

The obligation to maintain a child is set out in section 8(1) of the Maintenance Act:

> Subject to subsection (2), every parent has an obligation, to the extent that the parent is capable of doing so, to maintain the parent's unmarried child who –
>
> (a) Is a minor; or
>
> (b) Is in need of such maintenance, by reason of physical or mental infirmity or disability.

The obligation to maintain a child rests firstly on his or her parents.[55] It is only in the case of the failure of the parents to maintain due to death, physical, or mental infirmity or disability, that there is an obligation on grandparents to maintain their grandchildren.[56] Generally speaking, applications for grandparents to maintain grandchildren are rare. It would seem that parents who want maintenance for a child are not likely, in the face of any of the conditions stipulated in section 8(2), to direct their application towards the grandparents.

'Every parent...'

The structure of the act allows this phrase to encompass more than two parents to a child. In fact, under the Act, a parent can be anyone who comes into the categories set out in section 8(3). This is an important safeguard in the event of unavailability or incapacity of the biological parents. Section 8(3) extends the definition of parent not just to those who marry into a parental relationship but also a person who is in *loco parentis* to the child. There are eight paragraphs under which a person may be seen as a parent under section 8. The categories are self-explanatory and are of

55. Section 8(1).
56. Section 8(2).

significance because under paragraphs (c), (d), and (h), the person will not be a biological parent. Paragraph (c) recognizes the child of the family referred to in the MCA as the relevant child, without using this terminology. Paragraph (d) restates a long-established position that with adoption comes all the responsibilities of parenthood. Paragraph (h) is a far-reaching device for creating maintenance obligations, but it has its basis in the longstanding family practices of informal child care arrangements. Putting an obligation on these different categories of parent brings with it the right to apply for maintenance, if the need arises.

The purpose of casting the net so wide when it comes to responsibility for children is to ensure as far as possible that the child does not become a burden on the state. The practical effect of giving a wide circle of people the duty to maintain a child is that although a person may be a parent for the purposes of maintenance, he/she will not be a parent for the purposes of getting custody of the child. This may appear to be an incongruous situation, but it arises from the fact that custody law and maintenance law have taken separate developmental paths. In short, one has little to do with the other in the eyes of the law even though most parents who are obliged to maintain a child expect a corresponding right of access of the child.

Apportionment

The obligation of parents to maintain their child is joint, but not necessarily equal. Section 9(1)(a) states that the court 'shall' apportion the obligation according to the capacities of the parents. This does not entail explicitly the pronouncement of a sum for total support followed by apportionment between the parents. The court tends to assume the contribution made by the parent with whom the child resides, and quantify only the amount that the non-residential parent is to pay. It is not difficult to deduce from this approach that the quantified portion is unlikely to reflect a proportion that is genuinely based on a divergence of capacities or otherwise.

Apportionment also arises where the liability to maintain extends beyond the parties, for example, where the obligation arises by virtue of having accepted the child as a child of the family, in which case the other biological parent's obligation would be a relevant factor in apportioning the financial responsibility to maintain the child.[57] The child of the family, that is, by way of acceptance or adoption, is well recognized in law for the purposes of conveying custodial and child support responsibilities. However, although not expressed in statutory form, the notion that you look first and foremost to the biological parents is deeply ingrained. As such, our legislators are obliged to employ sensitivity when dealing with this issue.

Capacity

The obligation to maintain is couched in similar terms as spousal maintenance, that is, it is conditional upon the parent's capacity to do so. However, what if the parent is simply impoverished? In Jamaica, there are many instances where the maximization of earning capacity still leaves an unskilled or uneducated parent in poverty. State provision for those on the lowest rung of the social ladder is limited and may be made through poverty alleviation initiatives such as the Programme of Advancement Through Health and Education (PATH).[58] Often, these parties in the lowest stratum seek to augment their income by way of the receipt of maintenance payments. The futility of this endeavour is that (if the person who is being claimed against is in a similar state of impoverishment) it simply aggravates the cycle of poverty in which the parents and children are trapped. This is often lost on both the parties and the court. The determination with which the court seeks to extract 'blood out of a stone' often drives respondents at this economic level, to despair. Also, this can adversely affect the children because the parent may feel inclined to abandon any form of relationship

---

57. Section 9(4), see below.
58. PATH is a nation-wide Government of Jamaica programme providing health and education grants to poor families.

with the children because of his financial incapacity and how it is viewed by the court. It is easy, if not misguided, to hold the view that if you can't afford children you should not have them in the first place. Those who sit in our courts, even if they are cognizant of or interested in the link between poverty and fertility patterns, will recognize that their powers under the law of maintenance are limited with regard to addressing this issue.

Who is to be Maintained?

'the parent's unmarried child...who (a), is a minor...'

A minor, according to the Maintenance Act, is a person under the age of 18 years.[59] If a child was to marry at the age of 16, albeit with parental consent, the obligation to maintain will fall on the spouse.[60] Also the court only has the power to make an order where there is a dependant who is owed an obligation,[61] and since there will be no obligation beyond the age of 18, an application for a maintenance order is not permissible under the Act, once the child has attained the age of 18 years.[62] However, where the order is already in place, the court does have the power to extend the duration of the order to any period up to the child attaining the age of 23 years.[63]

'or (b), is in need...by reason of physical or mental infirmity or disability'.

It should be clear from the wording of this provision that the obligation in relation to a child with an infirmity or disability is not constricted to minors. The obligation is contingent on the level of dependency, that is, the extent to which the child is dependent as a result of the particular condition that he is suffering from, and not

59.   Section 2.
60.   Section 4. This is an expression of what is generally known as the married minor rule.
61.   Section 11.
62.   *Brooks v Brooks* 3652/2007, 28/10/2010.
63.   Section 16(3).

the existence of the condition itself. In addition, the obligation to maintain such a child exists for the duration of the child's life.[64]

The infirm or disabled child's capacity to support himself or contribute to his own support is therefore a decisive factor in considering entitlement, amount, and duration of any order made for this category of dependent.

What is Child Maintenance?

What is the nature of child maintenance? By way of contrast with spousal maintenance, the Act does not speak of needs when expressing the obligation to maintain a child, but in section 9 reference is made to what a maintenance order should achieve. As well as providing 'support',[65] it should take into account the child's 'reasonable prospects of obtaining an education',[66] and the 'need for a stable environment'.[67] Prenatal and expenses relating to the birth of a child can also be included.

The absence of any specific definition of child maintenance in the Act means that the court has wide powers in terms of making orders to meet the requirements of each child. Orders are routinely made for medical, dental, and optical expenses. If there are any particular needs that the child has, whether it is equipment for education, health, training, or expenses for a trip abroad, the court can make orders to address these needs.

Types of Orders and the Application of the Guidelines

Section 15(1) of the Maintenance Act sets out the range of different orders which can be made, but for child maintenance some of these options will be more suitable and therefore more frequently used than others.

---

64.   This is section exemplifies the fact that the Maintenance Act like the MCA does not equate the term 'child' as being someone who is under the age of 18. Child is used within the act to mean a person to whom a parent, as defined in section 8(3), has an obligation.
65.   Section 9(2)(a).
66.   Section 9(2)(b).
67.   Section 9(2)(c).

Generally, the support aspect of maintenance will be expressed as a monetary sum, payable on a weekly, fortnightly, or monthly basis, which is referred to in section 15(1)(a). Educational maintenance and any other expenses applicable to medical, dental, or optical needs are usually mentioned in the order and will usually be evidenced by receipts.

Lump sums are not the usual method of effecting maintenance orders for children, largely because the obligation is continuing. However, it could be that either in the course of property distribution or if the order will be of short duration, a lump sum payment might be appropriate.[68]

Maintenance is used in the Act to refer to 'such periodical sum'[69] which is payable to the dependant and, in the case of children[70] to 'the appropriate person'[71] who will normally be the person who 'has care and custody' of the child.[72] Whereas this may be convenient in most circumstances, the court's reduction of the means of maintaining a child to a monetary value can become an issue between the parents. It is sometimes put forward in court that the person who receives the money does not apply it to the benefit of the child, or that suitably nutritious food items are not provided. On the other hand, if food and other necessities are purchased by the payer instead of or in addition to a monetary sum, it is often not given any monetary value or seen as being capable of offsetting a monetary obligation. Unless the recipient, usually the mother, makes allowance for non-financial contributions to maintenance,[73] the respondent will get no credit in court for this. The provision of staple foodstuffs can play a significant role in the care and upbringing of a child. It also has a

---

68. This is to be compared with common law spousal maintenance, where a lump sum might be more appropriate, see *Parker v Parker*.
69. Section 14(2).
70. Increasingly the American term 'child support' is being used in reference to maintenance for children.
71. Section 14(2).
72. Section 12(1).
73. This is more likely to occur in rural communities, where the supply of farm produce, ground provisions, etc., is considered to be a valuable input.

powerful psychological effect on the child who is left with an image of the contribution that the absent parent is making to their well-being. The exchange of money, often when the child is not present, leaves the child with no enduring memory of the parent contributing to his needs and acting responsibly.

It is possible to interpret section 14(4)(d) as a provision that allows the court to view, for example, a farmer's capacity to provide support being evidenced by the provision of produce. It may also be possible to encourage the court to use section 14(4)(m) in a liberal way, so as to give recognition to these practical aspects of family life. While it may therefore depend on persuading a court to apply these guidelines in a particular case, it would be useful if Parliament could give the court specific guidance on the recognition of non-financial contributions towards maintenance. This would create a uniform approach. Undoubtedly, payment in kind can in some cases be used as a means of defeating the order and frustrating the applicant. Nevertheless, the exercise of the court's discretion can take this into account and balance the interests in each case, being mindful of the child's welfare.

Section 14(4)(e) is of significance as it relates to maintenance for children with a physical or mental infirmity or disability. The obligation to maintain such a person is conditional upon the extent to which they are in need. Therefore, it is expected that where that person can earn an income for themselves they will do so. As a factor in determining the amount and duration of a maintenance order, section 14(4)(e) is reinforcing the principle that a person with disabilities should use what skills and capacities they possess in order to support themselves. If they do not have the requisite skills, section 14(4)(f) and (k) bring in the option of getting trained and this can be an extremely useful feature in a maintenance order. These are important factors as an order for maintenance in these circumstances may be an order for life.

The circumstances which are referred to in section 14(4)(g), are not specified and therefore it may be another child, an elderly relative such as parents or even grandparents, or even someone else to whom the party is connected. It will inevitably depend on the practices and circumstances within that particular family.[74]

Quite often a person who has an obligation to maintain a child will also have other children and therefore will have an obligation to maintain them also. While applicants who are parents to the first born child or the child/children born in the marriage might seek to be ranked first, the law does not recognize any hierarchy of child dependents. Indeed, the court is mandated to consider that the respondent has a legal obligation to others in considering the amount and duration of an order,[75] and this would include not just a responsibility to other children but also parents and grandparents.[76] Even in section 9(3) and (4), when considering the responsibility of a parent who accepted a child of the marriage or cohabitation, the 'other' natural parent is not given a higher responsibility than that of the parent by acceptance. This is just something to which the court should 'have regard'. This is to be contrasted with the position in Barbados....[77]

By section 14(4)(j), the court may take into account 'any other legal right of the dependant to support other than (the right to support) out of public funds'. This means that the court should not take into account that the child is, for example, a beneficiary under PATH. This highlights an enduring dilemma faced by most countries of balancing the duty of the parent and the duty of the state when dealing with the alleviation of child poverty. Some Commonwealth countries have introduced a statutory child support regime, which brings with it a complex system of trying to 'claw back' money paid

---

74.   See *Marriage of Soblusky* (1976) 2 Fam LR 11.
75.   Section 14(4)(g).
76.   Section 10.
77.   No concept of 'acceptance' which underscores the priority of the biological father when applying section 42 of the Family Law Act.

by the state from the delinquent parent.[78] While highlighting that this social problem is not a simple matter, it would seem that at present, this approach is neither desirable nor feasible in Jamaica or the wider Caribbean.

Time to Apply and Duration of Orders

Section 9(1)(b) allows the court to make orders in respect of a period prior to the birth of the child. However, the application would normally be made subsequent to that event. A maintenance order will normally run until a child reaches the age of 18 years[79] unless the child has a physical or mental infirmity or the order is extended because the child will be engaged in further educational studies.

If a child 'is or will be engaged in a course of education or training beyond the age of 18'[80] and it is 'expedient' to continue payments under the order, the court can extend the order to any period up to the age of 23 years. However, the wording of the section directs that the court only has the power to extend an existing order[81] prior to its expiration, that is, before the child reaches the age of 18.[82] This clause raises concerns about the extent of the court's protection of young adults who continue their educational and/or career training. The linking of the court's power to award maintenance to children over the age of 18 who are studying, to the pre-existence of the order is a source of much frustration for would-be applicants.[83] The rationale of the legislature may have been that the applicant (whether parent or child) should have got their house in order by the time the child attains the age of 18 and therefore should have applied for and been granted a maintenance order. Also, from the standpoint of the respondent, one would ask: Are they not entitled to expect that there will be some finality when a child reaches 18?

78.   Australia, UK, Child Support Acts.
79.   Section 16(1)(a).
80.   Section 16(3)(a).
81.   *Brooks v Brooks* 03652/2007 28/10/2010.
82.   *Rowe v Brown* (2014) JMCA Civ 30.
83.   Often, parents do not realize that this is the case until after the child is over 18.

The court's approach may be viewed as a calculated demotion of the welfare principle, which may be justifiable on the basis that we are now dealing with an adult, despite the fact that the child may still be wholly dependent on the parents. However, the question remains as to why a young person who is still in full-time study should not be able to apply for an order to have a parent maintain him, unless there is already an order in place.[84] Sometimes there are circumstances where there would have been no need to make an order and possibly no basis for an order to be made prior to the child attaining the age of 18. Should a person who is now engaged in tertiary studies and therefore still fully dependant be penalized because the parents did not separate until they reached 18? Should that child be denied maintenance because the would-be respondent honoured his obligations up to the child reaching 18 without an order of the court, and suddenly stopped maintaining the child thereafter?[85] What compounds the injustice of this, is that none of these 'reasons' have anything to do with the conduct of the child. The exercise of the court's powers in such circumstances requires a broad-minded approach so as to provide some form of relief.

Welfare and Child Maintenance

Sometimes judges make broad declarations as to the welfare of the child being paramount in the course of a maintenance hearing. While it is understandable that the court is preoccupied with the welfare of the child by virtue of the nature of the proceedings, it is difficult to preserve the notion of paramountcy in the face of the economics of the case.

The statutory provision setting out the welfare principle in Jamaica is found in the legislation dealing with guardianship and custody, but the Maintenance Act is silent as to the status of the welfare principle

---

84.   See *Brooks v Brooks*.
85.   Or because the custodial parent was negligent and did not apply for maintenance for the child when they were under 18.

in maintenance applications. In looking elsewhere, for example, in England, in considering financial relief,[86] the court:

> need only give "first" consideration to the welfare of the child in question,...the court must simply consider all the relevant circumstances, always bearing in mind the important consideration of the welfare of the children, and then try to attain a financial result which is just as between husband and wife.[87]

While this is of particular significance in property matters, it should equally hold true to all questions of financial relief, including maintenance.

From a practical standpoint, the limitation on the application of the welfare principle becomes the only workable formula. It is possible to look at the cost of meeting all the reasonable needs of the child and apportion that cost between the parents, but there are a number of contingencies that undermine this idealistic scenario. First of all, it can only be fulfilled if the parents are earning enough to meet that cost. Secondly, certain expenses are necessary for one's survival and must come before the child's needs, because without that, the parent will not be in a position to go out and earn and thus provide for the child. These include food, shelter, transportation, and clothing.[88] Furthermore, there may be equally important but competing demands on a parent's resources, such as meeting the needs of an elderly parent or other children. If each child's welfare is paramount, then who gets the money, how much do they get, and what if the money cannot meet that parent's share of all the reasonable needs of all the children concerned? In short, someone's interests must yield. The wording of the relevant provisions in the act recognizes this: 'to the extent that the parent is capable of doing so' effectively spells out that capacity is a pre-condition to the obligation. So the welfare of the child can only be the starting

---

86. See *Suter v Suter* [1987] 2 All ER 336.
87. Cretney, *Principles of Family Law*, 355.
88. This might be called the 'put on your own oxygen mask, before helping others with theirs' phenomenon.

point [89] in any maintenance application, and the extent to which that principle can be paramount is usually defeated by certain inescapable financial realities.

MAINTENANCE OF PARENTS AND GRANDPARENTS

Under section 10 of the Maintenance Act, every adult is obliged to maintain their parents and grandparents 'who are in need...by reason of age, physical or mental infirmity, or disability'. Despite the fact that 'parent' according to section 8(3) has a wider meaning than biological parents, 'grandparents' is not defined for the purposes of the act, and presumably would be given its ordinary meaning.

Interestingly, the Act gives guidance as to the court's consideration of the circumstances of the dependant (parent or grandparent), section 10(2), but does not provide any other special circumstances applicable to this type of maintenance other than the general criteria under section 14(4) which are applicable. As such, under section 14(4)(l), the court should take into account 'the quality of the relationship between the dependant and the respondent'. This factor may be of significance where a person is brought to court to maintain a parent who did not maintain him when he was growing up. The notion that the delinquent parent can then, in years to come, make claim against a child who has done well in life, despite the non-involvement of the claimant, can be addressed within the factors listed under section 14(4) of the act. Similarly, it could be argued that the obligation to maintain a parent should be shared and apportioned among siblings, but this is not specifically recognized in the Act.

Needs

Needs for the elderly or infirm parent or grandparent can amount to a large sum, particularly when the cost of medical treatment and/ or home care is factored in. Is this the means by which, in the face of inadequate retirement pensions from the state, the obligation

---

89.   It is therefore a first consideration.

can now be re-directed back to the family? In some respects, this is simply a statutory acknowledgement of our cultural norms and practices and, as such, most Jamaicans would have little difficulty in accepting the moral imperative enshrined in this part of the law. Certainly, as the population ages, this particular obligation may gain greater significance.

MAINTENANCE AGREEMENTS

The Maintenance Act and the Property (Rights of Spouses) Act (PROSA) give statutory recognition to agreements between spouses or spouses to be. The Maintenance Act allows the parties to enter into maintenance agreements in relation to the settlement of their support rights and obligations as they think fit.[90] This is a specific endorsement of the power to make pre- and post-nuptial or cohabitation agreements, which is a common feature of the two Acts.[91]

The agreement may be in respect of the spouses themselves and/ or any children that either party has an obligation to maintain. It may, therefore, cover a child who is not a child of the union or a relevant child.[92] The agreement may deal with financial matters, but can also address the right to direct the education and moral training of their children. The latter area usually falls under the umbrella of custody, but it is understandable that this would be included. For practicality, many financial decisions relating to children are derived from a conviction as to how the child should be brought up, the education and religious training that they should receive, and as a consequence, who should pay for it. The scope is wide regarding matters affecting the settlement of the support obligations of the parties, and includes the power to vary previous agreements.[93]

---

90. Section 24(1).
91. See PROSA, section 10.
92. However, this provision does not appear to acknowledge the power to make agreements in respect of a child to whom there is no obligation under section 8.
93. Section 24(2)(b)(iii).

The Act sets up a framework of conditions in section 24(3) and (4) which, if complied with, will generally ensure that the agreement is recognized in law. However, in the event of non-compliance with the terms set out in section 24 or if the court believes that the result would be unjust, the agreement may be held to be unenforceable.[94] Even if the terms of the section have not been followed, if the court is satisfied that there has been no material prejudice to the interests of either party, the agreement may still be effective, whether fully or partially.[95]

An agreement should not be made unless each party has obtained independent legal advice. This is important because, apart from the need to explain the legal effect of the terms and conditions of any proposed agreement, it brings a measure of balance to the negotiations. All too often if there is one party who has considerably more assets or some other advantage over the other, then that party will assume a dominant position in any settlement negotiations.

The agreement must be in writing and signed by both parties, and their signatures must be witnessed by a justice of the peace, attorney-at-law in Jamaica, or a person with the requisite legal authority as listed in the Act if it is made elsewhere.[96] Since it is possible for minors to be spouses within the meaning of the Act,[97] it is stipulated that their legal capacity to enter into the agreement is the same is if they were adults.[98]

The rest of the section deals with miscellaneous matters in relation to the validity of the agreement. Section 24(8) gives guidelines to the court regarding the question of whether an agreement will be considered unjust. The consequence of this provision is that the validity of the agreement will be affected by matters outside of its terms, such as the passage of time and changes in circumstances since the agreement was made. In addition, the court is entitled

94. Section 24(5).
95. Section 24(7).
96. Section 24(4)(a) and (b).
97. Also under PROSA.
98. Section 24(6).

to consider 'any other matter which it considers relevant'.[99] Once again, the court is bestowed with an extremely wide discretion.[100] Even though it is important to allow the court to maintain fairness, this type of discretion has the effect of undermining the ability to predict the outcome and therefore give reliable legal advice on the likely outcome of such a challenge to the validity of an agreement.

Section 24(11) introduces another criterion for the consideration of arrangements in an agreement in relation to a child. If the court finds that the arrangements in respect of a child are not proper or are no longer adequate, the court may make an order for maintenance of the child in accordance with the Act. The question as to what is not proper is not explored and may provide scope for further deliberation by the courts. The law in this area will be further honed and developed as more agreements become the subject of judicial scrutiny.

MAINTENANCE UNDER OTHER STATUTES

Maintenance under the Matrimonial Causes Act

Section 23 (1) of the MCA states, inter alia:

> The Court may make such order as it thinks just for the custody, maintenance and education of any relevant child or for the maintenance of a spouse:
>
> In any proceedings under section 10, or in any proceedings for dissolution or nullity of marriage before, by or after the final decree
>
> Where such proceedings are dismissed after the beginning of the trial, either forthwith or within a reasonable period after the dismissal....

This provision advises when applications for maintenance[101] can be made. A careful reading discloses the necessity to commence proceedings either by way of a petition for the marriage to be

---

99. Section 24(8)(e).
100. For an example of the exercise of the court's discretion in relation to a post nuptial agreement, see *AH v JH* [2014] JMSC Civ 68.
101. And other forms of ancillary relief.

terminated or by way of an application for injunctive relief under section 10.

The court's powers under the specific legislation of the Maintenance Act are drawn into the ambit of the MCA.[102] This gives the high court jurisdiction to make orders that are consistent with the Maintenance Act in the course of proceedings brought under the MCA. Prior to the 2005 Act, the court's powers under the MCA were divergent from the court's powers under the old Maintenance Act. While these powers were being exercised in different courts, that is, the high court for the MCA and the RM Court for the Maintenance Act, there was seemingly no logical basis for applying different principles in the different courts.[103] Incorporating the principles under the 2005 Act into the MCA by way of section 23(2) has rectified this anomaly. The court's powers in this regard are contingent upon the commencement, though not the completion, of either an application under section 10 or an application for termination by way of dissolution or nullity. Where proceedings are completed or even if they are discontinued, the court has the power to make orders after the final decree or within a reasonable period as the case may be.[104]

Section 23 incorporates the court's powers under the Maintenance Act to make orders for the benefit of a spouse and any relevant child. This section becomes a general statement relating to the court's powers, which is particularized in sections 20 and 22. While section 20(1) allows for making lump sum orders, and for securing such (other) payments by drawing up the necessary deeds or instruments, these powers are now encapsulated in the Maintenance Act and apparently render this provision superfluous. Section 20(2) provides for periodical payments between spouses, and subsection (4) directs the court to regard the factors set out in section 14(4) of the Maintenance Act. The combination of section 23(2)–(5) and

---

102.   See subsections (2)–(5).
103.   This was pointed out in the case of *Samuels v Samuels* 0131/ 1997 5/10/2000.
104.   Section 23(1)(b).

section 20(4) is that the Maintenance Act applies in all respects. Section 22 of the MCA is procedural in nature and is in keeping with section 23 that applications under section 20 may be commenced at any time after the presentation of the petition.

Section 23(3), (4), and (5) incorporate the law in relation to agreements[105] into the MCA, and they appear to cement the court's power to recognize and endorse pre- and post-nuptial agreements in the course of terminating marriages, particularly by way of divorce.

Notably, where a disposition is made with the intention of defeating a claim for maintenance under section 20 or 23 of the MCA, section 26 of that Act gives the court extensive powers of redress. The Maintenance Act 2005 now includes powers to make all the orders which can be made under section 20 and 23 (and more), but it contains no such express provisions as set out under section 26. Is this an intentional distinction for the added protection of those who are married? Or is this an inadvertence that is not expected to make any real difference between the rights of the parties when applying in the high court and when applying in a court of summary jurisdiction?

Maintenance under the Children (Guardianship and Custody) Act

When the court grants custody of a child to the mother it can also make an order for the father to pay maintenance in respect of the child.[106] The court may make such an order for maintenance whether or not the mother and father are living together; however, the order will not be enforced while the parents are together and will lapse if they continue to live together for more than three months.[107]

In considering how much the father should pay under the maintenance order, the court is to have regard to the means of the

---

105.   As set out in section 24 of the Maintenance Act.
106.   See the Children (Guardianship and Custody) Act, section 7(3).
107.   Section 7(4).

father.[108] Under section 7A, the court may order the continuation of payments beyond the age of 18 up to the age of 21. The court may also order that any payments beyond the age of 18 be made to the child directly 'instead of the person to whom it was previously paid'.[109]

These provisions are not consistent with the Maintenance Act in a number of respects. Under the Maintenance Act, maintenance for children may be extended to the age of 23 years and under that Act the extension is contingent on the child being 'engaged in a course of education or training after attaining the age of 18 years'.[110] It may be that under the Children (Guardianship and Custody) Act the court would not exercise its discretion under section 7A to extend the duration of the order unless the circumstances were similar to those expressed in section 16 of the Maintenance Act. There is, it would appear, nothing to restrict the court to such an approach. It could be argued that this advantage is offset by the shorter number of years that the order can extend to under the Children (Guardianship and Custody) Act. It is difficult to see any justification for the difference in ages in the respective legislation.[111]

Once again, under sections 7A and B provisions, the criteria for the court to decide what is to be paid is 'the means of the person ordered to make the payment'. The failure to amend the Children (Guardianship and Custody) Act during the passage of the Maintenance Act to incorporate the terms of the Maintenance Act has become a matter of query for the courts.[112] In some instances, the court has been prepared to rely on the common law.[113] As yet, the question has not been dealt with by way of a comprehensive statutory approach.

---

108. In *Jones v Jones* 0003/2006 16/12/2008, the court took into account the means of the mother, applying the reasoning of Harrison J(Ag) in *Butler v Butler*, which in turn, relied on *Re T (Infant)* [1953] Ch D 789.
109. Section 7A(b).
110. Section 16(3)(a) of the Maintenance Act.
111. There may be some guidance from the case of *Campbell v Campbell* (below).
112. See *Campbell v Campbell* 528/2000 4/4/08.
113. See *Jones v Jones* 0003/2006 16/12/08, applied in *Butler v Butler* 099/1982.

Section 17 of the Children (Guardianship and Custody) Act offers a gallant but now outdated attempt to grapple with the issue of enforcement. The creation of a criminal offence is noteworthy but largely ignored in practice. Under section 17(2), the court can make attachment to pensions or 'income payable to the person', subject to the opportunity being given for the person to be heard. This section shows the recognition by Jamaican legislators that enforcing maintenance orders requires an effective means of addressing this issue outside of the standard punitive measures.

Finally, sections 13 and 14 of the Children (Guardianship and Custody) Act allow the court to order a parent to pay the whole of the costs reasonably incurred in bringing up the child where another person has brought up the child. This provision is largely obsolete due to the expansive of powers of the court under the Maintenance Act, outlining who is deemed to be a parent.

The discrepancies between the Maintenance Act and the Children (Guardianship and Custody) Act means that the desirable objective of consistently applied principles is yet to be achieved.

Maintenance under the Property (Rights of Spouses) Act

The Maintenance Act refers to the fact that a maintenance order may be made when the court is hearing an application for division of property.[114] This provision reinforces the link between the two pieces of legislation, and is also another example of the extension of the court's jurisdiction in maintenance matters beyond the summary court level.

This is important as so often the needs of children, in particular, are caught up in questions of property division. Furthermore, frequently the parties to an application for division of matrimonial property have obligations to children that may not as yet be formalized in a court order. This provision gives the court the opportunity, when dealing with property, to make orders that deal with these contingent

---

114.   Section 3(2).

matters and thus address all the relevant issues comprehensively. Any maintenance order is to be made in accordance with the provisions of the Maintenance Act,[115] thereby ensuring a consistency of approach by the courts wherever the question of maintenance arises.

Even where the court is making a property order, the order may take on the appearance of a maintenance order by virtue of the terms. For example, where money is to be paid by one spouse to the other, 'the court may direct that payment be by a lump sum payment or by instalments, either with or without security....'[116] It is often difficult for one party to access the funds to pay off the other for their interest in a property. This provision allows the court to make an order that makes such transactions manageable for parties with limited means. It may be that if payment is by way of instalments, the receiving party will not have full compensation for his interest until some time has passed, but the sum can at least be secured by way of a charge on the property. This may not be appropriate in many cases, but in circumstances where limited financial means has to be set off against the need to provide a secure home for the children, and the right to move on with one's life, such options give the court the power to strike a balance.

In addition, the factors to be taken into account when the court is looking at property division include 'such fact or circumstance which in the opinion of the court, the justice of the case requires to be taken into account'.[117] Of course these facts or circumstances can be the matters which concern the maintenance of the children. This allows the court to 'set off' obligations to maintain against declared property interests. For example, if the parties each have a 50 per cent interest in the family home, and one will stay in the home with the children, the other may wish to be paid off. In such a case, it is open to the court in ordering payment to take into account the fact

---

115.   Ibid.
116.   Section 23(2) of PROSA.
117.   Section 14(2)(e) of PROSA.

that the leaving spouse would have to maintain the children and, with the agreement of the parties, quantify that obligation into a sum that can then reduce the amount he would be paid and allow him to make a 'clean break'. This is useful if the person is leaving the jurisdiction and enforcement of maintenance issues might present certain procedural challenges thereafter.

Maintenance under the Domestic Violence Act

When a protection or occupation order is being made under the Domestic Violence Act,

> the Court may at the same time, of its own volition or upon the application of any party applying for the order, make an order, in accordance with the provisions of the Maintenance Act ...[118]

Such an order can be in respect of anyone who is a member of the household to which the respondent would have an obligation to maintain under the Maintenance Act. Presumably, when the occupation and/or protection order is made in respect of persons in a visiting relationship, the court might be restricted to orders in respect of the children because, in such a case there would be no duty to maintain an adult victim as a spouse. Any maintenance order made under these provisions cannot exceed the duration of the protection or occupation order and is therefore in the strict sense ancillary to the main order.

PRACTICE AND PROCEDURAL ASPECTS OF MAINTENANCE

The Commencement of Maintenance Proceedings

Which Court and Why

Section 3(1) of the Maintenance Act states that applications for maintenance orders are subject to Subsection (2), to be made in the Resident Magistrates' (now Parish) Court or in the Family Court.

---

118.   Domestic Violence Act, section 4(5).

Where maintenance is being applied for in other proceedings, the court that is hearing those proceedings may make the order for maintenance. So, in the case of applications for division of property under the Property (Rights of Spouses) Act (PROSA), the court that is hearing the case, whether Supreme Court or summary court, can make orders for maintenance.[119] Similarly, under the Children (Guardianship and Custody) Act, the maintenance orders under that Act[120] can be made by whichever court is hearing the matter, which may be the Supreme Court or the lower court. In contrast, proceedings under the Domestic Violence Act, like the Maintenance Act itself, are dealt with only in the lower courts and, therefore, the power to make maintenance orders in the course of dealing with a domestic violence matter under that Act rests in the lower court solely.

In divorce proceedings under the Matrimonial Causes Act (MCA), applications for maintenance of spouse and/or of a relevant child can be made, but only as ancillary applications to the main action for terminating the marriage.[121] The practical effect of this is that when a marriage or cohabitation relationship breaks down, the parties can only make applications for maintenance in the lower courts. It is only when parties who are married have started divorce proceedings or make an application for injunctive relief under section 10, that the Supreme Court can make maintenance orders under the MCA.

In some jurisdictions, the lower court is limited in the amount of maintenance that a respondent can be ordered to pay.[122] However, this is not the case in Jamaica. There is no monetary limit on what either the lower court or the Supreme Court can order as a maintenance payment. This does not affect the general perception that the Supreme Court tends to make higher maintenance awards. The summary courts by their very nature are supposed to be quicker in dealing with matters generally, and certainly if a consent order

---

119.   Maintenance Act, section 3(2).
120.   Children (Guardianship and Custody) Act.
121.   Matrimonial Causes Act, section 23(1). The only exception to this is if an application is being made under section 10.
122.   For example, Antigua and Barbuda.

can be arrived at, the process is undoubtedly speedier than the high court. However, if the matter goes to a contested hearing, then the lower court may take just as long in adjudicating as the Supreme Court. These are the considerations that have to be weighed when deciding where to commence proceedings of this type.

Who May Apply

Under the Maintenance Act anyone who is a 'dependant', can apply for maintenance.[123] A dependant is a person who is owed an obligation to be maintained.[124] Therefore, in cases of spousal maintenance, it is the spouse who is claiming that they are in need of maintenance from the other spouse who can apply to the court.

In relation to child maintenance, although the child is the dependant, it is the parent, custodial, or any other person with care and custody of the child, who is also given the right to apply for a maintenance order.[125] In light of the expansive character of section 8(3), it is expected that 'care and custody' would be given its ordinary meaning. In this way, an aunt, for example, with whom a child resides, could apply for maintenance from either one of the biological parents. This is reinforced by the use of the phrase 'or any other person'. If the child is in the care of the state, an application may be made for maintenance to be paid by the parents towards the upkeep of the child.[126]

The Forms for Commencement

In the Family Court or Parish Court, maintenance proceedings will be commenced by way of a summons[127] to the respondent to attend court in relation to the claim. The summons is issued on the basis of a sworn complaint that the named dependant is in need of maintenance from the respondent. If the respondent, having been

123. Section 11.
124. Section 2.
125. Section 12(1).
126. Section 12(2).
127. Section 13(1).

served with the summons, does not attend court, then a warrant will be issued. The court does have the power to make orders in the absence of the respondent,[128] but will normally try to secure the attendance of the respondent whether willingly or otherwise.

The Process of the Court

The vast majority of maintenance cases are dealt with in the lower courts. Most orders in the Family Court circumvent the adjudication process by having the parties sign and thereby consent to the order that is being made. The powers of the court to hear an application for maintenance and make an order are set out in section 14(1):

> The court shall act in accordance with subsection (2) if satisfied that:
>
> The dependant is entitled under this Act to be maintained by the respondent named in the application, and
>
> The respondent has failed to fulfil the obligation to maintain the dependant.

It is then necessary, if the power is to be properly invoked, to look at whether or not the respondent has fulfilled the obligation.[129] The failure to maintain, in most cases, seems to be established by virtue of an application being made. It is probable that if the tribunal was met with the response that adequate maintenance was already being paid and this was proved, or admitted by the applicant, that the court would still make an order. However, this is not what a strict reading of section 14(1) would dictate. It would appear that the power to make an order exists only where the obligation is not being met. Indeed, the court is quite amenable to formalizing an existing arrangement.[130] Clearly, a failure to fulfil an obligation may be established by irregular or insufficient payments, and this is frequently the issue before the court. Few respondents would

---

128. Section 13(2).
129. Section 14(1)(b).
130. 'Since you say you are paying x amount Mr. P, I am going to make an order that you pay x per week to ensure that you continue to pay it.' This sentiment is often expressed without recognizing that it is not consistent with section 14(1)(b).

dispute, as a matter of principle, the duty to maintain their child. Most fall foul of the provisions by not making adequate payments, whether in the eyes of the applicant or the court, or not being able to maintain a regular schedule of payments.

In any event, formalizing an existing arrangement will be necessary to ensure that the court has the power to extend, enforce, or vary the order according to the circumstances which may arise. It also allows the court to specify the way in which payments are to be made and ensure that those particulars are adhered to.

In the Supreme Court, the judge will try to encourage the parties to come to a settlement whether by way of mediation at the case management stage, or simply with the assistance of counsel.

Adjudication

The method that the court should use to decide on an application for maintenance is set out in section 14(2) of the Maintenance Act:

> The Court shall enquire into the matters referred to in subsection (4) and if the Court is satisfied that the respondent is able to maintain or to contribute to the maintenance of the dependant, the Court shall make a maintenance order....

Once it is satisfied that there is an obligation, then the next question is whether the respondent is able to maintain or contribute to the maintenance of the dependant. In child maintenance cases, the court tends to lean heavily on the respondent to pay an amount often just above what he claims he can comfortably afford. This is a strategy that needs to be employed with care, because it is just as likely to achieve the optimum level of child maintenance as it is to push a respondent to a point of desperation. The challenge for the court is to identify which situation is occurring and draw the line between them. Parish Judges will no doubt say that they can astutely detect the respondents who are not being candid from those who are genuinely restricted in their ability to pay, but some respondents would say otherwise.

'...to maintain or contribute to the maintenance of....'

Where the obligation is shared with another parent, or in some cases with the dependant themselves, the calculation should consider the responsibility that the other person has. So, if as in acceptance cases, there is another biological parent, then some effort should be made to find out what that parent could pay.[131] Ideally, that person should also be before the court, but this will not be possible or indeed desirable in every situation. Undoubtedly, such an approach would impede the timely disposition of these matters, even if it would allow for obtaining more relevant information and, hence, a fairer result. In such circumstances, the payment would be a contribution to the total maintenance figure, provided that the other person is ascertainable and capable of paying. The act does, however, envisage that there will be circumstances when the whole of the obligation may, of necessity, fall on one person.

'...that the respondent pay, either to the dependant or to some other appropriate person named by the court in the order.'

Where the dependant is an adult, it is to be expected that, apart from reasons of convenience or capacity, the respondent will pay the dependant directly by cash in hand, or indirectly by paying into a bank account, or to the collecting officer at the court. Furthermore, there is no restriction placed on the court from ordering payment directly to a minor dependant if it is considered appropriate in the circumstances. While a court might baulk at the idea of significant sums of money being paid directly to a child, there is no reason why lunch money and other manageable sums should not be paid in this way.[132]

---

131. Section 9(4).
132. The real difficulty is keeping an acceptable record of the payments that are made outside of payments to the Collecting Officer or to a bank.

'...such periodical sum...or such other order under Section 15 (1) as the court considers appropriate.'

A maintenance order is for a sum of money to be paid periodically, either weekly or monthly. The distinction between a weekly sum which may be paid monthly and the payment of a certain sum monthly is often not highlighted when the order is being made, and can lead to misunderstanding when arrears accrue. Another area where there may be a misunderstanding of payment obligations is where a custody order has been made and the child spends all or part of the long holidays with the respondent. What is the responsibility of the respondent during this time, in light of the fact that in calculating arrears, these periods are routinely included and accepted by the court?[133] These matters should be clearly addressed by the judge when the order is being handed down, but time is limited and they may often be overlooked.[134] Similarly, with regard to spousal maintenance, while the Court of Appeal has deliberated on the question of the effect of obtaining a decree absolute during the subsistence of a spousal maintenance order,[135] the commonly held view is not in line with the court's approach in that case.

'Such other order' under section 15(1) could be a lump sum order,[136] or the transfer of property to be held in trust.[137] An example of this can be found in the 2010 case of Heywood v Heywood.

After applying sections 14(1) and (2), the court is to take into account the factors in section 14(4) and can make different types of orders as set out in section 15(1).

133. Opinions vary where this is concerned, some parish judges will regard it as a deductible, while others take the view that the 'custodial' parent will still have expenses in relation to the child, notwithstanding that the child is not staying at the home during this time.
134. It may be that there should be a mandatory counselling session following the making of the order, to address these matters, but this would have to be in the context of a consistent approach from the bench.
135. Jarrett v Jarrett RMCA 5/99, 20/7/2000.
136. See Hughes v Hughes (1993) 45 WIR 149.
137. Sections 15(1)(b) and (c).

The Factors

The factors set out in section 14(4) are designed to bring a measure of consistency to the deliberation process.[138] The tribunal can look to these guidelines and consider the matter knowing that although every case is unique, they should all be dealt within the same framework.

Those set out in section 14(4) are also to be applied in conjunction with those that relate specifically to certain types of maintenance. So, in the case of spousal maintenance, the matters set out in section 5(2) should also be taken into account. In cases of child maintenance, the matters set out in section 9 also provide guidance for these claims.

Each guideline is self-explanatory, and they cover a wide range of situations. The final factor in section 14(4) gives the court a wide discretion to consider 'any fact or circumstance which, in the opinion of the Court, the justice of the case requires to be taken into account'.[139]

Characteristics and Features of Maintenance Orders

Periodical Payments

The different types of maintenance orders that the court can make are listed in section 15 of the Act. The most common type of maintenance order is the periodical payment, which is described in section 15(1)(a) as:

'...an amount...paid periodically whether for an indefinite or limited period, or until the happening of a specified event'.

Most orders for spousal maintenance are for a definite period, while most orders in relation to children are until the child reaches the age of 18.[140]

---

138. The legal content of section 14(4) is examined above.
139. Paragraph (m).
140. The court does have the power to extend maintenance for a child who is in tertiary studies, see pages 147 and 170.

The act refers to the respondent being required to pay 'such periodical sum as the court thinks fit',[141] and therefore seems to be primarily thinking of monetary payments. Whereas the court may order quite routinely that expenses of a particular kind be paid, it is less common for the court to order that specific items be provided except in relation to medical or educational needs (for example, a computer, or a wheelchair, or the cost of a particular surgical procedure). As discussed under child maintenance, it is possible for the court to take into account the provision of specific items, which could be treated as being in lieu of monetary payments,[142] but this discretion is generally exercised cautiously.

The court can order that payments be made by the respondent to the dependant, or, as is usually the case with a child, 'some other appropriate person named by the court in the order'.[143] It may be more convenient for the dependant for payment to be made to the collecting officer at the court rather than directly to that person. The court will keep a record of payments and if there is failure to pay, the enforcement process can be activated quickly.[144]

Lump Sums

A lump sum may be ordered to be paid or held in trust. This mechanism is useful when funds are to be applied to a specific requirement such as medical treatment. A lump sum payment may also be a means by which there can be a 'clean break' between the parties, such as when the marriage is of short duration.[145] Section 15(1)(b) and (c) allow the court to create a trust, whether it is for the purposes of holding money or real property, for example. These provisions are likely to be invoked when the court is also dealing with division of matrimonial property.[146]

---

141.   Section 14(2).
142.   Section 14(4)(m).
143.   Section 14(2).
144.   Section 20, see below.
145.   *Hughes v Hughes.*
146.   Section 3(2).

Where a government agency has provided assistance relating to a child, the court can make an order for the reimbursement of those funds.[147] This is limited to government agencies as set out in section 12(2), and does not extend to third parties generally.

Maintenance payments can be secured against property by way of a charge. This procedure, which is also found in section 20 of the MCA, can be useful in ensuring that payments are met notwithstanding default, such as leaving the jurisdiction. In such an instance, it is necessary to have a lawyer draw up the necessary documents and submit the application to the Office of Titles. It is the sort of provision which, if used appropriately, could obviate the need to embark on costly and often futile enforcement proceedings. Although the provision can be utilized, there are conflicting views as to its application and, in some instances, the tribunal may regard securing the order as an additional burden or constraint on the respondent.

Attachment Orders

Under section 17, in the event of non-compliance with a maintenance order and provided that there is an income or pension available, the court may make an order of attachment. This allows for the money payable under the maintenance order to be deducted from this income or pension before it is paid to the respondent. The court has general powers to make attachment orders under section 15,[148] but also under section 17 the power is demarcated as a penalty that arises upon default. Quite often, respondents express relief at the measure being applied because the burden of making regular payments is lifted from their shoulders. While the respondent receives less money in their wage packet, that may be considered a small price to pay for the removal of constant demands or disagreements with the applicant. This mechanism should be promoted as a sensible option whenever the circumstances allow for it.[149]

147.　Sections 15(1)(f) and 14(3).
148.　Section 15(1)(g).
149.　This clause was taken from the previous act.

The Duration and Extent of Maintenance Orders

A maintenance order may commence at the time that the court is making the order or at the earliest convenient time in the future. This will often be the end of the pay cycle of the respondent, for example, the end of the week or month. Sometimes the court will order that the order be back-dated to the date that the application was filed. Under section 15(1)(e), a payment can be ordered in respect of a period prior to the date that the order is being made, and this could cover the period just referred to, that is between the filing of the application and the date of the order. This will be of use where the proceedings have been protracted. This provision also takes in payments under section 9(3)(a), where the order is not being back-dated as such, but the terms of the order cover a prior period. However, despite the word 'any', it is difficult to view the terms of section 15(1)(e) as giving a general power to make awards for periods prior to the application being made. It would have the effect of changing the character of a maintenance order from something that is designed to address current and future needs or expenses into something that is more akin to a judgment debt. This paragraph in section 15 may need to be clarified by the court and/or amended by Parliament to avoid misconstruction. Section 15(1)(f) as previously mentioned extends this power to government agencies that have responsibility for the child.

Maintenance orders will normally last until the dependant reaches the age of 18 in the case of child maintenance and for anyone else for the time that is specified in the order.[150] Section 16(2) gives the power to make orders for life where someone is of old age or suffering from a permanent infirmity or illness. The growing independence of women, (which manifests itself quite swiftly in the small societies that we see in the Caribbean), is recognized by the courts and, as such, spousal maintenance is no longer to be viewed as a lifelong entitlement, unless there are exceptional circumstances.

---

150. Section 16(1).

The question of extending child maintenance is discussed above at page 147.

It is possible that if an application for spousal maintenance is before the court, that a liberal interpretation of sections 4(b), 5(1)(a), and 5(2)(e)[151] might be of assistance in these circumstances.

The court's power to hear applications to vary and make further orders is contained in section 18. There are also powers to suspend orders, revive orders which have been suspended, and cancel orders if necessary.

Section 19 of the Act provides for the court to include in the order that payments be made to the collecting officer. The power of the collecting officer to disburse the money that is collected is also set out here.

Enforcement of Arrears

General Provisions for Enforcement of Maintenance

Where there is a failure to pay amounts specified in a maintenance order and arrears accrue, the procedure to collect these outstanding sums is found in sections 20–22 of the Act.

In the first instance, when an amount that is ordered to be paid to the collecting officer is 14 days overdue, the collecting officer can apply for a warrant of distress.[152] In practice, this rarely happens because of the collecting officer, and hence, the application to the court is prompted by the complaint of the person in whose favour the order was made that the sum has not been received. Furthermore, even though the Act provides for swift pursuit of the defaulter who need only to be 14 days in arrears, often applicants will allow several years of arrears to accrue before taking action. Whether it is by default or oversight on the part of the collecting officer or the applicant, many cases of 'disobedience of maintenance order' are for substantial amounts stretching back over a lengthy period

---

151.   Particularly the generalized phrase "or other cause…."
152.   Section 20(1).

of time. Section 20(5) lends support to this approach by expressly stating that the general limitation rules do not apply. However, if the collecting officer acted conscientiously and alerted the court soon after the 14-day trigger, the question of limitation should never arise. It should also be borne in mind that a maintenance order is supposed to be for ongoing needs, and if the amount payable is allowed to accrue over a lengthy period even running into years, it suggests that the sum is not really required to meet the daily needs that were the basis of the initial order. In this regard, arrears of maintenance are not to be seen in the same light as a judgment debt, and the general approach of the court could benefit from a more balanced perspective.[153]

When the warrant of distress is issued, a bailiff is directed to attend at the respondent's address in search of anything that can be subject to distraint in order to satisfy the amount of the outstanding sum. Invariably, there will be a statement from the bailiff that upon attending the address of the respondent, nothing of value was found. This declaration allows the parish judge (formerly resident magistrate) to issue a warrant for the respondent to be brought before the court.[154] If upon being brought to court the respondent neglects or refuses without reasonable cause to pay the arrears and the legal costs, the judge may commit the respondent to prison for any period up to three months.[155]

According to section 21(1), 'a person shall not be committed to an adult correctional institution for default in payment under a maintenance order unless the court is satisfied that the default is due to the wilful refusal or culpable neglect of that person.'

In many instances where a person is committed for non-payment of maintenance in the lower court, the court gives little or no consideration to this provision, or at best, the basis upon which the court could possibly be satisfied that the default is due to the wilful

---

153.   See further comments in 'The Way Forward' on maintenance.
154.   Section 20(2).
155.   Section 20(3).

refusal or culpable neglect of the respondent remains obscure.[156] What is clear, however, is that when considering such an issue, the court is obliged to have a hearing.[157] The fact that the respondent's liberty is at stake and should therefore be advised to get legal representation may not always be at the forefront of the judge's mind when dealing with these matters.

In the Supreme Court, however, under the procedural notice of motion to commit for breach of a court order, at least one of the parties will be represented. In the case of *Gardner v Gardner*,[158] the court explored fully the legal and procedural requirements to make out a case of contempt in civil proceedings. It is by no means a straightforward matter, as is inevitably the case when the liberty of the subject is at stake.

Section 21(3) stipulates that no arrears will accrue during the period of incarceration, but at the same time, the time spent does not operate to discharge any of the outstanding sums. However, the court is given a wide discretion to remit the whole or part of the sum at any time after the respondent has been committed. The court may look to the applicant to exercise the discretion to remit all or part of the claim, but it would appear from the wording of the section that it is properly a matter for the court, albeit that the views of the applicant should be taken into account.

Section 22 allows the court to deduct from the respondent's income or make an attachment order during the period of incarceration. In most instances, however, the period is relatively short, much less than the three-month maximum,[159] and this renders the application of section 22 impracticable.

---

156. The Court of Appeal had sought to clarify this in the case of *Fairweather and Lawes v A. G.* [2014] JMCA 40.
157. *Campbell v Sterling* (1963) 8 JLR 225, *Martin v Martin* (1982) 19 JLR 394 and *Abiram v Ramjohn* (1964) 7 WIR 208. This was recently confirmed in *Morgan v Williamson-Morgan* [2016] JMCA Civ 53.
158. [2012] JMSC Civ 160.
159. About seven to 10 days.

Enforcement of Orders Abroad

Under the Maintenance Orders (Facilities for Enforcement) Act, the Government of Jamaica, through the Ministry of Foreign Affairs, has entered into reciprocal arrangements with certain countries for the purposes of enforcement of maintenance orders. This allows an order to be pursued by way of registration in the appropriate court in another jurisdiction.[160] The same procedure applies in the case of orders obtained in the reciprocal countries that are to be enforced in Jamaica.

Section 23 provides for appeals to the Court of Appeal.

THE WAY FORWARD

One of the significant features of the act is the standardized list of persons who are deemed to be parents for the purposes of having an obligation to maintain. With the exception of section 8(3)(h), there appears to be a biological connection or a step-parent-type relationship between the child and the person who is deemed to be a parent. However, (h) prescribes that one who is not a parent in any sense other than the fact that they are caring for the child may have a duty to maintain that child.[161] In Jamaica, the largest contingent of this group is likely to be other family members, in particular, grandparents. While it is an important step to make such persons liable for maintenance, and equally able to sue for maintenance on behalf of the child, it seems anomalous that such a person should not be able to apply for custody. Although there is good reason for this, it would be worth taking the extended definition of parent under the Maintenance Act into account when the custody laws are being reviewed.

Furthermore, it becomes necessary, as a result of this clause, to consider whether some parents should be placed in a position that is more proximate to these obligations than others. In other

---

160.   Section 12.
161.   For example, de facto adoptions and other informal child care arrangements.

words, there should perhaps be good reason for by-passing a direct biological parent in pursuit of one whose link is indirect. Therefore, the first in line for a claim should be the biological parent, and if the parent being claimed against is non-biological, the applicant should have to account for why the claim is not being pursued against a biological parent. It may not be necessary to resort to a hierarchy of parenthood, but at the same time the court should not be put in a position where, because the group has been expanded, some are able to offset their obligations on others.

The court, in dealing with extended and overloaded court lists, has to efficiently manage its time. While it is easy to say that the court should have clear, accurate, and reliable information about the parties, this may be difficult to achieve when resources are strained. What is feasible is for the support services – social workers, court officers, probation officers – to get in depth training in the workings of the law and a comprehensive rubric in which to insert information. If a detailed form could be devised to capture the financial circumstances of the parties in every case, the court would be better equipped to act. In this way, the judges would be seized of the necessary data to make at least an interim order, without being influenced or affected by a first impression or gut reaction to the individuals appearing before them.

The courts, when applying the Maintenance Act, have a tendency to dismiss payments in kind and only count monetary contributions. The way in which such methods of maintaining children are treated discloses an unbalanced approach, in that the court has no problem assuming a contribution of the parent with whom the child lives (usually the mother) which is based on non-monetary care, but will ignore the groceries or the farm produce which is brought by the non-residential parent (usually the father). When children see their parents maintaining them, especially if the parent is not living with them, they will be more likely to recognize their own obligations in the future. It should also be appreciated that children see 'things' rather than money, and this is far more meaningful to them than the collection of a cheque or the handing over of money that may make little impression on them. At present, the system is unwittingly engaged in creating the next generation of deadbeat parents by an inflexible approach that ignores the life practices which are still common in many rural communities. It is possible to interpret the existing provisions to take these contributions into account, but it may be necessary to deal with this explicitly rather than implicitly to achieve a measure of consistency in the courts.

Another area of concern, as it is in most jurisdictions is the question of enforcement. Sending a delinquent to jail is one of the least efficient ways of collecting arrears of maintenance. Whereas in Jamaica, most persons (men) who default on maintenance payments are assumed to be deliberately evading their responsibilities, the application of this punitive measure is often the first rather than the last resort of the court.[162] It tends to increase the level of bitterness between the parties, and it becomes a wedge between the father and the children, which is difficult to remove. Sometimes the enforcement process is not activated until huge sums have accrued. A responsible approach would not, if it recognizes that maintenance has the purpose of meeting daily needs, allow years of maintenance to go uncollected without considering whether or not it was appropriate to enforce. If it were the case that only arrears up to a period of say 12 months could be collected,[163] then applications for enforcement would be made promptly because there would be nothing to gain by waiting. It would allow for an assessment of the financial circumstances of the delinquent, triggered by the calculation of arrears. It would also mean that when a person is brought before the court for arrears, the amount would

---

162. This is ironic given that our society exhibits a significant level of poverty arising out of a lack of economic performance.
163. See *Hosein v Hosein* [1964] 7 WIR 466, concerning similar provisions in Trinidad and Tobago.

be realistically repayable.[164] Judges of the Family Court should be given specific training as to hearings when a person is alleged to be delinquent. Matters where the liberty of the subject is at stake should be handled with clarity and fairness.

Alternatives to incarceration need to be explored, including travel restrictions, restrictions on driving or licensing motor vehicles and other measures to encourage payment. There are other methods of enforcement such as restrictions on leaving the jurisdiction or driving bans that could be highly effective if properly enforced. Community service is also an alternative that could be explored as a penalty in this area rather than imprisonment. It is important to try to break what can become a cycle, by enlightening the person as to the irresponsibility of their neglect, rather than adversely affecting their ability to repay with a custodial penalty.

---

164. For an interesting criticism of legislation making the payment of certain arrears unenforceable, see Leighton M. Jackson, 'Family Law and Domestic Violence in the Eastern Caribbean: Judicial and Legislative Reform.'

5. Matrimonial Property

INTRODUCTION

Janet and John started living together in 1995. They had two children in the next three years and were very happy together. When John got a job on a ship, he rented a house for Janet, the two children and his elderly widowed father, Edgar. Janet, a simple woman but very industrious, looked after the children and Edgar well and even managed to find a job at a factory nearby. She saved diligently. John was very proud of Janet and having decided that she was clearly 'wife material', the two of them set about planning their nuptials for when next he returned to Jamaica.

When John returned, Janet explained that the landlord was about to give them notice, and suggested that the money for the wedding along with her savings should be used to pay down on a house. In late 2001, two days before they were to sign the purchase papers, Janet and John had a big argument and Janet left to stay with her sister in the country for a week. Since John was left with the children and his father, he took Edgar to the lawyer's office, and the house was signed over to Edgar and John as joint tenants. The night before he left to resume work duties, Janet and John made up and decided to get married on his next shore leave.

Early in 2002, Janet, the children, and Edgar moved into the new house, and when John returned later that year, they were married. John, in his wedding speech declared, 'This house is for me, my bride, and the children.' John sent money for the mortgage payments, and Janet used her money to run the house, care for the family, and effect whatever repairs were necessary. Edgar died in 2006.

When in 2011, John lost his job and returned permanently to Jamaica, the marriage started to deteriorate. Janet moved to the 'small side' of the house in 2013, and all marital relations ceased at that time.

Six months ago John obtained a decree absolute. Janet now sits in your office. She has been served with a summons to vacate the property. She admits that she did receive a notice to quit 'some time ago', and further explains, 'since is my house too, I didn't pay it any mind'.

HISTORICAL DEVELOPMENT OF THE LAW: THE MARRIED WOMEN'S PROPERTY ACT

The Married Women's Property Act (MWPA) came into effect in the late nineteenth century along with the Maintenance Act as legal measures to address the plight of women and children. They came about as a direct result of agitation for recognizing the rights of women in England and passed into Jamaican law and other Commonwealth Caribbean territories at the same time. The MWPA expressly recognized the right of the married woman to a separate legal identity with respect to property holdings from her husband,[1] and consequent upon that, the right to sue and be sued, to own property and other assets in her own right, and to be liable in contract tort and other areas of law.[2] Although the MWPA is primarily recognized because it gave the courts specific power to deal with property matters in relation to a married woman, the far-

1.	Sections 2(a) and 3.
2.	Sections 2(b), (c), and (d).

reaching effect of this legislation by virtue of giving married women a separate legal identity cannot be underestimated. Although sections 16 and 17 of the Act have now been repealed by the Property Right of Spouses Act (PROSA), the rest of the Act is very much in force and is, in fact, the implicit foundation of the legal basis for most proceedings and legal rights of redress concerning married women.

Property Applications under the MWPA

Sections 16 and 17 of the MWPA allowed applications to be made to the court to decide questions of ownership in property with which a married woman might be concerned. Although it is these applications to the court which provided the procedural gateway for the development of the law on division of matrimonial property, the principles by which the judges should be guided when hearing these applications was something that was to evolve over time through the decisions and judgments in various cases.

Initially, the courts followed the basic rules of property ownership with the result that invariably the husband would be declared the sole legal owner. This approach left the wife and children in an extremely vulnerable position with little safeguards.[3] This led the courts to develop and protect the wife's occupation rights, and the concept of the matrimonial home was fashioned to provide a safe place for the wife and children to reside, initially, as a form of protection from domestic violence. We see, therefore, the court's efforts to ensure that the wife could remain in the property of which the husband was trying to get exclusive possession or when by his financial negligence, a third party might seek to gain control over the property. Thus, the wife's interest in the matrimonial home was primarily seen to be a right of occupation, not a right of ownership. The reason for this apparently lopsided approach was that, usually, all transactions as to ownership were in the name of

---

3.   *National Provincial Bank v Ainsworth* [1965] AC 1175.

the husband. Furthermore, in circumstances where the wife often did not work outside of the home and whose role it was to look after the home and the children, the question of ownership did not readily arise from a legal standpoint.[4] Even though this rationale did not necessarily apply to the situation that existed in the Caribbean, English decisions, as a part of our common law, found their way into Jamaican law bolstered by the application of the MWPA in both jurisdictions.

As will be seen in a later chapter, efforts were also made to extend the occupation rights of the wife in circumstances where there was domestic violence. The courts were concerned with whether the occupation rights of the wife when her personal safety was in issue could go so far as to exclude the other party. It is in circumstances such as this[5] that we see the emerging reasoning behind what was to become the ouster order in the Domestic Violence and Matrimonial Proceedings Act in the United Kingdom (UK) and the occupation order in the Domestic Violence Acts across the Caribbean.

Emerging Principles of Ownership: The Trust Concept

It was understood that occupation rights alone were inadequate, insufficient, and, in many cases, inappropriate to address the question of matrimonial property rights. Therefore, the courts were forced to contend with the question of ownership. There was a sense in which the courts began to understand that, morally, it was right to give the wife something. But in the face of the rules in relation to legal ownership, how was that to be achieved? From this dilemma emerged cases such as *Wachtel*, where the court tried to establish rules of division of property with little legal foundation. When looking at the 'one third rule' in *Wachtel* and later propositions that followed it,[6] what we see is the court struggling to do the right thing.

---

4.   See Megarry J in *Wroth v Tyler* [1974] Ch 30.
5.   *Richards v Richards* [1984] 1 AC 174.
6.   *Duxbury v Duxbury* [1987] 1 FLR 7 and *Piglowska v Piglowski* [1999] 3 All ER 961.

In *Pettitt v Pettitt*[7] and *Gissing v Gissing*,[8] the equitable trust came to the fore as the mechanism by which some proprietary recognition could be given to the wife. These cases set the standard, although there remained some uncertainty about what was sufficient to amount to a common intention and hence create a trust. That was until the decision in *Lloyds Bank v Rosset and Rosset*,[9] which took a strict position.[10] The equitable trust, as a concept to be applied to matrimonial property was useful up to a point, but having found that there was a trust – resulting or constructive – where does the court go from there? The English Matrimonial Causes Act of 1973 gave judges a wide discretion, and the cases coming out of the UK under this legislation was widely adopted in the Caribbean. Similarly, the Matrimonial Proceedings and Property Acts that are to be found all over the Caribbean, having been exported from England, are a statutory acknowledgement of the trust concept, and go on to enunciate the powers of the court which flow from the adoption of such an approach.[11] There is, however, in these acts, no formula noting how these powers are to be exercised.[12] So a framework emerged from common law and fortified by statute which states:

a. that the legal owners hold on trust for the equitable owners, though the circumstances in which that arises are for the courts to decide, and;

b. in such circumstances, the court has certain powers,

but no guidance as to the means of apportionment between the equitable owners.

---

7.   [1969] 2 All ER 385.
8.   [1970] 2 All ER 780.
9.   [1991] 1 AC 107.
10. For a useful summary, see Tracy Robinson, 'Family Property Regimes in the Caribbean,' *Caribbean Law Review* 295 (2001).
11. For example, section 53 of the act in Anguilla.
12. Section 53(1)(a).

Resulting and Constructive Trusts

Resulting and constructive trusts are both attempts to determine apportionment by how the trust is conceptualized; it ascertains what was the intention of the parties when creating the trust or acquiring the property. The cases of *Pettit v Pettit*[13] and *Gissing v Gissing*[14] looked at how the beneficial interests can be established in light of the irrefutability of the legal title. Thus, a resulting trust can arise if the legal title to the property is in one name, but the other party actually contributed all or a substantial part of the purchase money. This, however, led directly into the question of direct monetary contributions as opposed to indirect contributions. Lord Denning led the charge to recognize indirect contributions and was quite forthright in seeking to explain how it should work:

> It is sufficient if the contributions made by the wife are such as to relieve the husband from expenditure which he would otherwise have had to bear. By so doing, the wife helps him indirectly with the mortgage installments because he has more money in his pocket with which to pay them. It may be that he does not strictly need her help – he may have enough money of his own without it – but, if he accepts it (and thus is enabled to save more of his own money), she becomes entitled to a share.[15]

Once the courts had embraced the doctrine of trusts as a means of getting around the legal title, they were then confronted with the problem of how the mechanism of the trust should be applied, particularly in circumstances where on the facts there had been no express intention to create such an arrangement. Was there a difference between a constructive trust and a resulting trust and did that mean a difference in outcome? What of the intention of the parties, could it be imputed or inferred? Did it make any difference if the parties were married or not? Did it make any difference if the land was registered or not? Is the presumption of advancement subject to cultural nuances which bring about a

---

13.   [1969] 2 All ER 385.
14.   [1970] 2 All ER 780.
15.   *Hazell v Hazell* [1972] 1 All ER 923.

different interpretation? What effect do statutory measures have on the courts' powers of interpretation? The case of *Stack v Dowden* [2007] UKHL 17 is indicative that, rather than clarifying the law, Lord Diplock, in *Gissing* provided a whole new avenue for the pursuit of legal and intellectual discourse. In *Gissing*, Diplock was not concerned with such distinctions:

> A resulting, implied or constructive trust – and it is unnecessary for present purposes to distinguish between these three classes of trust – is created by a transaction between the trustee and the cestui que trust in connection with the acquisition by the trustee of a legal estate in land, whenever the trustee has so conducted himself that it would be inequitable to allow him to deny to the cestui que trust a beneficial interest in the land acquired (790, para. a–b).

The case of *Grant v Edwards and Another*[16] is a good example of the court's reasoning behind the establishment of a constructive trust. Nourse LJ at page 431, paragraph h, states:

> In order to decide whether the plaintiff has a beneficial interest in 96 Hewitt Road we must climb again the familiar ground which slopes down from the twin peaks of *Pettitt v Pettitt* [1969] 2 All ER 385, [1970] AC 777 and *Gissing v Gissing* [1970] 2 All ER 780, [1971] AC 886. In a case such as the present, where there has been no written declaration or agreement, nor any direct provision by the plaintiff of part of the purchase price so as to give rise to a resulting trust in her favour, she must establish a common intention between her and the defendant, acted on by her, that she should have a beneficial interest in the property. If she can do that, equity will not allow the defendant to deny that interest and will construct a trust to give effect to it.

Useful Presumptions: Unjust Enrichment

It has been said that, 'The principle of unjust enrichment lies at the heart of the constructive trust.' And further, 'The equitable principle on which the remedy of constructive trusts rests is broad and general; its purpose is to prevent unjust enrichment in whatever circumstances it occurs.'[17] What can be seen clearly is that the court

---

16.   [1986] 2 All ER 427 (CA).
17.   Per Dickson J, in *Pettkus v Becker* 117 DLR (3rd) 257 Supreme Court, Canada.

is prepared to employ whichever mechanism and apply whatever legal principle in order to ensure that justice is served, and that a party is not unfairly deprived of an interest that is derived from equitable rather than legal status. In *Drake v Whipp*,[18] the artificiality of the distinction between the different types of trust was highlighted, because when they can be seen as the means to the end which is really to do justice between the parties in respect of the property which has been acquired, the debate on terminology can then be put into some context.

But in *Stack v Dowden*,[19] the court took the time to examine all the distinctions as a means of providing some measure of clarity, at least in so far as the use of the various terms, and it is instructive in that regard.

In looking at recent cases in Jamaica, distinctions still need to be made between the different forms of trusts relating to marital or spousal property as we strive to retain some semblance of the common law, notwithstanding the enactment of PROSA.

With the ultimate goal of doing justice between the parties, other concepts have also been employed as a means of bringing about a suitable result, such as proprietary estoppel[20] and, as just mentioned, the presumption of advancement.[21] The court will look beyond the interests in real property and will consider the position of ownership in relation to bank accounts, etc.[22] This also came up for consideration in the protracted proceedings in *Stockert v Geddes*,[23] where the court was called upon to look into assets and investments made in different countries.

---

18.   [1996] 1 FLR 826.
19.   [2007] UKHL 17. See also *Muschinski v Dodds* [1985] 62 ALR 429.
20.   See *Griffith-Brown v Brown* [2015] JMSC Civ 172.
21.   *Whitter v Whitter* (1989) 26 JLR 184 and *Lynch v Lynch* (1991) 28 JLR 8.
22.   *Lynch v Lynch, Jones v Maynard* [1951] 1 All ER 802 and *Re Bishop deceased* [1965] 1 All ER 249.
23.   [2004] UKPC 54.

The Presumption of Advancement

The presumption of advancement as applied in Jamaica was an important tool used to assist the court in resolving property issues between husband and wife. According to Lord Evershed in *Silver v Silver*:[24]

> There is a rule of equity which still subsists, even though in this day and age one may feel that the presumption is more easily capable of rebuttal – a rule that if a husband makes a payment for or puts property into the name of his wife he intends to make advancement to her.

Reliance was placed on a transfer or disposition or gift, whether or not there was any monetary contribution, so as to protect or enhance the rights of the wife.[25]

Proprietary Estoppel

In the case of *Henry v Reid*,[26] the trial judge took time to examine the doctrine of proprietary estoppel. In *Principles of Family Law* the authors state:[27]

> If a party to a relationship incurs expenditure or does some other act to his or her detriment in the belief, encouraged by the other, that he or she already owns or would be given some proprietary interest, an equity will arise to have the expectations which have been encouraged made good so far as may fairly be done between the parties.

There are many similarities between proprietary estoppel and the constructive trust as was noted by Lord Bridge, in *Lloyds Bank plc v Rosset*.[28] This case shows that the facts should not be defeated by the need to categorize under one definition or another.

---

24. [1958] 1 W.L.R. 259, quoted in Stephen M. Cretney and J. Moussaieff Masson, *Principles of Family Law*, 6th ed (London: Sweet & Maxwell 1996), 130.
25. See *Whitter v Whitter* and *Lynch v Lynch*.
26. [2012] JMSC Civ 109.
27. Stephen M. Cretney, Judith M. Masson and Rebecca Bailey-Harris, *Principles of Family Law*, 7th ed., (London: Sweet & Maxwell) 136.
28. [1991] 1 AC 107, 132.

Fairness, Equity, and Equality

While the need for certainty was evident, it was also recognized that no sooner was a formula for division established, a factual situation would arise which if the formula were to be applied to would render a nonsensical or gravely unjust result. *Duxbury v Duxbury*[29] was an example of taking a mathematical approach.[30] In *Gissing*, Lord Diplock referred to the maxim 'equality is equity', but only as a last resort. This shows that judges were, and still are, reluctant to have their judicial discretion reduced to applying a standard arithmetical formula which does not take into account the particular features of a case. At the other end of the spectrum, even though judicial discretion can be useful in these circumstances, there is still a need for guidelines to fetter what could become a dangerously unbridled power. The question then becomes: what are all these rules and formulae trying to achieve? The answer that most readily comes to mind is fairness and justice between the parties.

The case of *White v White*[31] tackled this issue of fairness directly. In that case, it was said that fairness demanded that equality be the starting point from which the court should seek to decide matters of property division. Reasons should be given whenever the courts depart from a position of equality. It was also said that the court should not discriminate between the parties, which meant that financial contributions would not weigh more heavily than non-financial contributions. This case gave much insight into how the courts should deal with the question of property division by way of interpreting the statutory provisions in the UK,[32] but in so doing it provided a beam of clarity that was easy for the Caribbean, including Jamaica, to follow.[33]

---

29. [1990] 2 All ER 77.
30. To the point of being able to produce a software program, this mathematical approach is still favoured in many states in the US.
31. [2000] UKHL 54, also *Cowan v Cowan* [2001] 2 FLR 192.
32. Section 25 of the MCA (UK).
33. See a useful summary of the application of *White* in M.E. Birnie Stephenson Brooks, 'What Does Equality Mean in Relationship to Property Division?'

Prior to the introduction of PROSA, the Jamaican courts enjoyed a similarly wide judicial discretion as is still exercised in many Commonwealth jurisdictions. The disadvantages of the so-called wide discretion as exercised in Jamaican law were highlighted in two cases which exposed the need for parliamentary intervention in this area, in a resounding manner: *Stoeckert v Geddes* and *Chin v Chin*.[34]

In *Chin*, the parties were married in February 1986. Audrey, a chartered accountant and Lascelles, a successful businessman, formed a company that was originally called Versatile Packing Limited, but which in 1992 became Lasco Foods Limited. At the time that the company was formed, they each had one share. Over time, the business prospered and the marriage deteriorated. In the course of the demise of the marriage, the share distribution was altered to give Lascelles, 249,999 shares, while Audrey remained with a single share.

At first instance, the case was treated as if the only considerations were matters of company law as to whether or not the enlargement of the share compliment was lawful and therefore binding on the parties as shareholders in the company. That the parties were married or that the company might be matrimonial property and therefore subject to different or additional principles regarding ownership was ignored until the case went to the Court of Appeal where the respondent Audrey Chin was held to be entitled to half of the net assets of the value of the company. However, as a result of some pronouncements as to the evidence of Mr Chin, the case made its way to the Privy Council.

The case was then remitted for re-hearing in order to be dealt with by the application of the principles set out by the Privy Council in the judgment.[35]

accessed April 19, 2018, http://www.eccourts.org/wp-content/uploads/2013/10/What-Does-Equality-Mean-in-Relationship-to-Property-Division-by-Justice-Birnie-Stephenson-Brooks.pdf

34.   [2007] UKPC 57.
35.   [2001] UKPC 7.

After being heard a second time, the case went to the Privy Council on a further point,[36] but the board declined to reconsider the decision of the Court of Appeal on that occasion.

While the *Chin* case exposed the limitations of being able to bring about equality between married spouses by way of applications under the MWPA, the case of *Stoeckert v Geddes* highlighted the singularly disadvantageous position of the unmarried spouse when it came to division of property matters.[37]

In *Stoeckert v Geddes*, the parties had a common law relationship that extended over decades. The respondent was a successful businessman with considerable assets and the applicant lived with, travelled with, cared for, and claimed to give business advice to the respondent throughout the many years of their relationship.

At first instance, the trial Judge, Clarke J, found that the applicant was entitled to a one-sixth share in the assets of the respondent. On appeal, however, the decision was reversed. In the words of Rattray P:

> There is no evidence of any contribution made by the plaintiff to the acquisition by the defendant of property or any sacrifice, deprivation or act done by the Plaintiff to her detriment as would raise a constructive trust in her favour.

The case continued its way to the Privy Council[38] and was sent down for re-hearing and ultimately made its way to the Privy Council for the second time.[39] The result had the effect of exposing the deficiencies in the law as it currently stood. Despite the fact that the decision was entirely in keeping with the law, there seemed to be a general feeling according to ordinary people, that Ms Stoeckert had not received any legal or proprietary acknowledgement of the

---

36.   [2007] UKPC 57.
37.   See Margaret E Forte, 'Rights of Women in 'Common Law' de facto Unions in Jamaica'. Presentation at the Norman Manley Law School, Mona, Jamaica 1982. See also Anthony Bland, 'How constructive is the trust? The use of the trust concept in relation to property rights of de facto spouses – a comparative study.' 1977 *West Indian Law Journal* 34.
38.   [1999] UKPC 52.
39.   [2004] UKPC 54.

time and effort that she had put into the relationship and that justice between the parties had not been achieved. The common law as it had developed by virtue of applications made under sections 16 and 17 of the MWPA had created as many problems as it had solved, and most notably for a country such as Jamaica, it failed to specifically recognize a spousal relationship between unmarried couples who merely lived together, no matter for how long or how many children were produced from such a union. This represented a significant difference from the societal arrangements in England and meant that the option of making applications under the MWPA, especially when the relationship comes to an end, was not open to a considerable number of couples in Jamaica. Apart from not being available to the average Jamaican couple who happened to be unmarried, it also led to what many considered to be injustice as exemplified in the case of *Stoeckert v Geddes*.[40] It was this case, more than any other, which exposed the perilous position of women who were not married.[41]

The *Stoeckert* case, and to a lesser extent the *Chin* case, may well have been the motivators behind the steps taken by Parliament to establish a new regime for division of matrimonial property in the form of the PROSA. However, from as far back the 1970s when the Family Law Committee was established, it was recognized that there were inherent problems with a strict application of the legal principles:

> The present law relating to ownership of matrimonial property is unsatisfactory, creates injustice between the parties and is out of touch with the social realities.[42] It recognizes only money contribution to the acquisition and ignores the contribution

---

40. See Tracy Robinson, 'The Application of the Common Intention Constructive Trust in Family Property Disputes in the Commonwealth Caribbean: Geddes v Stoeckert,' *Caribbean Law* 45 (1997): 2.

41. The case of *Stack v Dowden* was decided in the UK in 2007 after Jamaica had embarked on the process of codification by way of PROSA.

42. This seems to be a clear reference to the prevalence of common law unions in Jamaica.

made by a wife in the performance of her role as a mother and a homemaker.[43]

The working paper and the final report of the committee were produced in 1990, but it was not until 1999 that the Family Property (Rights of Spouses) Act was tabled in Parliament. The committee considered the statutory position regarding matrimonial property from a broad swath of the Commonwealth, and the New Zealand Act was viewed favourably. The committee was mindful of the dangers of a wide judicial discretion in this area, so as well as curtailing the discretion in relation to the family home, it also ensured that the discretion relating to other property was hemmed in by guidelines. Finally, in 2004, the Property (Rights of Spouses) Act became law.[44]

THE PROPERTY (RIGHTS OF SPOUSES) ACT (PROSA)[45]

In essence, the purpose of the Property (Rights of Spouses) Act 2004 provided a consistent approach to this area of the law and, most importantly, sought to ensure fairness. In the case of *White*, the Law Lords in England sought to tackle the issue of fairness head-on and, in so doing, took time to analyse the different legislative mechanisms by which different countries have employed to achieve that end. The following statement of Lord Nicholls in *White* summarizes the efforts to achieve the notion of fairness in different jurisdictions:

> So what is the best method of seeking to achieve a generally accepted standard of fairness? Different countries have adopted different solutions. Each solution has its own advantages and disadvantages. One approach is for the legislature to prescribe in detail how property shall be divided, with scope for the exercise of judicial discretion added on. A system along these lines has been preferred by the New Zealand legislature, in the

---

43. The Family Law Committee Report on Matrimonial Property Law Reform.
44. For a full account of the salient issues and the developments leading to the new law, see Robinson, 'Family Property Regimes in the Caribbean.'
45. For an excellent summary of the development of the law and a review of how the act came into being, see the judgment of Morrison JA in *Brown v Brown* [2010] JMCA Civ 12.

Matrimonial Property Act 1976. Another approach is for the legislature to leave it all to the judges. The courts are given a wide discretion, largely unrestricted by statutory provisions. That is the route followed in this country. The Matrimonial Causes Act 1973 confers wide discretionary powers on the courts over all the property of the husband and the wife.

The codification of the law in Jamaica strikes a happy medium between the two legislative mechanisms mentioned by Lord Nicholls. As Brooks JA stated in *Stewart v Stewart*:[46]

...the Act provides the courts in this jurisdiction with less flexibility than English courts are allowed, in apportioning interests in the matrimonial home, but more flexibility than that afforded in the New Zealand courts...Despite the difference in approach by the respective legislation, it is said that each seeks to achieve fairness.

Behind this notion of fairness, we see in the Jamaican legislation two hallmark features: the concept of spouse and the concept of the family home.

PROSA 2004[47] recognized that it was necessary for the concept of spouse to go beyond the confines of marriage for the purposes of resolving property issues, if there was to be 'fairness' according to societal norms in Jamaica. The act also addressed the huge discretion vested in the judge under the common law by defining and providing paths along which the trial judge might proceed in order to resolve disputes concerning the division of matrimonial property. To the extent that the law has brought about the recognition of common law unions, it has been a huge success, yet still maintaining a hierarchy of spousal relationships with marriage at the apex.[48] However, as a law which has sought to bring clarity and consistency to the exercise of judicial discretion, after more than a decade of enthusiastic judicial activity, it continues to develop and grow.

46. [2013] JMCA Civ 47 at paras 17 and 18.
47. Which did not come into effect until April 1, 2006, at the same time as the Maintenance Act 2005.
48. Although many still believe that the Act erodes the status of marriage, this was a risk that Parliament was prepared to take.

The Concept of Spouse

PROSA, along with the Maintenance Act enlarges the concept of spouse in this area of the law by expressly extending the definition to include a single man and a single woman who live as man and wife for a period of not less than five years.[49] The definition of a single man or woman includes a widow, widower, or divorcee.[50] The provision also states that the parties to this type of spousal relationship should have been living together 'immediately preceding the institution of proceedings under the Act'. Section 13 of the Act extends the period in which applications can be made, as of right, to 12 months after cohabitation has ceased.[51] It may be argued that if more than 12 months have elapsed since non-marital cohabitation has ceased and no application under the Act has been made, this is not merely a case where leave would be necessary, as, under the Act, they are no longer deemed to be spouses.[52] However, section 13(3) precludes this interpretation. It would appear that the intention of Parliament was that it should become increasingly difficult to make (even though it remains open to apply for the leave of the court) a claim years after the unmarried parties have ceased to cohabit. Therefore, it is reasonable to expect that the court may not be so easily persuaded to grant leave in such circumstances. This is to be compared with married spouses who would not be subject to this condition and, therefore, even when the marriage is over and more than 12 months has elapsed,[53] the court could still entertain an application under the Act as long as leave was obtained to do so.

The legal concept of spouse as set out in PROSA is deliberately hierarchical, with marital partnerships being superior. As well as

---

49. Section 2(1). This extension came about in relation to succession in The Intestates Estates and Property Charges Act, section 1d(ii) and The Inheritance (Provision for Family and Dependents) Act with a slight difference of wording.
50. Section 2(2).
51. Section 13(1)(a).
52. Section 2(1).
53. And possibly even where they have married someone else, see *Wills v Wills* (2003) 64 WIR 176.

distinctions such as discussed in the last paragraph, there are other obvious differences such as the fact that married couples can invoke the provisions of the Act as soon as they are married. The parties to a non-marital or common law union can only qualify after at least five years have elapsed. Also, a person cannot establish a spousal relationship outside of (or in addition to) an existing marriage for the purposes of the Act. This means that the husband or wife will be recognized by the Act and not the non-marital partner, even if they are cohabiting with the non-marital partner or had been for a period in excess of five years.[54] Clearly, the intention behind this formulation is that the Act should provide relief in a commensurate manner for established common law unions, but not to the extent that such informal unions should compete with or oust the primacy of a marital union in the eyes of the law.[55] In addition to the required minimum of five years, the nature of the relationship can be subjected to the scrutiny of the court in order to decide whether a spousal relationship will be recognized under the Act.

What then are the essential features of a non-marital spousal relationship? Is it that the parties should have children or share bank accounts? Inevitably, the question finds itself being answered in the context of marriage and harks back to marriage as a point of reference when describing a spousal relationship as 'living together as man and wife'. The case of *Bowes v Taylor*[56] considered this question and, in an adaptation of the case of *Kimber v Kimber*,[57] sets out a number of features from which the court can deduce whether or not there is a spousal relationship. These features are not ranked in importance, and the absence of one or two will not be fatal.[58] In short, the court will view each case according to its

54. *Murray v Neita* 0176/2006, 18/8/2006.
55. Compare with Barbados, Trinidad, and Guyana's Family Law Act, Cohabitational Relationships Act and Married Persons Property (Amendment) Act, respectively.
56. 05/2007 19/1/2009.
57. [2001] 1 FLR 383.
58. Similarly, the fact that a 'spouse' is sexually involved with someone else will not necessarily affect the way that the court decides the question of whether there is a spousal relationship: *Declaration of Spouse of Dexter Ogilvie Harriott* [2016] JMSC Civ 15.

own circumstances and precepts. As seen in the case of *Williams*,[59] where Evan Brown J stated:

> It requires to my mind, a thorough examination of the circumstances of the parties' interaction with each other as well as their interactions with others while bearing in mind that there will always be variations in the personalities, conduct, motivations and expectations of human beings. The court, indeed, will have to make a value judgment taking into account all the special features thrown up by a particular case to see whether the lives of the parties have been so intertwined and their general relationship such that they may be properly regarded as living together as if they were in law , husband and wife....

The Family Home

The concept of the family home is the other cornerstone of the Property (Rights of Spouses) Act. It is understandable that the legislation singles out the family home[60] since often the only asset of any real value a couple may own is the home in which they live or have lived in together. By having a separate and relatively straightforward formula for division of the family home, Parliament no doubt anticipated that the vast majority of matrimonial property disputes could be resolved under this part of the Act. This has been termed the 'composite approach' to matrimonial property and was summarized by Brooks JA in *Stewart*:

> In this approach the family home is treated differently from other property owned by either or both of the spouses. Such other property will, on occasion, be referred to...as "other matrimonial property". Unlike its treatment of other matrimonial property, the Act creates a statutory rule of equal entitlement to the beneficial interest in the family home.

---

59. *Williams v Thompson* 03404/2010 15/7/11, and more recently *In the Matter of Olive Adams* [2016] JMSC Civ 15.
60. The term 'family home' is found in the Property (Relationships) Act 1976 of New Zealand, as well as the presumption of equal division, and the Canadian Family Relations Act 1979 took a similar approach and was the legal mechanism recommended by the Family Law Committee.

The family home is defined in section 2 of PROSA as:

> A dwelling house that is wholly owned[61] by either or both of the spouses and used habitually or from time to time as the only or principal residence…and used wholly or mainly for the purposes of the household, but shall not include such a dwelling house which is a gift to one spouse by a donor who intended that spouse alone to benefit….

The physical limitations to this definition are explored in the case of *Weir v Tree*[62] where the Court of Appeal made it clear that the acres of land surrounding the family home were not to be included in light of the circumstances of the case.

There are a number of issues which arise from this definition. If a third party's name is on the title for the property, it would appear that the property will not generally[63] be treated under the Act as the family home.[64] Similarly, if the property was given to one party whether before or during the relationship, then it would seem that out of deference to the donor, the property will not be treated as the family home.[65] In referring to 'the only or principal family residence', the definition seems to import that there can only be one family home at any given time, even if it may change from one property to another depending on the circumstances of the couple. It may also be argued that if the property was treated as the family home in the past, even though it may no longer be used as such, that this should be taken into consideration when division is taking place, even if the property is now being divided on the basis of contributions. What must be recognized is that because the circumstances of acquisition and use of the purported family home may differ widely, and because of the consequential presumption which flows from

61. See *Johnson v Johnson* [2012] JMSC Civ 142.
62. [2014] JMCA Civ 12.
63. See *Gordon v Gordon* [2015] JMCA Civ 39.
64. Of course, the circumstances by which the third parties' name comes to be on the title will itself open up further consideration of this point. See *Lambie v Lambie* [2014] JMCA Civ 45.
65. It has long been accepted that property which is given or bequeathed to one of the parties should be treated differently from general matrimonial property. See Lord Nicholls in *White v White*.

a property being defined as the family home, there will often be challenges as to whether or not the particular property falls within the definition. This will have to be dealt with by the courts on an ongoing basis.

By singling out the family home with a particular formula for division, the legislature may have anticipated that this would be the central issue in the vast majority of cases and, once resolved, the relative interests would fall into place. This is not unreasonable as stated before, in most cases, the only property of any significant value that the parties own will be the family home. However, there are two substantive factors which impinge on an otherwise relatively straightforward resolution of these matters: First, the Act sets out circumstances in which the court may side-step or depart from the presumption and secondly, if the property does not fall within the definition of the family home, it is likely that it will nevertheless be the subject of another part of the act that invokes different principles.[66]

Shares and Division of the Family Home

On Separation or Termination of Marriage or Spousal Relationship

Upon the breakdown of the marriage or cessation of cohabitation, a presumption of equal shares is employed. So, where the relationship is terminated by circumstances other than death, that is:

1. on dissolution or upon termination of the cohabitation; or

2. upon the grant of a decree of nullity; or

3. where there is separation and no likelihood of reconciliation;

each spouse is entitled to a half share in the property.[67] This formulation is subject to the court's power to vary the shares according to the criteria set out in section 7 and the provisions of section 10.

---

66.   Section 14.
67.   Section 6(1).

The time when a marriage is dissolved or annulled can readily be identified, but termination of cohabitation, may be a matter of dispute. Similarly, to determine when there is no likelihood of reconciliation by a separated couple may be extremely difficult to judge. This provision also needs to be read in conjunction with section 13.

On Death

If the spousal relationship comes to an end by the death of either of the parties, then the survivor will be entitled to half of the family home as long as there was no joint tenancy.[68] Of course, if the spouses own the family home as joint tenants then the right of survivorship would apply and the survivor would be entitled to the whole of the property. But, in any other circumstances, it would appear that any will or exercise of the provisions of intestacy would apply subject to this provision, and would therefore take effect only in relation to the remaining half.

The Equal Share Rule

It is useful to look closely at the legal formula for division of the family home and how it has emerged to understand how the courts apply the law relating to what is often the most important aspect of matrimonial property division. Each spouse is presumed to be entitled to a one-half share in the family home upon the occurrence of any of the circumstances set out in section 6(1).

In the case of *Carol Stewart v Lauriston Stewart* [2013] JMCA Civ 47, the Court of Appeal carefully reviewed the history behind the legal principles applied to the family home, drawing from the dicta of several judges in Jamaican cases, both at first instance and in the Court of Appeal. In relying on English, Canadian, and New Zealand cases, the Jamaican judges, in considering the question of what fairness and equality means in the context of the family home, will

---

68.   Section 6(2).

employ and apply legal principles common to all Commonwealth jurisdictions. This is the case, notwithstanding that the statutory provisions will differ from country to country.

Quoting Lord Nicholls in *Jones v Kernott*, Brooks JA at para. 20 of *Stewart* stated:

> The presumption of a beneficial joint tenancy is not based on a mantra as to 'equity following the law'…There are *two* much more substantial *reasons* (which overlap) why a challenge to the presumption of a beneficial joint tenancy is not to be lightly embarked on. The **first** is the *implicit nature of the enterprise.* If a couple in an intimate relationship (whether married or unmarried) decides to buy a house or flat in which to live together, almost always with the help of a mortgage for which they are jointly and severally liable, this strongly indicates an emotional and economic commitment to a joint enterprise. That is so even if the parties, for whatever reason, fail to make that clear by any overt declaration or agreement.

The **second** reason is enunciated by Lady Hale in *Stack v Dowden*:[69]

> The notion that in a trusting personal relationship the parties do not hold each other to account financially is underpinned by *the practical difficulty*, in many cases, *of taking any such account*, perhaps after 20 years or more of the ups and downs of living together as an unmarried couple. That is the second reason for caution before going to law in order to displace the presumption of beneficial joint tenancy.

The adoption of this principle was underscored by McDonald-Bishop J, in the case of *Graham v Graham*,[70] the following being quoted with approval by Brooks JA in *Stewart*:

> It is recognized that the equal share rule (or the 50/50 rule) is derived from the now well established view that marriage is a partnership of equals (see *R v R* [1992] 1 AC 599, 617 per Lord Keith of Kinkel). So it has been said that because marriage is a partnership of equals with the parties committing themselves to sharing their lives and living and working together for the benefit of the union, when the partnership ends, each is entitled to an equal share of the assets unless there is good reason to the contrary; fairness requires no less…The object

69. [2007] UKHL 17.
70. 03158/2006 8/04/08.

> of the Act is clearly to attain fairness in property adjustments
> between spouses upon dissolution of the union or termination
> of cohabitation....

So when the notion of fairness is combined with the notion of marriage as a partnership of equals, certain rules of guidance can be deduced:

1. Whether the parties are married or not is not a valid platform upon which to base a departure from the presumption of joint tenancy or 50/50 rule because if what lies at the heart of it is 'sharing lives and living and working together for the benefit of the union' or 'a trusting personal relationship...with the ups and downs of living together' as a basis for the presumption, then whether the union is 'churched' or not is immaterial.[71]

2. The fact that the property is legally in the name of one party alone is not a valid basis for departure from the 50/50 rule because the presumption is concerned with the beneficial interests. The reasons for a property being legally in the name of one party alone are many and varied. Whereas most circumstances are not necessarily going to provide a basis for departure from the equal share rule, the law has nevertheless singled out property that is gifted to one party and property that is owned by one party prior to the union as being worthy of separate consideration.

3. Importantly, unequal financial contributions are not a reason to depart from the presumption of a beneficial joint tenancy because parties contribute in different ways and to place greater significance on financial contributions than non-financial contributions would be discriminatory.

This 'distillation' or encapsulation of the hallmark features of the 50/50 rule are codified PROSA.

---

71. The legislature has in any event sought to maintain the higher status of marriage by virtue of the five year cohabitation rule for non-marital spouses.

Exceptions to the Equal Shares Rule

Section 7 of PROSA allows the court to depart from the 50/50 rule, if it believes that it would be unreasonable or unjust,[72] and to make such order as it thinks reasonable.[73] In *Stewart v Stewart*,[74] it was settled that this does not include a mere disparity in contributions.[75] In the exercise of this right to depart from the 50/50 rule, the court may take into account that the family home was inherited by one spouse,[76] that the marriage was of short duration,[77] or that the home was already owned by one spouse at the commencement of the marriage or cohabitation.[78] This section selects certain criteria that have been identified in case law as warranting special consideration, and in *Stewart*, it was said that a disparity in contributions, once one of these criteria was established could then be taken into account, but not in their absence.

The respect for the wishes of the testator in the case of inherited property has long been recognized, although it should not be assumed that this will necessarily mean that the spouse who is the beneficiary will keep it entirely. Although this will often be the case, it is evident that the court also has the power to depart from the equal share rule without vesting the property in one party solely and can also depart from the 50/50 rule by way of granting unequal shares, since it may 'make such order as it thinks reasonable....'

The application to invoke the court's powers under section 7 can be made by 'an interested party' and the definition of such a person is wide. In fact, the court has stated on more than one occasion that there may be great significance in including 'interested parties'

72. See *Christian v Christian* [2012] JMSC Civ 36, for consideration of the legal meaning of these words.
73. Section 7(1).
74. [2013] JMCA Civ 47.
75. This issue was explored previously in the case of *Christian v Christian* by Campbell J who provides an excellent summary of the theory behind the operation of the law in this regard.
76. Section 7(1)(a).
77. Section 7(1)(c).
78. Section 7(1)(b).

to the proceedings, and the court's powers relating to the property may be affected by whether or not others have, in fact, been so joined.[79] For example, in cases where it is being alleged that the property is not the family home because it is legally held by a third party along with one of the parties, it is important that the third party is joined as an interested party in order for the court to hear his position and also to allow for the opportunity for that person to be cross-examined.[80]

In section 8, the family home is given special attention with respect to protection from certain transactions that could defeat the interest of a beneficial owner. A caveat may be lodged, and any transaction concerning the family home requires the consent of both parties. For practical purposes, it is necessary that the matter be brought to the court's attention to bind the parties to the stipulation that the consent of both is required in any dealings with the property.[81] In the first place, the mere lodging of a caveat may put a third party on notice, and the caveat itself also requires that further legal action be taken. The statement in section 8(1)(b) cannot prevent a party from entering into a transaction without the consent of the other spouse, particularly if the other spouse's name does not appear on the title. It is only by invoking subsection (3) that the court may, upon application, set aside the transaction, unless the interest is acquired by a bona fide purchaser for value without notice. This is not dissimilar to the more extensive provisions in sections 20–22, and it was probably thought useful to repeat these safeguards with specific reference to the family home.

Where property is declared to be the family home the shares in the property will be substantial unless section 7 applies and, as such, the thrust of many applications for division of property rests on the assertion that the property is, first and foremost, the family

---

79. *Greenland v Greenland* 02805/2007 9/02/11 and recently, *Gordon v Gordon* [2015] JMCA Civ. 39.
80. *Lambie v Lambie* [2014] JMCA Civ 45; per McDonald Bishop JA (AG), see below.
81. This is mirrored in section 20(1).

home. Recently, the court has acknowledged the factual issues in relation to this categorization: Was it used in the manner specified in section 2? What are the legal issues regarding the nature of the ownership? Are any third parties present? How did they come to be 'owners'? So far, the court has gone no further than to look at the situation where there is a legal interest because someone other than the parties is named on the title.[82] However, the court may yet have to look at the situation where a third party is an equitable owner and consider what effect this will have on whether or not the property can be defined as the family home.[83]

Property 'Other Than the Family Home'

Any property which does not come within the definition of the family home will be treated as other property. Property is defined separately in section 2, and is given a very wide meaning. Section 14 (1)(b) states that the court may divide property other than the family home, as it thinks fit, having regard to certain factors. Section 14(2) lists a number of specific factors and concludes by allowing the court to take into account: 'such other fact or circumstance which, in the opinion of the court, the justice of the case requires to be taken into account'.

This gives the court extremely wide powers and many would say that this is entirely justified. It could, however, lead to a measure of uncertainty since within each case can be found 'such fact or circumstance...,' which can then be used to justify a singular decision. This provision and, to some extent, the similar power to depart from the 50/50 rule in respect of the family home makes it difficult to successfully appeal a case of division purely on the merits if the trial judge relies on these discretionary mechanisms. In the interests of finality in these matters, this may not be a bad thing.

---

82. *Lambie v Lambie* [2014] JMCA Civ 45.
83. See *Duncan v Duncan* [2015] JMSC Civ 75.

Value of the Property and Shares in the Property

The value to be placed on any property and the means by which that value is to be ascertained is dealt with in section 12 of PROSA. The pertinent value is the value at the time that the order is being made.[84] The court does have the power to alter the effective valuation date presumably in circumstances where there might otherwise be an injustice. On the other hand, the determination of the respective shares in the property takes place a the date of separation. The case of *Hogg*[85] exemplifies the difficulties, in this area, when the parties have been separated for many years. The property may have been substantially altered or sold by the time of the hearing, and it may be difficult to trace the shares back to the situation at the time that they separated. It is for this reason that the court has restated what was urged in the case of *Wills*[86] that parties take steps to sort out the issues pertaining to matrimonial property as soon as it becomes clear that they will not be continuing their lives together.

In the case of *Wills*, G and E, who had been married since 1935 and had three children, were the owners of several properties which they sold and consolidated into two properties, one of which was held by the parties as joint tenants from 1966 – 'the property'. In the early 1970s, the couple separated. They eventually divorced in 1985. The wife, E, who lived abroad, visited Jamaica occasionally, but the last time she went to the property was in 1976. In the meantime, the husband, G, became acquainted with a woman, M, who came to reside at the property from about 1971 or 1972. When the divorce was granted G married M in January 1986, and they lived together until his death in 1992. G and M collected the rent for part of the property and M signed receipts as co-owner. No money was paid over to E during this period, and later G offered to pay E for her share in the property for $25,000 but she refused. Upon G's death, E sought to evict M from the property on the basis that she was now

---

84.   Section 12(1).
85.   [2013] JMSC Civ 7.
86.   Privy Council Appeal (2003) 64 WIR 176.

the sole owner by virtue of the right of survivorship. At paragraphs 28 and 29 of the judgment, Lord Walker of Gestingthorpe concluded that:

> 28. Shorn of these accretions, the issue does in the end come down to reasonably simple terms. It was established by the evidence that Elma never set foot in Sunrise Crescent after 1976…She never positively challenged Myra's evidence that none of her possessions (except her abandoned wedding ring) was to be found at Sunrise Crescent after 1971. In the Court of Appeal, counsel for Elma conceded as recorded in the judgment of Langrin JA (Ag) that George had been exclusive possession since 5th January 1974. Was there any basis for the conclusion that Elma had not discontinued her possession, or been dispossessed more than 12 years before the issue of the originating summons?
>
> 29. …Elma no doubt wished to maintain her claim to co-ownership, not least because she expected to outlive George and hoped to take by survivorship. But such an intention however amply documented, cannot prevail over the plain fact of her total exclusion from the properties.

This decision has been viewed with some concern because of the effect that it could have generally on the law in relation to joint tenants, whether in marriage or otherwise. However, their Lordships were at pains to make it clear that this was a decision based on its own somewhat peculiar facts. At paragraph 32:

> Their Lordships do not therefore see the outcome of this appeal as likely to cause trouble for the large number of Jamaican citizens who work overseas and contribute to their families' welfare and the Island's economy. Most of them will come home on a fairly regular basis, will retain the bulk of their possessions at home, and will not (on coming home) be treated as guests in their own houses. *But if (as must sometimes happen) a Jamaican working overseas forms new attachments and starts a new life, and entirely abandons the former matrimonial home, he or she will (within the ample period of 12 years) have to consider the legal consequences of that choice.*

The question is: What is the effect of PROSA on this decision? It may be that where the joint tenancy is, in fact, abandoned in a situation such as *Wills*, the provisions of section 6(2) could be applied to give the abandoning spouse at least a half share provided that the property was, in fact, the family home.

In the case of *Hogg*, the land upon which the family home was built was a gift to the defendant from his father and was not the subject of a joint tenancy. However, because of the length of time from the separation of the parties and the claim being made, there had been considerable alteration to the property. The parties were married in 1990 and separated in 1998. However, the divorce was not granted until 2010, and the application for division of property was made subsequent to that and was heard between 2012 and 2013. This was in keeping with section 13 of the Act which allows a spouse to make a claim within a year of the dissolution of the marriage. In the words of Edwards J,

> The practical effect of this is that either spouse may make such a claim for property rights even if they have been separated for thirty years. The blatant possibility of injustice this state of affairs may cause to one or both sides, in a case where they have sat upon their laurels for lengthy periods whilst the status quo may have changed several times over, seemed to have escaped the legislators. Be that as it may. The claim was made by virtue of the statutory provisions and therefore, unlike equity and the Statute of Limitations, delay does not defeat it.

What needs to be clearly understood is that it is foolhardy to allow these matters to remain unresolved in some instances for decades, because this can make it difficult for the court to apply the law to the changed circumstances.[87]

On the other hand, the question of the respective shares in the property, that is how much of the property that each party owns, is a separate issue. *Hogg v Hogg* also considered the question of the time when the shares in property will vest, and it was confirmed in keeping with the wording of section 12(2) that the shares are established at the time that the parties separate.[88] In this regard, it

---

87. A recent decision where these issues resurfaced was in the case of *Fullwood v Curchar* [2015] JMCA Civ 37.
88. See also *Stewart v Stewart* [2013] JMCA Civ 47.

is often alleged that because one party has left and the other party continues to make mortgage payments or improve the property, then those contributions should have the effect of increasing that person's share in the property. The fallacy of this approach was examined by Brooks JA in *Stewart*, which quite usefully contains a comprehensive review of judicial opinion in this area.

The court will usually order a valuation of the property by a valuator from an approved list. Generally, the cost of the valuation is split between the parties, though of course the court may direct a deviation from the usual practice if there is sufficient reason.

Taxes and Charges

Section 9 is important as it allows for transactions between spouses pursuant to the Act to be exempt from transfer tax. The remaining taxes and charges would still be applicable and would ordinarily be divided equally. If the interests in the property are being apportioned unequally, in some cases, the slavish adherence to the general rule could operate as a penalty to the party who is of limited means. The general rule is that parties to a transfer cannot contract out of their obligations to the tax authorities but in matters such as division of matrimonial property, as distinct from 'arm's length' transactions, this rigidity deprives the court of an additional tool with which to balance the justice of the case.

Agreements

In section 10, the PROSA allows agreements to be made at two stages in a spousal relationship. An agreement may be made:

1. In contemplation of marriage or cohabitation, or

2. 'For the purposes of settling their differences which have arisen between them'.

Agreements can therefore be made, and subject to the terms set out in section 10, will be recognized by the courts, either, in anticipation of, or after the marriage or cohabitation has taken place, as the parties see fit. This suggests that the parties would not be restricted to the rules of ownership as specified in the Act when making such agreements. So, if the parties wish to agree that the family home will become the property of a third party (a child, for example), they would be perfectly entitled to do so and, subject to the court's powers, there is no reason why such an agreement should not be upheld in court. The generality of the provision is augmented by giving the parties to the agreement not only the power to define the share but also to say how a share will be calculated.

The process by which an agreement can be made is set out in the Act. The parties must get independent legal advice and the agreement must be signed by both parties and witnessed. The court's powers to review or set aside or disallow the agreement or parts of an agreement and the factors to consider when so doing are also set out. In keeping with the age of marriage, and presumably the age of consent, the Act recognizes agreements where one or both of the parties are minors, between the ages of 16 and 18.

This section of the Act corresponds to section 24 of the companion legislation, the Maintenance Act, and sets out a process that was anticipatory of the developments which were likely to take place in society as we adopt methods of protecting property that have become commonplace elsewhere.[89] While the courts in Jamaica have had cause to adjudicate on agreements made elsewhere for sometime,[90] it may be a while before the courts consider the agreements made pursuant to the Act,[91] certainly regarding those that have been drawn up in Jamaica.[92]

89. In *Pino v Pino* 03869/2009 1/7/2011, both the parties were Cuban and the Deed of Separation was executed before PROSA came into effect. It was upheld by the trial judge.
90. *Ebanks v Ebanks* (1968) 10 JLR 464.
91. *Fearon v Fearon* (1995) 32 JLR 161 is a case prior to PROSA where the court upheld the agreement.
92. The case of *Miller v Miller* [2016] JMCA App 1, addresses the issue of property not included in a separation agreement that was effected in the US. As an aside, the court's recognition of the agreement was accepted without challenge.

Types of Applications

Applications to the court in respect of property rights can be made under section 11 and under section 13. Section 13 applications are made when the marriage or cohabitation has broken down or come to an end; while section 11 applications can be made 'during the subsistence of the marriage or cohabitation'.

A section 11 application can be made in order to resolve 'any question (which) arises between the spouses as to the title to or possession of property'. The application may be made by either party or a third party, including any bank, corporation, public body, or society to either the Supreme Court or to the Parish Court of the parish where either spouse resides.[93] This introductory passage is reminiscent of section 16 of the Married Womens Property Act (MWPA) and to some extent replicates the powers of the court under that section which is now repealed. The application can be made in the Resident Magistrate's (now Parish) Court regardless of the value of the property that is the subject of the application. This is extremely far-reaching considering that the court has wide powers under this section, including making an order for sale.[94] The application can be made in respect of property, which is no longer under the control of the other party, and this suggests that even where the property has been sold, the court can make orders concerning it, in particular, the payment of money in lieu of the spouses' share or interest in the property.[95]

Interestingly, the court may make orders for partition[96] that can be useful when dealing with family property, so that a property held as joint tenants may be converted to being held as tenants in common, thereby extinguishing the right of survivorship. The application of the Partition Act to these types of proceedings has also been considered,[97] and careful consideration should be given to the desired outcome when drafting the claim in these matters.

93. Section 11(1).
94. Section 11(2).
95. Sections 11(3) and (4).
96. Section 11(5).
97. *Belnavis v Belnavis* [2013] JMSC Civ 39.

The court also has the power to make orders as to the possession of the property and determin who will occupy the property, on what terms, and for how long.

While it is to be expected that the powers of the court upon division will be much greater, the orders that can be made when an application under section 11 is made[98] are interproted with little to differentiate between the court's powers at either stage. It may also be that with the current restriction on when proceedings may be commenced under section 13 according to the ruling in *Saddler*,[99] if the parties have exceeded the 12-month time limit and the marriage is still subsisting, they may nevertheless invoke their powers under section 11 as a means of settling their issues. Justice Campbell, in the case of *Sandcroft v Sandcroft*,[100] alluded to this option.

> It may become necessary for the court to define the limits of the orders which a court can make when hearing an application under Section 11, because in the absence of such limits, it is easy to see that the jurisdiction of the Resident Magistrate could have been unwittingly increased in a way that parliament had not intended. In particular, this would seem to run contrary to the provisions of section 5 of the Act. But for this uncertainty as to the extent of the court's powers, applications under Section 11 clearly provide a very useful avenue for spouses to resolve any issues in relation to property prior to the termination of the marriage or spousal relationship.

Contributions

Section 14(2) of PROSA provides a list of the factors to be taken into account when the court is considering applying for division of 'other property'. Here, we can find the first reference to contributions, what form they may take, and what they may be applied to. These factors apply whether or not the property is still owned by the spouses.[101] Importantly, the contributions may be 'financial or otherwise', and there are several examples of non-financial contributions. These are

---

98.   Sections 11(2) and (4).
99.   *Saddler v Saddler* [2013] JMCA Civ 11.
100.   [2013] JMSC Civ 184.
101.   Section 14(2)(a).

not to be seen as being of lesser value than a financial contribution and these provisions are the encapsulation of a non-discriminatory framework.[102]

When considering an application under section 13 and there is no family home,[103] the courts must carefully consider a case where there are relevant children, as it is necessary to ensure that one of the spouses is in a position to provide a home for the children to live in.

The duration of the marriage is a well-recognized factor when considering division of matrimonial property,[104] and where the marriage is of a short duration, it tends to reduce the share of the spouse when claiming against the party who has been in possession of the property before the marriage. The cases vary in this regard, from nothing,[105] to a substantial amount.[106] However, sometimes the court is prepared to consider the period of cohabitation prior to the marriage.[107] When considering the duration of cohabitation however, this principle may not work in the same way. In the first place, for the cohabitation to create a spousal relationship as recognized by the Act, it has to be in existence for no less than five years, which means that no cohabitation can be viewed as 'short' by the same yardstick that could be applied to a marriage. At this point, the Act, although recognizing 'common law' relationships, does not (as many mistakenly believe) put them on an equal footing with marriage. Parties who are married to each other can exercise their rights under the Act immediately after signing the marriage certificate – subject, of course, to the provisions of the Act. On the other hand, for a spousal relationship to be recognized based on cohabitation, the parties have to have been together for a minimum

---

102. This is an adoption of the principle of non-discrimination which is set out in *White* [2000] . See *Christian v Christian* per Campbell J at paragraph 53.
103. Section 14(1)(b).
104. See *Gardner v Gardner* [2012] JMSC Civ 160, marriage prior to separation four years.
105. *Krystman v Krystman* [1973] 1 WLR 927.
106. *C v C* [1997] 2 FLR 653 and *Foster v Foster* [2003] 2 FLR 299.
107. *GW v RW* [2003] 2 FLR 108.

of five years, and even then the court is able to examine the nature and quality of the relationship in order to decide if it will qualify.[108]

The next factor[109] that appears in section 14(2) gives specific endorsement to agreements, and serves as an encouragement to enter into such arrangements. It seemingly implies that even if the court does not uphold the agreement and follow its terms explicitly, the court may still look to those terms as possibly being indicative of either the intention of the parties or their respective mindsets at the time.

The court is not limited to the factors that are listed, and may take into account 'such other fact or circumstance which, in the opinion of the Court, the justice of the case requires'. This open-ended approach is understandable and useful, but if it is not closely monitored by the appellate court, it could also lead to uncertainty. Such an approach can make it difficult to give advice on the law in this area, and may encourage opportunistic ventures into court. The question of costs in this area must be a significant consideration because the law should not support vexatious claims based on the antagonism between the parties, which can be the effect if costs are not applied judiciously. However, where the parties are of moderate means, an exorbitant bill of costs from the other 'winning' side can have a devastating effect on the well-being of the parties and the children, and should be uncompromisingly discouraged by the courts.

Alteration of Property Interest

Section 15 allows for the creation of trusts whether by or at the direction of the court, in substitution for an existing interest, whether for the benefit of one or both spouses or a relevant child. In this way, a life interest or a right to occupy until the children reach adulthood can be established;[110] see also section 23(3). The court will generally

---

108. *Bowes v Taylor.*
109. Section 14(2)(d).
110. These are referred to as Mescher and Martin orders in the UK. Generally, the court in Jamaica has been less sympathetic to the option of postponing the

impose what is effectively a deferral of a party's proprietary interest only when necessary, and the caution to be exercised before ordering such re-arrangements is expressed in section 15(2).[111] The factors to be taken into account are set out in section 15(3), whereby the criteria in section 14(2) are brought in. Section 16 permits the court to dismantle or set aside a trust created by order under section 15(1). The provisions in section 16 would raise the question of whether the court would not, in any event, have a general power to set orders aside where there has been 'fraud, duress, the giving of false evidence or the suppression of material facts'. Perhaps it was thought specifically necessary in reference to this section because of the consequences of the transfer of legal (and not necessarily equitable) ownership.[112] There is no time limit or requirement for leave specified in this section relating to an application for the orders to be set aside.

Location of the Property

The definition of property under PROSA is not qualified by location and therefore according to the ordinary rules, the court would have jurisdiction, depending on the domicile of the parties. This means that if a party who is domiciled in Jamaica wishes to apply to the Jamaican court to decide the question of division of property in another country, he may do so. However, the enforcement of the Jamaican court's decision in relation to that property would have to take place in the country where the property is located.[113] The difficulty of enforcement, as discussed in this case, means that since enforcement would have to take place in the country where the

---

sale of the property until a child reaches adulthood; see *Belnavis* [2013] JMSC Civ 39.

111. Here you have the competing interests of the welfare of the child and 'clean break'.

112. It may be considered that whereas sections 8 and 22 refer to the setting aside of transfers made on the initiative of either of the parties, section 16 is really dealing with the power to revoke orders.

113. See the converse situation in the case of *Sterling v Sterling* SCCA 55/2009, 13/11/09, where the property located in Jamaica was the subject of an order made in Canada.

property is located, it may be more efficient to institute proceedings in that jurisdiction where the orders can be readily carried out. Although, if the substantive law would bring a different effect in one place rather than another, the parties may embark on a contest to determine the most advantageous jurisdiction in which to institute proceedings.[114]

The Applicability of PROSA on the Death of Either Party

The PROSA is concerned with the adjudication of property rights when a spousal relationship comes to an end by some form of termination other than death, and does not purport to interfere with the intestacy provisions which are to be found in other legislation. This also means that the death of a party to proceedings under PROSA does not alter the validity or effect of anything done or suffered in pursuance of its provisions.[115] In short, with the exception of sections 3(2), (3) and 6(2), death and termination under this PROSA are mutually exclusive. Parliament clearly seemed to believe that it should not be possible for one party to weigh up the advantages of proceeding by way of property division or probate in the case of the death of a spouse or former spouse.[116]

Jurisdiction and Scope of the Act

The Savings Clause and the Retroactivity of the Act

For some years, the question of how the provisions of PROSA affected property that had been acquired during unions, marital or otherwise, which had come to an end before the Act came into force was a live issue. Some believed that the common law would apply in such circumstances, and this was expressed in a number of cases, for example, in *Shirley-Stewart v Stewart*.[117] The case of

114. *Radmacher (formerly Granatino) v Granatino* [2009] EWCA Civ 649.
115. Section 3(2).
116. Except in respect of the family home.
117. 0327/2007, 6/11/07.

Annette Brown v Orphiel Brown[118] brought matters to a head and gave the Court of Appeal the opportunity to consider the matter. The court considered the concept of retroactivity in its broadest legal sense, drawing from authorities outside of family law. The court decided that the factor of time would not exclude the application of PROSA. Therefore, regardless of when the decisions pertinent to the acquisition of the property had been made, the current law at the time that the application was being made would apply.[119] This decision, of course, took section 12(2) of the act into account and rejected the case of *Stewart* in the course of arriving at its conclusion.

The Powers of the Court outside of PROSA

The Common Law

Section 4 of the Act states: 'The provisions of this Act shall have effect in place of the rules and presumptions of the common law and of equity to the extent that they apply to transactions between spouses in respect of property....'

In several instances, the argument has been advanced, and in some cases successfully, that there will be certain situations when the PROSA will not apply. It has been posited that there will inevitably be some circumstances where the provisions of the Act should not apply, for example, if the acquisition of the property, the breakdown of the marriage, or the termination of the marriage took place before the Act came into force, then the common law should apply.[120] This question of whether the Act is retrospective was considered in detail in the case of *Brown v Brown*,[121] and it was decided that every significant milestone had taken place before the Act came into force was not sufficient to oust jurisdiction.

---

118. [2010].
119. While all three judges came to the same conclusion by different legal routes, the judgment of Phillips JA adopts a common sense approach which is readily grasped.
120. *Shirley-Stewart v Stewart* 0327/2007 6/11/07.
121. [2010] JMCA Civ 12.

It has also been suggested that if the stipulated time for bringing applications has expired and an application for leave has not been made, then the claimant cannot seek any remedy under the Act.[122] Generally, the circumstances in which the common law can be resurrected will be limited. The court sometimes refers to circumstances in which if the act is not applicable, then the court has powers under the common law. The question is what are those circumstances to which they refer. If, for example, an application is so far out of time that leave is (quite exceptionally) refused, would that be such a situation where the court would resort to the common law?

In cases where the parties have been found not to be spouses within the meaning of PROSA, the court will go back to the common law and look at whether or not there is evidence from which a constructive trust can be inferred,[123] and in so doing the court may draw from cases which clearly lie outside the ambit of the Act, such as *McCalla v McCalla*.[124] In the recent case of *Tapper v Taylor*,[125] the court again resorted to the 'common law' in a case where the parties would have fulfilled the requirements for being spouses but for the fact that one of them was married.

In *Greenland v Greenland*,[126] the court considered the question of what might happen if the property in dispute did not come within the definition of 'family home' under the act. It was postulated that if it did not, then PROSA would not be applicable, and the matter would fall outside of the scope of the Act. The court however took the view that even if the property was not the family home, it would then be in the category of other property and would be subject to the factors set out in section 14.

---

122.   *Bernard v Bernard* 01865/2006 2/4/08.
123.   *Henry v Reid* [2012] JMSC Civ 109.
124.   [2012] JMCA Civ 31. *McCalla* was a case that concerned members of the same family but not spouses.
125.   [2017] JMSC 101.
126.   SCCA 71/08, 20/1/09.

In *Bernard v Bernard*,[127] the court looked at the situation where the Act was not applicable by virtue of the application being out of time. The court decided that in such a case, 'if the Property (Rights of Spouses) Act does not apply, then the court would have to apply the common law principles existing on the issue before the Act was passed.' This has been stated repeatedly by the Supreme Court and the Court of Appeal.[128]

The court has also considered the applicability of the Partition Act to this type of application, in the case of *Belnavis v Belnavis*.

Practice and Procedural Aspects of PROSA

Applications under PROSA are made to either level of the courts in a summary way, by way of fixed date claim in the Supreme Court or by summons on complaint in the Parish Court. There is nothing to prevent a claim under PROSA being made by way of a complaint in light of the fact that the lower court is not a court of pleadings, and whichever format lends itself to greater edification, the better.[129] In addition, the statute allows such matters being dealt with in the lower court to be heard in chambers.[130]

The fixed date claim must be accompanied by an affidavit in support, and will be heard as with most family matters in chambers. The question of matrimonial property arises naturally when a marriage is coming to an end and, therefore, it is important to have an understanding of how the Matrimonial Causes Act (MCA) and PROSA interact. The MCA, in defining matrimonial proceedings, seems to encompass property matters and therefore the scope for an application under this Act is clearly present. Furthermore, part 76 of the Civil Procedure Rules (CPR) include property matters in the definition, but the rules predate PROSA. The issue is, how do property proceedings interact with proceedings for termination of marriage?

---

127. 01865/2006, 2/4/08.
128. As recently as in the case of *Stewart v Stewart* [2013].
129. Unfortunately this court is becoming rigid as to the use of appropriate forms in set circumstances.
130. Section 5(2).

As a preliminary point, the MCA was amended when the PROSA was passed to limit the scope of orders which could be made under section 10, by way of injunctive relief. Nevertheless, as stated, the definition of matrimonial proceedings in the rules means that it is procedurally possible to include an application for division of property as a form of ancillary relief in a petition for termination of marriage.[131]

It is therefore possible to apply for division of property by way of an application for court orders in the course of divorce proceedings. This has raised the question of what is the correct method of commencing proceedings for property in the course of MCA proceedings.[132] The question in *Gordon* was whether or not it was permissible to apply for matrimonial property orders in the course of divorce proceedings when the claim had not been included in the petition. The court was not in favour of the technical approach being taken on behalf of the appellant, and was at pains to stress that an objection which simply leads to 'the generation of more paper' would not be supported. In any event, the essence of the problem is how quickly a matter can be adjudged once the marriage has broken down and it is being dissolved. The case did not addressed the question of the implications of section 13 on the timing when the application is made by application for court orders in the course of divorce proceedings. However, this decision once again addressed the requirement for leave/extension of time, the need for evidence in support, and whether the 'common law' or PROSA will be applied by the courts.

It is for these reasons that it is preferable to commence separate proceedings outside of the divorce by way of a fixed date claim form and proceed to a hearing before a judge in chambers without any possible dispute as to the proper mode of commencement.

131. See Rule 76.2. This (in light of *Allen v Mesquita; Saddler*, etc.) assumes that the time limitations expressed in section 13 PROSA can be addressed by an accompanying application for leave.
132. *Gordon* [2012] JMCA Civ 51.

Certainly, it should be open to proceed in this way from the time that the decree nisi is granted since a judge has pronounced on the irretrievable breakdown of the marriage and, therefore, arguably, section 13(e) has been complied with regardless of if or when the decree has been made absolute. However, the safer course (and certainly for the avoidance of any dispute), is to file the claim within 12 months of the granting of the decree absolute. This, of course, does not preclude an earlier application if the conditions of section 13(1)(d) are evident.

Furthermore, the court will not usually hear an application for property division in the course of dealing with another issue such as custody of children and maintenance, but will generally sever such a claim and deal with the property separately.[133] The complexity of property claims is sufficient justification for this, and although the court is empowered to make maintenance orders when dealing with property,[134] it is not necessarily appropriate to do so in the reverse. The question of costs will also be a factor in deciding what claims should be included in such proceedings and the extent to which the consolidation of issues, even where permitted by the rules, makes for efficient and economical use of the court's time.

The Time for Making Applications for Division

Division of property is a fundamental step towards permanent severance of the spousal relationship and, as such, it should not generally be entertained while the union is likely to continue. Section 13 of PROSA acknowledges this premise and sets out the stages at which the court will entertain an application for division of property.

The first juncture is upon the grant of a decree of dissolution or the termination of the cohabitation. The first instance can be readily identified, and is extended to nullity proceedings in section 13(1)(b).[135] However, the question of when cohabitation has come to an

---

133. This is another reason why the claim should generally be dealt with separately.
134. Section 3(2) of the Maintenance Act.
135. This points to yet another reason for parties to a void marriage to formalize the annulment rather just walking away from the relationship.

end may, as previously stated, be a matter of disagreement between the parties. *Bowes v Taylor*[136] examined the cohabitation in terms of its characteristics so as to be able to identify such a relationship from a legal standpoint. It followed the UK case of *Kimber v Kimber*.[137] By listing a number of features, the court set out to establish that cohabitation for the purposes of the Act was taking place. The case did not go so far as to say whether all or any of the stated features needed to be extinguished in order to say that the relationship had come to an end. It is quite reasonable to expect that some features may diminish or end without bringing the relationship, as a whole, to an end. This is especially the case where there is no hierarchy of characteristics and each couple may place greater or lesser emphasis on different aspects of their relationship. In short, it may be difficult to say exactly when the relationship has ended other than to say that it can be no later than when none of the features are any longer present, but that is not sufficient to establish the earliest time at which it can be said that the cohabitation has ended and hence when proceedings for division can be commenced. In the absence of agreement between the parties on this, it will be for the court to examine the particular circumstances of each case. This is a similar situation to the court having to decide when there has been a loss of consortium so as to be able to say that separation has taken place or that the marriage has broken down irretrievably.[138]

Section 13(1)(c) is, indeed, a logical development of the issue in that it recognizes separation where 'there is no reasonable likelihood of reconciliation', as an appropriate stage at which an application for division of property may be made. The question then arises as to what extent a party who is reluctant to accept that there is irretrievable breakdown may contest an application for division on the basis that a reasonable likelihood of reconciliation still exists. While this may be dealt with from a legal standpoint without too

---

136.   05/2007 19/1/09.
137.   [2001] 1 FLR 383.
138.   *Heron-Muir v Heron-Muir* 00144/2004, 21/10/05.

much difficulty, it may cause unnecessary procedural delays and additional costs. *Saddler* attempted to address this overly legalistic approach by stressing that the emphasis should not be on technical points of striking out (for want of leave or an extension of time, etc.) in order to incur additional costs for the other side.

Section 13(1)(d) allows the court to entertain an application for division to deal with emergency circumstances where the property, and hence the applicant's interest in it, is under threat. In such a situation, the primary remedy would be injunctive relief in order to preserve or protect the property and restrict any dealings which undermine the maintaining of the status quo.

The principle that applications regarding matrimonial property should be brought promptly is underlined by the provisions in section 13(2), by setting a 12-month limit from the time of the separation or decree, etc., in which proceedings should be commenced. While the court can hear an application brought after this time, it is essentially a matter of the discretion exercised by way of leave. This question came up for consideration in the case of *Allen v Mesquita*[139] where the Court of Appeal looked at the court's powers in this regard, in light of the emerging practice of treating an out-of-time application as being rectified by an application for extension of time rather than an application for leave. As stated before, the court has said that an overly technical approach is not necessarily to be encouraged in these matters.[140]

By virtue of section 13(3), it is not open to argue that a person who is no longer a spouse (presumably as a result of having obtained a decree) is not a 'spouse for the purposes of making an application under section 13.

It has often been the practice in Jamaica for parties not to deal with these issues and go their separate ways. This problem arose for consideration by the court in the case of *Wills v Wills*[141] and

---

139.   SCCA 8/2011, 7/10/2011.
140.   *Saddler v Saddler*, per Phillips JA.
141.   (2003) 64 WIR 176.

continues to be an issue.[142] The act seeks to address this, but is met with lethargy by those who look no further than terminating the marriage and do not to resolve property matters. As a result, cases continue to come before the court where many years have elapsed and the practice had developed where the claimant would make an application for extension of time in order to bring the case outside of the 12-month period. In the case of *Allen v Mesquita*, the Court of Appeal made it clear that the correct approach, in such circumstances, was to apply for leave to commence out of time, and that the court did not have the power to extend time that had already expired.[143] It is important for attorneys who are handling the dissolution of the marriage to broach the question of matrimonial property and advise their clients of the necessity of settling these issues expeditiously.

Applications for Division of Property

An application for division of property may be of two types:[144]

1. An application in respect of the family home where the court has powers under sections 6 and 7 as stated in section 14(1)(a),

2. Or as stated in section 14(1)(b), an application in relation to 'such property other than the family home' which the court may deal with as it thinks fit subject to section 17(2), but taking into account the factors set out in section 14(2).

Where the matrimonial assets consist of both the family home and other property, the court may act in accordance with both paragraphs (a) and (b). It would appear, therefore, that if what was being used as the family home does not come within the legal definition, then such property will fall to be dealt with under paragraph (b). It has been suggested that if the property thought to be the family home

---

142. *Hogg v Hogg.*
143. The distinction between an application for extension of time and an application for leave to proceed out of time may have been somewhat eroded as a result of the dicta in *Saddler*.
144. Section 14.

does not in law fall within that category, then the 'common law' will apply.[145] The better conclusion may be that, in such circumstances, the admittedly wide powers set out in section 14(1)(b) will apply. In other words, the statute itself gives the court similarly wide powers as is exercised at common law before the passing of the Act, but they are nevertheless statutory powers and should not be confused with those obtained previously.[146]

We see a similar approach in section 7 of the Act when the court is minded to depart from the one-half share principle. In such a case, the court may 'make such order as it thinks reasonable, taking into consideration such factors as the Court thinks relevant....' Once again, these are wide powers that can easily be mistaken for the re-emergence of the common law, but they are, in fact, wide powers granted by statute. In short, it is unlikely, upon close reading of the Act, that there is any preservation of the common law as alluded to in some early decisions. The common law, such as it is, could foreseeably be revived by virtue of the ownership of the property. This is not an appropriate option simply because the case does not fall within a specific category under the Act or because there has been non-compliance with the stipulations if the Act, for example, that leave has not been obtained under section 13.[147]

Types of Orders

PROSA gives the court extensive powers to deal with matrimonial property, and as such, the combinations of orders that can be made are limitless. However, there are certain types of orders that are frequently sought. To start with, the court is usually asked to make a declaration about the ownership of the property, that is, who owns it, and in what proportions it is held by the parties (or others), as

---

145. Per Morrison JA in the case of *Greenland v Greenland* SCCA 71/08, 20/1/09.
146. This was addressed by Brooks JA in the case of *Gordon v Gordon* [2015]. This was also applied by Campbell J in *Christian v Christian* with a full explanation as to why the Act is intended to work in this way.
147. In any event, *Saddler v Saddler* [2013] JMCA Civ 11 makes it clear that leave will usually be a formality and the absence of it will not defeat a claim nor if submitted will give rise to the exercise of powers outside PROSA.

beneficial owners. Then the court will often be asked to make an order for sale, either on the open market or by one party buying out the other's interest. Then there will follow orders that allow the order for sale to take practical effect, such as an order for the valuation of the property, an order as to the carriage of sale, and an order giving the registrar of the Supreme Court the power to sign on behalf of the parties in certain circumstances. This will be the pattern for each item of property that is the subject of the application. Sometimes the court will be asked to make orders about the occupation of a property. Sometimes the interests that parties may have had in institutions connected to the property[148] will also be the subject of directives from the court.

In the future, we can expect that agreements (both pre- and post-nuptial) will be put forward for ratification, modification, or be set aside by the courts.

Interlocutory Orders

As family proceedings are more closely integrated into the CPR, the general powers of the court that are exercised in relation to ordinary civil actions are increasingly being used in family matters. The court's powers regarding discovery may be gravely important in cases concerning matrimonial property. In the case of *Hart-Chang v Chang* [2012] JMSC Civ 56, orders for full disclosure of property owned by the defendant were made, and as has been stated,[149] the importance of disclosure in matrimonial proceedings is emphasized in the case of *Bromfield v Bromfield* [2015] UKPC 19.

The court has also considered the power to grant injunctions outside of PROSA, that is, under the Judicature (Supreme Court) Act in proceedings under the Act.[150]

---

148. Such as the National Housing Trust.
149. Sherry Ann McGregor, 'Laws of Eve,' *The Gleaner*, October 19, 2015.
150. *Cain v Cain* [2014] JMCA Civ 3.

Interim Orders

In many instances, the status quo needs to be maintained in order for a court to be able to meaningfully adjudicate on a case. This can involve restricting third parties such as mortgagees or one of the parties to the action from dealing with the property. In the case of mortgagees, although the act is adequate in protecting any interest that they may have, they may seek to argue that they should not have to wait for the court to decide the matter before they are able to take steps to recover the debt, particularly where the parties are in default. Where one of the parties is trying to deal with the property, the issues are usually clearer, although if matters have progressed to the point where a purchaser or lessee has come into the picture, the court may have to look beyond the interests of the parties.

Increasingly, the question of trying to discover the number of properties in a marriage is being raised before the court. The court is extending its powers of discovery in general civil cases to this area.[151] Consideration should be given to the fact that the nature of property extends beyond real property and includes other assets. The notice of application for court orders with supporting affidavit(s) would be employed in these instances so that an interlocutory hearing can be set to obtain any required order.

Other Orders

The court is challenged to use creativity in the pursuit of resolving property issues by the terms of section 23. If there is any extent to which the court may feel that it is limited with regard to the type of order or combination of orders that can be made in order to do justice between the parties, this section should serve to remove any such misgivings. The list is extensive and covers the vesting of property between the parties and their children, making orders with conditions as to future events, and the transfer of property other than land, such as stocks, shares, and other securities. Interestingly,

---

151.　CPR, part 28.

the Act gives the court powers to make orders in relation to 'rights or obligations under any instrument or contract', which seems to suggest that the court can readjust insurance policies and pensions for the mutual benefit of the spouses.[152] There is also the issue of the extent to which a court could dissect such an arrangement and take funds in order to allow a party to make a clean break.

Similarly, the variation of trusts or family settlements[153] is something that could cause much consternation, although it is possible to see why the court might wish to do so in certain circumstances. The role of trustees is effectively being circumvented although it should be recognized that their powers were always subject to the supervision of the court.

The court can order the payment of a lump sum[154] and can make orders relating to the occupation of any property,[155] including the exclusion of a party from the premises.[156] This could be used as an interim or a final order as the case may require. The status of a consent order was considered in the case of *Richardson*.[157]

Protection of Property

a. Protection of Spousal Interests

Section 8 of PROSA specifically addresses the means by which a spouse's interest in the family home can be protected, that is by way of lodging a caveat under section 139 of the Registration of Titles Act. Under section 8(1)(b), 'any transaction concerning the family home shall require the consent of both parties'. The generality of this statement gives rise to a number of interpretations, and the court may be required to provide some degree of specificity in the future. If, for example, there has not yet been any claim by one of

---

152. This power raises questions about privity of contract and how it is to be preserved in such circumstances. See *Ministry of Finance v Bennett* [2018]JMCA Civ 9.
153. Section 23(1)(m).
154. Section 23(2).
155. Section 23(3).
156. Section 23(4).
157. *Richardson v Richardson* [2012] JMSC Civ 12.

the spouses that the property is the family home, then is a sole owner, in such circumstances, to presume (contrary to his own legal interest) that an equitable interest (created by statute), exists, which requires the permission of the other spouse?

The court is given powers to set aside a transaction that is in breach of section 8(1)(b)[158] or otherwise to direct that a spouse whose interest has been defeated is to be compensated from the proceeds of the transaction. These provisions appear to be in respect of the family home and not 'other property'.

Although the court has wide powers under section 15 to make orders in respect of 'other property', these powers are subject to section 16 of the Act:

> Where the Court is satisfied on an application made by a person affected by an order made under section 15 that the order was obtained by fraud, duress, the giving of false evidence or the suppression of material facts, the Court may set aside the order and make another order under subsection (1) of that section in substitution therefore.

This is itself subject to the interests of a bona fide purchaser for value without notice.[159]

b.   *Protection of Creditors*

Section 17 of the Act preserves the rights of creditors and the trustee in bankruptcy in relation to the property of a spouse and, in this way, ensures that the priority of the creditor's interest is not disturbed by the legislation. To the extent that the satisfaction of a personal debt may affect the interest of the 'innocent spouse', the other spouse can be ordered to compensate that spouse, or his/her interest in the property can be adjusted as necessary. Personal debt is defined within the section so as to exclude certain joint purposes.[160]

Section 18 specifically states that any order of the court regarding the distribution or apportionment of the property shall be subject

158.   Section 8(3)(a).
159.   Section 16(2).
160.   Section 17(4).

to the interests of any third party whose interest in the property is registered before the order was made. This, of course, does not apply to transactions where the third party knowingly acts to defeat the interest of the other spouse, particularly relating to the family home,[161] and presumably those that are entered into after the commencement of proceedings without leave of the court. The balance between the interests of creditors and the need to ensure that the interests of a party are not defeated by inappropriate transactions must be delicately managed, and whether the court's powers are adequate as currently framed in the legislation remains to be seen.

Disposal of Property

The commencement of proceedings imposes a freeze on transactions affecting the property under consideration,[162] and this is a logical provision since it is necessary to preserve the status quo to enable the court to adjudicate. A criminal offence is committed if a person acts in contravention of this provision.[163] However, in practice, a person may not be aware of when proceedings are instituted since there is a lapse of time between when the application is filed in court and when the documents are issued by the court to be served on the respondent. It would appear that the legislators have taken a firm position that does not take into account ignorance that proceedings have been instituted on the part of the person dealing with the property, certainly in so far as the court's power to intervene in such circumstances[164] is concerned. The criminal offence created by section 20(2), however, would require mens rea and, therefore, the offence could not be committed where there is no knowledge that proceedings have been commenced. The offence is apparently reserved for those who act in flagrant, rather

---

161. Section 19.
162. Section 20(1).
163. Section 20(2).
164. Of course, the period of ignorance may be argued by way of defence to subsequent proceedings for rescission under section 22.

than inadvertent, disregard for the court. Transactions are permitted where the permission of the court or the consent of the other party has been obtained.

The adequacy of the penalty for the offence is debatable and would be so almost as soon as the act came into law because of a combination of factors that have the effect of diminishing the perceived severity of these measures. In the first place, it was always debatable, even at the time the law was enacted, whether a fine of one JMD$1 million would be an effective deterrent to such activity, and as time goes by, this is even more doubtful. This needs to be reviewed regularly to avoid injustice.

The court is given extensive powers of tracing in section 21, so that where a transaction has already been completed, the court can take control of the proceeds and direct them as necessary. The court is also empowered to set aside a disposition, but the priority of the bona fide purchaser for value without notice is specifically recognized.[165]

Costs

The questions of legal costs in family cases, along with the expanding powers to litigate, have come to the attention of the court. Increasingly, the court is being asked to make orders along the lines of the rules that apply in ordinary civil matters which, in general terms, are that the winner is entitled to costs, although the judge does have a discretion to depart from the general rule. The case of *Williams v Williams*,[166] in deciding to grant leave to appeal, looked in a limited way at this issue. Once judicial discretion is more willingly exercised when apportioning costs in family matters, this opens the door to considerations such as the conduct of the parties in relation to each other or in relation to any of the property. The conduct of the parties in relation to how the matter has been pursued in court (whether there was full cooperation or unnecessary

---

165.   Section 22(1)(a).
166.   [2015] JMCA App 48.

delay) may well be a valid consideration as to the apportionment of costs in future. Does the fact that one party will have continuing day-to-day responsibility for any children have a bearing on this issue, and what about the disparity in financial standing of the parties? Increasingly, the time honoured notion that unless there are exceptional circumstances the usual order in family matters would be 'no order as to costs' is not a reliable assumption.

THE WAY FORWARD

PROSA represents a significant step forward in the development of the law, but in some ways it has not gone far enough. The presumption of 50 per cent share of the family home needs to be bolstered. There must be sufficient certainty in the law to deter those whose determination to go to court is fuelled by personal antagonism rather than an understanding of the law. Judges who may feel that the Act curtails their discretion too much may, in time, recognize that contested property hearings take up a lot of court's time and judicial energy that could be deployed in other more useful areas. In many instances, where the only asset is the family home, the only reason why the case is being heard in the high court is because of inflated property values, and from a legal standpoint, there is little or no justification for the case to be heard at this level. Since this forms the bulk of cases brought before the court, an amendment to have these cases dealt with in the lower court would have major impact on the court list. The judicious employment of costs orders could go a long way in sending a message that parties, in matters of this nature, should use every available means to settle and thereby avoid several trips to court. One of the methods of avoiding court proceedings that has not been adopted to the fullest extent is separation agreements. Where the marriage or cohabitation has come to an end, it is an act of responsibility and maturity to resolve issues regarding children, maintenance, and property by coming to an agreement before proceeding. The courts can do a lot by referring to this avenue and encouraging it even at the stage where proceedings have already been initiated.

Pre-nuptial agreements are becoming more commonplace particularly where the parties have acquired property before contemplating marriage to each other. This will become increasingly the case as people marry later in life. Those who have a business or substantial business interests will also gravitate towards making pre-nuptial agreements. It will, however, take some time for the court to get the opportunity to consider and rule on these agreements.

The present definition of family home does not seem to entertain the notion that people can live permanently in two different places, whether by spending an equal amount of time in both homes, or by the parties living in separate residences but spending time together in both. Although Parliament used a conventional lifestyle pattern as a guide in this area, the fact is that it has become a norm of sorts for happily married people to live in different countries and, in time, the number of variations to this theme will increase.

In this legislation, Parliament has shown that it will enact laws which are cognizant of Jamaica's lifestyle patterns rather than borrowing from a country whose society is quite unlike Jamaica's. Some have been critical of this legislation (and the Maintenance Act) for recognizing common law unions, saying that it undermines marriage. It can be equally posited that Parliament had little choice and to continue to ignore these couples was unrealistic.

In *Brown v Brown*, the legislation has provided the court with the chance to address some far-reaching questions, and it is hoped that this will continue. For example, it may be that to encourage people to clear up property issues as soon after the break of the marriage or cohabitation, the courts should consider using the concept of abandonment within the context of the Act. This might have avoided the somewhat invidious position that the court found itself in the case of *Hogg*. The tendency to leave property unassigned is a source of considerable problems, not only regarding matrimonial property but also in the area of probate and succession. Untraceable or neglectful owners encourage squatting and are a significant impediment to the economic progress of the country. To that extent, the interpretation of the law, including PROSA, has an important role to play.

The question of costs in family property cases is likely to take on greater significance in the future. In many cases, there is no order as to costs and each party will, therefore, be responsible for their own legal costs. It was, in the past, rare for the court to make an order for one party in the family case to pay another's costs, even if on the face of it that party had 'won'. This meant that there was generally little incentive for a party to act responsibly and not waste the court's time with protracted hearings. This can be a source of considerable frustration, not only in property cases but also particularly in matters where maintenance is at stake.

In the realm of matrimonial property, the wording of the law invites a challenge to the 50 per cent presumption, and many still think it is worth their while to take their chances and try to get a larger share, particularly when the level of acrimony is high. Not only can this attitude be reined in by the appropriate orders for costs, it can also make it easier to advise clients and thereby forestall unnecessary litigation. To avoid being burdened with unexceptional cases, the court must not only encourage mediation but also ultimately be prepared to penalize where necessary, in the form of costs, because everyone thinks their case is exceptional and is otherwise unlikely to compromise.

Attorney's costs in land/property transfer matters are applicable as a percentage of the value of the transaction. Once again, it could be helpful to parties who are in the process of dismantling their marital assets if attorney's costs were at a fixed percentage, rather than somewhere on the scale to be decided by the attorney.

It is far from settled whether PROSA has had the effect of reducing the amount of division of matrimonial property actions. The need for interpretation and clarification of new legislation provides ample scope for cases to be pursued with interesting results. Also, there remains something interminably contentious about division of family property that prompts parties to ignore the advice of their attorney and spend years in court (and a great deal of money in the process). Lawyers will need to acquire the skills to direct their clients towards more conciliatory methods of resolving these matters, such as agreements and mediation.

6. Domestic Violence

INTRODUCTION

David came home from a gruelling day at work to a house that was a mess. There was no dinner and the children were still in their school clothes. It was 8:00 p.m. As he entered the kitchen, he saw his wife Sonia on her cell phone. He was tired and furious. He could not understand why he worked so hard to provide for his family and yet his wife could not keep her side of the bargain and look after them properly. As she turned to greet him with a sheepish smile, he slapped her soundly and she fell back against the kitchen counter. That is how the fight started, and yes, he did take it a bit far, and it is right that he did not stop even when he saw that she was bleeding. It was only when the children were crying and begging him to stop that he let go of Sonia and went into the bedroom.

Sonia dragged herself up and walked to the police station nearby. She reported what had happened to the desk sergeant, who was not particularly interested. However, when he saw the blood on her clothes, he dispatched two police officers to accompany her back to the house and speak to David.

The police stood in the front yard and told Sonia to go inside and get David. Sonia was a bit fearful, but since the flashing lights of the police car was lighting up the whole place, she did not think he would do anything. She explained to David that the police just wanted to talk to him, and after some time David agreed to come out. As David and Sonia emerged, the police were struck by the disparity in size: David is at least 6' 4", and Sonia is no more than 4' 10" or 4' 11". As they stepped off the veranda, in full view of the two policemen, David turned to Sonia and said 'Is dis you bring down pon me?' and punched her in the face. Sonia collapsed and lost consciousness. David was taken into custody and charged with assault occasioning bodily harm.

At court, Sonia tried to have the charge dropped, but because it had taken place in front of the police, who were present in court and ready to give evidence, the judge would not entertain her. David pleaded guilty and is further remanded. The judge and, indeed, everyone in the court are astounded at such a brazen attack. A probation report is ordered.

In the two weeks between David's guilty plea and his sentencing, a message is sent through an intermediary to the judge that Sonia really does not want David to go to jail because he is the sole breadwinner and the family cannot manage without him.

Domestic Violence – A Brief History[1]

From a social perspective, the greatest act of domestic violence was the wholesale assault on the family called slavery.[2] Not only was the family as a social unit completely and utterly decimated, but the dehumanizing treatment left many of the Jamaican population with no reference point to conduct intimate relationships in a respectful,

---

1.   For more in-depth historical discourses on the history of domestic violence, there are numerous books and articles on this topic.
2.   Interestingly, in more recent times, domestic violence has been likened to a form of slavery by feminist commentators.

loving, non-violent manner.[3] The traditional legal approach to the history of the law in this area is set between Jamaica to England. The concept of the sanctity of marriage created an institution that was like a fortress into which the law was reluctant to pry. This meant that the law and society would turn their backs on physical abuse on the basis that what went on within the confines of a person's, more specifically, a man's home, was his own business.[4] Short of murder,[5] what took place within the family walls was of no concern to the law,[6] although there were what came to be accepted as common law rules that disallowed a man from beating his wife with a stick of greater thickness than his thumb.[7]

The law has made steady inroads into the domestic environment and has done so using different areas to curtail this type of behaviour. Nevertheless, the cases of imprisonment and cruelty persist into modern times.[8]

Criminal Law and Domestic Violence

The criminal law all over the world has been at the forefront of the challenge to acts of domestic violence over an extensive period of time. Since the nineteenth century, the criminal courts have been concerned about where the line should be drawn between a man's right to control those in his household and an unlawful interference

---

3. Historically, domestic violence has been seen as both the enemy of and, in earlier times, a necessary component of family security.
4. Law of Coverture, 1860: A husband may physically and verbally chastise his wife and children to control their behaviour.
5. Renaissance France: 'All the inhabitants have the right to beat their wives so long as death does not follow.'
6. Except to the extent that others may be inconvenienced: City of London Bye Law, 1895, introduced a 'Curfew on Wife Beating' rule between the hours of 10:00 p.m. and 7:00 a.m. so that neighbours would not be disturbed.
7. This was supposedly based on the comments of a judge in 1857 and is referred to in later twentieth-century English judgments with doubt and, in some cases, derision.
8. 'One woman's account of imprisonment describes how her jealous husband who could not bear the possibility of his wife talking to another man, locked her in a coal shed every time he went out, subjecting her to a 50-year ordeal of cruelty.' Daily Mail, February 1992 – Welstead and Edwards, Family Law, 2006.

with the person.[9] In England, the case of *R v Jackson*[10] looked at whether or not a husband had the right to imprison his wife and keep her away from her family, in order to compel her to fulfil her conjugal duties. The case *of R v Clarence*[11] looked at the wilful transmission of a venereal disease.[12] The culmination of the debate as to the scope of the criminal law was whether or not a man can, in any circumstances, be guilty of rape in relation to his wife, and a considerable amount of case law has dealt with this issue.[13] In Jamaica, steps have been taken to devise a statutory offence,[14] which bears some relation to the position at common law as set out in the case of *R v R*.[15] To date, it is doubtful that a conviction under this section of the law has been secured, and the debate as to its possible modification or enhancement continues with the parliamentary review committee.

Civil Law and Domestic Violence

The civil law of tort has also been employed as a means of seeking to control instances of domestic violence. An assault is a tort as well as being a crime, and it has long been recognized that the remedies available to the court in the case of tortious claims can be effective in restraining and preventing the further occurrence of these actions. Sometimes the nature of the activity does not lend itself to being defined within the ambit of an established tort, and in such circumstances, the courts have tried to address the problem by creating new torts or extending the scope of those which already

---

9.   In the case of *Fulgham v The State of Alabama*, 1871 46 Ala 143, it was said
       'The privilege, ancient though it may be, to beat her with a stick, pull her hair,
       choke her, spit in her face or kick her about the floor, or to inflict on her other
       indignities, is not now acknowledged by our law.'
10.   [1891] 1 QB 671.
11.   (1889) 2 QB 23.
12.   With recent concerns about HIV transmission, the criminal law has had cause to
       revisit this issue.
13.   *R v Jackson; R v Clarke* 1949 2 All ER 448; *R v Miller* [1954] 2 All ER 529.
14.   Sexual Offences Act, section 5.
15.   [1991] 4 All ER 481.

exist.[16] In other jurisdictions, Parliament has stepped in to create new actionable torts[17] to bolster the powers of the court in defining certain activities in a way that is actionable and therefore allows the courts to apply the remedies that will then be at the court's disposal. The problem with civil actions as a means of addressing domestic violence is that such claims can be unwieldy, expensive, and not sufficiently comprehensive as to be an effective response to such behaviour. In some states in the US, actions have been brought against the authorities, in particular the police department, for failure to respond or non-intervention to protect a victim of domestic violence, and juries have made substantial monetary awards. This, of course, is a condemnatory action to what has already taken place, and is not protective or prohibitive in nature.

The real problem with addressing domestic violence lies in the nature of the activity. It involves people who are related and often dependent on each other. It frequently involves people who have children together and, if only for the sake of the children, may have to maintain an ongoing parental relationship. Domestic violence may take place in the home in keeping with its name, but it may also take place at the workplace, on the street, at a school, or other institution that is frequented by one of the parties. The effect on the children, on the economic stability of the family, and on the psychological well-being of the family are all additional factors arising from the violent actions and also from the legal response to such actions. Finally, the heavily-slanted biases based on deeply ingrained cultural beliefs simply add to a potent mix of influences in these matters.

The fact that these actions often take place in the home also led to the law in relation to the matrimonial home taking a detour along the route of trying to provide a safe place for victims of domestic violence, notwithstanding the legal ownership of the property.[18]

16.   *Needham v Clarke and Senior* HCV 0852/2006, March 24, 2006.
17.   Protection from Harassment Act 1997, UK.
18.   The Matrimonial Homes Act 1967, UK.

When it became clear that there were real legal impediments to taking this approach, legislators began to look at specialized laws to deal with the issue of domestic violence. This, in itself, gave rise to two broad issues: balancing ownership/occupation rights in relation to property with the need to provide a safe space for victims, and defining domestic violence. In the Caribbean, the latter question has been the main concern, whereas in some other Commonwealth jurisdictions the emphasis has been on addressing the former question.

Throughout the region,[19] domestic violence legislation is becoming more sophisticated in defining and providing remedies for domestic violence. We are seeing that a considerable amount of effort and ingenuity can be brought to bear by perpetrators who are determined to prevail. Countries such as Belize have pronounced a state-sponsored zero tolerance to domestic violence which espouses (at least in the legislation) a conscious effort to retrain and reshape the societal values and norms that surround the perpetuation of this behaviour.

Another question that inevitably arises is: How far should the court be allowed to go in terms of inflicting penalties which may strike at the heart of highly valued freedoms and privileges and, at the same by their very nature, infringe on the liberty of the subject or his rights protected by the constitution in a significant way?

THE DOMESTIC VIOLENCE ACT

The Domestic Violence Act 1995 is the cornerstone legislation for the protection from domestic abuse in Jamaica. The Act uses two main tools as a means of providing security for those who have been affected by domestic violence: protection orders and occupation orders.

---

19. Roberta Clarke, 'An Evaluative Study of the Implementation of Domestic Violence Legislation: Antigua and Barbuda, St Kitts/Nevis, St Lucia and St Vincent and the Grenadines.'

An application for either of these orders can be made by:

a. a spouse or parent of the respondent;

b. in the case of children or dependents, by a person who lives with the child or parent, or guardian, a dependant, an approved social worker, or a constable; and

c. a person who is a member of the family or in a visiting relationship with the respondent who has acted or has threatened action against that person.

In the case of a) and c), the application can be made by a constable or any other person who has the leave of the court.

The range of persons who can apply to the court was considerably extended by amendment to the Act in 2004. A significant amendment was the inclusion of visiting relationships as a basis upon which applications could be made. This brings in the widespread practice in Jamaica of parties to an intimate relationship not necessarily living together but conducting an ongoing relationship for years and often decades. Usually, one party, the man will visit the other on a regular basis and often the couple will have a number of children together. There may or may not be an impediment to the parties residing together or an expectation of marriage. Often, such relationships last until the death of one of the parties. The exclusion of such persons from the scope of the original Act was a glaring anomaly. With this and an exhaustive list of permutations of the definition of 'child', the 2004 amendment ensures that anyone who has some connection with the family can apply either directly or on behalf of another family member. In addition, the state in the form of a constable or an approved social worker is also given powers to apply for either protection or occupation orders.

What is Domestic Violence?

Domestic violence is not defined under the Jamaican Act in a comprehensive manner, and no attempt is made to describe certain types of violence that may come within the definition. On one hand, it can be argued that this gives the tribunal of fact a wide discretion in terms of applying the law to what it may deem to be objectionable conduct, but in practice, the court is inclined to be quite conservative in the exercise of its powers. They may make a protection order where there has been a 'threat to use violence or cause physical or mental injury to' a person prescribed under the Act. This formulation is results orientated in that it looks at the effect on the victim rather than the actions of the abuser or perpetrator. Indeed, to put the offence in terms of causing a certain effect on the victim is to introduce a measure of subjectivity which is undesirable. The Act in Jamaica is to be compared with the domestic violence acts of other countries in the Caribbean where the legislators have gone to great lengths to encapsulate terms like domestic violence, emotional and psychological abuse, and financial abuse.[20] Although it is right to say that there will generally be a subjective element in proving typical instances of abuse.

PROTECTION ORDERS

Where the court is satisfied that:

a. the respondent has used or threatened to use violence against or caused physical or mental injury to a prescribed person and is likely to do so again; or

b. having regard to all the circumstances, the order is necessary for the protection of a prescribed person;

then a protection order may be made.

While the vast majority of cases will fall under paragraph (a), the court is given wide power under paragraph (b). Paragraph (b) is also a useful device to get around the credibility deadlock where, as is often the case, the evidence rests on the word of one spouse against the other. Where there is no bruise, scar, or other evidence

---

20.   Domestic Violence Act, section 3 (Trinidad); Domestic Violence Act 2007, section 2 (Belize); and Domestic Violence (Protection Orders) Act 2016 (Barbados).

of harm, a tribunal may find it difficult to decide who is telling the truth without a witness, especially when both parties have ulterior motives.

If so satisfied, on the balance of probabilities, the court can make any or all orders contained in section 4(1). In practice, the parish judge, when making the order, will specify which paragraphs and subparagraphs will apply. The problem may be that as this is being recited in a perfunctory way by reference to the statutory clauses, the parties may not necessarily grasp the exact restriction that is being placed on their actions.

In section 4(3), the court is empowered to make ex parte protection orders where the personal safety of the prescribed person is at risk. The second criterion for making an ex parte order is an alternative to the first and states that if the process of hearing the matter *inter partes* would result in serious or undue hardship, then the matter can be heard ex parte. It would seem that the first factor – that there is a risk to the personal safety – is repeated in section 4(2)a, but in this case arises as a preliminary question before going to the merits of the application.

A person who breaches a protection order commits a criminal offence for which he/she is liable on conviction to a fine of up to $10,000 or imprisonment for up to six months. Quite apart from whether or not a criminal charge ensues, the police have the power to arrest anyone who is reasonably believed to be in breach of a protection order. This power should only be exercised where it is necessary for the protection of the prescribed person. The discretion when making an arrest is guided by section 5(4), and the rights of the person arrested are set out in section 5(5).

The summary in the margin of section 6 suggests that this section gives us information on the duration of a protection order. However, it is misleading since the section actually deals with discharging the order.

OCCUPATION ORDERS[21]

An occupation order is an order granting the prescribed person the right to live in the household residence – section 7(1). In practice, to be able to live undisturbed in the household residence, the prescribed person will usually be granted a protection order as well as the occupation order, section 8(3).

An occupation order may be made when the court deems it is a necessary step to protect the prescribed person or when it is in the best interest of a child. It would appear, therefore, that the substantive grounds for granting a protection order, section 4(2), are sufficient for an occupation order to be made along with either of the stipulations set out in section 7(3). So, essentially, when the court is presented with circumstances upon which it could ground a protection order, it is also necessary to consider if an occupation order should also be granted to ensure the prescribed person's complete protection.

It is only when an ex parte application is being made that the court is required to be satisfied that the respondent has used violence or caused physical or mental injury to the prescribed person, section 8(1)a. In addition, the court must be satisfied when an ex parte application is being made 'that the delay that would be caused by proceeding on summons could or might expose the prescribed person to physical injury', section 8(1)b. In short, for the court to entertain an ex parte application there must have been physical or mental violence to the prescribed person, and the risk of physical injury if the order is not made. The usual restrictions with regard to ex parte orders, as found with protection orders, are also included in the provisions dealing with occupation orders. Interestingly, section 7(2), provides that an occupation order may be made 'for such period or periods and on such terms and subject

---

21.   For an interesting assessment of this type of order from an Australian perspective see Rachael Field, Belinda Carpenter and Susan Currie. 'Issues in the making of Ouster orders under the Domestic Violence (Family Protection) Act 1989 (Qld).' In *Family Law: Processes, Practices, and Pressures* edited by John Dewar and Stephen Parker, 99–116. West Sussex: Hart Publishing, 2003.

to such conditions as the court thinks fit'. This is a sweeping power, particularly considering that it is being exercised by a parish judge. While in practice duration of an occupation order maybe from six months to one year, the Act places no restriction on the powers of the court in this matter other than either of the parties having the right to have the period reduced or discharged as set out in section 10.

An ex parte order will, of necessity, be an interim order and will therefore come to an end either by the setting of an *inter partes* hearing or by the discharge of the order under section 8(4). The respondent can apply for an ex parte order to be discharged under section 8(5). In addition to an extremely liberal power in the length of the occupation order, the court also has the power to extend the period of the order under section 10.

Granting an occupation order against someone who is an owner or joint owner of the premises represents a serious interference with their proprietary rights, albeit justified in law. Even if the person against whom the order is made is merely a lessee, it can still be seen as an intervention by the courts, into the contractual arrangements involving third parties.[22] On the other hand, it can be argued that domestic violence is so serious that this kind of intervention is entirely warranted. It should, however, be considered that the duration of the order may defeat the interest in the property.[23]

While it may be further argued that, in practice, this would present strong grounds for discharge of an occupation order, there is nothing in the Act that dictates or gives guidelines for such an outcome. When one looks at the domestic violence acts enacted in the Caribbean after the Jamaican Act, there is at least the recognition that for rental premises it is necessary to consider these issues, but the Jamaican Act remains silent on this question, except for the generalized provisions of section 11. Where the person affected is the respondent, rather than a third party, the prevailing sentiment

---

22.   Except by way of sections 11 and 20.
23.   Furthermore, the court-imposed separation often signals the legal separation that is a prerequisite to divorce proceedings.

seems to be – you deserve to be deprived of your occupation rights because of your actions against the prescribed person. This goes somewhat further than simply providing a safe space for the victims of domestic violence and takes on an almost punitive character.

OTHER ORDERS

Where the court makes either a protection order or an occupation order, the court can of its own volition or if the applicant applies, make an order for maintenance of the applicant or any member of the household. This is provided that the application could be entertained by the court according to the terms of the Maintenance Act, section 4(5). This would mean that it would have to be established that the respondent has an obligation to maintain the person, and so on. This means that it is not necessary for the applicant to take out an additional summons claiming maintenance and the order can be made at the same time as the protection and/or occupation order. This is essentially a temporary measure designed to alleviate immediate hardship because there is a proviso that the maintenance order will only last for the duration of the protection or occupation order that is being made at that time. If the order is of a short duration, it may be necessary for the applicant to initiate proceedings under the Maintenance Act itself in order to receive maintenance on an ongoing basis. This facility is, of course, only be open to the applicant in circumstances where there is no pre-existing maintenance order.

Section 12 of the Act permits the court to make orders in respect of furniture, household appliances and household effects, when an occupation order is made. A time limit of three months is set in respect of a furniture order. This presumably, is on the basis that this should be sufficient time for the applicant or any other member of the household to obtain replacement furniture. However, it is difficult, in practice, for a respondent to remove furniture from the premises upon the expiration of such an order if an occupation order and protection order are still in place. This necessitates an application from the respondent to suspend or vary the terms of the order(s) in order to allow the furniture to be removed from the property. What will often happen in such a case is that the respondent will leave the furniture and household effects in the property, unless they are of particular value to the respondent or he is minded to enforce his rights regardless. Surprisingly, the Act does not make any provision for the prescribed person to be restrained from damaging any of the furniture or household effects in the course of their exclusive occupation of the premises. It may well have been thought by Parliament that the potential for such misconduct can adequately be dealt with by way of warnings from the court.

As stated previously, it is open to a third party with an interest in the property to apply for an occupation order to be discharged.

General Provisions under the Act

Part 3 of the Domestic Violence Act provides guidance as to the conduct of the hearing. If it is an ex parte application, an interim order will be made and the orders must specify a return date which will be 'as soon as reasonably practicable thereafter'. The interim order must be served on the respondent and at that hearing the court may discharge the interim order and/or replace it with another order, or adjourn the matter to another date. The question of service is important because this is a prerequisite to any proceedings for enforcement in the event of a breach of the order, section 5(1)a.

Privacy is addressed in sections 14 and 16 of the Act. Section 14 deals with the hearing itself and restricts the number of persons who may be present to those listed in the section. This does not apply to any criminal proceedings under the Act. The court also has the power to send out a witness, exclude any person, and hold the proceedings in camera.

There are restrictions with regard to publishing 'any report of any proceedings' under the act without the leave of the court.

Since the media is not generally admitted to the Family Court, this stipulation may be infringed only when proceedings take place in the parish court. Even then, the provisions of section 14 forbid reporters being in court when such matters are being dealt with. Section 16 does not exclude criminal proceedings under the Act and therefore even if section 14 does not apply, the reporters would nevertheless be restricted under this section. There is a criminal penalty of a fine of up to $25,000 for being in breach of section 16(1). This is understandably more than the $10,000 that may be imposed on an errant respondent under section 5, because it is directed at members of the media. However, there is an urgent need to increase the penalties under both sections 5 and 16. The court's powers under section 16 are in addition to any other general powers to restrict publication that the court may have, as well as the power to punish for contempt.

There is an important exemption from the restrictions on publication as set out in section 16. This is in circumstances where the publication is of a 'professional or technical nature' or is intended for circulation among professionals connected with the court and public officials.

In any proceedings under the Act other than criminal proceedings, the court needs to be satisfied on the balance of probabilities.[24] In light of the sweeping powers that the court possesses to limit the activities and alter the living circumstances of any respondent, the standard of proof being a civil standard represents a major concession to the applicant.

The court can make consent orders and quite often uses this mechanism to impose orders where there has not been a full hearing in the matter. In addition, sometimes in making a protection order in favour of the applicant, the applicant may be asked to consent to a corresponding order in the face of counter-allegations from the respondent. Not only do consent orders allow the court to deal

---

24.   Section 15.

with these situations seamlessly but also it is the generally held view that parties are more likely to adhere to an order that they have consented to. This may be of particular significance in domestic violence cases, but often in the Family Court, the consensual nature of these types of orders is far from apparent.

By section 18, the court also has the power to recommend that either or both parties participate in counselling as specified by the court.

The right of appeal is set out in section 19.

The Domestic Violence Act is the main piece of legislation dealing with violence and abuse in familial relationships. The jurisdiction is entirely summary and this provides access to the courts for those most in need of protection, without the necessity and expense of legal representation. The Act applies whether the parties are married or not and extends to provide universal coverage of most domestic relationships. It also provides the most comprehensive means of responding to this problem, and is set out in such a way that it is relatively easy for the court to exercise its powers. For this reason, even though there are additional measures to deal with domestic violence in marital unions in section 10 of the Matrimonial Causes Act (MCA), most instances of domestic violence, even where the parties are married are dealt with summarily under the Domestic Violence Act.

DOMESTIC VIOLENCE RELIEF UNDER SECTION 10 OF THE MATRIMONIAL CAUSES ACT

Section 10 of the MCA states, inter alia: '...the Court may, upon application made by either party to the marriage, whether or not an application has been made...for any other relief under this Act, grant an injunction or other order....'

There then follows a list of the types of orders which can be made.

First of all, it is clear that as with an application under the MCA, generally, relief can be sought only by a party to the marriage. That is a major distinction between these provisions and the Domestic Violence Act. Most forms of ancillary relief under the MCA require that proceedings to terminate the marriage have started. This section is an exception to that general rule and allows for an application to be made by either party for any other relief. This means that, although there is no other proceeding under the MCA, the court will still entertain an application for orders to be made pursuant to section 10. The court, in this instance is the high court, and these proceedings are quite separate from proceedings under the Domestic Violence Act that are entirely summary and heard only before a parish judge. Persons who are married, therefore, have to choose whether they seek relief in the high court or in the lower court when domestic violence occurs. The basis for deciding which court is appropriate may be the fact that proceedings in the high court, being a court of pleadings, usually require the services of an attorney. However, the Domestic Violence Act addresses this issue comprehensively, and the court is better equipped by the Act to tailor orders to meet a variety of situations. Interestingly, the application under section 10 must be made by the party whereas the Domestic Violence Act allows applications to be made on behalf of prescribed persons by other specifically designated officials.

The Orders

The types of orders that the court can make under section 10 of the MCA vary from personal protection to occupation of the matrimonial home. They are:

i.   Orders for the personal protection of a party to the marriage or a relevant child.[25]

This would be in the form of a non-molestation order. The legal provisions are expressed generally, and would therefore require that the wording of the order be specifically drafted by the lawyers for the applicant. This is to be compared with section 4(1) of the Domestic Violence Act where an array of activities and actions are

---

25.   Section 10(1)(a).

specifically restricted or prohibited, and all that is required of the court is to identify the part of the section, which is then adopted to form the wording of the order.

ii. Orders restraining a party from entering, remaining, or being in the vicinity of the matrimonial home.[26]

Orders under this section would generally be described as restraining orders comparable with sections 4(1)(a)–(d) of the Domestic Violence Act. This part of section 10 refers to the matrimonial home which, in the absence of a specific definition, can be given its ordinary meaning. This term is not used in the Domestic Violence Act, nor in the Property (Rights of Spouses) Act (PROSA), which instead speaks of the 'family home'. Once again, it would be for the applicant's legal representatives to frame the application in terms of the orders that the court is being asked to make.

iii. Restraining a party from entering the workplace of the other party or the workplace or school of any relevant child.[27]

This part of section 10 does not envisage that a party to the marriage may need protection in places other than their home or place of work. Many adult spouses are also engaged in further education, or may attend a place of worship, gym, or have taken refuge with a relative or friend. It would appear that both the Domestic Violence Act and the MCA are deficient in respect of family and friends. Even though this section is a laudable attempt to cover the usual locations, the later Domestic Violence Act once again, provides comprehensive protection in this regard.[28]

iv. Orders in relation to the use and occupation of the matrimonial home.[29]

This is the equivalent of an occupation order under the Domestic Violence Act and would allow the court to grant exclusive occupation to an applicant.

26. Section 10(1)(b).
27. Section 10(1)(c).
28. Sections 4(1)(a)–(d).
29. Section 10(1)(e).

Section 10(2) establishes that the court may make an order relieving a party of any obligation to perform marital services or render conjugal rights. These rights, though in some instances recognized, theoretically, have not been enforced by the courts for a long time. The provision is also somewhat anomalous in light of section 35 of the MCA. This passage can address the possibility of the enforcing of 'rights' being advanced, as a defence to an allegation that there has been a breach of the order. It can also be used to relieve a party of such duties in circumstances such as marital rape.[30]

If there is a breach of any order under section 10(1), subsection (3) sets out the powers of the court to respond to the breach. There is no criminal offence as there is in the Domestic Violence Act, but the court's extensive powers of contempt, being a court of inherent jurisdiction, are firmly endorsed. Section 10(3)(d) enables the court 'to make such other orders as the Court considers necessary to enforce compliance with the injunction or other orders'. These are extremely wide powers, but are not inconsistent with the general powers of the high court. They are also in keeping with the fact that the court takes these matters seriously or at least is directed to do so by Parliament.

PRACTICE AND PROCEDURE IN DOMESTIC VIOLENCE

In practice, where there is domestic violence within marriage, the parties will avail themselves of the Domestic Violence Act. It is cheaper, faster, and more expansive in terms of the protection options. Nevertheless, the provisions in the MCA are necessary and, in some instances, vital to the proceedings under this legislation. In particular, where proceedings for termination have already commenced, it is important that the court has the power to deal with any threats, intimidation, or violence that may occur. It is also important that, in such circumstances, the victim who is already a

---

30.   These provisions preceded the Sexual Offences Act.

party to the original proceedings should not have to seek relief in another court by way of a separate claim in order to take action against what is taking place. While the ability to bring an originating action under the MCA is logical, it is not so much for this purpose that the section is usually invoked, and in practice, it tends to be used as an interlocutory tool to remedy or deter the occurrence of violence or threats between the parties after the commencement of proceedings.

The Domestic Violence Rules 1996 set out the procedural process for making applications under the Domestic Violence Act. Proceedings are commenced in the Family Court or in the Parish Court by way of a plaint and the issuing of a summons. The Parish Court, of which the Family Court is a part, is not a court of pleadings and therefore the failure to adhere strictly to the rules will not nullify the proceedings. The court does have the power to set aside but need not exercise it. Furthermore the court, when dealing with proceedings, should seek to achieve 'the just, speedy, simple, and inexpensive determination of the proceedings'.

The forms to be used for a protection order, an occupation order, and an ancillary order, are prescribed in the schedule to the rules. There is a separate form for when the application is being made ex parte.

The procedure is primarily civil in format. The respondent may serve a notice of defence, but may also put a defence to the application on the day of appearance without having previously filed or served the defence.

Proceedings under the Domestic Violence Act may be transferred if it is felt that it would be more convenient for the matter to be dealt with elsewhere, namely in another parish. If transfer is mutually agreed between the parties, the clerk of the court (rather than the parish judge) may transfer the proceedings. The Domestic Violence Rules are generalized and rely on the Resident Magistrates' Court rules to guide the court when these specific rules are silent.

In practice, domestic violence proceedings usually require the court to decide which of the two sides has the preferred account of the incident, which is the subject of the complaint. Often, this incident is the culmination of ongoing violent behaviour between the parties, or that something has occurred since the plaint was filed. For some reason, in cases of domestic violence, the perpetrator may be less inclined to submit to or abide by the orders or directions of the court. On the other hand, it is also found that in front of the court, the parties present themselves in a way that is designed to obtain their objectives and elicit sympathy from the court. This may, in fact, bear no relation to their true violent, cowardly personality. It is thus easy for the court to be misled as to who is the real victim and make orders simply to try and keep the parties away from each other.

Cases will often drag on with numerous court appearances, and it starts to become clear that at least one party may relish the opportunity for engagement that is afforded by protracted proceedings.

The procedure for making an application under section 10 of the MCA is guided by part 76 of the Civil Procedure Rules (CPR). If the application is the start of proceedings under the MCA, then the application would be made by way of a fixed date claim form, with an accompanying affidavit in support. The application may be made ex parte if the circumstances demand it. The matter will, therefore, be heard before a single judge sitting in chambers.

Section 23 of the MCA enables the claimant to apply for maintenance for himself/herself, and for any relevant child, as part of the section 10 proceedings. As with the Domestic Violence Act, the court's powers to make maintenance orders in these situations are in accordance with the Maintenance Act 2005. Where termination proceedings, such as divorce have already commenced and the court is being asked to make interlocutory orders, the application would be by way of a notice of application for court orders, form 7, with an affidavit in support.

The vast majority of applications in relation to domestic violence are made in the Family Court or Parish Court under the Domestic Violence Act. The Domestic Violence Act does not preclude obtaining orders in the high court under section 10 as well, but it is unlikely that this would be permitted by the court, and generally parties would not wish to incur the additional and unnecessary expense.

On a final note with regard to procedure, at common law the high court retains the power to grant injunctions in any proceedings. This means that, technically, in proceedings for custody, for example, if either party acts in a way that is violent or unlawfully interferes with the other party, especially in relation to compliance or non-compliance with court orders, the court still has inherent powers to make such orders to protect the innocent party and, if necessary, bring proceedings against the offending party for contempt. This process is rarely used, because it is rare for persons to act in this way in the course of proceedings, but it does exist. Similarly, if the action of the person amounts to a tort for which a claim may be made, the court will then have the power to grant injunctions as it sees fit either as an interim or as a final remedy to the claim: see *Needham v Clarke and Senior*.[31]

THE WAY FORWARD

While the domestic violence legislation is rightly gender neutral, the vast majority of complaints brought before the court are commenced by women against their male partners. Even if this is obvious to anyone who simply sits in court, it is important if legal reforms are to take place that policymakers and legislators have current and accurate information as to what is taking place in the courts.[32] It is also important to look at the laws in other countries

---

31.   0852/2006 24/3/06.
32.   The Ministry of Justice is now furnished with data from the courts as to the number and type of cases, but for policy purposes beyond the provision of resources, such as law reform, it may be necessary to obtain a more comprehensive study.

in this area to see what kind of innovative steps are being taken to combat violence between domestic partners. This is a worldwide problem and in this respect, Jamaican society is not different. It is tempting to give in to the cries for a draconian response, but while this problem must be taken seriously, there needs to be a multifaceted approach. The legislation in Belize is exemplary because not only is there an incorporation of a 'zero tolerance' attitude in the form of progressively harsher penalties, there is also an appreciation that the police have a vital role to play in controlling the outbreak of violence in the home. The 'hands-off' stance of the police has caused unnecessary injury and loss of life and has been assiduously challenged in the Belizean Act. The police are also charged with the responsibility of keeping records and furnishing those records to the authorities, and in this way the new role that they play will help to re-shape the prevailing attitudes at the root of their previous reluctance to get involved with domestic violence cases. The Belizean Act also deals extensively with the responsibility of the political directorate to develop programmes that will educate the society about domestic violence and, in this way, it is recognized that the battle that is faced reflects deep-seated beliefs and, if these are not addressed, future generations will behave in exactly the same way as their forefathers. Anger management, family intervention, counselling, and other forms of social support for the family afflicted by domestic violence are costly, but the cost to society when domestic violence is not addressed is already too great.

At present, the law concentrates on protection of the victim at the expense of property rights. Whereas it is important to maintain this emphasis, it may be necessary to consider the weight of the balance. All too often the imposition of an occupation order signals the departure of the man and the irreversible break-up of the family. There are, of course, situations where this is absolutely necessary, or inevitable, but nevertheless, there are some cases where it would appear that the breakdown of the marriage was prompted by the orders of the court. The sanctity of the marriage in the face of ongoing occurrences of domestic violence clearly comes into question. It must not be forgotten that the criminal law also plays a part by extending the definition of rape to include circumstances where the parties are still married to each other. This remains a controversial area because, on one hand, there is no doubt that a wife in these times must be afforded the protection of the law from a husband who abuses her in the same way that any other woman is so protected. Similarly, the law and those who apply it, must create a climate that deals sympathetically with abuse of men by women so that such a prescribed person is not daunted by prevailing attitudes.

This leads to considerations of the protection of the children who, in most cases, are the real victims. Not only may they have witnessed the violence, but it is likely that they will also be deprived of interaction with one of their parents after the court has dealt with the matter. Views differ widely in this area. There are those who say that the interaction between adults, whether violent or not, does not necessarily affect their ability to parent, and that even where it takes place in the child's presence, the child is resilient enough to understand that a momentary outburst has nothing to do with the offender's continuing love for him/her. On the other hand, there are those who say parents who are violent should not be allowed access to the children because they have been shown to turn the abuse onto the children in order to manipulate the family and retain power. Relevant agencies should engage in this debate and collect information on such studies to ensure that judges are provided with sufficient knowledge to act informatively, rather than react emotionally. When dealing with domestic violence cases, it may be hard to prevent a natural sense of outrage from taking over and determining the course of proceedings. Hence, training should not only be provided, but enhanced.

Finally, perhaps more use should be made of the exemption under section 16(4) as a means of keeping all concerned aware of what is taking place when these matters are being heard. It would also allow the courts, social workers, and police to move towards greater consistency when dealing with these cases.

HELPLINES FOR VICTIMS OF DOMESTIC VIOLENCE

Woman's Inc. & Crisis Centre
4 Ellesmere Road, Kingston 10
Telephone: 876-929-2997

Sam Sharpe Square,
Montego Bay
Telephone: 876-952-9533

Deaconess House
4 Caledonia Avenue, Kingston 5
Telephone: 876-926-8856

Sisters United for Prayer, Healing, Empowerment and Restoration
Contact: Marie Berbick
Telephone: 876-832-4867

Missionaries of the Poor (Jacob's Well)
74 Hanover Street, Kingston
Telephone: 876-922-4414

7. Custody

INTRODUCTION

Upon the death of Desmond, his wife Mary found herself in poverty, with more children than she could properly take care of. The solution was that two of the children were 'adopted out' into what turned out to be two different families. The boy found himself in a family that had some money and spoilt him. He was indulged and petted, with little emphasis placed on the importance of getting a sound education. At an early age, he joined a small band of musicians who played at local dances. His youth was spent in jollification and libation. The girl, on the other hand, was fortunate enough to find herself in a reasonably 'well-to-do' family that nurtured her intelligence with proper schooling and ensured that she took all the public examinations to further her ability. She did spend an occasional weekend with her birth mother and the remaining siblings, but she still slightly resented that her mother had given her away, and her siblings were openly jealous and excluded her. At the appropriate time, she was 'boarded out'[1] in Kingston in order to attend a prestigious high school. After leaving school, she went to a teachers college so as to be able to enter the main profession open to women at that time.

Unfortunately, in many situations as the one described, there were different and more serious results. Many a teenage pregnancy has had its origin in inadequate family supervision due to the absence of a parent, and many instances of juvenile delinquency can be attributed to distant or non-existent parenting. At the same time, many children have found themselves to be the beneficiary of well-meaning caregivers, some related, who have taken them in, brought them up, and launched them into a successful life.

In Jamaica, as in most Caribbean countries with a population which is predominantly of African descent, the issue of child care is a battleground between the received norms of the former colonial masters enshrined in the law and the social and cultural values of child-rearing, originating from Africa.[2]

The importance of family as an extended, rather than a nuclear concept, is the foundation of the Jamaican approach to raising children.[3] When the issue of child care is compounded by that constant feature of island living – migration[4] – a potent mix of

1. Persons would (and still do) provide lodgings for children from the country who were/are attending school in certain main towns.
2. For some reason, it would appear that the child custody norms of the other population strands have not played a significant role in shaping the law in Jamaica.
3. Caribbean Families-Extended Families, http://family.jrank.org/pages/204/Caribbean-Families-Extended-Family.html.
4. This took the form of 'intra-Caribbean', hemispheric, and later intercontinental migration; see Verene Shepherd, 'On the Move: Caribbean Women and Emigration,' in *Women in Caribbean History: The British-colonised Territories* (Kingston: Ian Randle Publishers, 1999).

motivation, ambition, and largely good intentions[5] is constrained by inflexible legal definitions and categories that most people do not identify with at all.

What may appear to be a fairly casual approach to 'who goin' look after di chile' [Who is going to look after the child?] masks what is basically an assumption that one's family is available as a child care resource when the vicissitudes of life impede direct parental involvement.[6] Interestingly, migration, whether from country to town, or from one island to another, or from Jamaica to America, Canada, or the UK – is an enduring occurrence, but not the only factor that influences child care practices. In Jamaica, as with anywhere else, parents may get sick, die, or go to jail, but there are also some situations and features which prevail in the Commonwealth Caribbean that are less typical.[7] Women who perform domestic work on a 'live-in' basis are forced to leave their own children in the care of others while they keep house and look after their employer's children. In such circumstances, the prolonged absences of the biological parent cause children to look upon their day-to-day caregiver as parent, rather than the person who comes periodically bearing apologetic gifts.[8] In situations where the parent is in another country the children wait patiently for the parent to send for them, and even when this dream materializes, it often becomes difficult for the parent and child to resume their respective roles in relation to each other because they simply do not know each other.

In the circumstances described, the concepts of custody, guardianship, and adoption are terms that bend and flex to suit the circumstances. Adoptions in Jamaica are often informal and do

---

5.   'Better wages, educational opportunities, and for self-improvement'.
6.   Leaving children with grandparents remains an enduring feature of Jamaican family life.
7.   Teenage pregnancy, see Pauline A. Russell-Brown, Beverly Norville and Cheryl Griffiths, 'Child Shifting, a Survival Strategy for Teenage Mothers,' in Caribbean Families: Diversity Among Ethnic Groups, eds. Jaipaul L. Roopnarine and Janet Brown, 223–242 (Greenwich, CT: Ablex Publishing Corporation,1997).
8.   This is seen up to the present in the phenomenon of 'barrel children'. See notes under 'Children and the State' chapter.

not affect birth registration or ties with blood relatives. Generally, in these informal adoptions, a family member will become the guardian or adoptive parent.[9]

Many grandparents, aunts, and cousins see themselves as having custody and may well wish to apply for an order from the court to that effect.[10] Similarly, people often act in the position of guardian – with or without the blessing of the court – in circumstances which do not square with the situations envisaged by the Children (Guardianship and Custody) Act,[11] that is, in the event of the death of either or both parents. In many instances, both parents are alive and well but simply poor. The courts have, therefore, had to interpret and apply the law taking full cognizance of the familial realities in Jamaica.

From these examples, one can see that the notion of parenthood is an all-encompassing concept borne out of family tradition and custom. Of course, there are the usual custody disputes between estranged parents that are every bit as protracted and aggressively pursued as anywhere else. Like other jurisdictions, the cases which attract attention, and hence make law, are those where the parties have the resources to pursue cases in the high court or to subject the result to the appellate process. Parties with such resources at their disposal frequently have strong ties abroad or may actually live outside of Jamaica. As a result, landmark cases in the area of custody are often compounded by jurisdictional issues.[12]

The welfare principle that governs custody and care proceedings, while masquerading as a panacea for all ills is, in practice, deeply subjective and has been open to considerable criticism.[13] Feelings

---

9. This is akin to the open adoption model which has now been recognized in adoption legislation elsewhere in more recent times.
10. This does not appear to be what section 7 of the Children (Guardianship and Custody) Act that envisages applications by 'the mother or father'.
11. See Sections 3 and 4 Children (Guardianship and Custody) Act.
12. See *Panton v Panton* 2079/2004 16/9/2004; *Forrester v Strong Forrester* SCCA 51/2007 2/5/2008; and *Grant v Edwards and Another* [1986] 2 All ER 426.
13. See chapter 8, Sonia Harris-Short, Joanna Miles, and Robert H. George, *Family Law: Text, Cases and Materials* (Oxford: Oxford Press, 2015); and M. Freeman, 'Taking Children's Rights More Seriously,' *International Journal of Law and the Family* 6 (1992).

run high as to what is in the best interest of the child, and these feelings are coloured – almost commanded – by the personal convictions, experiences, and motivations of the judge, lawyer, or parent involved. This is apparent as custody submissions or decisions can easily be influenced as much by anecdotal or biblical reasoning as professional reports, to justify the stance that is being taken.

There is, in fact, no shortage of national, regional, and international works that examine the Caribbean and the Jamaican family from all perspectives.[14] The difficulty arises when one has to forge the links between the social scientist in the strict sense and the legal/social reformer who has drafting and/or legislative responsibility. As such, the main statutory provisions in this area are in need of review.

CUSTODY LEGISLATION IN JAMAICA

Jamaica follows a pattern that is found in most Commonwealth Caribbean jurisdictions where there is legislation specifically designated to address custody and guardianship,[15] and additional powers to grant custody found in other statutes such as divorce legislation.[16] This will usually have the effect of giving the high court and the summary courts the power to make custody orders depending on the nature of the proceedings. However, in Jamaica, the Children (Guardianship and Custody) Act itself allows for applications to be made in the Supreme Court and also in the Parish or Family Court. This is to be compared with countries such as Antigua and Barbuda, St Kitts and Nevis, and Anguilla where the Minors Act which deals specifically with custody and guardianship questions restricts applications to be made in the high court alone. In those countries, the power to make custody orders in the Magistrates'

---

14. See Bibliography, for example, Mary DeChesnay, 'Jamaican Family Structure: The Paradox of Normalcy,' 1986; Delores E. Smith and Gail Mosby, 'Jamaican Child Rearing Practices: The Role of Corporal Punishment,' *Adolescence* 38, no. 150 (2003).

15. See Minors Act, Antigua and Barbuda; Guardianship of Infants, St Kitts and Nevis, etc.

16. Divorce Acts of Antigua and Barbuda and St Kitts and Nevis; Supreme Court of Judicature Act, Belize.

Court is derived from the Magistrates' Code of Procedure Act. In this way, the same result is achieved by a different route, which is essentially that the power to grant custody orders is vested in both tiers of the court in every jurisdiction.

The Children (Guardianship and Custody) Act

The Children (Guardianship and Custody) Act 1957 is the statute which, in keeping with its title, governs the court's powers to make custody orders and grant legal guardianship.

The provisions regarding custody are preceded by those that deal with the appointment of legal guardians.[17] The Act gives jurisdiction to both the high court and lower courts and most importantly, sets out the welfare principle. The Act also gives some guidance to the court when dealing with custody matters and allows the court to make maintenance orders persuant to certain custody orders.

The Matrimonial Causes Act

The court is also given the power to make custody orders as ancillary relief in matrimonial proceedings under the Matrimonial Causes Act (MCA).[18] This Act, therefore, allows parents who are married to have the court adjudicate and settle the question of custody of any relevant child at the time that they are seeking to terminate the marriage.[19] Unlike the Children (Guardianship and Custody) Act, there is no guidance given to the court as to applicable principles, and the court is simply permitted to 'make such order as it thinks just'.[20] Proceedings under the MCA can only be heard in the high court, so this represents an additional power to the main Act since it will always be convenient for the court to entertain all matters concerning the family at the time that the parties are

---

17. Sections 3, 4, and 5.
18. Section 23.
19. Sections 23(1)(a) and (b) speak of before, by or after the final decree, and within a reasonable time of the dismissal of any proceedings.
20. Nevertheless, the application of section 18 of the Children (Guardianship and Custody) Act would be applicable.

getting divorced. Proceedings under section 23 of the MCA are, by definition, ancillary to the central proceedings concerned with the termination of the marriage, so that proceedings for termination of the marriage or an application under section 10 must be started before the court can hear an application for custody. Under the MCA, either party to the proceedings can apply for orders under section 23 and, therefore, where a child becomes a relevant child through acceptance into a family, it would still be open to the non-biological parent to apply for custody if he/she so wishes.

THE CHILDREN (GUARDIANSHIP AND CUSTODY) ACT – DEFINITIONS

Child, under the Children (Guardianship and Custody) Act, is an unmarried person under the age of 18.[21] However, when the Act deals with the court's power to grant maintenance pursuant to making a custody order, the court can extend the order beyond the age of 18 under the provisions of sections 7A and 7B.[22] It can only be presumed that, under this Act, a child is the biological or adopted child of the mother or the father, since these terms are not defined in the interpretation section.

Unlike the MCA that recognizes the parental status of the parties by virtue of marriage and hence the right to apply for custody,[23] under the Children (Guardianship and Custody) Act there is no requirement for the parties to be married, the Act simply uses the terms 'mother' and 'father'. While the term 'parent' is used in the body of the Act, neither father, mother, nor parent is defined. Perhaps this is because at the time that the law was enacted neither science nor the perspective of the court had advanced to where it is today. By comparison,[24] the Maintenance Act recognizes a person as a parent

---

21. Section 2.
22. Payment of maintenance pursuant to a custody order.
23. Section 23 MCA.
24. Although it can also be argued that because two laws arise in different ways, they should not be compared.

by virtue of several other relationships in addition[25] to a biological connection. In a historical context, it is understandable that the Children (Guardianship and Custody) Act should be consistent with the common law of the times which was that custodial rights vested in the biological parents.[26] The later legislation is less restrictive and reflects the shift in perspective to a 'child-centred' approach where parents do not automatically get custodial rights to a child but instead a duty or 'parental responsibility' to care for the child. So, under the Maintenance Act, a child may not be the child of the person who has a duty to maintain him/her; and under the MCA a child may not be the child of the person who may apply for custody of him/her. This is because the later law is directed towards the care of the child rather than the exercise of rights by the parents.

THE WELFARE PRINCIPLE

'The welfare of the child is paramount'. This phrase is intoned with monotonous regularity in the practice of family law. It is usually stated by a judge in a manner that brooks no argument and most practitioners will accept this proposition as sacrosanct and not subject to qualification. However, the Children (Guardianship and Custody) Act which codifies the principle in Jamaican law is quite specific about the circumstances in which the welfare of the child is, in fact, paramount. These circumstances are any proceedings before any court where:

i.   the custody or upbringing of a child, or

ii. the administration of any property belonging to or held in trust for a child or the application of the income thereof[27] are being considered.

---

25.   Section 8(3).
26.   Having previously been vested in the father alone for a child born in wedlock, see *Re Agar-Ellis* (1883) 24 Ch D 317 and the mother alone for a child born out of wedlock, see *Clarke v Carey* (1971) 18 WIR 70.
27.   Section 18.

Custody or Upbringing

The welfare principle is the first and paramount consideration in the case of applications made under the Act,[28] and also custody applications under section 23 of the MCA. So, in the main applications – custody and guardianship – and in the subsidiary questions such as access, education, religious training, and medical treatment, the welfare of the child is once again first and paramount. Interestingly, no reference is made to the principle in the adoption legislation although there is reference to acting 'in the best interests of the child', and this is usually treated by the courts in Jamaica as an interchangeable statement of the welfare principle if only because adoption is central to the question of upbringing.

Administration of Property

This second area of application of the welfare principle concerns children's property. This is defined broadly to include trust property and the income therefrom. This situation will often arise where a child is the beneficiary under a settlement, in which case the trust deed will appoint persons to handle the assets with the welfare of the child being at the forefront when making their decisions. If the need arises, a trustee can refer a question to the court which may give directions or even appoint trustees to ensure the proper management of the assets (property or shares, or accounts) so as to provide the child with the funds that he needs, but at the same time to make sure that the money is not frittered away or siphoned off for the benefit of others. The same would apply to the situation where a child receives payment for musical or dramatic performances.

Probate and Damages

The principle will intrude on other areas outside of family law such as tort where, for example, as a result of personal injuries sustained by the child, damages are awarded. It will also have application

---

28.   *Forsythe v Jones* SCCA No 49/1999 6/4/2001.

where an estate is being administered and there are beneficiaries of tender years. In both these examples, the property that belongs to the child is easy to ascertain. The court should, therefore, have little difficulty in applying this principle and ensuring that the welfare of the child is at the forefront of any arrangements that have been put in place which will ensure that the child gets the benefit of the assets in question.

Matrimonial Property

The question of what belongs to the children of a marriage is not so readily ascertainable when family property is being divided upon the termination of a marriage or at the end of cohabitation. The Property (Rights of Spouses) Act, like the Maintenance Act, does not acknowledge the welfare principle in any respect and follows a similar format to the Maintenance Act of listing facts and circumstances that are to be taken into account, which do not include welfare.[29] The need to provide a home for the children of the marriage or cohabitation is recognized as a priority without resorting to the application of the welfare principle.[30] In this regard, the Jamaican law does not even make this factor a first consideration.[31] The courts in the UK have been at pains to stress that welfare as a first consideration does not mean paramount, and to explain how this works in practice.[32]

Welfare and Maintenance

The question then arises, are there proceedings apart from those mentioned that would come under 'upbringing' to which the welfare principle applies?[33] The courts in Jamaica routinely include maintenance in this category. It is certainly possible to argue that

---

29. Section 14(2).
30. Section 7(2)(b), section 15(1)(c), and section 23(1)(n).
31. Compare with section 25(1) of the UK MCA.
32. *Suter v Suter and Jones* [1987] 2 FLR 232.
33. Or is the term 'upbringing' broadly or narrowly construed?

if the maintenance order is being made under this Act[34] that is pursuant to a custody order, then the welfare principle should not lapse simply because the court is dealing with financial aspects of care. However, the Maintenance Act itself does not acknowledge the welfare principle at all.[35] Even while listing exhaustively the factors to be taken into account in sections 9 and 14, there is no incorporation of the welfare principle.

There are good reasons for not imposing the welfare principle as paramount when maintenance is in question, even if it can properly be seen as a first consideration. First, maintenance is always set in the context of the financial capacity of the person who has an obligation. This, it may be argued, is the paramount principle when it comes to these proceedings, which automatically subordinates the welfare principle. Second, being a dependant or person to whom an obligation is owed, cannot put that person (even if he is a minor) in a position of first and/or paramount consideration because there may be others who are equally entitled. In the Family Court, respondents frequently claim in response to an application being made against them that they have other children to maintain and cannot find the additional funds to support yet another child. While the court is anxious not to encourage an irresponsible lifestyle and recognizes that no child whether born first, last, in wedlock, or out of it, is any less entitled to be maintained,[36] it is difficult to see how the paramountcy of the welfare principle can comfortably be housed in such circumstances. The absence of the principle in the Maintenance Act may be said to be a recognition of this. Of course, it is possible to contend that the welfare principle would be included under the 'catch all' provisions of paragraph (m) of section 14(2), but it would be less than ideal to incorporate such an important principle in this manner. In any event, it would probably have to be

---

34.   Under Section 7(3).
35.   Section 18 of the Children (Guardianship and Custody) Act speaks of 'any Court' but not applications under any act.
36.   While the court might frown on such irresponsibility, the question is, is maintenance imposed to punish the father or provide for the children?

recognized as a 'first' rather than a 'paramount' consideration in such circumstances.[37]

Is maintenance pursuant to a custody order under the Children (Guardianship and Custody) Act any different from one made under the Maintenance Act or the MCA in respect of the applicability of the welfare principle? In other jurisdictions, it has been stated that the welfare principle, although obviously a factor to be taken into account when considering applications for maintenance, it will not be paramount.[38] This has not been specifically acknowledged by a court in Jamaica to date. It is easy to see that the urge to do what is right from a practical standpoint could prompt a court towards concluding that the welfare principle should indeed be applied as paramount in maintenance cases simply because a child is involved. However, the court may need to resolve the particular issue some other way.

Even in strict custody questions, the issue of competing interests has given rise to some exceedingly difficult cases elsewhere, such as the case of the conjoined twins in the UK,[39] with which, the Jamaican courts fortunately have not had to contend. The judgments in cases like this make it clear that the welfare principle is by no means a simple concept or a panacea for all ills.

The Welfare Checklist

Following a recommendation in a law commission report,[40] the English law introduced a checklist of factors to be considered when applying the welfare principle. They were set out in the Children Act 1989 and have been adopted elsewhere both expressly in statute[41] and impliedly through the common law in custody decisions throughout the Commonwealth. They are:

37. UK, Domestic Proceedings and Magistrates' Courts Act, section 20.
38. *K v H* (Child Maintenance) [1993] 2 FLR 61.
39. *Re A* (Conjoined Twins) [2001] 2 WLR 480, see also *Birmingham CC v H* (A Minor) [1994] 2 AC 212, and *T and E* (Proceedings: Conflicting Interests) [1995] 1 FLR 581.
40. The Law Commission, 'Family Law, Review of Child Law: Custody' (London: Her Majesty's Stationery Office, 1986).
41. Families and Children Act, Belize.

1. the ascertainable wishes and feelings of the child concerned (considered in the light of his or her age and understanding);

2. his or her physical, emotional and educational needs;

3. the likely effect of any change in circumstances;

4. his or her age, sex and background and any characteristics of his or hers which the court considers relevant;

5. any harm which he or she has suffered, or is at risk of suffering;

6. how capable each if his or her parents – and any other person in relation to whom the court considers the question to be relevant – is of meeting his or her needs; and

7. the range of powers available to the court in the proceedings in question.[42]

This deconstruction of the welfare principle has been adopted by the courts in Jamaica in deciding cases where the principle is applicable.[43] Although not officially set out, it provides a useful reference to guide both practitioners and the court towards comprehensively examining the issues. This is to be contrasted with Belize where a welfare checklist has been adopted into statute.[44]

The Jamaican courts have fully embraced the welfare principle, as have most Commonwealth jurisdictions. Its standing is almost unimpeachable, and the courts have relied on it as a powerful weapon in support of any of its pronouncement or otherwise. As the judiciary reaches further and further, taking the welfare principle along as a willing but sometimes overstretched talisman, the principle itself will come under greater scrutiny. Furthermore, the welfare principle can be used to entrench antiquated positions, or break new ground, with equal cogency. As such, we may begin to question whether the welfare principle is the objective criterion that it professes to be or simply a cloak with which to cover our prejudices and agenda, albeit along with our best intentions.[45]

42. The Children Act 1980, UK.
43. *F v B* 2702/2010 19/09/11.
44. Families and Children Act.
45. 'The Paramountcy Principle: Consensus or Construct?' H. Reece, CLP 49 (1996) 267.

CUSTODY

Section 7 of the Children (Guardianship and Custody) Act gives the court the power to make custody orders. The court[46] is the Supreme Court, the Family Court, or the Resident Magistrates' (now Parish) Court. In the summary courts, the power exists where the applicant, respondent, or the child lives in the parish over which the court has jurisdiction.

The term custody is not defined in the Act and as such, the nature of the duty that a custodial parent has to a child is all-encompassing and entirely unspecified.[47] The practice of the Jamaican courts, in recognizing that questions such as where shall the child live, how is the child to be educated, etc., fall under the ambit of custody comes about through the application of the common law. The right to decide on the child's religion is given singular attention in the Act.[48]

The application for custody can be made by the mother or the father of a child. There is, however, no definition of the terms used, and there is no mention of whether this includes persons who assume the responsibilities of parent by marriage.[49] By comparison, the definition of relevant child under the MCA includes a child who has been accepted by a party to a marriage. Section 23 of the MCA, therefore, would permit a custody application by a step-parent. It would appear, however, that notwithstanding an expanded definition of parent in sections 12–14 of the Children (Guardianship and Custody) Act, in the absence of a liberal interpretation of mother and father, step-parents may not apply for custody under the Children (Guardianship and Custody) Act.

The law was enacted in the 1950s at a time when the mother's status before the court was not generally considered to be equal

---

46.   Section 2.
47.   Compare with the Child Care and Protection Act, sections 2(2) and (3) and 51.
48.   Section 15.
49.   See the definition of Relevant Child in the Matrimonial Causes Act.

to that of the father.[50] This Act can be seen as a forerunner to legislation such as the Maintenance Act and the Property (Rights of Spouses) Act (PROSA) by seeking to erase the distinction between fathers and mothers for the purposes of applications for custody. This is continued in section 7(1) of the Act, but when considering the award of maintenance after the court has determined the question of custody the traditional assumptions resurface.[51] This was entirely in keeping with the legal norms of the time, but is archaic in the twenty-first century.

Legal Custody

Legal custody,[52] which is the right to make the important decisions regarding the upbringing of the child, is not usually uppermost in the minds of the parties to a custody dispute. They may be more concerned with the issue of 'care and control',[53] that is, who the child is to live with. Nevertheless, the question of legal custody is the starting point for the court in considering an application for custody. It is usually only upon separation, termination of the marriage, or cohabitation that the court is called upon to decide issues of custody. At that time, the court is looking at which of the parents should take responsibility for the child. The general view in the past was that if the parties were in conflict and antagonistic towards each other, a joint legal custody order – that is, custody to both parents with care and control to one of them – was not advisable.[54] The thinking behind this approach was that the level of co-operation required for a joint order to be effective did not exist, and therefore it was better to have the person making the decisions to also have legal custody.[55] This view has been superseded in recent times by a different approach, namely that joint custody orders are

---

50.   Section 6.
51.   Section 7(3).
52.   This is not defined in the Act.
53.   This is not defined in the Act. See UK, Australian, and New Zealand legislation.
54.   *Clissold v Clissold* (1964) 108 Sol Jo 220.
55.   *Jussa v Jussa* [1972] 2 All ER 600.

in the best interests of the child.[56] From a practical standpoint, the wisdom of this way of resolving the matter depends on the maturity of the parties and the state of their relationship, and the court has been inclined to place much weight on this factor.[57] Even so, such orders can serve as a catalyst in bringing about a more collaborative approach to parenting by separated parties. In some cases, however, the court's tendency to grant joint legal custody in the majority of cases can be exploited by a party who delights in being as contentious as possible, as a means of maintaining a presence in the other parent's life, rather than out of concerns for the balanced development of the child. However, each case is essentially decided on its own merits and to that extent the court may, depending on the circumstances, arrive at the view that there is full justification for a sole custody order to be made.[58] A notable exception to the tendency to grant joint custody orders is in the case of allegations of sexual molestation. In such circumstances, the court is likely to take a more cautious approach and will lean in favour of granting sole custody even where the allegations are not established.[59] In these situations it can be difficult to identify a trend.

The court's readiness to grant joint legal custody is frequently applied when the parents are not married to each other, even though traditionally the custodial right to a child born to unmarried parents lies with the mother alone.[60] In this situation, the father may apply for an order for custody that brings him into the child's life in a legally recognizable and enforceable manner. The application will be heard applying the welfare principle, and in this way if an order for joint custody is made the father will acquire the same rights as those which vest automatically in the father where the parents are married.

---

56. See Ormrod LJ in *Dipper v Dipper* [1980] 2 All ER 722 CA. Also see *Hurst v Hurst* [1984] FLR 867.
57. *Fish v Kennedy* [2003] 0373, per Marsh J. For a recent example, see *F v D* [2017] JMSC Civ. 9.
58. See the case of *Mrs. S v Mr. S* [2016] JMSC 224.
59. *AH v JH* [2014] JMSC Civ 68.
60. For example see *Re Lewis* (1970) 15 WIR 520, per Douglas CJ at 521.

A father who shows interest and willingness to be involved in the child's upbringing and is candid to the court, is unlikely to be denied custody according to the new custodial dispensation because it will generally be in the child's best interests to have contact with both parents. In this way, a balance can be struck between the interests of the child and parental rights. At present, in Jamaica, the courts have been content to allow the welfare of the child to override every position that is in keeping with the terms of section 18. This issue is exemplified in the UK in *Re E* 1997 FLR 638 and is mirrored in the case of *BP v RP* in the Jamaican Court of Appeal.[61]

In these cases, the Court of Appeal in both countries accepted that the welfare principle itself must, to some extent, take into account other factors concerning the parents.[62]

In Jamaica, the required co-operation and consultation that is necessary from the parents when a joint custody order is made tends to be sorely tested when questions of schooling and residency arise. In the former case, the question is as much a financial issue as it is an upbringing issue. The court may be asked to order the payment of expensive educational fees to fulfill the ambitions of one parent who also expects to be financed by maintenance payments from the other parent, who was not in agreement with the educational plans in the first place, particularly where there are satisfactory and less costly alternatives.[63]

In relation to residency, whereas the courts were at one time more inclined to the view that the chance to live abroad was a positive factor, this is no longer the case. The courts are increasingly cognizant that, for some families, the standard of living, and particularly of education, may be higher for the child if he remains in Jamaica.[64] In

---

61. SCCA 51/2008 30/07/09 .
62. *Smith v Orrigio* (1989) 26 JLR 561; competing parental interests versus the welfare principle.
63. The courts have devised imaginative formulae for arriving at a fair approach to these questions.
64. Unfortunately the instances of children who are sent to parents abroad being abused are beginning to rival those of children achieving academic success, see *Daily Gleaner*, December 1, 2014.

this way, the court becomes a useful check on the parent's unbridled desire to live in a foreign country, and balances it with a careful assessment of the best interests of the child.[65] This, of course, is also applicable to the wishes of the state in deportation cases.[66]

Care and Control

This is the heart of the contention in most custody disputes between parents – who will the child live with. In several other jurisdictions care and control is now termed 'residence'. The Jamaican courts, as in all jurisdictions that have embraced the welfare principle, have been at pains to disabuse the parties of the notion that the child is a prize to be fought over. It is not about 'who gets the child', but what residential circumstances suit the best interests of the child. The courts recognize that a parent's suitability to have the child reside with him/her is not automatically determined by the degree of affluence, even though a lot of parents, particularly fathers, believe this to be the case and may use their superior position to intimidate the one who is in a weaker financial state. In the case of *Re McGrath* (Infants),[67] it was stated 'the welfare of the child is not measured by money only, or by physical comfort only. The word welfare must be taken in its widest sense….' Similarly, a parent who lives in the city is not automatically in a better position than a parent who lives in a rural community, though there may be other factors that tip the balance one way or another. Legal principles such as reluctance to separate closely bonded siblings and close scrutiny of separating a young child from its mother[68] are routinely applied.[69] In short, what in other jurisdictions, including Belize, is called the welfare checklist,[70] is readily embraced and employed by the Jamaican

---

65. See below.
66. See *N and N v AG* (2004) 65 WIR 372.
67. [1893] 1 Ch. 143.
68. But see *Lord v Lord* (1981) 18 JLR 288; and *Simpson v Condappa* (1988) 25 JLR 44.
69. Not found in the custody legislation, but see Child Care and Protection Act, sections 2(2) and (3).
70. Belize, Families and Children Act; First Schedule, paragraph 3.

courts when making these decisions. Therefore, as set out in the Belize legislation, in determining any question to which the welfare principle applies, the court or any other person shall have regard to the checklist.[71]

This is to be compared with section 2(2) of the Child Care and Protection Act in Jamaica that reflects a similar set of criteria under the head of 'the best interests of the child'.[72] That several statutory renditions of what is essentially the welfare principle are available to the Jamaican courts shows a need for comprehensive custody and child care legislation to simplify this area.

Nevertheless, the care and custody circumstances of many children may be determined without the intervention of the court. In the past, particularly in rural environs, it was not unusual for parties to agree that the mother would take the girls, and the father, the boys. There are many reasons for this which would have as much to do with traditional child-rearing mores as with views about division of labour.[73] While this is by no means always the case, the situations where girls end up in the care of the sole male parent generally occur when the mother is either unwilling or unable to care for them, rather than as a decision arrived at by mutual agreement.

We see, therefore, that the welfare checklist has made its way into Jamaican case law other than by statute, but nevertheless, in a practical sense, it operates alongside the personal practices and convictions of the parents who will apply their own test in arriving at the best way to raise a child.

Custody, Child Abduction, and the Jurisdiction of the Court

The courts in Jamaica have had to turn their attention to the impact of the parents living in different jurisdictions in the course of deciding custody disputes. The court's approach to this has

71. *F v B.* 2702/2010 19/9/11.
72. This terminology is supported by article 3(1) of The Convention of the Rights of the Child, 1989.
73. Children assisting with 'marketing', light farming, etc.

developed through a number of cases. The case of *Thompson*[74] was concerned with an application for custody by a father in Jamaica, in circumstances where the mother had been granted custody in another jurisdiction in the course of a divorce settlement. The judge in awarding custody to the father put great emphasis on the domicile and nationality of the applicant and the child. Even though it is only right that the courts should recognize the rights of its citizens where access to the courts is concerned, it does not follow that the matter will be decided in their favour because of this. The cases decided after *Thompson* did not place the same level of significance on domicile as a deciding factor.

The case of *Grant v Robinson*[75] took the issue a step further in setting the factors of nationality and domicile against each other and introducing *forum non conveniens* to this branch of the law. Both parties were Jamaican nationals, but (then) Sykes J's view was that the proper forum ought to be either of the countries in which they resided. This meant that in the ordinary scheme of things, the mere fact of Jamaican nationality would not determine the appropriate jurisdiction in which the case should be decided. In finding for the respondent father, the judge said, 'a court does not lightly deny it's nationals, but given that the overriding concern must be the welfare of the child, if there is some hope of enhancing the welfare of the child by declining jurisdiction then that ought to be done.' Sykes' reliance on the welfare principle in order to decide whether or not the court would accept jurisdiction to hear the custody application was the starting point from which this concept was fully developed in the case of *Panton v Panton*.[76]

Panton is evidence of the court beginning to reject *forum non conveniens* as an unhelpful import from private international law, which did not necessarily assist in the proper resolution of these applications. It was in this case, that the welfare of the child was

---

74.   (1993) 30 JLR 414.
75.   2079/2004 16/09/2004.
76.   SCCA 21/06 29/11/06.

confirmed as the paramount principle at the stage of deciding which court the case should be heard in; even before getting to the merits of the case itself.[77] A matter of months later, the Court of Appeal once again had reason to deliberate on custody and jurisdiction in the case of *Forrester v Strong Forrester*.[78] The intensity of the parties' allegations against each other was considerable, and the court was being asked to consider if there was kidnapping or wrongful retention of the children. This raised the question of whether or not a summary return order should be made and finally whether or not Jamaica was the appropriate forum to hear the substantive claim. The case highlights the difficulty for countries like Jamaica that did not have an established protocol for dealing with child abduction, or are not signatories to international treaties such as The Hague Convention.[79] The fact that Jamaica is a signatory to the Convention but had not enacted legislation to give effect to its provisions in the local law allowed for the possibility of an inconsistent approach by the courts, and in these cases where time is of the essence,[80] adjudication could be protracted because whichever way a judge at first instance decides, the 'loser' is likely to have the means to take the matter to appeal. There has recently[81] been an amendment to the Children (Guardianship and Custody) Act to incorporate the terms of the Convention.[82]

Consideration of the cases in this area would be incomplete without reference to the case of *B.P. v R.P.*[83] This is an example of the Jamaican Court of Appeal recognizing that although welfare is

---

77. See also *Williamson v Williamson* SCCA 51/2007 and see M. Georgia Gibson-Henlin and Suzanne Risden-Foster, 'Flight or Right? Custody and Access in International Child Abduction Cases: Emerging Issues in Jamaica,' http://henlin.pro/uploads/articles/Flight%20or%20Right.pdf.
78. SCCA 101/2007 2/05/2008.
79. Convention of October 25, 1980 on the Civil Aspects of International Child Abduction: www.hcch.net.
80. The longer the child stays with the abductor, the greater the chance of a court saying that the welfare demands that the child should not be uprooted again, see Australian case, *Kress and Kress* (1976) 2 Fam LR 11,330 per Golstein J.
81. January 2017.
82. Children (Guardianship and Custody) (Amendment) Act 2017.
83. SCCA 51/2008 30/07/2009.

paramount, other factors, in this case the wishes of the mother to return to her homeland, could affect the welfare of the child and have a bearing on the court's decision. Another way of looking at the decision in this case is that the wishes of the parent, in this regard, has a substantial impact on the welfare of the child and therefore cannot be ignored. In this case, it was held that the mother's psychological and emotional stability would be adversely affected by having to remain in Jamaica and this, in turn, would not enhance the welfare of the child. This case also shows how the courts' views have changed since the case of *Hohn v Hohn and Robinson*.[84]

Custody, Residence, and Third Parties

The wording of section 7 allows the court to 'make such order as it may think fit regarding custody'. This allows for custody to be granted to a third party, such as a grandparent, even if the application had been made by the father or the mother. It would appear that if the application is being made after the death of either parent or of any guardian, then according to the wording of section 7, the application may be made by someone other than the father or mother of the child as well as the order being in favour of someone other than the father or mother. Generally, if both parents are alive, the court will grant custody to one or both of them, but could grant care and control to a third party, which will mean that the child would actually live with someone other than the parties to the proceedings. This is usually another relative such as an aunt or grandparents, so that the decision-making power (custody) would remain with the parents with care and control to the third party.

Care and control devolves from legal custody and, as such, it is the parent (or parents) with legal custody that authorizes care and control. In several other jurisdictions, care and control is now termed 'residence'. It is because care and control is a derivative of legal custody that the court is unlikely to make an order granting

---

84. (1979) 16 JLR 364; children to stay in Jamaica.

legal custody to one parent and care and control to the other as it is would undermine the exercise of the powers implicit in both terms. The Act at sections 12–14 makes reference to third parties bringing up a child and a parent's right to re-claim the child in the circumstances outlined. If a parent is unfit to care for a child then the court may allow the child to stay with that person by virtue of not making a custody order in favour of the parent. The Act nevertheless stops short of allowing that person to apply for or be granted legal custody except under the circumstances prescribed under section 7. This position is to be contrasted with section 29 of the MCA,[85] which seems to be a statutory provision that acknowledges the court's power to act to protect children.[86] In such proceedings, the court assumes parental powers over the child, which are then exercised by placing the child with someone who is subject to the control of the court.[87]

Financial Support when Making Custody Orders

When the court makes a custody order in favour of the mother, it then has powers to make an order that the father pays maintenance.[88] The maintenance order may last until the child is aged 21,[89] and once the child is 18 years of age, the money is payable directly to the child. Even if the order made prior to the child attaining the age of 18 has lapsed, it can be renewed and remain in force until the child is 21.[90] Orders under this section cease to have effect if the parties live together for three months or more, and are unenforceable for any period that the parties are living together.[91] Either of the parties may apply for variation or discharge of the order.[92] The court's

---

85.   Where the court has the power to commit a child to the care of an independent
        person under the supervision of a welfare officer.
86.   Wardship.
87.   This has come to the attention of the court when considering guardianship
        applications, see below.
88.   Section 7(3).
89.   Section 7A(c).
90.   Section 7B(1).
91.   Section 7(4).
92.   Section 7(5).

power to award maintenance under section 7(3) in subsections 7A and 7B is an extremely important provision. It provides the convenience of accompanying financial relief with granting custody orders. However, the court's power to grant maintenance only arises if custody is given to the mother, in which case maintenance is to be paid by the father. As such, it would appear that these provisions are inconsistent with the gender-neutral approach of the Maintenance Act that promotes joint responsibility as between the mother and father of a child. Interestingly, when the Act turns to the extension of such an order under section 7B, it states, inter alia, that:

> The Court may...make an order requiring either parent to pay to the other parent or to the said person...such sums towards his maintenance as having regards to the means of the person ordered to make the payment, the Court thinks reasonable.

Also, the criteria to be used when deciding the question of maintenance are somewhat basic when compared with the extensive and varied criteria in the Maintenance Act.[93] Indeed, the court has had to rely on old common law cases to get around the limiting effects of phrases such as 'having regard to the means of the father'.[94] At the time that this Act came into force, the duty to maintain rested entirely on the father unless certain exceptional circumstances existed.[95] The need to have a consistent approach to custody and the consequent maintenance orders in the face of the disparity between the Children (Guardianship and Custody) Act and the Maintenance Act 2005, has led to a liberal, and perhaps inappropriate, application of the court's inherent jurisdiction and the welfare principle in order to fill the lacunae left by Parliament's failure to enact suitable amendments.

The confused position as to custody and maintenance is further compounded by the fact that section 23 of the MCA allows the

---

93.   This should have been addressed when the Maintenance Act was being considered in Parliament.
94.   Section 7(3), for example *Re T (an infant)* [1953] Ch D 789.
95.   Maintenance Act 1881, section 2.

court to make custody and maintenance orders in the course of divorce proceedings. Therefore, the range of options detailing which orders to seek, under which statutes, in which court, and in the course of which proceedings are all relevant questions to be carefully considered in the process of deciding how to proceed.

Custody Agreements

Custody agreements are recognized in Jamaican statute by section 11 of the Act. The section acknowledges agreements in the form of 'separation deeds', and states the circumstances in which their validity will be upheld. It may be that the implied nature of the recognition given in section 11 has contributed to a seeming reluctance to embrace separation agreements as a standard procedure in Jamaica.[96] However, one explanation may be that agreements properly arrived at and adhered to, have resulted in little court intervention indicating that these agreements are being used successfully.[97] Section 11 supports the position that a separation agreement cannot oust the jurisdiction of the court. Under the Act, the court will not allow an agreement to take effect if it runs contrary to 'the benefit of the child'.[98] It is not clear why there is a departure from the phraseology of the welfare principle as enunciated in section 18. Even after the agreement has taken effect, it will still be open to the court to reconsider the arrangements and replace them with its own orders.[99] Leighton Jackson[100] endorses the parent's power to make custody agreements, recognizing that the parties are more likely to honour an agreement. Certainly it would appear that, this is a mechanism that could be utilized more with proper training for social workers and legal representatives.

---

96. Compare Barbados where agreements are positively endorsed under the Family Law Act.
97. For a notable exception, see *Edwards v Edwards* (1990) 27 JLR 374.
98. See the proviso under section 11.
99. *AH v JH* [2014] JMSC Civ 68.
100. 'The Law Relating to Children in Jamaica: Report on Guardianship and Custody,' Ministry of Justice , Jamaica - UNICEF.

It was not until 2005 in the Maintenance Act that agreements were given express endorsement in law. It is stipulated that maintenance agreements inter alia, 'make provision in respect of the support rights and obligations of the parties with regard to…any child that either party has an obligation to maintain….'[101] The Act goes on to specify that the provisions of the agreement may include: 'the right to direct the education and moral training of their children'.[102] So, in this way, it would appear that the close association of custody with maintenance dictates that custody matters can properly be dealt with maintenance agreements.

Section 24 of the Maintenance Act states that agreements can be made by spouses 'in contemplation of their marriage to each other or of cohabiting…' and are therefore pre-nuptial or pre-cohabitation. For the purposes of custody therefore, agreements in anticipation of a union are recognized under the Maintenance Act, but it is only agreements on separation that are referred to in the Children (Guardianship and Custody) Act. Furthermore, this raises the question of whether the courts will impute the conditions for the making of a valid agreement from section 24 into section 11. That agreements arise in a piecemeal way in the Jamaican family legislation may present the opportunity for fine distinctions to be made, requiring a creative approach if technical objections to validity are to be avoided. For example, what would be the status of an agreement which addresses property and custody and maintenance of children and spousal maintenance? By which act would it be interpreted and how would this be affected by the nature of the proceedings and how the action commenced? The preferable course would be for Parliament to bring coherence to the issue with consistent statutory provisions in all the relevant legislation.[103] Without legislative intervention the court is likely to deal with these issues in an ad hoc and therefore unsatisfactory way.

---

101.   Section 24(2)(a).
102.   Section 24(2)(b).
103.   As has been the case with the Maintenance Act and the Property (Rights of Spouses) Act.

Custody and Inherent Jurisdiction

The inherent jurisdiction of the high court exists because that court derives its powers from the English sovereign. In historic times, the inherent power of the court was considerable but was reined in by statute dating as far back as the Magna Carta. Over the centuries, statute has almost completely superseded the inherent jurisdiction of the court with a few notable exceptions. In family law, a particular type of inherent power, namely the court's power to act in protection of the vulnerable, especially children, continues to be of considerable importance. It is derived from the power of the monarch to act as *parens patriae*. In the UK, inherent power finds expression in wardship proceedings when a child may be made a ward of court so that the court can then exercise parental powers in relation to the child.

Inherent powers are residual and, as such, can only be invoked where there is no statutory provision enabling the court to act in such circumstances. It is not a means by which legislative powers are enhanced or lacunae filled; that is a matter for Parliament. Inherent powers are essentially what remain of those powers which have not been specifically curtailed, whether impliedly or explicitly, by the passage of law. This limitation ensures that the court does not trespass on the legislative responsibility of the state.

In recent times, the Jamaican high court has demonstrated a willingness to resort to the inherent jurisdiction of the court and its equally useful mechanism, the welfare principle, as a means of filling loopholes and 'doing justice to the case' where children are concerned.[104] This is an area that could benefit from further examination and measured consideration by the court where the reasoning of the court is not overshadowed by the desire to achieve a particular result in the case. In *PEC v DRC*, the court expressed reluctance to 'be hampered by procedural trappings'; but is the

---

104.   The case of *Campbell v Campbell* 528/2000 4/4/2008 is an example of the application of this type of reasoning.

application of an express statutory provision to be relegated to a mere procedural trapping simply because it does not produce the desired result?

In this case the court sought to remedy Parliament's failure to amend the Children (Guardianship and Custody) Act when the Maintenance Act became law. The court imputed the factors applicable under the Maintenance Act into consideration where an application was being heard pursuant to the Children (Guardianship and Custody) Act under what was declared to be its inherent powers. The welfare of the child was put forward as justification for this approach. Despite the good intentions of the trial judge, this is not the best way of resolving the problem at hand. The court has, in some instances, relied on its inherent powers to overcome substantial procedural deficiencies to make an order that was thought to be appropriate. To commandeer inherent jurisdiction to wield and shape the legislation to a desired result is a forthright step. Not only can the court be led into dangerous waters, but using the welfare principle as the reason for taking this route makes the exercise look more like the waving of a magic wand than the application of a legal principle.

A more legally stringent approach was taken in the case of *Butler v Butler*[105] where Harrison J (Ag) relied on the common law[106] rather than inherent jurisdiction.

So where is the inherent jurisdiction to be found and how is it to be exercised? It is expressly preserved for guardianship under the Children (Guardianship and Custody) Act but not in relation to custody.[107] It would therefore appear from that Act that no inherent jurisdiction remains in pure custody cases. In addition, the Matrimonial Causes Act also recognizes and retains the inherent powers of the court.

Section 23 of the MCA states inter alia:

---

105.   1982/B099.
106.   *Re T (Infant)* [1953] Ch D 789.
107.   Section 20.

> ...in any case in which the court had power by virtue of paragraph (a) to make an order in respect of a child, the court may if it thinks fit, direct that proper proceedings be taken for placing the child under the protection of the court.

The phrase 'under the protection of the court' is a clear reference to the inherent jurisdiction of the court as *parens patriae*. The provision indicates that it is not a general power, but one which may be exercised if making orders for 'custody, maintenance and education of any child...' where they arise in proceedings set out in paragraph (a). Furthermore, the power is to be exercised by way of a direction that 'proper proceedings be taken' which does not allow for random invocations without more.[108] It would be expected that, in such circumstances, the court would alert the parties directing that proceedings be instituted to place the child under the court's protection. The similarity between this provision and wardship proceedings in other jurisdictions is marked. The court would also presumably give reasons for directing such a course. The question then arises as to what would be proper proceedings, and section 29 of the MCA provides the answer; the child may be placed with 'an independent person' under the supervision of a welfare officer.

As a matter of practice, the court is rarely inclined to exercise those powers under sections 23 and 29 because it places a heavy burden on the social services. The scope of the court's inherent jurisdiction has only recently come to the attention of the appellate court[109] and in the meantime the question remains whether the inherent jurisdiction of the court is being effectively utilized in family cases.

Access

The parent who does not have care and control will generally be granted access to the child because it is considered the basic right

---

108. It may sometimes be the case that the Court assumes that because it is exercising inherent jurisdiction that all procedural requirements may be swept aside.
109. *B v C.*

of a parent;[110] although in the modern child-centred dispensation, it could be viewed more correctly as the basic right of every child to have access to his/her parent. Access may be liberal (sometimes called reasonable), that is, unspecified by the court. In such circumstances, it is left up to the parties to decide how and when access will take place. Access orders may also be specified according to the duration, frequency, time and location that the child is to be collected. All of these matters can be decided by the court and contained in the order. Sometimes relatives will be drafted in to play a role in the process as some sort of intermediary.

Access is the aspect of parental involvement in the upbringing of a child that is most likely to be a casualty of the severance of relations between mother and father. Whether it is simply to get away from the other parent, or because it is thought that the other parent is a bad person and should not have any influence over the child, or as a means of exacting revenge, the custodial parent may prevent or obstruct access to the child. Often, parents make a connection between maintenance and access to the child and conclude that if maintenance is not forthcoming then there is no reason why the other parent should enjoy access to the child. Or the converse of that position is employed, which is: 'If I'm being denied access, why should I pay maintenance for a child who I'm not allowed to see?' Generally, these opinions labour under the misconception that access is a privilege or entitlement for the parent rather than a right of the child. This was the position of the court until as late as 1985.[111] Once the parties have overcome this misconception, they will often redirect their aims towards getting terms of access that are most advantageous to themselves.

Residential Access

A weekend stay-over is usual except for young babies or in situations where the parent's accommodation is unsatisfactory.

110.   *B.A.M. v C.G. re D (An Infant)* (1985) 22 JLR 9.
111.   Ibid.

For school age children, major holidays – Christmas, Easter, and summer vacations – are usually split, with alternation of the split in the Christmas holiday to ensure that the child is with one parent for Christmas and with the other for the New Year. The court will often tailor the conditions of access to suit the circumstances, so that if the child is living in another country, communication can be maintained by cell phone or video conferencing such as Skype.

Supervised Access

Where the court seeks to ensure that the safety and well-being of the child is not compromised by access to the parent, a designated person will oversee them during the access period. This person, who may be a relative or a professional such as a social worker, is usually specifically appointed by the court and will have the responsibility to the court, not to either of the parties, to ensure the safety of the child. In *AH v JH*,[112] the court delegated the selection of a suitable person to supervise the access to the Family Life Ministries, an approved counselling services provider. This type of access can also be utilized when the child is not familiar with the parent and needs time to get acquainted with and comfortable around him/her.

In the case of *Stockhausen v Willis*,[113] the option of supervised access was considered novel by the presiding judge. Although there has never been any express reason for not making supervised access orders, the matter of resources has to be factored in to the court's decision. In *Stockhausen*, the court relied on a person accepted by the court-approved agency to be the 'accompanist'. This may have been because the claimant was to pay those expenses. Notwithstanding that the court seemed to have no difficulty with this arrangement, obvious objections could have been raised had the respondent been involved in the proceedings. The fact that accompanist's time is being paid for by the claimant and as a result his impartiality must have been compromised did not

---

112.   [2014] JMSC Civ 68.
113.   02920/2004 16/7/2008.

seem to trouble the court. The difficulty is that, in the absence of more social workers attached to the court,[114] the power to impose such conditions will be severely constrained. It can, however, be countered that, in practice, the number of orders for supervised access should be relatively small and would not impose too much burden on public resources.[115]

Access and Violence

Acts of intimidation or violence may be a factor in custody/access disputes on occasions. The victims of domestic violence will often consider it their right to prevent the child from spending time with the other parent either out of revenge or because of a genuine belief that, in such circumstances, rights of access are forfeited. A knee-jerk reaction to violence in the home can lead to a loss of perspective on the issue. If it is recognized that the question of access in this situation, as in all custody cases, is guided by the welfare principle, then it becomes clear that there is no general answer to the problem and it depends upon the circumstances in every case. Distinctions may be drawn between violence that takes place in the presence of the child and instances where it does not. However, often the child, even if not present, becomes aware of what has taken place – sees bruises – or is sensitive to the change in atmosphere in the home. What then are the possible effects of violence on the welfare of the child? Furthermore, even if the child is adversely affected by the occurrence, does it follow that it is in the best interests of the child for there to be no access to the parent perpetrator? The answer to the second question involves the consideration of whether there is more harm to the child as a result of the interruption of his relationship with a parent, and the level of exposure to violence and its effects. Cases are inevitably decided on their own facts in this area, but it is possible to identify certain

---

114. This is the kind of responsibility which can be quite readily assigned to the CDA, although more resources may be necessary.
115. For a recent example of this, see *AH v JH* [2014] JMSC Civ 68.

trends in how judges respond to these matters.[116] So many cases of this nature are dealt with in the Family Court, and few of them will find their way into the law reports unless the matter is taken to appeal. Also, the approach to the law is left up to the presiding Parish Judge who may not be familiar with the guiding principles, for example, from decisions of a higher court.

Violence towards or abuse of children is viewed seriously and is the most likely reason for access to be denied. There may, however, be a distinction between 'lawful chastisement' and unwarranted physical abuse.[117] This is a controversial area where the views of the court may run ahead of the views of society as to the rights of parents in relation to the upbringing of their children.

The courts are mindful that allegations of sexual abuse are often made just to gain an advantage in the hope that the court will be so horrified that access will be refused. This is rarely the case, because while the court is extremely sensitive to the seriousness of this issue, it will seek to ensure that such complaints are fully investigated before coming to a decision.[118]

Access and Lifestyle

Access to a child was considered to be the basic right of a parent,[119] however, the right is not inalienable, and the court will determine from the particular facts of every case if, and in what circumstances, access should take place. In *Forsythe v Jones*,[120] the lifestyle of the father caused the court to scrutinize whether access should be allowed.

In *Stockhausen v Willis*,[121] the court was asked to re-consider access to the mother in light of her home circumstances where the child was 'continuously exposed to the smoking of marijuana by his

---

116. See *Re L* (Contact: Domestic Violence) [2000] 2 FLR 334.
117. The Child Care and Protection Act is silent on this.
118. *AH v JH*.
119. *BAM v CG and Re D* (an Infant) 1985, Court of Appeal.
120. SCCA 49/1999 6/4/2001.
121. 02920/2004 16/7/ 2008.

brothers'. There were also allegations of exposure to pornography. As a result of the medical and psychological effects of these issues on the child, an application for variation was put forward. In this case, even where the court was extremely perturbed by the allegations against the mother – who did not take any part in the proceedings – it was not enough for the court to curtail the previous access order. Instead, the trial judge went to great lengths to put in place a mechanism by which the mother's access to the child would be closely supervised. A restraining order on the mother was also made to further protect the child. In *AJ v JH*,[122] as well as allegations of sexual molestation, there was admitted drug use by both parents. Nevertheless, the court was able to ensure the continued input of both parents in the child's upbringing by way of sole custody and supervised access orders.

In Jamaica, the court has not yet been approached to consider questions of access where the sexual orientation of the parent is the basis of an objection to access. The scope and application of the criminal law in this area, as well as rights under the Constitution, have been an ongoing topic of debate and, therefore, it is to be expected that the courts will have to consider this issue eventually.

PRACTICE AND PROCEDURE IN CUSTODY MATTERS

The Children (Guardianship and Custody) Act allows for applications to be made in both the Supreme Court and at the summary level in the Parish Court and the Family Court for the respective parish.[123] With respect to custody applications, the choice of being able to make those applications in the high court or in a court of summary jurisdiction is of considerable importance. This is because, whether for reasons of cost or the comparative speed, the lower court is where the majority of custody matters are heard. Also, where custody matters arise out of maintenance applications made in the Family Court, in such circumstances they are most conveniently dealt

122.   [2014] JMSC Civ 68.
123.   Sections 2(a)–(d).

with before the same court.[124] By contrast, custody applications in the high court frequently arise as an application that is ancillary to divorce proceedings and are therefore made under the MCA. Applications in the high court under the Children (Guardianship and Custody) Act as opposed to the MCA can be made by unmarried parents who prefer to have the matter heard there and sometimes by married parents where divorce proceedings have not yet been instituted. The high court may also hear an application for custody pursuant to an application for injunctive orders under the MCA.[125] Whereas it would be open to the high court to consider custody applications whether the proceedings under the MCA have been completed or terminated,[126] couples who have ended their marriage in another jurisdiction could only make an application if it is to be heard in the Jamaican high court, under the Children (Guardianship and Custody) Act.[127]

Custody Applications and Forms

Applications in the high court under the Children (Guardianship and Custody) Act are made by way of the fixed date claim procedure, and the hearing will therefore be in chambers. In circumstances where applications for custody are made in the course of divorce proceedings or otherwise under the Matrimonial Causes Act, the appropriate form would be the notice of application for court orders.[128] As stated previously, the Civil Procedure Rules state that even if the application is made by way of fixed date claim form, the court will nevertheless proceed to hear the application.[129] In either case, the hearing will be in chambers.

In the lower court, custody applications under the Children (Guardianship and Custody) Act are made by summons issued for

---

124. In practice, this happens quite often even though logically one would expect it to happen in the reverse.
125. Section 10.
126. Section 23.
127. As in the case of *Panton v Panton*.
128. Rule 76.6(1).
129. Rule 76.4(15).

the respondent to attend court as a result of the applicant laying an information or complaint on oath.

The precise content of affidavits in custody cases will be peculiar to the circumstances in every case, but in every case the court expects fulsome and detailed information. In the absence of a guardian *ad litem* or some other means by which the child's interests might be represented independently, it is the attorneys for each party who should be mindful of the welfare principle and how this affects their ethical position. Affidavits should refer to the current living conditions of the child and what is proposed, with alternatives if necessary. The affidavit should indicate who will be living with the child, what school, church and other activities he, she or they will be involved in. If there is a special issue, for example, education, religion, or medical treatment, this must be addressed so as to put the court in a position where it has sufficient information to make a decision. When maintenance is being granted under section 7(3), it does not appear to require a separate application but is instead housed within the court's powers to make a 'further order', as long as the custody order is made in the terms specified. The court might request further evidence regarding the financial details of the parties, if this issue arises.

The Hearing

In the high court evidence is presented primarily in affidavit form although, if the matter is contested, orders can be made for oral examination of the deponent to take place. The judge will often speak directly to the parties and, depending on the age, may hear from the child in the absence of the parties. In the high court, social workers or probation officers are not present at the hearing, and it is only where the judge makes a request for such assistance that a report or other supervisory duties will be undertaken. This is to be compared with the lower family court where probation officers are a constant presence in court and are called upon routinely, particularly in custody matters. This is to investigate the parents' home circumstances and report to the court on such matters. In the Family Court, access to the reports prepared by the probation officer is restricted, and although the attorneys are allowed to read the reports, they are not supposed to retain or make a copy of the report. In particular, the court prevents the parties from reading the reports. Those parties that appear before the court unrepresented will be at a material disadvantage in such a situation.[130]

Where the central issue is the care and upbringing of a child, the paramount consideration is the welfare of that child, and the court will generally require the attendance of the applicant at the hearing in order to assess the demeanor of the parties notwithstanding the existence of affidavit of evidence.[131] The judge may also take a more active part in questioning the parties directly, and this will not necessarily be restricted to the end of cross-examination by counsel, but can take place during the questioning period according to the inclination of the judge. The wide discretion that the judge has in the fixed date hearing means that the hearing will follow the format in keeping with the requirements of the judge. Generally, the applicant's case will be heard first and after the opening the applicant will be cross-examined,[132] and if necessary re-examined, followed by the cross-examination of any witnesses who the court has given permission to be cross-examined. The respondent's case will then be heard in the same way followed by closing submissions from both sides, whether orally or in writing.

In the lower court, the hearing is quasi-criminal in that the procedural features that are peculiar to civil trials in the Parish Court jurisdiction are absent. The applicant will give oral testimony and may be cross-examined by the respondent or his attorney. This will be followed by any witnesses the applicant wishes to call. Then the

---

130. Whether this practice conforms with the rules of disclosure or natural justice or even standard court practice is questionable.
131. *Biggs v Biggs* 1883/2004 17/09/04.
132. Assuming that leave has been granted for the parties to be cross-examined.

respondent's case will follow the same pattern. If either or both parties are unrepresented, the court will assist to some extent sometimes by way of questioning by the clerk of courts. At the close of the evidence, the applicant will address the court followed by the respondent, irrespective of whether witnesses have been called. As in the high court, the parish judge may speak with the child, and this would be in the absence of the parties.[133] The extent to which a parish judge may take reports from social workers into account is uncertain. Some parish judges make it clear that they will be read, others say that such information will not fall within the ambit of the court's consideration during a trial. This area needs specific regulations so judges can come to a uniform decision. Arguably, if the reports are to be taken into account, then the lawyers should be able to question the social worker who authored the report. Social workers or probation officers are not usually called to give evidence on the grounds that the reports, like the information given during interviews, are confidential. On the other hand, reports from child psychologists as with any other medical evidence will be heard and taken into account by the court.

Judgments in the high court are delivered orally, even if a written judgment is subsequently issued. It is then for the applicant's attorney – unless otherwise directed by the court – to perfect the orders flowing from the judgment. In the lower court, the judgment is given orally, and the court's office will generate a written order that is available to the parties.

In the courts, at both levels, there is considerable encouragement of the parties towards consent, recognizing that the best chance of compliance exists where the parties have put their own agreed orders in place. In the lower court, this encouragement takes the form of an automatic order for a report in contested cases. When the report is before the court the parties are invited to come to agreement, or at least to abandon the prospect of a trial, based

---

133.   The Clerk will be present on such occasions.

on the recommendations of the probation officer in the social enquiry report. It is usually only in the absence of agreement that the matter will proceed to trial. In contested hearings where lawyers appear there is often a tendency to cite numerous legal authorities in support of one position or another in custody cases, but the courts have been at pains to stress that more so than in other areas, applications for custody are decided on their own facts.[134]

Types of Orders in Custody Cases

1. **Custody Orders**
2. **Access Orders**
3. **Special or Ancillary Orders**

Custody Orders

At common law, when the parents of a child are married to each other they will have joint custody that can only be set aside by an order of the court granting sole custody to one or the other. Often, the court will maintain the status quo by endorsing the pre-existing joint custody by way of a formal order. This was a statute-endorsed development[135] from the historical position where the father was in a dominant position.[136] It is upon separation or divorce of a married couple that the issue of custody of the children will usually arise. If the children lived with one party, it had become routine in the past for that parent to be granted sole custody. This will also be the case when a parent agrees to the other parent having sole custody of the child; or if good reasons are put forward for a sole custody order, it will be granted. The premise that joint custody would not be granted unless the parents could work together was superseded by the view that the welfare of the child is the first and paramount consideration. This view recognized that generally, the welfare of

---

134. *B.A.M. v C.G. re D (An Infant)* (1985) 22 JLR 9; recently, *F v D* [2017] JMSC Civ 9.
135. Children (Guardianship and Custody) Act, section 18.
136. *R v de Mannerville* (1804) 5 East 221, *R v Greenhill* (1836) 4 Ad & E 624, culminating in *Re Agar-Ellis* (1883) 24 Ch D 317.

the child is enhanced by contact with both parents, and the parents are expected to work things out for the good of their offspring. As a result joint custody orders became the norm.

By contrast, if the parents were not married, at common law, it was the mother who had de facto custody of the child. This was for the simple reason that, in the absence of any presumption of paternity, there remained an issue as to who was legally the father. There could be an affiliation order or some other prima facie evidence of paternity, but the question was not conclusively settled. Therefore, in such circumstances, the father will have to apply to the court for a custody order. In so doing, the father may rely on the record of his particulars on the birth certificate, as well as actions taken in acknowledgement and support of the child.[137] Often, the issue would not arise because it was accepted by the mother that the applicant is the child's father, and the court would proceed to hear the matter having put the question of paternity to one side. Historically this would then allow the father to assume a traditionally superior position as having a primary right to custody over the mother. As stated above, it was the Children (Guardianship and Custody) Act that had a profound effect on the common law position by giving statutory recognition to an equal right to custody of both mother and father.[138] Following on from there, the Status of Children Act rendered the parent's marital status immaterial to the question of custody, as well as other issues. That combined with the best interests of the child as determined by the court, will often result in an order for joint custody. It remains to be seen if the recent swing towards sole custody orders (see *F v D* [2017] JMSC Civ 9) will materially affect this position.

Legal custody is the right to make the important decisions pertinent to a child's upbringing.[139] The problem with joint legal custody is that

---

137. See Status of Children Act, section 8.
138. Sections 6 and 18.
139. This definition is not supported by Jamaican statute, but is readily assumed by the court in all cases.

it assumes a level of cooperation on the part of the parents, which will enable them to collaborate in the decision-making process for the overall good of the child. Too often, however, the exercise of this joint responsibility becomes yet another basis for dispute between 'warring factions', with the interests of the child being a minor consideration.

Access Orders

Liberal or reasonable access has as its hallmark complete flexibility. This type of order leaves it up to the parties to decide when and in what circumstances the child will have contact with the parent who is to have access. Liberal access is frequently ordered by the court, notwithstanding the fact that this type of access places a burden to cooperate, which may or may not be honoured. For this reason, Jamaican courts have been leaning in favour of specified terms of access when called upon to make orders in this regard. Specified access orders will set out precisely when and where access is to take place, and will also state who is to collect the child and at what time. The aim is to create a framework that allows the parties to operate systematically, civilly, and in the best interest of the child. This, of course, does not stop parents who are really determined from frustrating the process. What is hoped is that they will subordinate their own impulses for the benefit of the child. Specified access generally gives parents a workable format to which they can adhere until such time as they are able to develop flexible arrangements of their own, being mindful of the primacy of the needs of the child. Crafting appropriate access orders may call for considerable ingenuity on the part of the legal representatives and the court. Supervised access may be required and can be ordered by the court. The court may also order that access takes place at the home of a relative, provided that the relative consents and is prepared to cooperate with the arrangements that are put in place by the court.

Special or Ancillary Orders

There are occasions when the dispute in relation to the care and upbringing of a child concerns a particular feature of his/her care, such as education or rarely some other aspect (such as immunization). In such cases, the court will address the specific issue raised.

Where general custody orders or orders regarding education give rise to financial needs, the court, under the Children (Guardianship and Custody) Act, has the power to make ancillary orders. The anticipated need for maintenance can be specifically pleaded in the fixed date claim form although the wording of the section does not seem to require it, because it would appear that the power is vested in the court.[140] In the lower court, maintenance orders flowing from custody can be granted either under the Children (Guardianship and Custody) Act section 7, or under the Maintenance Act, which gives even wider powers to the court. Since the lower court is not a court of pleadings, the distinction is largely ignored, although increasingly there is insistence that a formal application for maintenance be made. In many instances, the application and orders for custody are simply the means of getting to the point where the court will order maintenance.

In both the high court and the lower court, interim orders can be made pending final resolution. One of the more significant interim orders that may be sought is that the child is not to be removed from the jurisdiction without the leave of the court. This is invoked primarily to maintain the status quo for sufficient time for the court to be able to adjudicate. Sometimes, such a term might be included in a final order. In some cases, the application is for the child to be allowed to live outside of the jurisdiction with the custodial parent.[141]

To the extent that these orders concern children, and therefore circumstances may change, the label 'final order' is a misnomer since the court always has power to re-visit the issue, generally by way of an application for variation[142] or enforcement by one of the

---

140.   'The court may further order…' section 7(3).
141.   As in the cases of *BP v RP* and *F v B* 2702/2010 16/09/11.
142.   See *Richards v Richards* (1980) 17 JLR 225; welfare principle applicable.

parties. As such, the order will almost invariably be concluded with the phrase 'Liberty to Apply'.

Enforcement

In practice, the courts in Jamaica give quite a lot of latitude to parties in custody disputes in the area of compliance. Where access is specified by the court, the rules that are set out in the order often become a battleground of misunderstanding, misinterpretation, and flagrant disregard. The court's approach may stem from the recognition that the parties are interacting with each other and the child is a mere pawn who provides the opportunity for a point to be made or a score to be settled *inter parentes*. So the question of who collected or dropped off the child at what time and at what place will often be treated with a firm reminder of the terms of the order and no more. However, when a party removes a child from the custody of the other parent or does not return the child as required, the court is likely to take a more serious view. Usually, a stern directive to comply or, if necessary, that the child be produced to the court is sufficient, rarely does the court have to remind the parties that non-compliance is a contempt of court and may be visited with imprisonment. The issue of enforcement in custody cases arose in *Adjudah v Lalor*,[143] where an application to commit was dismissed by the court at first instance and the applicant appealed to the Court of Appeal. He contended that the respondent was in breach of a court order to allow access every second Saturday between the hours of 9:00 a.m. and 3:00 p.m. The court looked carefully at the procedural steps to be taken as well as the merits and concluded that the Resident Magistrate had been correct in dismissing the application.

---

143.   [2016] JMCA Civ 52.

GUARDIANSHIP

Introduction

Seven years ago, Sophia Jennings decided to stop at the corner shop on her way home from work and in so doing got into a lengthy conversation with a teacher from the local basic school. She was informed that her brother James's child, Teisha, aged 4 was attending school sporadically and her uniform was always dirty and her hair uncombed. Despite requests for Teisha's mother, Angie, to attend school, she had not done so, although she was seen at all the local dances and had got into a number of altercations that seemed to be prompted by drink and/or drugs. As a result of the teacher's intervention, Sophia convinced Angie to let Teisha come and live with her. Angie, who has never worked, and had three other children for different fathers, was more than happy for Sophia to take Teisha, because she knew that the child would be properly looked after in a comfortable setting. Sophia's brother, James, was a seaman who spent extended periods of time outside Jamaica. He gave what support he could until he was killed during a robbery several years ago. Sophia is married, has two children, and Teisha has been fully accepted into the family. However, Teisha is unable to travel abroad with the family when they go on vacations, and has been refused medical insurance benefits enjoyed by the other children. Sophia has no wish to exclude Angie, who has moved away from the district and sees Teisha infrequently, but she finds it difficult to keep in contact with her and get her to co-operate when it comes to making decisions about Teisha.

This scenario is typical of the sort of case which leads to an application to the court for the appointment of a legal guardian. Whereas the first application that might spring to mind would be for custody, it would appear from the wording of the Act that only the mother or the father of a child can apply to the court for custody unless particular circumstances arise.[144] The question then arises as to how a third party may legally assume the responsibility of being a parent to a child. This dilemma may arise in any number of situations such as when the parent is unable to look after the child due to incapacity, impoverishment, or absence. In this situation, other family members or persons in the community may, for practical purposes, take on the obligation of caring for the child, sometimes for an extended period of time. This may present little difficulty on a day-to-day basis, but there will still be some 'official' requirements that the stand-in parent is unable to fulfil even though, in many instances, he/she may be closely related to the child. For example, the family may wish to travel abroad,[145] but is unable to get a passport or a visa for the child or is unable to show the necessary legal connection that will allow them to travel with the child. Sometimes, a school trip or international travel to a sporting event may be open to the child, but the person or family who is caring for the child is unable to provide the required consent.

Another reason why there may be the need to formalize a parental relationship between the child and a third party (whether a relative or not) is in the event of the death of a parent. The Children (Guardianship and Custody) Act specifically addresses the appointment of guardians upon the parent's death. In a situation where there is sufficient time, a parent may specify who he would want to act in his place when he dies,[146] and this may be done by deed or will. A testamentary guardian so appointed will act jointly with the surviving parent.[147] However, if there is no testamentary guardian or the guardian who is appointed dies or may not wish to take on the duty, then the court is empowered to appoint someone.[148] Interestingly, it would appear that the court does not have to wait until someone puts himself forward to be appointed as guardian,

---

144. Section 7.
145. Whether or not the guardian will in fact acquire the power to take a child out of the jurisdiction is, in fact, in doubt as a result of the decision in *B v C* (below).
146. Section 4.
147. Section 4(3).
148. Section 3.

but may do so 'if it thinks fit' so that provided that the matter is brought to the attention of the court, it may act accordingly.

The circumstances specified by the Act in sections 3 and 4 are to be read in conjunction with section 20 where it clearly states that these powers do not have the effect of curtailing the jurisdiction of the Supreme Court to appoint or remove guardians. In the case of sections 3 and 4, the historical perspective is clear: wills could be made, but where a parent died, someone had to fill the gap, not only in relation to the care of the child, but (just as importantly) to control the assets which concerned the child.

Leighton Jackson states: 'The early philosophy of the law of guardianship was almost wholly related to the exaggerated concern for property in feudalism'.

However, the law extended itself into other situations and section 20 appears to be a direct reference to the court's inherent powers that could be triggered in circumstances other than death and by which the court's general power to appoint guardians is expressly preserved in the Act. The inherent powers of the Supreme Court, when exercised in relation to children (and the vulnerable, such as lunatics), is derived from the power of the monarch as *parens patriae*.[149] So the court retains the power to act as a parent in relation to minors whose interests are not being protected by their biological parents. In this regard, the powers of the court in guardianship are not dissimilar to the powers of the court when making a child a ward of court. In wardship proceedings, once a child is made a ward of court, the parental decisions are exercised by the court, and the powers of the parents are usurped by the court. By comparison, guardianship is a mechanism that allows the court to exercise its powers as *parens patriae* through the person who is appointed as legal guardian. That the court still has the power to remove the guardian or to adjudicate in any dispute between guardians or the guardian and the parent clearly implies that the court does not divest itself of the inherent power simply because a guardian is appointed.

---

149.   For a detailed review of *parens patriae* in Jamaica, see Jackson, 'Fi Wi Law'.

In effect, the court remains the parent and the guardian is akin to an agent through whom the court will exercise its power to protect and provide for the child according to the welfare principle. As was recently acknowledged by the court, the effect of an application for the appointment of a guardian, therefore, is that the child becomes a ward of court.[150]

Guardianship is a procedure that allows a person to take responsibility for a child without severing the legal relationship with the biological parents. This distinguishes guardianship from adoption as currently defined in Jamaican law. So, if one parent has died the guardian will act in conjunction with the surviving parent to provide for the needs of the child.[151] In such a case, the co-operation of both the guardian and the surviving parent is required. The difficulty that may arise is where the surviving parent is inaccessible, disinterested, or uncooperative. The court is given the power to adjudicate where a dispute arises and may make either the parent or guardian the 'sole guardian'. In the case where the guardian, rather than the parent, is made sole guardian, the court may grant custody to him/her with access to the natural parent.[152] The court may even order that, in such circumstances, the parent should pay maintenance to the guardian, having regard to his means.[153] This power to grant maintenance is rarely exercised and is generally overlooked; furthermore, there is no reference to ensuring that the factors and principles included in the Maintenance Act when such orders are being made.

What presents more difficulty is where both parents are alive. The question will inevitably arise as to what is the legal status of the each of the adults in relation to the child. Does the child now have three parents? Are the parent's powers in relation to the child diminished by the introduction of a third party? If the appointment of a guardian

150.   *B v C and the Office of the Children's Advocate* [2016] JMCA Civ 48.
151.   Sections 3(1) and (2).
152.   Section 4(4).
153.   Ibid.

was made on the grounds of a biological parent's incapacity, is this not an implied, if not explicit, curtailment of the parent's powers in respect of the child? In this regard, it has been decided[154] that the powers of the court in guardianship are akin to the powers of the court in making the child a ward of court, that is, the court retains the right to make decisions as *parens patriae*. However, the powers of a guardian as expressed in section 5 encompass powers over the estate as well as the person, that is, over the child and his property 'as a guardian appointed by will or otherwise has in England'.

Statutory Provisions

The Children (Guardianship and Custody) Act codifies the court's powers to appoint legal guardians while preserving the court's inherent powers to provide protection and supervision of children. Section 5 is a declaration that the responsibilities of guardianship are exercised in line with English principles.

Section 8 allows the court to remove any guardians whether testamentary or appointed by the court, if that is consistent with the welfare of the child. It also gives the court power to replace those who have been removed. The following section allows the court to resolve any dispute between joint guardians according to the welfare of the child.

The court's inherent jurisdiction to appoint or remove guardians is specifically preserved.[155] This facilitates the court's power to appoint legal guardians outside of the stipulations of sections 3 and 4 of the Act. Therefore, applications are often the means by which arrangements that are already in place are formalized. For this reason, section 20 is an important provision that allows the court to appoint guardians in situations not specifically covered by the Act but which arise far more frequently in the lives of ordinary Jamaicans than testamentary appointments by the court upon the death of a parent.[156]

---

154. *B v C.*
155. Section 20.
156. As recognized in *B v C*, the inherent jurisdiction of the Supreme Court is also set out in the Judicature (Supreme Court) Act, section 27.

Practice and Procedure for Guardianship

In guardianship matters, the court may exercise its powers under section 3 and 4 of the Act, that is, in circumstances where one or both of the parents have died. More commonly, applications are made where the parents are alive and therefore the court's inherent jurisdiction, which is preserved by section 20 is being invoked. As a result of this, applications for the court to appoint a guardian are generally made in the Supreme Court, since the lower court does not have such inherent powers. In practice, the Family Court will routinely refer guardianship applicants to the Supreme Court.

Since guardianship is generally dealt with in the high court, the fixed date claim procedure is applicable, and the matter will be heard before a judge in chambers. The affidavit in support must set out all aspects of the child's life and how the proposed guardian will meet the child's needs. Often, these arrangements are already in place, but they will still be subject to the review of the court. The court will also want to know what has happened to the parents and whether they know about the proceedings or are in a position to consent or give their views[157] about the application. This, of course, would not arise in circumstances where a testamentary guardian is being appointed. While not specified in any rules, it is a matter of practice that the court will require supporting evidence as to the suitability of the prospective guardian, and such a report will also provide the court with information relating to the biological parents.[158] Also, in making custody or guardianship orders, the court will expect that even if the evidence is primarily in affidavit form, the applicant(s) will be present.[159]

If at least one of the biological parents is still alive when the application is being heard, the question of how the rights of the

---

157.   It has been said that where the parent(s) are alive, they should be made parties to the application, *Re: Application for Guardianship of a Minor Child F* [2016] JMSC Civ 193.

158.   The court will ask the Child Protection and Family Services Agency (CPFSA) to investigate and provide a report in these cases.

159.   *Biggs v Biggs* 1883/2004 17/09/04, per Mangatal J.

guardian are to be exercised alongside the existing parental rights may arise.

However, where both parents are alive, the question of who is to exercise parental responsibility over the child may have to be decided specifically by the court. In particular, if it is the lack of involvement or incapacity of one or both of the parents that has prompted the applicant to take over the responsibility in the first place, then the format of acting jointly may be unworkable for all practical purposes. Some parents who are not in any way prepared to take responsibility for the upbringing of the child may nevertheless refuse to yield to or co-operate with a legal guardian. Even though the Act allows for further applications to the court for this to be resolved, it may be prudent for the court to consider putting orders in place, addressing this issue from the outset, so as to avoid the expense of further applications. In any event, the court will, as long as the child remains below the age of majority, retain the right to hear applications and in the course of so doing, vary or discharge any previous orders in keeping with the best interests of the child.

Finally, in relation to the court's inherent jurisdiction in relation to children, it remains uncertain as to why in Jamaica, the court has not developed its powers in wardship.[160] As Jackson states:

> As said earlier, the wardship jurisdiction of the Supreme Court plays virtually no role in the law relating to children today. It is difficult to accurately account for this, but one of the reasons must be the difficulty and uncertainty involved in invoking the jurisdiction.[161]

This to be compared with Barbados, where in cases such as *P v P* (1977) 30 WIR 8, the court is willing to apply its inherent jurisdiction in such proceedings.

---

160. The only reported case being *MacKintosh* (1871) Eq. J. B. Vol 2 113, Vol 1 Stephens Reports 106.
161. The Law Relating to Children, 53. This is to be compared with Barbados where wardship is more frequently invoked.

ADOPTION

Introduction

In Jamaica, up to about a generation ago, adoption was a process which was referred to without stigma and often with a sense of pride. Adoption meant that the adoptive parent or parents had opened their home to a child or children who were in need. Adoption meant that the adoptive child was plucked from unfortunate circumstances and given a stable home life and an opportunity to succeed. Most adoptions prior to the Children (Adoption of) Act were informal and rested essentially on an agreement between the natural parent(s) with the adoptive parents for the latter to bring up the child.

The informal adoption of a child by a 'well to do', childless couple could then be a turning point in a child's life. She might be able to get a good education and have a career, which, in turn, will enable her to jettison her children into their own professions by way of good quality education. This springboard to upward social mobility is to be found over and over again throughout the length and breadth of Jamaica. It is a truism that the middle-class Afro-Jamaican owes much of his/her social standing to education, which may have been acquired with or without the direct input of his/her biological parents. Childless couples and single women have traditionally taken in a child, whether related or not, to whom they could offer 'a chance in life'. It is only in modern times with the spectre of child trafficking that the attention is being paid to the less than ideal aspects of guardianship and adoption.

Largely as a result of influences outside Jamaica, adoption has become an intricate and quite daunting process. There is much less of the informal adoptions that have just been outlined. Adoption has been formalized in the traditional Western manner where the rights of the natural parents and their connection to the child are extinguished, and the child embarks on a new life with a new family. The Adoption Board was created pursuant to the Children (Adoption of) Act[162] and tends to carry out its functions outside of the scrutiny of the court and lawyers. It is only at the final stage when the judge makes the adoption order that the case comes before the court. This approach does not appear to be accidental and may be borne out of a desire to protect the adoption process from the wrangling of lawyers and legal procedure. So, on a daily basis, interpreting the rules of practice in adoption applications may be informed by the law, policy, or a mixture of both as interpreted usually by non-lawyers. It is difficult to challenge the received wisdom of the all-powerful social worker/children's officer in this arena, and it is in the absence of proper monitoring and oversight by the court that misuse of power can thrive.[163] When the process is so protracted and the power to grant is concentrated in the hands of so few, there is always the danger that persons who want to adopt may become disheartened and resort to an unregulated private arrangement. The rarity of court intervention was acknowledged in the case of *In the matter of an Appeal against the decision of the Adoption Board* [2015] JMSC Civ 185.

The Children (Adoption of) Act

The procedure for adoption is the responsibility of the Adoption Board.[164] Since the establishment of the Child Development Agency (CDA) now the Child Protection and Family Services Agency (CPFSA), many of the duties of the Adoption Board have been delegated to that entity.

Under section 6 of the Act, legal adoptions in Jamaica are effected by means of an adoption order from the court. The Adoption Board oversees the arrangements with regard to investigation, notification and supervision.[165] The board initiates and pursues the application for an adoption order on behalf of the adopter. It is, therefore, not

---

162. Section 3.
163. 'Children's Officer Fined for Falsifying Adoption Papers,' *The Daily Gleaner*, September 5, 2014.
164. Section 5.
165. Section 6(2).

possible to adopt a child without the approval of the Adoption Board. It is a criminal offence to interfere or intervene in the actions of the Adoption Board, which carries a penalty of six months imprisonment or a fine.[166]

It is the board that decides whether or not a person is fit to adopt a child, and this decision is made according to what is in the best interests of the child.[167] A person may appeal to a judge in chambers against the decision of the board.

The overarching power of the Adoption Board is cemented by section 4 of the Act which makes it a criminal offence to arrange an adoption outside of the management and control of the board. The penalty, as with an offence under section 6(4), is imprisonment for up to six months or a fine.

After the application forms have been submitted and reviewed, the consent of the biological parents is sought. There will then be home visits and counselling and a home study report will be prepared and submitted to the board. There will be a period of supervision of the child and the prospective adoptive parents that may last for approximately three to four months. The case is then put before a review committee and thereafter a court hearing will be set. Once the court makes the adoption order, the process is complete. Where the consent of the biological parent cannot be obtained, an application to dispense with consent can be made. This application can also be made where the consent is being unreasonably withheld.

Adoption orders are made by the Parish Court or the Family Court.[168] The application is made by the Adoption Board, and in these proceedings the judge will hear the matter in chambers with only the parties and sometimes their legal representatives present.

---

166. Section 6(4).
167. Section 7.
168. The right of appeal under section 293 of the Judicature (Resident Magistrate's) Act does not apply to adoption orders; Re D.C., An Infant (1965) 9 JLR.

Under section 25(6) of the Act, a birth certificate in the prescribed form may then be issued upon the application of 'any person'. The fact that such a certificate will be stamped with the word 'ADOPTED' across the face of the document has given rise to objection[169] on the basis that it is insensitive and unnecessary. The Registrar General's Department maintains, however, that this is in compliance with the law and is therefore a matter for Parliament to address.

The Legal Effects of Adoption

The first and foremost effect of adoption is that it terminates the parental rights in respect of the child, which ordinarily vest in the biological parents. Rights relating to custody, maintenance obligations, as well as inheritance on intestacy that would apply in the absence of an adoption order, no longer exist between the biological parents and their child who is adopted by others. Correspondingly, all these rights pass to the adoptive parents from the time the order is made.

Interestingly, the prohibitive degrees of consanguinity and affinity apply to the adoptive parents, biological parents, and biological siblings and the child, but not to the adoptive siblings and child.[170] Thus, 'if an adopted person (however innocently) marries a child of the natural parents the marriage is void.'[171] The fact that the law in this regard is derived from 'the law of England from time to time in force' is cumbersome and presents another reason why this section of the Act[172] should be amended.

Adoption orders act as an irrevocable severance of the parental rights of the biological parents. It has been said that if adoption orders were revocable 'the edifice of adoption would be gravely

---

169. By the Kingston and St Andrew Foster Parents Association see 'Don't Label Our Children!' *Sunday Gleaner*, August 18, 2013.
170. English Adoption Act 1976, section 47(1), this rule comes into the law of Jamaica by virtue of the Marriage Act, section 3(3).
171. Cretney and Masson, *Principles of Family Law*, 6th ed., 881.
172. Marriage Act, section 3(3).

shaken'.[173] However, there have been cases in another jurisdiction where an adoption order has been nullified on appeal.[174]

Adoption will also convey the right to apply for citizenship based on the adoptive parent's nationality and/or country of residence. Of course, the specific rules in this area will be governed by the immigration and nationality laws of the particular country.[175]

Conclusion

Adoption can bring about the transformation of a child's life in an overwhelmingly positive way; however, the spectre of child-trafficking lurks behind the stringent procedures of adoption and guardianship. As a result, the genuine adopter may be deterred by obstructive and unsympathetic officials.[176] In the absence of adequate child support backed by the state, the issue of making children available to non-biological, adoptive parents remains open to exploitation by unscrupulous adults who are involved in the process.[177] Perhaps the most challenging defect of the process of adoption is the protracted time it takes to obtain a decision. Many would-be adopters are defeated by the length of time for investigations during which they may be travelling back and forth to Jamaica, to maintain contact with the child and thereby incurring considerable expense. If, after a number of years, the decision is that adoption is not recommended, not only is the child emotionally abandoned and effectively thrown back into the pool, but by virtue of being older, may have less of a chance of ever being adopted, and will therefore remain in state care.[178]

---

173. *Re B* (Adoption: Setting Aside) [1995] 1 FLR 1.
174. *Re M* (Minors) (Adoption) [1991] 1 FLR 458 and *Re K* (Adoption and Wardship) [1997] 2 FLR 221.
175. See report in *Daily Observer* on migration of biological parent to Canada 1/03/17.
176. Janet Cupidon Quallo, 'Adoption (in Jamaica) is a Very Tedious Process,' *Sunday Gleaner*, June 23, 2013.
177. 'Policy paper outlining recommended amendments to the Adoption Act' to be presented to the Ministry of Youth and Culture,' *JIS*, April 25,2014.
178. A comprehensive review of adoption on Ireland is found in Kerry O'Halloran, 'Adoption-a Public or Private Legal Process? The Changing Social Functions of Adoption in Ireland and the Wider Implications for Coherence in Family

The calls for reform of the adoption laws are becoming louder, but a major hindrance is the scarcity of resources to expand entities such as the Child Protection and Family Services Agency that undertake the investigating, reporting, and recommendations in adoption cases. As always, the question of resources is set within the context of the country's overall economic well-being.

THE WAY FORWARD

In the area of custody, guardianship, and adoption, the way forward is linked with the need for a comprehensive legislative instrument that explicitly addresses the welfare principle and sets out explicitly what it encompasses and when it is applicable.

Whereas, in some circumstances, welfare will remain the overarching principle – first and paramount – for custody and upbringing, it does not follow that in all family matters where a child is involved that will be the case. While this may be a deliberate course that one may wish to adopt, it should not happen without full consideration and it should not (as occurs at present) be assumed according to the convenience of the court. The Maintenance Act and the Property (Rights of Spouses) Act are two examples of the types of proceedings where, even though children are involved, welfare need not be paramount but should be the first consideration. The issue also arises in the area of status and paternity where it may not accord with the welfare of the child to be exposed to the scientific truth. This is an area where the welfare principle has to contend with developments in fertility treatment (which is changing day by day) and has somehow to be reconciled with human rights principles such as the rights of the child and the right to family life.

If children are to be adequately protected from the scourge of child-trafficking, we must be pre-emptive in our actions to secure

Law.' In *Family Law: Processes, Practices, Pressures*, edited by John Dewar and Stephen Parker. West Sussex: Hart Publishing, 2003.

and update the provisions regarding guardianship and adoption. The difficulty that applicants have experienced with adoption encourages private adoption arrangements that circumvent the safeguards the Act has put in place.[179]

The Children (Guardianship and Custody) Act needs to be comprehensively reviewed in light of the MCA, the Maintenance Act, and the Property (Rights of Spouses) Act and, most importantly, the Child Care and Protection Act. The inconsistent and sometimes contradictory provisions – what is a child, what is a parent, who can apply for orders, what are the factors to be taken into account – are questions that should not depend upon which act the application is being made under. The current position in the various pieces of legislation leads to ambiguity and places the courts in a position of uncertainty where the applicable law can be subject to manipulation and the courts may be tempted into a law-making role. It is in this area that the need for a comprehensive Family Law Act becomes apparent to address these matters appropriately.

---

179.   A review of the adoption laws is currently underway, The *Gleaner*, April 7, 2007.

8. Status of Children and Parentage

INTRODUCTION AND HISTORICAL OVERVIEW

'So who is this?' said the elderly aunt looking at the young woman with a slight smile and an inquisitive gleam in her eye. Her father and brother laughed nervously, but her sister stated defiantly 'this is Daddy's daughter, Sharon, she was in Toronto.' The aunt's eyebrows shot up, 'But I don't understand...' she cried, staring pointedly at the father, presumably for some kind of explanation. The sister took her a little way off and a few moments later she exclaimed 'Oh, I see.' Then she came and took both the young woman's hands, she stared into her eyes 'Sharon, is it? Well welcome, I am your Aunt Mattie, we are family, and this is where you come from.'

They were in southern St Elizabeth, high on a bluff inland from the sea, outside an old well-kept wooden house – with concrete addition (done by another aunt on her return from America). The graves of the grandparents a little way off silently witnessing what was taking place.

This scenario is put forward as just one example of the sort of incident which occurs in almost every family in Jamaica. People discover that they are related to people who they might not previously have met, or if they have met them they were previously ignorant of the fact that they are related. After a period of discomfort (short or very lengthy, depending on the circumstances and the type of family) everyone muddles along. There is, however, another aspect to this scenario which may not be readily apparent: If 'Daddy' migrates and then wishes to have his children join him, close inspection of the children's birth certificates may reveal some discrepancies. Daddy's name may be absent from Sharon's birth certificate or worse yet, the name of her mother's former husband may be inserted even though 'everyone' knew she was not his child. Furthermore, if 'Daddy' dies and there is need to establish who his children are for purposes of dividing his estate, once again it would appear that Sharon is not his child. So begins the legal journey to unravel the documentary suppositions and get to the truth. Such is the nature of paternity matters as they arise within the Jamaican family.

Historical Overview

In Jamaica, women frequently become mothers before getting married. The men who father the children of this early maternal phase are sometimes unable (unemployed) or unwilling (married to someone other than the mother) to take full responsibility for those children. This can lead to reticence in terms of having one's name recorded on a child's birth certificate as father.[1] In any event, given that registering the child may take place weeks after the birth, this delay should give ample time for decisions to be made as to the name and parentage of the child. In circumstances where the

---

1. This is to be contrasted with the account of the registrar general regarding the first Births and Deaths Registration Law, 1877 describing the 'almost universal practice' for the father of the 'illegitimate' child to come forward to register his offspring. See Jenny M. Jemmott, *Ties that Bind: The Black Family in Post-slavery Jamaica, 1834–1882* (Kingston: University of the West Indies Press, 2015), 186.

woman is in a relationship with one man – whether married, living together, or visiting – but becomes pregnant by another man, whilst there may be no doubt as the child's true parentage, it may not be considered prudent for that to be acknowledged in public records.

In Jamaica when a woman dishonestly passes off her child as the child of a particular man, she is said to give him a 'jacket'. While this phenomenon is documented as widespread, it is viewed as the ultimate betrayal by most men. This, however, is a superficial assessment of something that often involves the complicity of the true father. It sometimes occurs with the knowledge and acceptance of the 'duped' father because it would be embarrassing for him to do otherwise. In this landscape, principles like the presumption of paternity as encapsulated in section 6 of the Status of Children Act have little relevance to the circumstances of most women and the need to resolve these issues from a practical rather than a legal standpoint may not arise until decades after these decisions were taken.[2] Whatever arrangements are made at or around the time of birth may then need to be unravelled by way of a declaration of paternity sometime in the future, whether for the purposes of maintenance, migration, or inheritance. Usually, the nature of the problem is that a child's birth certificate does not have any information as to the father, or the information which was recorded is incorrect.

Until the Status of Children Act 1976, the only way to address these problems outside of the limited powers of rectification under the Registration of Births and Deaths Act was to bring some legal recognition to the father was by way of affiliation proceedings. This only provided relief in terms of maintenance and a declaration that one was the 'putative father' of a child meant little beyond the boundaries of that act.

---

2.   Interestingly, the Status of Children legislation in Barbados extends the presumption to common law unions – Status of Children Reform Act.

The history of bastardy laws in Jamaica started in 1881[3] when for the first time a single mother could go before a judge and affirm the paternity of her child on oath and having heard from the putative father the court could order that he pay maintenance for the child. While this represented an advance on the state of the law prior to its passing, this law introduced new perils for the single mother:

> Thus, the Bastardy Law of 1881 made the mother liable to imprisonment for a maximum of twenty-eight days if her child became a burden to parochial charity as a result of her negligence.[4]

The putative father, on the other hand, was merely liable to compensate the authorities in such circumstances. The use of these proceedings in England in the late nineteenth and early twentieth centuries is questionable on many levels, but their applicability to the colonies particularly Jamaica was subject to the additional societal considerations of a post-slavery environment. These laws and their subsidiaries became a longstanding source of discontent. The law still left children born out of wedlock largely unrecognized. If a man left his property to 'his children', that meant his legitimate children in the absence of specifically naming them. In time, there were piecemeal legislative changes such as the provision that allowed for the father of an illegitimate child to be included on the birth certificate[5] and the 1909 Legitimation Act, which went some way towards bringing some children born out of wedlock into legitimacy, but there was no comprehensive legal status accorded to the child born outside of marriage.[6] So, for example, Leighton Jackson stated:

> The natural father (of a child born out of wedlock) was therefore denied recognition and any means of applying for custody of his child.[7]

---

3. The Bastardy Law 1881 is followed by the Bastardy Amendment Law 1882.
4. Jemmott, *Ties That Bind*, 183.
5. Registration Law 1877.
6. See Eileen Boxhill, 'Jamaica: Recent Developments in Family Law,' *Journal of Family Law* 28, no. 3 (1989–90): 551.
7. 'The Law Relating to Children in Jamaica: Report on Guardianship and

Effectively, a child born outside of marriage was primarily a child of the mother, rather than a child of both parents.

Finally, in the 1970s, Jamaican post-independence legislators seized the opportunity to address illegitimacy among other social ills. Measures were enacted that were appropriate to the vision of a new Caribbean society borne out of the country's newly independent status, with the status of children within the family being at the heart of this definition of nationhood.

The passage of the Status of Children Act was deeply rooted in the belief that the stigma of illegitimacy and bastardy had no place in a developing nation such as Jamaica.[8] The Act erased the legal distinctions between children based on whether their parents were married or not. However, the Act does not interfere with the existing law in other areas and, therefore, the notion of children of the marriage versus 'outside' children still lurks in intestacy and divorce, for example. Similarly, the law expressly recognizes the presumption of paternity, which itself is premised on protecting the child from the scourge of illegitimacy.[9] As a result, there remain some anomalies,[10] but overall it was and still is considered to be a successful and transformative piece of legislation.

THE DEVELOPMENT OF PARENTAGE THROUGH STATUTE

For centuries, the question of a child's parentage was confined to resolving paternity. To determine who the child's father was effectively gave the child an identity for most legal purposes. Contrary to the dispute that comes to Solomon in the Bible as

Custody,' Ministry of Justice, Jamaica – UNICEF. See also *Clarke v Carey* (1971) 17 WIR 69.

8. The slogan which accompanied the passage of this act is 'Nuh bastard nuh deh'.

9. Likewise, the legislators did not interfere with the process by which illegitimate children became legitimized by the marriage of their parents under the Legitimation Act and, as a result, there is tacit acknowledgement of the different status of children born in wedlock as opposed to children born outside of wedlock.

10. Leighton Milton Jackson, 'Some Difficulties with the Status of Children Acts.'

to which of two women was the baby's mother, the usual bone of contention throughout the ages has been the identity of the child's father. The reason for the emphasis on paternity is that fatherhood, first according to cultural norms[11] and the common law, and then according to statute[12] was synonymous with responsibility, that is financial responsibility and inheritance rights. Issues such as the right to family life and the importance of knowing one's heritage[13] were not taken into account, and would have been considered highly esoteric. The question was, and to a large extent in the Caribbean still is, who is going to pay for this child? The Affiliation Act[14] set out the limits of responsibility for those whose paternity was in question, and the strictures were daunting for the woman, but what role could such laws play in deterring such 'questionable' behaviour in a society where marriage was the exception to the rule? The drive towards respectability as a useful civilizing tool of the colonial masters included the encouragement of marriage.[15] The campaign of Lady Hutton to persuade common law partners to marry is well documented,[16] but what accompanied it was a disdain, (readily embraced by the newly initiated), for less formal unions and the progeny of such arrangements. Despite the efforts of the well-intentioned, children born as a result infidelity[17] or children born of 'unchurched' relationships remain a regular feature of family life that the court has had to address. The recognition of the child born out of wedlock, at least to a limited degree, could only be achieved by statute.

11. Patriarchy, although this question also plays a part in resolving disputes in matrilineal societies.
12. Maintenance Act 1881.
13. Which we see reflected in human rights conventions and the in particular the rights of the child.
14. Repealed by the Maintenance Act 2005.
15. See chapter on Marriage, for discussion on earlier efforts to encourage marriage in a post-slavery society.
16. 1945–46, Mass Marriage Movement.
17. Known as 'Outside' children.

The Bastardy Laws, Including the Affiliation Act

The Affiliation Act allowed applications to be made in the Resident Magistrates' Court by a 'single woman'[18] for a man to be declared the putative father of a child and therefore to be liable to pay maintenance in respect of that child. This Act predated scientific testing and therefore relied on an elaborate framework of evidential rules so that even though the standard of proof was on the balance of probabilities,[19] the intricacy of the law was daunting. There were restrictions on the time when an application could be made,[20] there was a requirement for corroboration,[21] and a requirement to be the child of a putative father did not give rise to the same rights of inheritance as possessed by a child born in wedlock. An application under the Affiliation Act could not result in a conclusive means of establishing paternity,[22] and this often presented the courts with the opportunity to reinforce the humiliation that was meted out socially.[23] The nature of Affiliation proceedings deterred many from asserting their right to support,[24] so that unless the man admitted paternity the woman could be faced with a protracted and expensive route to obtaining support for her child.[25] The Status of Children Act, while not repealing the Affiliation Act, rendered such proceedings unnecessary. A statutory and procedural usurpation had taken place by providing a new form of declaration: the declaration of paternity. In addition, the prevailing sentiment behind the legislation – that the legal distinction between children born in wedlock and children

18. See *Mooney v Mooney* [1953] 1 QB 38, *Jones v Evans* [1944] KB 528, *Giltrow v Day* [1965] 1 All ER 73 for example.
19. *H v B* (1977) 30 WIR 25.
20. *Smith v Finnikine* (1972) 12 JLR 705.
21. *Cracknell v Smith* [1960] 3 All ER 569, *Elliott v Elliott* (1945) 4 JLR 244, *Chambers v Taylor* (1967) 10 JLR 45, etc.
22. The man would be deemed to be 'the putative father'.
23. Terms such as 'a woman of ill repute' were applied to applicants in court at least until the mid-1990s.
24. See *Mooney v Mooney* [1953] 1 QB 38 cf *Giltrow v Day* [1965] All ER 73, *Smith v Finikine, Davis v Rumble* RMCA 142/1977 21/11/77, *Jeffrey v Johnson* [1952] 2 QB 8, *Cracknell v Smith* [1960] 3 All ER 569, *Thorpe v Molyneaux* RMCA 163/1977 31/7/79. Also article by Dennis Morrison 1981 WILJ 17.
25. *Elliott v Elliott* 1945 4 JLR 244; *Thorpe v Molyneaux.*

born outside of wedlock was untenable – began to permeate the approach of the courts with the result that affiliation orders were more readily granted.[26] Finally, the redundancy of affiliation proceedings was assured, not least because under the Status of Children Act,[27] an affiliation order was only prima facie evidence of paternity in any subsequent proceedings; while the declaration of paternity would henceforth 'for all purposes, be conclusive proof of the matters contained in it.'[28]

The Status of Children Act 1976

This Act established a new basis for determining parentage of a child in Jamaica. Although the Act speaks of the relationship of the person to his father AND mother, it is primarily concerned with the relationship between the person and their father.[29] Sections 7, 8, 10, and 11, which are the main sections dealing with evidence and the powers of the court, all refer to paternity, in particular, the keynote provision, section 10, whereby the court can make a declaration of paternity.

This statute will be examined more closely below.

WHO IS A PARENT?

The call for gender equality has had unforeseen consequences. The notion that equal rights brings with it equal responsibility is a concept that Parliament has been quick to embrace, but society has been slow to appreciate. The passage of the Maintenance Act 2005 is a classic case of the legislature and policymakers leading the march towards a progressive society and leaving the courts and the rest of the population to catch up. In particular, the legislation's clarion

26. Ultimately, they became a mere formality that was a necessary precursor to the maintenance orders which were being sought; that is, rarely contested and almost invariably granted.
27. Section 8(3).
28. Section 8(4).
29. Compare with the Status of Children Act in Barbados, which allows for declarations of maternity.

call for joint parental financial responsibility made the terminology of the earlier legislation such as the Status of Children Act and the Children (Guardianship and Custody) Act sound archaic. If the law now recognizes that a mother may be just as well or even better positioned to maintain her child as the father, then what place does the old law with its obsession with paternity have in this new social dispensation? This question is relevant even now because in maintenance, for example, the vast majority of maintenance claims are still made against the man. In any event, the move to a non-gender specific definition does not absolve fathers of their responsibility; it simply extends the responsibility to mothers. The trend then as evidenced by section 8(3) of the Maintenance Act is towards ascertaining parentage whether you are male or female, but in this journey many statutory provisions need to be revisited.

The question of who is a parent can only be answered from the standpoint of the responsibilities or rights that the law recognizes or bestows on that person who we look to as the parent of a child.

Maintenance

Under the Maintenance Act 2005, the prime position of the father that featured in the previous legislation has disappeared and been absorbed into the general obligation of the parent. Section 8(1) provides that 'every parent has an obligation to the extent that the parent is capable of doing so to maintain the parents unmarried child who

a. Is a minor; or

b. Is in need of such maintenance...'

A parent is defined for the purposes of the Act in section 8(3). Even where reference is made to declarations of paternity, there is no mention of the word 'father'. In section 8(3), a child's status for the purposes of entitlement to maintenance is not dependent on the gender of the parent. The marital status of the parent in relation to each other is similarly ignored under section 8(3), and marriage or cohabitation is only employed as a means by which someone who would not otherwise be a parent – a step-parent – may be accorded with responsibility.[30] Frequently, upon an application for maintenance being made, the respondent father will raise the question of paternity, and the court will direct that a paternity test be done. Increasingly, a woman will summon two men to court, and the court will have tests done on both men in order to decide who is the father and should therefore be financially responsible for the child.[31] However, sometimes the man who has accepted paternity and has paid maintenance over a number of years may subsequently find out and be able to prove that he is not the father of the child. The question of paternity fraud is an issue which the Jamaican courts have yet to consider comprehensively, although there is no reason to believe that the court would depart from the reasoning in the cases like *P v B* (Paternity: Damages for Deceit) [2001] 1 FLR 1041. In that case, the court in England held that the tort of deceit could apply to paternity cases, stating that the law should 'encourage honesty rather than condone dishonesty' in such matters.[32] Where the circumstances involve making false declarations or the falsification of documents, there is scope for a criminal prosecution

Custody

The Children (Guardianship and Custody) Act gives the mother and father the right to make applications to the court for custody orders regardless of whether the mother and father are married to each other. If the issue of paternity is raised, the court is empowered to order tests.[33] Furthermore, the Children (Guardianship and custody) Act is at pains to balance the position of mother and father relating to the right to apply for custody and to ensure that the

---

30.　　See section 8(3)(c).
31.　　The court may need to consider parental hierarchy more precisely as expressed in section 9 of the Act.
32.　　See also 'Laws of Eve: Paternity Fraud,' *Daily Gleaner*, January 18, 2010 and Sherry-Ann McGregor, 'Father by Fraud.' *Daily Gleaner*, June 19, 2017.
33.　　Section 11(1) Status of Children Act, 'In any civil Proceedings....'

applicable principle (the welfare of the child) is not overshadowed by any previously held views of the pre-eminence of the father's claim.

The Children (Guardianship and Custody) Act does not define mother, father, or parent, the question of who is the mother or father, for the purposes of custody applications, and it is expected that in giving these words their ordinary meaning, a biological connection would be necessary. In such circumstances, establishing parenthood by way of the Status of Children Act will remain pertinent. When the application is being made under section 23 of the Matrimonial Clause Act (MCA), that is, in the course of divorce proceedings, parent seems to include step-parents because the definition of relevant child under section 2 of the MCA encompasses a step-parent/step-child relationship.[34]

Often in Jamaica, when a step-parent wishes to acquire parental rights to a child, adoption is advised as the use of the term mother and father in the Children (Guardianship and Custody) Act has not been definitively interpreted to include step-parents. The same would appear to be true of grandparents. So, it can be seen that this area of the law, despite the inroads made by the MCA and the deliberate extension of those deemed to be parents under the Maintenance Act, needs to be updated to reflect the different pieces of legislation that address it.[35]

Inheritance and Succession

It was in this area of the law that common law unions were first recognized. The Inheritance (Provisions for Family and Dependants) Act 1993 in Jamaica recognized unions where cohabitation of five years or more had occurred. It was not until 2005 that non-marital

34. Although recently the standardized forms appear to modify the law multilaterally by departing from the full definition of 'relevant child'.
35. In practice, the Family Court will, in fact, make custody orders to grandparents whereby care and control is vested in them. The legal basis upon which these orders are made is sometimes unclear; although, it could be that the application is actually being made through one of the parents. Since such orders are usually entirely consensual such questions will not usually arise.

unions were recognized as spousal in other areas of family law in the Maintenance Act and Property (Rights of Spouses) Act (PROSA).[36] The Status of Children Act, on the other hand, was directed at children and was not motivated by the need to recognize adult relationships.

In matters of probate and succession, the law attaches considerable weight to legitimacy[37] as a means of classifying children's status in relation to their parents, particularly the father as the means of determining disposition on death. In Jamaica, under section 7 of the Status of Children Act, the concept of legitimacy is retained as a basis for recognizing the relationship of father and child.[38] Presumably, this recognizes that to disregard legitimacy in its entirety would not be practical since it would involve overturning a substantial body of case law and the repeal of certain statutory provisions. The complexity of the law in this area was acknowledged in the case of *Birthwhistle v Vardell* (11) (1835) 2 Cl. & Fin 595 (cited in the *Aga Khan* at case):

> That a man may be a bastard in one country and legitimate in another seems of itself a strong proposition to affirm; but more staggering is it when it is followed up by this other, that in one and the same country he is to be regarded as a bastard when he comes into one court to claim an estate in land, and legitimate when he resorts to another to obtain personal succession.

So although section 3 declares that '...for all purposes of the law of Jamaica the relationship between every person and his father and mother shall be determined irrespective of whether the father and mother are or have been married to each other...', this is subject to a major proviso in the case of sections 4 and 7. Section 4 made transitional provisions for the application of wills and other dispositions already in existence to be honoured even if the testator

---

36. The provisions for recognition of common law relationships in the area of inheritance have recently come to the attention of parliament which is moving to bring consistency to the definition of spouse in all branches of the law.
37. Rebuttal of Presumption of Legitimacy see *Re Estate of Princess Nina Aga Khan* (dec'd) 19 WIR 102.
38. Section 7(1)(a).

died after the act came into effect; and section 7, extended the law to allow inheritance where 'paternity has been admitted by or established[39] during the lifetime of the father....' That allows for the circumstances set out in section 8 to be relied on and in particular a declaration of paternity to be conclusive proof of the relationship.

While the requirement that paternity be established 'during the lifetime of the father' may appear to present difficulties, a careful reading of this section in conjunction with section 10(2) seems to empower the court satisfactorily. The possibility that a declaration of paternity sought for other reasons may affect the interests of beneficiaries may cause the court to require that the application be served on those who may be affected before it is considered.

Jamaica, like other countries in the Caribbean which have enacted Status of Children legislation, has sought to find a balance between the established law of succession[40] and the elevation of a parental relationship over a marital relationship of the parents. Different Caribbean jurisdictions placed different emphases in their status legislation.[41] In particular, countries such as Montserrat have until quite recently placed such weight on legitimacy as a condition for recognition, that it has restricted people in questions of nationality and hence obtaining a passport. In an effort to address this and the inadequacy or absence of legislation in several Caribbean jurisdictions, the Organisation of Eastern Caribbean States (OECS) has coordinated the introduction of a common Status of Children Act for most countries in that grouping.

Migration

In the past, producing a birth certificate with your parents' names recorded was sufficient to establish parentage for the purposes of migration. However, in Jamaica, certain factors call the authenticity

---

39. Presumably, this means relying on events or occurrences during the life of the father to form the basis of a declaration which could be made after the death of the father.

40. See *Seetaran v Powell* (1985) 37 WIR 37 for consideration of the effect Status of Children Act in Trinidad on inheritance.

41. See Zanifa McDowell, 'Status of Children: Legitimacy v Illegitimacy'.

of this documentary evidence of parentage into question as the system for obtaining a birth certificate was not regulated as strictly as necessary and had become compromised. This compromised system has since been addressed by the complete reform of the registration process coupled with the creation of a new registration certificate for births, deaths, and marriages.

Another factor which has had significant bearing on the attitude of consular officers when considering applications to migrate where there is a need to established paternity is a heightened awareness of child trafficking. The spotlight of international concerns in this area has forced countries all over the world to address the laxity of their registration system and those countries to which people traditionally want to move have become particularly sensitive to child trafficking as just one form of illegal immigration with which they have to contend.

For these reasons, and possibly others, the requirement of establishing a parental connection in the process of immigration in most instances has become obtaining DNA evidence and/or a declaration of paternity from the court. In the case of a declaration of paternity, while the court is empowered to take other evidence into account, where the alleged parent and child are both alive, the court tends to rely on scientific tests as a means of resolving the question without having to resort to hearing other evidence. This clarification of parentage by DNA testing has, in some instances, led to devastating consequences when the results of the test show that a child whose parentage was never in question suddenly finds out that they do not belong and as a consequence will not be allowed to migrate with other members of their family.

An interesting aspect to how the Jamaican legislation is perceived by another country was recently publicized in a newspaper report.[42] In an appeal[43] from the Board of Immigration in the United States dealing with deportation, the question turned on the interpretation

---

42.   Sheena Stubbs, 'Bastard still deh!' *Gleaner*, May 3, 2015.
43.   Matter of Shawn Theodore HINES, Respondent 24 I & N Dec. 544(BIA 2008).

of section 320(a) of the Immigration and Nationality Act, in which the court looked at the Status of Children Act and Legitimation Act of Jamaica. What is clear is that when the Status of Children Act that became law in 1976 was being promulgated, there was no evidence of any consideration of its impact on the preceding Legitimation Act that was passed in 1909 and last amended in 1961. While this may have been of little or no consequence locally, the fact that in another jurisdiction it should be an issue upon which the rights of a person born in Jamaica are affected is cause for concern.

In the case of a child who is adopted, the adoptive parents will become the legally recognized parents for all purposes, and it is only to the extent of the rules of consanguinity and affinity that there remains an acknowledgement of the connection between the adopted child and the birth parents.

Fertility Treatment

The legal aspects of Assisted Reproductive Treatment (ART) have at its heart the determination of who will be the child's parents assuming that treatment is successful. Traditionally, the mother of a child is the person who gave birth and the father is the person who supplied the sperm. However, depending on the type of treatment, it may be that neither of the persons who have acted in the traditional way (supplied sperm or given birth to the child) actually wish to have any parental role in the child's life. They may be performing these services to assist a couple who are having reproductive challenges, with the full intention that the couple will assume the role of parents going forward. Where the law in a particular country does not acknowledge the medical advancements that have taken place and their implications on questions like parentage, there is a measure of uncertainty. If the parties agree to put aside the traditional definitions and put others into the position of parents, can a contract to that effect be enforced if one side reneges on the agreement or will the court say that such an agreement is void because it is contrary to public policy? Even where the country does recognize ART such as surrogacy contracts, the question of public policy still raises its head in various aspects of the contract's terms.[44] In particular, the law in many jurisdictions continues to view the notion of payment for these services (rent a womb) as being fundamentally repugnant, and only recognizes 'altruistic' surrogacy.[45]

In Jamaica, there has yet to be any legal acknowledgement of ART, and as a result contractual arrangements for such services must inevitably look to a legal framework from another country or state, that appears to be suitable to the needs of the parties. It is time for the legislature to enact provisions that recognize agreements made pursuant to ART, and to state who the mother and father will be in the case of each of the various medical procedures that are available. This is a sensitive area, which calls for the balancing of several contending interests: the welfare of the child, protecting surrogates from exploitation, meeting the needs of infertile couples, and the economic implications of treatment such as insurance, etc. The usually cautious approach of the law is justified, but no one's interests are served by uncertainty.

ESTABLISHING PARENTAGE: THE STATUS OF CHILDREN ACT 1976

The question of child's parentage has been an issue since time immemorial and prior to the advent of scientific testing the methods of resolving this issue were both varied and uncertain. A distinction between a matrilineal and a patrilineal social arrangement is that in a society governed by patrilineal lines of descent, the question of who is the father, becomes central to the issue of who is to inherit or succeed and therefore becomes a significant source of dispute.

44. Carla Spivack, 'National Report: The Law of Surrogate Motherhood in the United States' (report, University School of Law, 2010). This provides a good summary of some of the leading cases in the US.
45. 'Should Contract Law Be Used To Enforce Surrogacy Arrangements?' www.keepcalmtalklaw.co.uk/contract-law-used-surrogacy-arrangements/ 5 December 2013.

The only fundamental difference between the two systems is the route which is taken to resolve the question of to which side of the family does the child belong for the purposes of defining that child's status, namely their identity, their right to inherit, and their right to succeed.[46] In Jamaica, a patrilineal approach is one more feature of the colonial experience and prior to the statutory recognition of blood tests in the Status of Children Act, the law relied on the presumption of paternity through marriage and where it was not applicable for the purposes of maintenance, affiliation proceedings. In essence, the question of parentage rested on marriage, and the necessary starting point was whether or not the parents were married, that is whether or not the child was born inside or outside wedlock.[47] With the passing of the Act, there was a fundamental change of approach.

The Status of Children Act 1976

The guiding principle of the Status of Children Act is to be found in section 3(1):

> Subject to subsection (4) and the provisions of sections 4 and 7, for all purposes of the law of Jamaica the relationship between every person and his father and mother shall be determined irrespective of whether the father and mother are or have been married to each other, and all other relationships shall be determined accordingly.

The landmark significance of the Status of Children Act is that it almost erased the legal distinction between children born of the marriage and those born outside the marriage. The court was vested with the power to make a declaration of paternity that had the effect of granting legal recognition or 'status' to the child in question. Thus, for the purposes of maintenance, migration and significantly in matters of inheritance, etc., the child's paternity would be resolved with certainty by way of the court's declaration.

---

46. A well-known example of matrilineal descent is that a child is Jewish by virtue of the mother or grandmother being Jewish not the father.
47. Legitimation Act.

The Act relegated this arrangement of determining parentage through the marital status of the parents and set out a number of circumstances where there is evidence of parentage. In this scheme of things, the presumption of paternity is just one means of establishing such a connection. There is evidence of paternity under the Act in the following general circumstances:

1. The Presumption of Paternity.
2. Paternity Recognized for Purposes of Succession.
3. Other Prima Facie and Conclusive Evidence of Paternity.

The Presumption of Paternity

1. The first instance of evidence of parenthood in keeping with its historical pre-eminence is the presumption of paternity and so the presumption of paternity remains enshrined in the Status of Children Act at section 6:

> Subject to subsections (2) and (3), a child born to a woman during her marriage, or within 10 months after the marriage has been dissolved by death or otherwise, shall, in the absence of evidence to the contrary, be presumed to be the child of its mother and her husband, or former husband, as the case may be.

The presumption applies 'in the absence of evidence to the contrary' and is therefore rebuttable on the balance of probabilities.[48] The presumption of paternity remains an important feature of marriage in the face of the advancing recognition of common law unions. It is a principle that can be easily overlooked by the courts when the issue of paternity is raised within marriage. An example of this is that in such cases the court orders tests, it will usually state that the costs of testing be shared equally. While the circumstances of each case may differ, acknowledgement of the presumption would militate against this practice of shared costs. That the presumption

---

48. Section 6(3).

exists is a clear statement that marriage has consequences. These consequences put the parties in a different position in relation to the children of the marriage than where couples simply live together. The presumption provides an additional element of security for children, which is an important safeguard for their overall welfare. If there is an attempt to go behind the presumption, it would be fair for the applicant husband to bear the full cost if the presumption is borne out by the results.

Paternity Recognized for the Purposes of Succession

2. The next instance of evidence of paternity is where paternity is recognized for the purposes of succession.[49] According to section 7 of the Status of Children Act, the relationship of father and child will be recognized for the purposes of inheritance if

    a. The father and the mother of the child were married to each other at the time of conception or at some subsequent time;[50] or

    b. Paternity has been admitted by or established during the lifetime of the father (whether by one or more of the types of evidence specified by section 8 or otherwise).

Legitimacy provides evidence of paternity, and so the notion that relationships are determined under the law irrespective of whether the parents were married to each other is not entirely correct.[51]

Section 7(b) is wide in its application as a means of establishing paternity, because it allows an applicant to rely on evidence of acknowledgement from the father that was made during his lifetime,[52] and this evidence may take the form of the type of declaration described in section 8, or otherwise.

---

49. Section 7.
50. This is a recognition of the provisions of the Legitimation Act again.
51. This is acknowledged in section 3.
52. Even though the application may be made after his death.

Prima Facie and Conclusive Evidence of Paternity

3. The Act then goes on to consider paternity in general and what circumstances will be considered to be evidence of paternity. Section 8 provides a comprehensive list of types of evidence of paternity that can come about by virtue of orders in a court or by statutory provisions.

Section 8(1) of the Act states that the inclusion of the father's name on the child's birth certificate pursuant to section 19 of the Registration (Births and Deaths) Act is prima facie evidence of paternity. This Act was amended at the same time that the Status of Children Act was passed to allow the father to be registered on the child's birth certificate upon the sole application of the mother. The father will be notified and has the ability to deny paternity and possibly cancel the entry.

Secondly, under section 8(2), if a document acknowledging that he is the father is signed by such person in the presence of any of a number of listed officials, this will be prima facie evidence of the child's paternity. This is also the case where, by an order obtained in another jurisdiction a person is declared to be the father of a child, such order will be seen under Jamaican law as prima facie evidence of paternity.

Orders declaring or referring to paternity in Jamaica were previously of two kinds, affiliation orders under the Affiliation Act, and Declarations of paternity under section 10 of the Status of Children Act. However, the Affiliation Act has been repealed[53] and section 8(3) which recognized affiliation orders as prima facie evidence of paternity has been deleted. While it is clear that after the repeal of the Affiliation Act such orders would no longer be made, it does not necessarily follow that subsection (3) should have been deleted since there are affiliation orders that remain applicable to children who are still alive and who may in the future need to put forward evidence of paternity. It is hoped that the court would still regard such orders in the way that the deleted subsection stipulates. In any

---

53.   Maintenance Act 2005.

event, the only conclusive proof of paternity[54] recognized as such under Jamaican law is a declaration of paternity made pursuant to an application under section 10. Interestingly, the evidence relied on in seeking a declaration of paternity may take the form of any of those types of evidence listed under sections 6, 7, or 8 of the Act or otherwise including the results of blood tests under section 11. The hearing of the application prior to making the order provides the opportunity for the challenge to, and testing of such evidence and allows the court to arrive at a finding that can be relied upon as conclusive. It becomes clear, therefore, that except in the case of a declaration of paternity all other forms of evidence of paternity that are merely prima facie are capable of being refuted.

The Declaration of Paternity

A declaration under section 10 of the Status of Children Act conclusively establishes whether or not a relationship of father and child exists.[55] Section 8 lists the various circumstances that are prima facie evidence of paternity, but declarations of paternity rank above all the rest.

The courts powers to make a declaration of paternity are set out in section 10.

'Any person' listed under section 10 (1) a, b, or c, who 'wishes to have it determined whether the relationship of father and child exists between two named persons' may apply. Since the court is empowered to determine this question in the broadest sense, as well as being able to declare paternity, it may decline to make any order, or it may make a declaration that the relationship of father and child has been found not to exist. This latter power is, on one hand, an important safeguard for a man who may want conclusive proof that he is not the father of a particular child, but it also provides the scope for a child to be left legally fatherless, on the other. Indeed, in a climate where the government encourages, if not mandates, the record of both parents on the child's birth certificate, a negative

---

54. Or otherwise.
55. Section 8(4).

declaration flies in the face of such a policy.[56] The application may be made before the birth of the child,[57] although as a matter of practice it is likely that the court would not request blood tests until the child is born. The significance of this provision is that it facilitates an order that will include pre-natal expenses.[58]

Where the declaration is being sought after the death of the father, the court may make a further declaration as section 7(1)(b) at the same or a subsequent time.[59]

Establishing Paternity by Way of Blood Tests

The Status of Children Act gives power to the court to:

> give direction for the use of blood tests, and for the taking within a period to be specified in the direction of blood samples from the subject, the mother of the subject, and any party alleged to be the father of the subject, or from any two of those persons.

The phrase 'give direction' rather than order is an acknowledgement of the fact that the lawful taking of a blood sample requires consent, and therefore cannot normally be ordered by the court. Nevertheless section 11(1) is expressed in such a way that it may not necessarily be obvious to the layman and in practice the court tends to behave as if consent is not in issue. In this regard, section 12(1) does make it clear that the blood sample is not to be taken in the absence of the person's consent, and this provision underscores the absence of mandatory powers, but the authority of the court particularly when persons are unrepresented, is almost impossible to challenge. Furthermore, the Act reinforces this position in section 13 where the court is empowered to draw inferences where there is a failure to comply with a direction under section 11(1). Section 13 also provides for the court to prevent a claimant using a presumption of legitimacy as a means of defeating a result from a blood test.

---

56. Though it may not be an official position, staff at the RGD have shown reluctance to remove the name of a man who has been declared not to be the father of a child for this reason.
57. Section 10(3).
58. Section 9(1)(b), Maintenance Act.
59. Note, however, *Seetaram v Powell and Another* [1985] 37 WIR 371.

In recent times, the court has tended towards reliance on DNA testing as the means by which paternity may be ascertained largely for reasons of convenience and saving court time. Whether or not a DNA test comes within the definition of 'any test made with the object of ascertaining the inheritable characteristics of blood'[60] is probably not a question that the courts are anxious to entertain, and thus far it does not appear to have been raised by any litigant. The question could be of some legal significance because if section 11 does not include DNA testing, then the court could not invoke section 13 against a party who refused to undergo such testing.

Another perspective on the impact of DNA testing on provisions such as section 11 is that the objection to mandatory testing is that taking blood without consent is an assault. The collecting of samples for DNA testing, however, does not require such an invasion of the person. This observation coupled with the development of rights of the child point to those rights weighing more heavily than the rights of an uncooperative adult.

Therefore, the court's decision to order blood tests in Jamaica is aimed at getting to the truth. This is usually for the purpose of ascribing liability for maintaining the child. However, cases are arising where a man seeks to assert his claim to have custody or at least access to the child. Where the mother is involved with or even married to someone else, such an application can be highly disruptive to the family unit. In such cases, the court may have to look beyond the simple question of getting at the truth in order to decide whether or not to make a section 11 direction. The welfare of the child may not support testing where the result can be harmful to the family structure. Similarly, the circumstances of the conception, for example rape, may not be conducive to a beneficial parent–child relationship. It is in cases such as this that the welfare principle, the rights of the child, the right to family life, and the societal norms of this country, may not be consistent which each other.

---

60.   Section 2.

Consent and Failure to Comply with Court Directions

The scientific test prescribed in the Status of Children Act to provide evidence of paternity is a blood test. By its very nature, this requires a puncturing of the skin and is therefore deemed to be an assault in the absence of consent. Where a blood sample is to be taken from a minor the consent of the person who has care and control of that minor is required[61] unless they have attained the age of 16 in which case they can give their own consent.[62] This is the reason why the court's power in section 11 is described as a power to give a direction rather than the making of an order.[63] However, the application of DNA testing to this area of the law has negated the significance of this provision since it is possible to obtain a sample for DNA testing without extracting blood. Nevertheless, to comply with the power under section 11, it is a blood sample which is to be tested and, in such circumstances, the requirement for consent is still applicable. There have been recent developments in respect of the DNA testing in criminal proceedings, but Parliament has yet to address this issue comprehensively in the area of family law cases where the impact of such testing is equally far-reaching and far more widespread.

The need for consent brings with it the question of how the court is to deal with the circumstances in which there is a failure to comply with the directive of the court, particularly in the form of a refusal of consent. Section 13 states that in such circumstances 'the court may draw such inferences, if any, from that fact as may appear proper in the circumstances.'[64] Section 13(2) ensures that where the success of a party's claim could rest on a presumption in law, if such a party refuses to comply with the direction of the court having been given an opportunity to submit to testing, the court will not allow the

---

61. Section 12(3).
62. Section 12(2) – this is another example of a person below the age of majority being able to make 'adult' decisions.
63. In any event, most people are unaware of this distinction and the court itself tends to convey a degree of compulsion.
64. *McVeigh v Beattie* [1988] 2 WLR 992; *Walker v Tulloch* (1992) 29 JLR 253.

presumption to be the determinant in the claim and will 'dismiss his claim for relief notwithstanding the absence of evidence to rebut the presumption'.

Challenging the Test

The person responsible for carrying out the test is required to produce a report which 'shall be received by the court as evidence in the proceedings of the matters stated therein.'[65] There is provision in the Act for the person making the report to explain or amplify any statement in the report at the direction of the court[66] and also for persons to be called to give evidence and be cross-examined provided that they are served with notice of intention within 14 days or as the court otherwise directs.[67] Clearly, the result of the test is simply evidence that should be considered by the court along with whatever additional information may be available. It may appear (and is often concluded) that the result is itself conclusive. While this is likely to be the case depending on the nature of the test, particularly if it is accepted by the parties, it is possible to challenge the integrity, regimen, or cogency of the conclusion that is deduced from the test.

Consequences of a Negative Test Result

Where the DNA test results disclose that the child is not the child of the man who is before the court, unless there is a challenge as to the integrity of the test or the interpretation of the test results in the report as stated above, the court will act in reliance of the result. In maintenance cases, this will usually mean that the man is found not to have an obligation to maintain and therefore may be discharged. The question is often raised whether a man found not to be the biological parent, can nevertheless be bound by virtue of having 'accepted' the child as his own.[68] Although it has not been

---

65.   Section 11(3).
66.   Section 11(4).
67.   Section 11(5).
68.   This will arise where the parties are married to each other.

specifically decided by a court in Jamaica, there are cases that seem to make it clear that such a child would not be considered relevant[69] by way of being accepted as a child of the family. In other words, the court is unlikely to find that there has been acceptance, and therefore impose the responsibilities of a parent, where it is premised on deception.

THE CONCEPT OF PARENTAGE

Historically parents, in particular the father,[70] owned and controlled their children[71] although such rights were accompanied by vaguely defined duties as to upbringing. The law was disinclined to pry into family affairs and just as this applied to husband and wife, so it was in respect of their children. Child labour was always a feature of agricultural society in England, and played a significant role in Britain's period of industrialization. In Jamaica, the fact that the children of slaves belonged to the slave owner not the biological parents, as well as the breeding of slaves with little regard for family structure accentuated the perception of child as a commodity and increased their plight. While the society rages about horrific cases of abuse that receive fulsome media attention, social workers, NGOs, state agencies, and ministry officials address these issues in the face of a society that wants quick answers and instant redress. Limited resources play a significant part the state's ability to address the abuse of our children.

The United Nations Convention on The Rights of the Child was adopted in 1989, and Jamaica as a member of the UN accepted the tenets of the convention. To be given legal effect, the Convention requires ratification in the form of the passage of domestic legislation. The Convention repeatedly acknowledges the importance of a child's relationship with its parents, and several articles within the

---

69.   *R v R* [1968] 2 All ER 608 per Park J, *Re L (an Infant)* [1968] 1 All ER 20 per Lord Denning MR and *Snow v Snow* [1971] 3 All ER 858.

70.   *Re Agar-Ellis* (1883) 24 Ch D 317.

71.   *R v de Mannerville* (1804) 5 East 221.

convention are devoted to strengthening, preserving, and protecting that relationship. It is recognized that ideally the primary source of care for a child is its parents and while the state must position itself so as to be able to step in if necessary, the role of the authorities should be supportive. It is important, therefore, for parentage to be ascertained, and it is important to provide mechanisms whereby parenting responsibilities and obligations can be defined and ascribed to those who are within the scope of this category.

In pursuit of ascertaining who is a parent from a biological standpoint, the law has been greatly assisted by scientific developments as seen when considering legal provisions as to testing. However, science has also developed in other aspects, in particular assisted reproductive treatment (ART). Other countries have found it necessary to enact legislation governing whether and in what circumstances a parental relationship exists. The legal recognition of these procedures raises complex ethical questions and perhaps for fear of waking a sleeping giant, both the church and Parliament have remained silent. In any event, it is to be expected that when the time comes for statutory pronouncement, Jamaica will, as in many instances before, take guidance from the legislation of other Commonwealth countries in this area. The concern at this stage is that the courts may be called upon to resolve an issue in this area before Parliament has enacted the requisite laws.

Automatic and Acquired Parentage

At common law parentage is established by the relationship between the mother and the father, that is whether they are married or not. Marriage brings the presumption of paternity. This has come to mean that married parents share parental responsibility (or in Jamaican terms: custodial rights) unless a court says otherwise. Where the parents are not married, there is no presumption that the man is the father, and his status as a parent is dependent on an admission by the 'father' or adjudication in court usually based on testing. It is only then that the court may assign parenting rights and obligations to the man in most cases. Even though this appears to be automatic for practical purposes, the court does have the power not to grant parenting rights even where a biological connection is established.[72] This is an issue that is fundamental to the contention made on behalf of men that they are not treated equally by the law in relation to children:

> The father of the child previous to the Status of Children Act 1976 had no rights with respect to his child born out of wedlock and could only be compelled to maintain the child under the restricted provisions of the Affiliation Act.[73]

Historically, the vesting of parental and hence custodial rights in the unmarried mother solely was a means of providing some protection for the child in the face of paternal uncertainty. This unquestioned assumption puts the mother at an advantage which, some may argue, is wholly justified given the transient nature of male commitment in some cases. Others would argue that, in most cases, the Jamaican courts in putting the welfare of the child first do, in fact, take a balanced approach to parentage,[74] which reflects a recognition of the prevalence of common law unions as the standard in the Jamaican society.

It was, therefore, the Status of Children Act which really put the parents on an equal footing, to the extent that it is now commonplace for fathers, regardless of marital status, to apply for, and sometimes be granted, joint custody.

Extending the scope of Parentage: The Maintenance Act 2005, section 8

For the purposes of creating an obligation to maintain their children, the legal definition of parent has been extended beyond biological boundaries under section 8(3) of the Maintenance Act:

72. *Finlay v Matthews* (1971) 17 WIR 69.
73. Leighton M. Jackson, 'The Law Relating to Children in Jamaica: Report on Guardianship and Custody,' (report, Ministry of Justice, Jamaica, UNICEF).
74. See *Carey v Clarke* (1971) 17 WIR 69, where the welfare principle was used to override the exclusive right of the mother to custody.

For the purposes of this Act, a person is the parent of a child if –

The person's name is entered as a parent in the general register of births pursuant to the Registration (Births and Deaths) Act, or in a register of births or parentage information kept under the law of ant overseas jurisdiction;

The person is or was a party to a marriage (including a void marriage) or cohabitation and the child is a child of the marriage or cohabitation;

The person is a party to a marriage or cohabitation and accepts as one of the family a child of the other party to the marriage or cohabitation;

The person adopts the child;

The person has admitted paternity or a court has made a declaration of paternity under section 10 of the Status of Children Act against the person in respect of the child;

The person is the child's natural mother;

The person has at any time in any proceedings before a court, or in writing signed by the person, acknowledged that the person is a parent of the child, and ta court has not made a finding of paternity of the child that is contrary to that acknowledgement; or

The person is in loco parentis to the child, including a person who has demonstrated a settled intention treat a person as a child of the person's family, except under an arrangement where the child is placed for valuable consideration in a home by a person having lawful custody.

The purpose of this provision is to close the loopholes regarding the obligation to maintain a child so that those who embark on or embrace parental responsibility in some way or another are visited with the attendant duty to maintain that child.[75] This is an attempt by the state to limit its obligation to the child as it ensures the financial protection of the child.

Whether by way of a Family and Children Act (Belize), or a Family Law Act (Barbados), or other examples of encompassing legislation that is found elsewhere, it is becoming increasingly necessary to

---

75.   This creates a situation where the person with custody will have a duty to maintain, but it does not give the person with the duty to maintain the corresponding right to apply for custody.

address the question of consistency in the area of parental rights and responsibilities head on. Clearly, the framers of the Jamaican Child Care and Protection Act did not regard the creation of a unified structure of parentage as a primary consideration.

Limiting the scope of Parentage

Should anyone with a connection to the child however tenuous be able to apply to the court for parental rights? Should persons who are already related to the child, such as siblings or aunts, be able to get parental rights, and if so, in what circumstances? Should there be a hierarchy of parentage with some classes of person ranking higher than others, or is it all about welfare? Does family life mean or include the extended family members? Are the alternative mechanisms of guardianship and adoption sufficient to cover any omissions? These are the questions that a Jamaican Parliament and the Jamaican courts must resolve in order to create a new landscape of parentage for children. Many grandparents act as parents, and the law only partially accepts this status. Most other institutions, for example, the church and schools respect this position and work along with it for the sake of the child's best interests.

PRACTICE AND PROCEDURAL ASPECTS OF THE STATUS OF CHILDREN LAWS

The Status of Children Act in Jamaica gives jurisdiction to both the high and lower courts to hear applications and make declarations as to paternity. Therefore, when applying for a declaration in the Supreme Court, a fixed date claim form would be used to initiate the proceedings. In the lower court, which can be a Parish Court or the Family Court, the application is made in the usual way, by summons on information or complaint.

Often, the question of paternity will arise as a sub-issue, for example, where an application for maintenance of the child is before the court and the respondent disputes liability on the grounds that he is not the father of the child in question. The court may in any civil proceedings give direction for blood tests 'on the application of any party to the proceedings'. This may be done orally in the lower court or either orally or by notice of application in the high court. Quite often in the high court, the trial judge will give directions for blood tests without an application being made by one of the parties. This practice could be called into question since it is not in keeping with the statute. However, a case could be made in these circumstances for such action to be covered by the overriding objective of the Civil Procedure Rules (CPR).

Evidence

In cases where the child and the putative father (to borrow a term from affiliation) are alive, the advent of scientific evidence has rendered most other forms of evidence as merely anecdotal. A DNA test tends to resolve the issue completely. In cases where the father is dead, however, the court will rely heavily on information about the deceased and his relationship with the child. This will usually come from relatives and, in some cases, the mother of the child. It is in cases such as this that the legitimation of the child by subsequent marriage of the parents can lend considerable support to the application. Similarly, if an affiliation order had, in fact, been made, although previously noted as prima facie evidence in itself, there is no reason why the court should not take it into account in deciding whether to make a declaration of paternity.

In cases where the child is born of the marriage between the parties who are now in dispute, the allegation that the man is not the father of the child is seeking to rebut the presumption of paternity. While the court in such circumstances will usually not make any order for maintenance until the matter is resolved, the presumption should operate to protect the child and an interim order should be made until the contrary is proved. Even though such an approach, which is rarely taken, would leave the mother at risk of having to repay monies advanced, this would be the lesser of two evils in that the interests of the child would be put to the fore.

Where the putative father is deceased and there are children other than the child who is the subject of the application, the court may order that those children be given notice of the proceedings. Where the application is made in the course of administering an estate this will be a natural part of the procedure. On the other hand, where the application is not made for these purposes and the other children are not witnesses, the court may decide that it is prudent to notify them because their interest in their father's estate whether realized or not can be affected by the outcome of the application.

Orders

The court may make a declaration of paternity and further orders as a consequence of the declaration. The court can order that the particulars of the person named on the child's birth certificate as father be removed or at least that a fresh birth certificate with the real father's particulars be issued. While the registrar general has usually been compliant with respect to orders from the court, in recent times that department has baulked at carrying out those orders that will leave the child without a registered father. It appears that while in many cases a father's name is not proffered at registration and a birth certificate is issued without this information, for policy reasons the Registrar General's Department (RGD) is less inclined to effectively delete particulars where someone is found not to be the father by the court, unless a substitution is being made. This is understandable because it leaves the child fatherless, and considering the paramountcy of the welfare principle, and the rights to family, this is not looked upon favourably.

Furthermore, the consequences of a man being excluded or being proven not to be the father go beyond matters of registration, which is only now being considered. In circumstances where the child has grown accustomed to the fact that 'x' is his or her father, and that person has been a fixture in their life, a declaration to the contrary may be devastating. The principle that a child is entitled to know their ancestry and therefore the truth in relation to these matters is not unimpeachable. There may be a lot to be said for a perpetuation of the falsehood and a continuation of the parental relationship at least until the child reaches adulthood, depending on the interpretation of what is in the best interests of the child. In fact, some fathers on finding that they are not the child's biological relative opt to remain responsible. Procedurally, the court has no power to compel good parenting, and ultimately it becomes a matter that is best pursued by way of public education, training, and exposure to positive family values that raise the bar of social norms across the board.

THE WAY FORWARD

A number of issues in the arena of parentage are in need of review. While Jamaica has signed on to the international conventions regarding the rights of the child, the counrty has not yet ratified by enacting legislation which addresses custody, parentage, and parental responsibility of children in the context of these overarching principles. The opportunity was disregarded when the Child Care and Protection Act was being drafted. The consideration of children in the care of the state and the restructuring of the courts[76] were important matters that had to be dealt with urgently, but the legislation could have been more comprehensive.

The rapid scientific development in the area of fertility treatment has outstripped the law in Jamaica. At present, there are too many parental options that have been introduced by these advances which are simply not recognized in Jamaican law. Surrogacy has, in some jurisdictions, morphed into a new industry, with attendant legal support in the form of contracts and insurance. The legal position of those who donate genetic and or reproductive material or receive it from others in the scientific environment should be clarified in law so that people are protected and the vulnerable are

---

76.   As well as Children's Courts, there have since been further legislative amendments to the Resident Magistrate's Court system, now called Parish Courts. However, the change of name and the lifting of certain conditions will not make much difference without the injection of resources.

not liable to exploitation. While these considerations are viewed as having little priority in the context of the society, it may be because of the absence of publicity so far. To ignore this area of the law is perilous and leaves the legal system open to ridicule by failing to address these issues. The law of contract by itself is not an adequate means of dealing with these matters.

DNA testing is now codified in legislation regarding its use in criminal proceedings, and while there may be a good reason why this law was drafted with strict parameters,[77] the fact remains that the specific and comprehensive recognition of DNA testing for ascertaining family relationships is long overdue.

The Registration of Births and Deaths Act should be revisited in light of human trafficking concerns and the emergence of sophisticated methods of identity fraud. The need to re-vamp the Children (Guardianship and Custody) Act, to set out specifically, who are parents and what parental responsibility entails must be addressed. How these responsibilities are to be apportioned between parents, and who, and in what circumstances applications can be made should be looked at. The disparity between who is a parent for the purposes of maintenance and who is a parent for custody purposes (admittedly originating from different legal sources with different considerations) should be made more coherent. In this context, it is understandable that so many countries have gone the route of all-encompassing laws such as family law reform acts.

The promotion of parental agreements whether for maintenance and generally regarding all aspects of care of children as an important means of addressing disputes is a feature of our recent legislation.[78] Agreements and family counselling, particularly in relation to parental obligations and paternity fraud, can go a long way in getting parents to take the necessary steps to avoid contentious court proceedings. However, such mechanisms need

---

77.   There is urgency to address this area where a criminal investigation is
       concerned.
78.   Maintenance Act, PROSA.

support in the form of lawyers and other family professionals that come with attendant costs that must be borne either by the parties or the state or both.

It is no longer sufficient to declare 'no bastard nu deh'. The law should keep pace with local and international imperatives.

9. Children and the State: Care and Crime

INTRODUCTION

Maxine and her 13 year old daughter, Paula stood before the Family Court. Maxine wrings her hands as she explains her plight to the judge. Paula has not been attending school regularly for the last four months, and it wasn't until the guidance counsellor at Paula's school notified her that Paula had been in a fight with another girl that Maxine became aware of it. When questioned about where she was going during school hours, Paula eventually disclosed that she was 'hanging out' with 'friends' in a dangerous part of the city. Maxine took drastic steps and began escorting Paula to school (after the two-week suspension for fighting had elapsed) and grounded her. Paula began to sneak out at night and when Maxine challenged her about it, a fight ensued. When Maxine went to the police, Paula stood in front of the police and threatened to burn down the house where they lived. Maxine ends her lament to the judge with the words 'I can't deal with it anymore, mi want yu just tek her!'

Throughout the time that Maxine is speaking to the judge, Paula is silent, brooding, and looks menacingly at Maxine.

Traditionally, parents in Jamaica (as in much of the world), have viewed their children as just another one of their possessions with which they could do more or less, what they pleased. Yes, there was the obligation to grow them in the 'right and proper way', but that was subject to the means, capacity, and benevolence of the overseeing parent. This person, quite often, was not even a biological parent of the child. The care of the child also could be affected by whatever exigencies arose along the way – the migration or death of a parent, the loss or change of the parent's employment, even weather conditions, particularly in farming communities, could affect the way a child was or was not cared for. In rural communities, children often have a part to play in the agricultural process, whether it is helping with sowing or reaping, or storage or selling, or, at the very least, accompanying those who do. Children may be required to care for younger children while the adults are outside of the home, and unfortunately, in some situations, they may be required to go out and undertake some income-producing activity, such as begging, in order to contribute to the household.[1]

Disciplining children is often seen in the context of the biblical edict 'spare the rod and spoil the child', and this may be used as justification, in some instances, for unconscionable physical abuse, which paradoxically, we may well boast of in adulthood. The danger, of course, is that this becomes the template for how we treat our children and the next generation will be similarly scarred.

---

1.   Contrary to section 41 of the Child Care and Protection Act.

THE CHILD CARE AND PROTECTION ACT

The Child Care and Protection Act has been in force for nearly 10 years, and in the initial stages of its enactment the country proceeded in much the same way that it had previously. There was much fanfare for the creation of the Office of the Children's Advocate, and the installation of its first head. In the courts, it was business as usual. There was a short period when judges were receiving training, and gradually the application of the new law became increasingly apparent. The terminology has changed and with that has come a different emphasis. Certain problem areas remain; however, the absence of resources to bring full meaning to the intervention capacity of the Office of the Children's Advocate and the Child Development Agency (CDA) now Child Protection and Family Services Agency, is a continuing source of frustration. The Children's Register took longer to establish than expected and the persistent categorization of children as being uncontrollable and the undesirable consequences of such a pronouncement brought Jamaica unwittingly into the spotlight. The tragedy of the Armadale Fire[2] was an indication of the continuing level of neglect and lack of control by the State where vulnerable children are concerned.

The objects[3] of the Child Care and Protection Act are, inter alia, 'to promote the best interests, safety and wellbeing of children'. Unfortunately, there are sections of the Act[4] that have failed to deliver in this regard. If anything, the relentless cry over time is that rather than affording protection of the child, the Act has been a tool by which vulnerable children have been victimized, punished, or exposed to abuse,[5] which detracts from their well-being in a radical way. In many respects, the Act does represent a significant advance

2.   Report of the Commission of Enquiry, 2010 and for a harrowing account, see 'Rising from the Ashes of Armadale: A Survivor Speaks – www.unicef.org/jamaica/violence_ 25474.htm
3.   Section 3.
4.   Section 24.
5.   Jamaicans For Justice (JFJ), a local human rights group has been consistent in calling for legislative development in light of incidents such as the Armadale fire and the detention of children in adult facilities.

in recognizing that the State has a fundamental responsibility to all children. However, in some respects, rather than addressing certain problems, it has simply repackaged them in new terms and procedures which, in the absence of public education and acceptance, can be viewed as draconian. The government appreciates the need to revisit this law and put the resources into addressing some of the deep-seated issues.[6] The Act was an ambitious piece of legislation that has not lived up to the expectations of many of its proponents.[7] Nevertheless, it has provided a learning opportunity for the courts, state agencies, social workers, and the government, which may auger well for developing the right attitudes that promote progress.

The Child Care and Protection Act and the Definition of 'Child'

The central component of the Act is the guidance by the State as to the care and protection, permissible and impermissible activities relating to children. The question, therefore, immediately arises as to what is a child from the standpoint of the law. On the face of it the Child Care and Protection Act is quite unequivocal in its definition and states that a child is 'a person under the age of eighteen years'.[8] However, even within the Act this demarcation line is significantly undermined.[9] For example, there has been a considerable amount of debate on the age limit for making certain important decisions in life, in particular the age at which a person may consent to sexual intercourse.[10] While this is not referred to in the Child Care and Protection Act, the standard, such as it may be, which is set in this Act, is increasingly being viewed as the prism through which all other legislation concerning children should be judged.

---

6. The security and suitability of detention centres for chidren has been an ongoing concern.
7. 'Committee on the Rights of the Child Considers the Report of Jamaica,' January 20, 2015. www.ohchr.org.
8. Section 2.
9. For example, section 34.
10. This was brought to the fore in submissions to the parliamentary committee which reviews the Sexual Offences Act, and in newspaper articles.

Despite the Law Reform (Age of Majority) Act, which is for the most part consistent with, but similarly equivocal as the Child Care and Protection Act, numerous other pieces of legislation which draw the line of maturity create as much confusion as consternation. For example:

1. Under the Maintenance Act, the entitlement to child maintenance ceases at 18, UNLESS;

   a. The child is in tertiary studies, in which case it can be extended to 23, or

   b. The child is dependent because of a physical or mental infirmity or disability, in which case it can apply indefinitely.

2. Under the Marriage Act, the minimum age of marriage is 16, BUT;

   a. Up to the age of 18, parental consent is required, UNLESS the person is a widow or a widower, and

   b. No one under the age of 21 can enter into a marriage *in articulo mortis*, UNLESS they are a widow or a widower, or the person whose consent is required gives it verbally.

3. Under the Children (Guardianship and Custody) Act, the age limit for the granting of guardianship and custody orders is 18, BUT

   a. Maintenance orders pursuant to certain custody orders can be extended up until the age of 21.

4. The Sexual Offences Act defines a child as a person under the age of 18 years, BUT

   a. For the purposes of offences committed under Part IV of the Act, a child is a person under the age of 16 years.

The use of the term 'minor' in some laws adds to the complexity of this question. So there are those who would seek a greater measure of consistency, and those who are not so troubled by the attainment of adult rights and obligations at different times depending on the nature of those rights and obligations.

PART I: PROTECTION OF AND OFFENCES AGAINST CHILDREN

The Children's Advocate

Section 4 of the Child Care and Protection Act establishes by commission of Parliament, the Children's Advocate. The rules as to the operation and powers of the commission are set out in the first schedule to the Act. Section 4(3) of the Act gives the Children's Advocate general powers to consider if a child is in need of legal representation, to have the court refer that matter to it, or for the court to grant a legal aid certificate. Whereas it would appear upon a general reading of this provision that the Children's Advocate might represent children in need of this type of assistance before the court, a closer reading may dispel this assumption: The court may:

i.   refer the case to the Children's Advocate, or

ii. grant a legal aid certificate, or

iii. adjourn the case for either I or ii to be pursued, or

iv. issue a notice for the Children's Advocate to make its determination under section 4(3).[11]

The practical distinction between (i) and (iv), that is, a reference and a notice in this context, is elusive. In either case, the matter will be brought to the attention of the Office of the Children's Advocate for them to consider whether to assist in keeping with section 15 of the first schedule. Notably, under section 15(4) of the schedule where the Children's Advocate grants an application for assistance in legal proceedings, 'he may arrange for the provision of legal advice or representation and any other assistance'. In short, the Children's Advocate becomes a clearing house, directing the responsibility of representing children to others. Indeed, section 15(3) makes it clear that the application should only be granted where 'there is no

---

11.   Sections 4(3)(a), (b), and (c).

other person or body likely to provide assistance'. The Children's Advocate may intervene in court proceedings, but only with the leave of the court, and only in circumstances where:

i.   The case raises a question of principle, or

ii.   There are other special circumstances.

The Children's Advocate is also given extensive powers to investigate complaints.[12] In the course of the investigation, evidence may be taken, a report compiled, and recommendations may be given on how to address the matter, whether by alteration of enactment, rule, or regulation. This report can be tabled before Parliament and if any criminal offence is uncovered, the finding can be referred to the relevant authority.[13]

The Children's Advocate is answerable to Parliament and must submit an annual report as to the exercise of its functions.[14] It is required to keep records and also to maintain confidentiality.[15] In summary, therefore, while the Children' Advocate may investigate, appear amicus curiae[16] and intervene[17] in proceedings in consideration of the best interests of the child, for practical purposes, the duties of this office are directed towards supervisory functions and as an aid to Parliament in the formation of child policy. Certainly, the responsibilities are wide-ranging and onerous, and without the provision of considerable resources with different departments and sections, it is difficult to see how these duties can be effectively discharged.[18]

The Children's Register[19]

A children's register is to be kept by the Children's Registry which is created by the Act. The purpose of the children's register is to

12.   Section 7 and Sections 16 and 17 of the First Schedule.
13.   Section 16(11) of the First Schedule.
14.   Section 21(2) of the First Schedule.
15.   Section 19(1) of the First Schedule.
16.   Section 15(1) of the First Schedule.
17.   Section 14 of the First Schedule.
18.   This is being addressed by the gradual provision of additional staff.
19.   Section 5.

enable persons, including prescribed persons to make reports of when they suspect that a child

a. has, is being, or is likely to be abandoned, neglected or physically or sexually ill-treated; or

b. is otherwise in need of care and protection.[20]

Where a person or prescribed person fails to make a report in circumstances where they should, a criminal offence is committed that carries a fine of up to $500,000 or six months' imprisonment or both.[21] The obligation to make a report to the Children's Registry differs between the general application to 'any person'[22] and the specific application to a prescribed person[23] in that, generally, the test is subjective for any person and objective for the prescribed person. The duty to report arises upon having information that causes 'that person to suspect....' On the other hand, the test as to the obligation to report which is placed on a prescribed person is objective: the provision refers to the acquisition of information 'which ought reasonably to cause that person to suspect...' The question then becomes: what would the reasonable physician, school principal, social worker, guidance counsellor etc. make of this information? Should it cause suspicion in such a person? In addition, if a person commits an offence under this section, the minister may direct the 'relevant regulatory entity' to conduct an investigation. [24]

Even if the information is acquired in circumstances which would make it privileged or confidential, the obligation to report remains unless there is no substantial risk of further endangerment.[25] This could give rise to some interesting scenarios, such as the lawyer who receives information from his client that he/she abused a child. The lawyer may not have to report the matter if the child and the

---

20.   Section 6(7).
21.   Section 6(4).
22.   Section 6(2).
23.   Section 6(3).
24.   Section 6(5).
25.   Section 6(9).

(alleged) perpetrator are no longer in contact. Since the privilege between lawyer and client belongs to the client, the strength of this provision remains to be tested.

Making a report has the effect of alerting the Children's Advocate and 'the government agency responsible for children',[26] namely the Child Development Agency to further investigate and, if necessary, initiate proceedings in court under section 13 of the Act. The person who has custody, care, and control of the child should also be informed unless it would endanger the child or impede the investigations.[27]

Children in Need of Care and Protection

Section 8 of the Act sets out the circumstances in which a child will be considered in need of care and protection. The circumstances stipulate the conditions in which a child finds himself/herself which are considered to be unacceptable by the Act.[28] This is a state of affairs that may or may not be the result of the actions of a responsible person, or the neglect of a responsible person, but the Act does not address it from that perspective but from the standpoint of the condition of the child, regardless of how that child finds him or herself in that condition.

Cruelty to Children

By contrast, section 9 sets out the criminal offence of cruelty as a first premise and explains the offence in the subsections that follow. The offence, which is triable summarily or in the high court on indictment, is punishable by a fine and or up to five years' imprisonment.[29] The neglect of a child is described under three headings:

   i.   Failure to carry out the parental duties prescribed by the Act;[30]

---

26.   Section 7(1)(a).
27.   Section 7(1)(b).
28.   Sections 8(1) and (2).
29.   Section 9(2).
30.   Sections 27 and 28.

ii.   Smothering a child;

iii. Exposing a child to water or fire or any noxious or flammable substance without adequate protection.[31]

There is also provision dealing with giving, selling, or supplying intoxicating liquor to any child, which will be deemed ill-treatment. The section also deals with those who, being convicted of an offence under section 9, have an interest in or knowledge of money accruing or becoming payable as a result of the death of a child. Substantial penalties[32] are imposed and the matter can be dealt with summarily or on indictment before the circuit court. The penalties do not include the power to intervene in the payment of such money in light of what may have taken place and the consequent responsibility for the death of the child.

Trafficking

There has been considerable international attention given to the problem of child trafficking for labour and sexual exploitation. Child trafficking takes place across international borders and within countries where children may be moved from rural areas to the cities. In some instances, Jamaica has been given specific attention[33] and recommendations on how to address the problem. Trafficking is linked to the commercial and agricultural sectors in some countries, but to the tourism and entertainment sectors in some countries such as Jamaica.[34] Combating trafficking requires co-operation with different sectors, including the internal security forces and the authorities responsible for border control. As such, it is a problem that requires a considerable amount of financial resources.

Trafficking of a child is a criminal offence under section 10 of the Child Care and Protection Act, although trafficking is not defined.

31.   Sections 9(3)(a)(b) and (c).
32.   Unspecified fine and imprisonment for up to 10 years.
33.   US Department of State, 'Trafficking in Persons Report: Country Narrative: Jamaica,' 2016.
34.   Like many countries there is also a household/domestic aspect to child trafficking.

The penalty for the offence that is to be tried on indictment before the circuit court is a fine or imprisonment for up to 10 years or both.

Warrants for Search and Detention of Children – the Powers of the Justice of the Peace

Where an information on oath is laid before a justice of the peace that a child has been or is being assaulted or neglected or that a schedule 2 offence is being or likely to be committed against a child, the justice of the peace may issue a warrant.[35] The warrant is to search for the child, remove the child to a place of safety, and thereafter have the child brought before the court within 48 hours.[36] The justice of the peace may also issue a warrant for the apprehension of any person who is accused of any offence in respect of the child's circumstances.[37] The justice of the peace may also prohibit a person who is accused of any offence arising from subsection (1) from entering or remaining in the household residence of the child or following or waylaying the child.[38] This would be an alternative to removing the child. This power could raise questions as to the extent to which the court can legitimately curtail the exercise of property ownership rights where the interests of the child are at stake.

Under section 12, a constable, children's officer or after-care officer may, without warrant, take a child against whom schedule 2 offences have been committed to a place of safety. The child should then be brought before the court within 48 hours. Thus, any child who is need of care and protection may be brought before a children's court and thereafter be dealt with by the court. There is a great deal of emphasis in sections 8–13 on searching for, taking control of, and producing before the court, the child who is to be protected from the various circumstances outlined in this part of the Act. It

35. Section 11(2).
36. Section 11(2)(a).
37. Section 11(3).
38. Sections 11(3)(a) and (b).

can easily be perceived that the child is the offender rather than the victim when these powers are being exercised, and subsequently when the court is exercising its powers under section 14. There is, essentially, a thin line between extensive powers to protect a child and the oppression or victimization of the child for what has been done to them. This may not be Parliament's intention, but it may well be the perception of those who are subject to the actions that are taken in furtherance of this part of the Act.

The Powers of the Court

The Children's Court is created by the Child Care and Protection Act and is defined as one which is established in accordance with its provisions.[39] The third schedule to the Act sets out the manner in which the court will be constituted. This contemplates the specialized training of justices of the peace who will form a panel from which its members will be drawn to sit with the parish judge (formerly resident magistrate), as the Children's Court.[40] Paragraph 4 of the third schedule allows any family court to be deemed a Children's Court, that is, a Parish Court Judge sitting alone.

Powers of the Children's Court in Relation to a Child

The powers of the Children's Court include:

a. The committal of the child to the care of any fit person who is willing to care for the child.[41] The fit person may be a relative, and according to section 26 of the Act has the same obligation for the maintenance of the child as a parent. A fit person is, in fact, by the definition, accorded in section 2, an impersonal entity and means 'the Minister, and any other person or body, whether corporate or unincorporated, designated by the Minister'.[42] In essence, a fit person is a person or institution

---

39.   Section 71.
40.   Paragraph 2(b) of the Third Schedule allows for the court to be constituted by an RM (now Parish Judge) sitting alone.
41.   Section 14.
42.   Section 2(1).

whose power to be so classified devolves to the minister. The court generally refers to the exercise of this power as a fit person order (FPO). There is, on the face of the act, no limit to the duration of an FPO.[43]

b. A supervision order placing a child under the supervision of a probation and after-care officer or some other person selected by the minister can also be made by the Children's Court.[44]

c. Detention in a Place of Safety – The Children's Court has the power to have the child detained in a place of safety, which is any place designated by the minister to be such.[45] This power is to be exercised where the Court...is not in a position to decide whether any or what order ought to be made under this section. This would be the equivalent of remanding an adult in custody for his own safety, but in the circumstances of the Act, this is being applied to a child who may be the victim of an offence[46] rather than the perpetrator under this subsection. These are interim powers, and orders made are not in force for more than 30 days although they can be extended by further order to 60 days.[47] If by reason of illness, accident, or 'other justifiable cause' a child is not able to come to court, the court may make any of these orders in their absence.[48]

d. Miscellaneous. The court may also order counselling for the child[49] or require a parent or guardian to enter into recognizance to exercise proper care and control over the child.[50]

e. Powers of the Children's Court Regarding Adults

The notion of being able to compel parenting is a debatable concept. Certainly, under section 14(2)(a) of the Act, this is precisely the power bestowed on the court by Parliament. It is generally used

43. Presumably, it would be curtailed at the time when the child attains majority.
44. Section 14(2)(c).
45. Section 14(5).
46. Section 14(1).
47. Section 14(6).
48. Section 14(7).
49. Section 14(2)(f).
50. Section 14(2)(a).

as a measure, short of detention of the child, and is to be exercised when the parent or guardian is co-operative and committed to the improvement of their parenting skills.

Adult Offenders

Apart from any of the penalties under section 9 or for the actual offences listed in the second schedule, the Children's Court has powers[51] to make orders in respect of adults as follows:

Section 14(d) – A person may be prohibited from entering the premises where the child resides for up to two years, despite that that person owning or having a right to occupy such premises. In addition, the person may be prevented from having any contact with the child even if he or she is a parent, except for when that parent may be granted supervised access by the courts.

Section 14(e) – The person brought before the court may be barred from contacting or interfering with anyone who has custody of the child.

Section 14(f) – If a person is found guilty of any of these offences then where that person had 'custody, charge, or care of the child', the Children's Court can require that they receive counselling by 'a fit person qualified by his knowledge of psychology or psychiatry who is appointed by the court'. The use of the term 'fit person' in this context is confusing, particularly where the emphasis of this provision is that the person be someone with appropriate qualifications.

Quite apart from the powers of the court under section 14, any constable has the right to arrest any person who commits a schedule 2 offence in his presence, or who he reasonably suspects of having committed such an offence.[52] The provisions of the Bail Act are applicable in these circumstances and it may be that, as a result, when compared with the options of the court in respect of children

51.　Sections 14(2)(d), (e), and (f).
52.　Section 15.

under section 14, the perpetrator enjoys greater protection of his rights than the victim.[53]

Sections 16–20 deal with procedural aspects of the court's powers, such as charging the adult in the case of schedule 2 offences, the presence or absence of the child, and evidential questions of the child of tender years. A child of tender years is a child who is under the age of 14.[54] The Act essentially codifies the common law position by saying that the question for the court is whether '…the child is possessed of sufficient intelligence to justify the reception of the evidence and understands the duty of speaking the truth'. The requirement for corroboration of the evidence of a child of tender years is also set out in this section.[55]

Medical Examination

The court may order that a child be medically examined whether on its own volition or upon the application of the parent or guardian of the child or a constable, authorized officer, or the Children's Advocate.[56] Presumably, a report from a medical practitioner pursuant to such an examination would be admissible in the proceedings before the court under the ordinary rules of evidence.[57] A person who is brought before the court and charged with offences specified may be ordered to submit to testing to establish whether he has any form of communicable disease.[58] The unauthorized disclosure of information regarding the testing of a person under section 22 is a criminal offence and carries with it a penalty of a fine of up to JMD$1 million and/or as much as 12 months' imprisonment.[59] This offence does not appear to be applicable to section 21 medical examinations of the child, and it is curious that the Act would include

53. See right to bail enshrined in the Bail Act, section 3 or 4.
54. Section 20(3).
55. Section 20(2).
56. Section 21.
57. Evidence Act.
58. Section 22.
59. Section 22(2).

an offence to protect the information with respect to the alleged perpetrator, but not the child.[60]

The Uncontrollable Child

The process by which a child is proven to be beyond the control of a parent or guardian and is then to be dealt with by the court is set out in section 24 of the Act. The child may be brought before a juvenile court[61] by the parent or guardian and if that person proves that they are unable to control the child, then the court may make an order in respect of the child. It would appear that the conduct of the child need not necessarily entail the commission of an offence. Furthermore, the stipulation is so subjective that it may be more of an indictment against the person's parenting skills than a valid complaint against the child. In any event, the parent's complaint to this effect, on condition that section 24(1)(a) and (b) are met, can result in the court making serious orders in respect of the child.[62] The question of what constitutes proof is an issue that might not trouble the court to the extent that it would if the procedure were explicitly set out. It would appear that, in many instances, the sworn evidence of a complaining parent would be sufficient, and natural justice considerations such as the right for the child to be heard[63] and/or represented[64] are conspicuously absent. This far-reaching provision has caused many children to be summarily placed in detention[65] and contributed to an unacceptable number of children being detained in the custody of the state.[66]

---

60.   It may be considered that the general restrictions on reporting are sufficient to protect the interests of the child.
61.   This may be a drafting oversight since there is no longer such a tribunal.
62.   Section 24(2).
63.   See Article 12(2) Convention on the Rights of the Child.
64.   See "Legal Aid for Children in Court for Being Uncontrollable." Press Release of the Legal Aid Council, August 15, 2013.
65.   Report on Uncontrollable Children, Office of the Children's Advocate.
66.   Human Rights Watch," Nobody's Children", Jamaican Children in Police Detention and Government Institutions, July 1, 1999.

The court may then make an expedient order with the consent of the parent or guardian.[67] The problem is that the parent or guardian who has brought the child to court because he or she is not able to control them is unlikely to withhold their consent to whatever measure the court proposes. Secondly, when the court is making the proposal, there is probably, in the absence of independent advice, a considerable amount of pressure on the complainant to consent. 'What, after all, did you bring the child to us for?' In practice, with the prevailing concern being the conduct of the child, it is easy for the parent to be swept along by the proceedings and barely realize that their consent was a condition upon which the order was being made.

The court may make:

a. A correctional order – an order sending a child to a juvenile correctional centre. It is not stated what the duration of the correctional order will be.[68]

b. A fit person order – commiting the child into the care of a person deemed suitable by the court, whether this is a relative or not.[69] Once again, there is no direction to the court as to the duration of the order.

c. A supervision order – The child may be placed under the supervision of a probation and after-care officer for up to three years.[70]

The application of section 24 of the Child Care and Protection Act and the general issue of children in police custody has resulted in a great deal of controversy and has attracted the attention of Human Rights groups, both locally and internationally.[71]

---

67.   Section 24(1)(b).
68.   Section 24(2)(a).
69.   Section 24(2)(b)(i).
70.   Section 24(2)(b)(ii).
71.   OCA Report on Children in Court, 'Armadale Report, Keating Report, CDA and OCA Annual Reports,' etc.

As a result, the government has come under intense pressure to introduce policy changes and legislative modifications to the act.[72]

PART II: EDUCATION AND EMPLOYMENT OF CHILDREN

Sections 26–32 of the Child Care and Protection Act address the responsibilities towards children by those who are entrusted with their care or who are financially responsible for them. Sections 27 and 28[73] explain what it means to provide care for a child, and it is set out as being the provision of adequate food, clothing, accommodation and medical care.[74] If the child is between the ages of four and 16, then it also includes ensuring that the child attends school.[75]

The duty to maintain as set out in section 26 is partially extended in the form of contributions to include those periods when a child is in a juvenile correctional centre. The duty encompasses biological, step, and adoptive parents, and any person cohabiting with the mother of the child.[76] Sections 30, 31, and 32 deal with the application and administration of contribution orders, including the transfer of maintenance payments and giving directions as to who is to pay and who is to receive these sums.

Children and Employment

Children under the age of 13 are not allowed to be employed for 'any work' unless a permit has been issued by the minister allowing the child to participate in 'artistic performances'.[77] The only exception to this is where a child has to work pursuant to a detention order, a community service order,[78] or as part of instructions from

---

72. Ministry of Youth and Culture, 'A Policy to Amend the CCPA, Appendix B: Legislative Gap Analysis.'
73. Sections 27(1) and 28 (1).
74. Section 27(1).
75. Section 28.
76. Section 29(1), no correlation with The Maintenance Act.
77. Sections 34 and 35.
78. Section 38.

an educational institution. Children are not to be employed in nightclubs[79] or sell intoxicating liquor or tobacco products, and the sale of these products to any child is also prohibited.[80]

A child between the ages of 13 and 15 may only be employed in the types of work specified in a list of prescribed occupations maintained by the minister.[81] In any event, even when a child may be employed, it should not be in any activity which is hazardous or may interfere with the child's schooling, or be harmful to their physical, mental, spiritual, or social development.[82] As such, night work, that is between the hours of 10:00 p.m. and 5:00 a.m., or any industrial work is specifically excluded.[83]

A constable may, if he is armed with a search warrant, enter any premises where it is believed that activities contravening sections 33, 34, 39, and 40 are taking place, and make all necessary enquiries that include a right to question those who are present.[84] These powers can then be used in conjunction with the powers concerning children who are need of care and protection, for them to be removed from the premises and brought before the court.

The use and involvement of children in begging, whether in any street, premises, or place is a summary offence triable in the Family Court.[85]

The remainder of this part of the Act is concerned with the procedure of the court[86] and the information that emanates from it when children appear before the court whether as witnesses or otherwise.[87]

---

79. Section 39.
80. Section 40(1).
81. Section 34.
82. Section 34(3).
83. Section 34(3)(b) and section 25.
84. Section 37.
85. Section 41.
86. Sections 42 and 43.
87. Sections 44 and 45.

PART III: CHILDREN IN CARE

Part III of the Act governs the regulation of children's homes and places of safety by the minister.[88] It sets out the process of applying for a licence from the minister and the process of appeal against the minister's decision. There is a power to inspect premises and to remove a child. The duties of the licensee who is running the home are also set out, as are the powers to apprehend who escapes from a person who under the act has care of the child.[89]

The minister's permission is required to allow a child who is committed to the care of a fit person to emigrate.[90] Importantly, under section 62, the rights of a child who is in a children's home, place of safety, or under the care of a fit person, are set out.

The term 'lawful guardian' is referred to[91] and defined by[92] part III of the Act as as including a 'person appointed according to law or by deed or will or the order of a court to be the guardian of a child'. They are excluded from the application of this part of the Act.

PART IV: CHILDREN DETAINED AND BROUGHT BEFORE THE COURT

Part IV of the Child Care and Protection Act stipulates what should take place when a child comes before the court. This part of the Act starts with declaring the age of criminal responsibility,[93] followed by the steps the court should take to ascertain whether someone brought before them is a child or not.[94] The court is to have regard for the best interests of the child, whether or not the child is charged with a criminal offence or otherwise.[95] While detained or awaiting

---

88. Section 47.
89. Sections 51–59.
90. Section 60.
91. Section 47.
92. Section 46.
93. Section 63.
94. Section 64.
95. Section 65.

attendance in any court, a child is supposed to be kept from associating with any adult other than a co-defendant or relative.[96]

A person who is apparently a child who is apprehended by the police is to be released once (the Child Development Agency (CDA) has been contacted,[97] and that child can be bailed from the police station, unless special circumstances exist.[98] Under section 68, if a court decides to keep a child on remand, he/she is to be detained in the custody of a named juvenile remand centre unless 'the court certifies' that the child is of:

i. So unruly a character that the child cannot safely be committed; or

ii. So depraved a character that the child is not a fit person to be detained";

in which case the child can be committed to an adult correctional centre.

A child's parents or guardians are required to attend the court when the child appears in court, unless it would be unreasonable to require that person's attendance.

Members of the press can be present during sittings of the Children's Court,[99] but presumably, reporting restrictions would be in place.[100]

The court must explain in simple language to any child brought before a court, the reason why he has been brought there, and the fact that he is entitled to assistance from the Children's Advocate.[101]

The terms and framework of a probation order, committal of a child to a correctional centre, and committal of a child to the care of a fit person are set out in this part of the Act.[102]

---

96. Section 66.
97. Section 67(2)(a).
98. See section 67(2)(i)(ii) and(iii). The condition in (iii) seems to be broad and unfettered.
99. Section 71(7).
100. As per sections 44 and 45.
101. Section 71(8).
102. Sections 80, 81, and 82.

PART V: ADMINISTRATION AND ENFORCEMENT

The final part of the Act sets up an advisory council to assist the minister with the preparation of regulations under the Act. The administrative powers of the minister are also set out. There is reference to the power of the minister to bring a child before the Children's Court in sections 87, and sections 88, and 89 of the act deal with the courts and the general powers regarding various offences.

Significantly, the penultimate section of the Act, section 95, recognizes the abolition of the sentence of detaining a child at Her Majesty's pleasure[103] by providing for a review of all existing cases under which the child may be released or given an appropriate alternative sentence.

PROCEDURE UNDER THE CHILD CARE AND PROTECTION ACT

The intervention of the State relating to children in need of care takes place almost exclusively at a summary level, that is, before the Children's Court. The State, in the exercise of this power, acts primarily through a central agency, which is the Child Protection and Family Services Agency (CPFSA). Legal officers of the Office of the Children's Advocate provide representation, and there is power for the Children's Advocate to intervene or have cases referred to it or decisions to be made. The CPFSA, or its predessessor the CDA, is not mentioned in the Child Care and Protection Act.

According to the Act, the powers of the court, including charging, hearing cases in the absence of the child, taking of statements, and the admission of evidence and special orders that the court can make, are set out in sections 14–24.

Often, cases come to court via the police, a social worker, or a parent. When this happens, the clerk of courts takes on a quasi-prosecutorial role and, in the early stages of the case, that role can be

---

103.   *Troy Gilbert v R* [2015] JMSC Civ 64.

critical. The court will make initial orders involving the curtailment of the child's liberty, usually where the child or the parent has no legal representation. Lawyers may be brought in after the case has been before the court on several occasions. The technical nature of the provisions of the Child Care and Protection Act will put the average lawyer at a disadvantage to the court and, as such, he or she usually becomes relegated to a mere advisory role in the proceedings. To be able to interface effectively with the court in these types of cases requires a degree of specialized knowledge that most lawyers do not possess. Furthermore, even with the extension of legal aid in cases concerning children, the average legal practitioner will not find it cost effective to invest any level of expertise in this area. Most families who are caught up in cases under the Act do not have adequate resources to obtain legal representation before the court, thus taking a passive role in the proceedings with little or no control over the outcome.

CHILDREN AND THE CRIMINAL LAW

Children interface with the criminal law in many different circumstances and capacities. The fact that the child will be a part of a family is something that may or may not be at the forefront of the judge's mind when dealing with cases where children are involved. Parents may be perpetrators of crimes against their children or facilitators of crimes committed by their children and, in occasional instances, may be victims of crimes committed by their children. Therefore, the significance of and need for family law interventions will vary according to the particular circumstances.

Child Offenders

Section 63 of the Child Care and Protection Act states 'It shall be conclusively presumed that no child under the age of twelve years can be guilty of an offence.'

The age of criminal responsibility is a matter which causes public concern as children become exposed to greater influences beyond the school and family environment. Television and access to the Internet have a considerable effect on children's awareness so that the original basis upon which criminal responsibility was ascribed, namely the level of mental development by way of age, becomes almost fallacious in light of the weight of external influences to which a child may be subject. Nevertheless, the age of criminal responsibility starts at 12, and up until the age of 18 the person will be treated as a child and therefore subject to the provisions of the Act, namely sections 63–84.

The presumptions in relation to the age of the child are set out in section 64 and essentially state that except where proof of age is an ingredient of the offence,

> the person shall for the purpose of this Act be presumed at that date to have been a child or to have been under or to have attained that age, as the case may be, unless the contrary is proved.

Importantly, child offenders remain children regardless of the nature of the offence, and there is no provision for charging or trying a child as an adult as is the case in some other jurisdictions.

At all stages, the court's treatment of child offenders or children charged with criminal offences is governed by the welfare principle.[104] Children, when detained, are to be kept separate from adult offenders and are not allowed to associate with any adult unless they are jointly charged with that adult or they are a relative.[105] The conditions under which a child may be allowed or refused bail are set out in section 67. However, if the child is over the age of 14 and of a particular character and disposition as set out in the Act,[106] then he can be 'committed to such place, including an adult correctional centre, as may be specified in the warrant'.

Parents or guardians are generally required to attend court when a child who is charged with an offence is before the court. Additional

---

104. Section 65.
105. Section 66.
106. Section 68(1)a.

protection is provided by the requirement that when a child appears in court notice should be given to a children's officer, a probation and after-care officer and the Children's Advocate, unless any of these officers are the ones who are bringing the child before the court.[107]

Section 71 of the act establishes the Children's Courts which, in essence, is another arm of the Parish Court system. Importantly, the child is to be addressed in simple language when explaining to him or her why they are before the court, and this should, and generally does, extend throughout the proceedings. If a child attains the age of 18 while the matter is before the Children's Court, that court may continue to hear the matter, exercising all the powers available as a court of summary jurisdiction.

Where a child is over the age of 14 and charged with certain offences,[108] the Children's Court can commit the child to stand trial at Circuit Court. Children who are found guilty may be remitted to the Children's Court for sentencing or that court may exercise the powers of the Children's Court.[109] The restrictions on punishment of a person under the age of 18 are set out in section 78 and 79 of the act.[110]

Child Victims and Witnesses

The plight of child victims has been a source of concern for a long time. The prospect of going into the witness box in open court with all the onlookers and not least of all the alleged perpetrator, being cross-examined by an intimidating lawyer is every child victim's worst nightmare. Legislation enabling such witnesses to give evidence by video link has been subject to rigorous criticism by many in the legal profession.

107. Section 70.
108. See Schedule 4.
109. Sections 74 and 75.
110. The restriction on the imposition of the death penalty was previously at common law, *R v Patrick Whitely* and *Lester Williams* (1986) 23 JLR 354.

A special unit of the constabulary – the Centre for Investigation of Sexual Offences and Child Abuse (CISOCA) – is charged with investigating cases, particularly cases of child abuse, and will in the course of investigating such cases, interview and take statements from children. Officers are specially trained and can, if necessary, get assistance from the CPFSA. Keeping child witnesses secure can be difficult where the accused is a member of the immediate family or even a member of the same household. It is frequently the children who are removed from the home for their own protection and they are the ones who then come to see themselves as being punished for speaking out about what has taken place. Even if the accused is remanded in custody, this person may be the breadwinner for the family, and the child can be made to feel responsible for the consequential financial deprivation of the family. If a child is put in a place of safety he or she comes into contact with young people who may be more disturbed than he or she is and, as a result, be subject to adverse influences. Where the child is placed with a family member outside of the immediate household, there is still the risk of pressure and threats being communicated to the child.

Quite apart from these logistical issues that can have a real effect on the outcome of any prosecution, there is also the matter of the psychological effect of being a victim of an offence, which may have been taking place over a protracted period. Counselling and, in some cases, more intensive psychological intervention may be necessary, but the resources in this area are often overtaxed, or are difficult to keep up over the lengthy period that criminal prosecutions may take to be completed.

THE WAY FORWARD

The Child Care and Protection Act is a reasonable first attempt at addressing the question of when the state needs to intervene in the care of children. It was anticipated that the Act would be subject to review on a regular basis and, as such, is considered a work in progress. The Ministry of Youth and Culture, through a policy paper by the CDA (now CPFSA), has undertaken an extensive review.[111] The paper concluded with an appendix that specifically addressed what it saw as the 'legislative gaps' in the current Act. There have been some recurring issues that continued to damage the country's reputation internationally, namely the detention of children in adult lock-ups, which seemed to persist regardless of the statutory provisions that were in place. The ministry recognized a need for significant expenditure in order to establish proper detention centres for those young people who it was absolutely necessary to incarcerate. Similarly, the ability of the CPFSA to function in the way that the act intended is primarily a question of resources, not law. Also, the need for proper facilities in which children can safely be housed, and properly trained staff within those facilities, is once again a matter of resources.

From a legal standpoint, it may be that the Act represents a missed opportunity. By seeking to confine itself to the narrower issue of children and the state, the Act, except for some generalized definitions, has unfortunately ignored the wider question of children and the law as a whole. This was the Act that could have replaced the Children (Guardianship and Custody) Act, which is overdue for a comprehensive overhaul. This is the Act that could have dealt with and replaced the out-of-date provisions on blood tests that currently reside in the Status of Children Act. This is the Act that could have signalled that 'care' starts with the family, and the law would have no hesitation in setting out the standards and duties of parenting within the family, as well as the duties of the State when it has cause to intervene.[112] This was the Act that could reasonably have included an expanded of the definition of the welfare principle as set out in section 18 of the Children (Guardianship and Custody) Act). The wide-ranging approach of the Belizean legislators in the Families and Children Act is worthy of attention.

---

111.   A Policy to Amend the CCPA, Ministry of Youth and Culture, December 2013.
112.   Sections 2(2) and (3).

The distinction between the responsibilities of the Office of the Children's Advocate and the CPFSA is far from clear and may overlap in some cases. If the CPFSA represents the social services arm of the Children's Court and the Probation Office represents the social services arm of the other courts, it may be time for the State to address comprehensively the role and status of social workers in court, the status of their reports, and the basis upon which their investigations can be admitted in evidence, and therefore challenged and rebutted. Maybe Parliament should revisit the way that these entities are structured, perhaps with the view that one should be subsumed into the other.

Finally, to the extent that the Child Care and Protection Act seeks to deal with the treatment of children in a broad way, for example, the employment of children (sections 33–36), it is important for the law to be made current by repealing legislation related to this area which remains in force.

10. Family Law: The Courts

INTRODUCTION

One of the best ways to understand how family law is practised is to become familiar with the courts and the types of family law applications that can be made in each court. Sometimes an application can be made in more than one court, which immediately begs the question: what are the advantages or disadvantages in choosing to apply in one court rather than another? The vast majority of family cases[1] are dealt with in the lower courts that is in the courts of summary jurisdiction. For over a century, these courts came under the title of Resident Magistrate's Courts, but by a recent amendment[2] to the legislation they are now called Parish Courts. The family law cases that are generally dealt with in the Supreme Court are divorce cases and matters ancillary to those cases, in particular, division of matrimonial property. As well as the usual hearings, some family cases may be the subject of an appeal and rarely an application may be made for judicial review. Where there

---

1. Maintenance applications.
2. Judicature (Resident Magistrates) Amendment and Change of Name) Act 2016.

is violence or some other criminal offence between family members, the case can be dealt with in the criminal courts and specifically under the Child Care and Protection Act cases concerning children are usually dealt with in the Children's Court.

The structure of the court system in Jamaica is set out on three levels or tiers. They are the summary level, the high court level, and the appellate level.

THE SUMMARY COURTS

The lowest level of courts that have jurisdiction to deal with family cases is the Parish Courts formerly the Resident Magistrates' Courts. This court is a court of summary jurisdiction, created and governed by statute namely the Judicature (Resident Magistrates') Act. As a creature of statute, the extent of the court's power is limited by the main act and the acts which in themselves recognize the jurisdiction of that court in dealing with certain matters. For example, the powers of the resident magistrate (now parish judge) to hear applications for maintenance are set out in the Maintenance Act 2005. The court is not allowed to go outside of the scope of its statutory powers and, if it does, the actions or orders of the court are liable to be struck down by a court of judicial review as being *ultra vires*. Family matters which can be heard at this level are listed in the Parish Court itself or in some parishes[3] there is a separate Family Court which is set up to handle them. The Family Court, which is established by the Family Court Act, is like its parent court presided over by a parish judge (formerly a resident magistrate). The Children's Court is another offshoot of the Parish Court, which is set up to hear cases where children are involved such as criminal cases against children and also offences under the Child Care and Protection Act. The Children's Court is also headed by a parish judge. These courts operate in such a way that persons who are not legally represented can conduct cases themselves. With the assistance of the courts

3. Kingston and St Andrew, St Catherine, St James, and Hanover.

office to lay a complaint or information[4] and get summons served, and also with the assistance of the clerk of court and, indeed, the judge when the matters are before the court for hearing, the court enables the ordinary citizen to exercise their legal rights.

The types of family cases which are generally dealt with at the summary level are:

Applications for Maintenance of Children

Applications for Maintenance of Spouse

Applications for Custody

Applications for Protection from Domestic Violence

Applications for Declaration of Paternity

Applications for Declaration of Property Ownership

Applications for Adoption

Applications for Maintenance

Applications for maintenance whether for a child, a spouse, or for any other dependent are made in the Parish Court or Family Court pursuant to the Maintenance Act.[5] The fact that these applications can be made in the summary court takes a tremendous burden off the Supreme Court and saves most applicants the cost of legal representation. The courts are summary in name and summary in nature in that matters are dealt with by a procedure that is designed to avoid a trial or a protracted hearing. Often the court will order the probation office to conduct a means inquiry and thereafter submit a report to the court as to the financial circumstances of the parties. The report will usually conclude with a recommendation as the order which should be made. The parties are encouraged to reach an agreement in the form of a consent order and will sign the court papers as an indication of this agreement. Unlike many summary courts in other jurisdictions, the Parish Court does not

4.   Essentially, this is an allegation of wrongdoing given on oath.
5.   Section 3(1).

have a financial limit for maintenance awards, although orders are often smaller than what may be ordered by a high court judge.

Applications for Custody

Applications for custody may be made in the Parish or Family Courts under the provisions of the Children (Guardianship and Custody) Act.[6] Under that Act, applications can also be made in the Supreme Court and, therefore, a decision has to be made to determine which court is most suitable to hear the matter in light of the circumstances of the case. In most cases the summary court takes less time to deal with a matter compared to the Supreme Court. As with maintenance applications, the court may order an investigation into the background and circumstances of the parties with a report to be submitted to the court that will include a recommendation as to what orders should be made. The parties are encouraged to accept the recommendation or to come to some other agreed arrangements so that a consent order can be made without having to resort to the more time consuming option of a contested hearing.

Applications for Protection from Domestic Violence

The Domestic Violence Act dictates that applications for any orders under this statute, for example, protection orders or occupation orders have to be made in the lower court before a parish judge. Applications are, therefore, made either in the Parish Court or in the Family Court. The court can make orders upon an ex parte application depending on the seriousness and urgency of the case as disclosed by the evidence. In such instances, an early return date will be set so that all parties can be present and heard by the court. Under this Act, the court has powers to impose criminal sanctions, including imprisonment if a party is found to have breached a protection or occupation order.

---

6.   Section 7 (also the section which denotes jurisdiction).

Applications for a Declaration of Paternity

Applications for a declaration of paternity can be and usually are made in what was formerly the Resident Magistrates, now Parish Court. In those parishes where there is a Family Court, applications will be listed in that court. A declaration of paternity is made by the court under section 10 of the Status of Children Act and is generally preceded by a direction for the relevant parties and the child in question to subject to genetic testing.[7] The need for clarification as to the paternity of a child may be the sole question for the court or it may arise as a preliminary issue to be decided before the court considers the merits of the substantive claim. In the latter cases, it may be contended that a man is or is not the father of a particular child in response to an application for maintenance, custody, or the distribution of an estate.

Applications for Declaration of Property Ownership

Applications for a declaration as to property interests under Property (Rights of Spouses) Act (PROSA) may be made in the lower court. Such applications may be made while the marriage or cohabitation is subsisting and regardless of the value of the property. The lower court also has power to deal with the division of property under PROSA provided that the value is not above the amount stipulated in the Act.[8]

Applications for Adoption

According to the Children (Adoption of) Act, the lower court judge is empowered to make the final adoption order. Adoption cases do not usually go before the court until the final order is to be made and the decisions that precede the final order such as suitability or unsuitability are made administratively. Since the court does not have a supervisory role as the case is progressing through

---

7.   Section 11.
8.   Section 5(1)(a), that is 'within the monetary limits prescribed by or under the Judicature (Resident Magistrate's) Act'.

the different stages, any challenge to such decisions may have to be made by way of judicial review in the Supreme Court.[9]

THE SUPREME COURT

The Supreme Court of Judicature of Jamaica is the title of the high court in Jamaica and was created by statute namely the Judicature (Supreme Court) Act. It is a court of pleadings as well as dealing with matters in common law, equity, statutory and miscellaneous claims. It retains the power to exercise its inherent jurisdiction. Most of the applications made in the Supreme Court now originate from statute, but there are significant powers which still rest on the exercise of the court's inherent powers. The family matters which can be dealt with in the Supreme Court are:

1. divorce, nullity, and all applications ancillary to those proceedings;

2. applications for division of matrimonial property;

3. applications for custody;

4. applications for the appointment of a legal guardian, and

5. applications for a declaration of paternity.

Divorces, Nullity, and Ancillary Proceedings

The Supreme Court alone has jurisdiction to dissolve and annul marriages. This is prescribed by the Matrimonial Causes Act (MCA). Divorce and nullity actions are generally commenced by way of a petition.[10] The MCA also states that this court can deal with any proceedings that come within the definition of 'matrimonial cause'.[11] Divorce petitions were heard in open court in the past, but now, by virtue of part 76 of the Civil Procedure Rules (CPR), the petition is considered by a judge or a master in the absence of the

---

9.   See *In the matter of an Appeal against the decision of the Adoption Board* [2015] JMSC Civ 185.

10.   Rule 76.4(1) CPR.

11.   Section 2.

parties by a 'default' process.[12] It is still open to a judge to refer the matter to the registrar to be heard in open court and to require the attendance of the parties, presumably if there are matters of law to be considered or if the judge wishes to test the evidence by way of further questions and/or assess the parties' demeanour. Similarly, the procedure of hearing divorces by way of notice of motion in open court remains.

It would appear from the rules that there is no default procedure for nullity petitions. The usual applications which arise in the course of an action for divorce are maintenance of spouse and maintenance and custody of the relevant children. Applications for maintenance and custody in the course of the divorce are specifically referred to in the MCA.[13] The applicable principles when the court is dealing with maintenance are those which are set out in the Maintenance Act,[14] so we find that both the Supreme Court and the lower court as mentioned above will be guided by the same legal factors. Ancillary matters in divorce will normally be heard before a judge or master in chambers by means of an application for court orders (Form 7) and supporting affidavits, although if the matter is brought by way of a Fixed Date Claim Form (Form 2) and supporting affidavits even though it is not an originating action it can still be accepted by the court.[15]

Applications for Division of Matrimonial Property

Applications for declarations of ownership and division of matrimonial property are normally made after divorce proceedings have commenced as is set out in PROSA.[16] The application is sometimes made as a notice of application for court orders ancillary to the divorce proceedings that are pursuant to the MCA, but is more frequently commenced as a separate action that is by way of a

12.   Rule 76.12(1).
13.   Section 23.
14.   Section 23(2).
15.   CPR, Rule 76.4(15).
16.   Section 13.

fixed date claim form with supporting affidavits. Quite apart from the complexities of law and fact which can arise in matrimonial property disputes, the venue in which these matters should be heard is set out in PROSA.[17] That is, if the value of the property (presumably the total value of the property) is below that set in the act, then the matter can be heard in the lower court, but if it is above the stipulated amount then it must be heard in the Supreme Court. The challenge for the legislation is to keep pace with current property values. Importantly, it is open to parties (and significantly third parties) to get a declaration during the subsistence of the marriage or cohabitation under section 11 of PROSA. This application can be made in the Parish Court regardless of the value of the property in question, and the court has considerable powers in terms of the range of orders that can be made consequent on such an application being heard and determined.

Applications for Custody

The Children (Guardianship and Custody) Act allows applications to be made in either the summary court or the high court and, as such, its jurisdiction straddles the two tiers. Custody applications as stated above can be made in the lower courts in the Parish Court or in the Family Court as is appropriate in the particular parish, but the matter can also be commenced in the Supreme Court to be heard before a judge in chambers. In the latter instance, the case will be commenced by way of a fixed date claim form with supporting affidavits. Of course if the custody application is ancillary to divorce, it can be heard by way of notice of application for court orders with supporting affidavit. In all matters concerning the custody and upbringing of a child as well as the management of a child's property and assets, the welfare principle guides the exercise of the court's powers.[18]

---

17. Section 5(1)(a).
18. Section 18.

Applications for the Appointment of Legal Guardian

Under sections 3–5 of the Children (Guardianship and Custody) Act, the court has powers to deal with guardianship of children. Although the Act does not specify these matters be heard in the high court, the practice is for a judge of the Supreme Court to make such orders because it may entail the exercise of the court's inherent jurisdiction.[19] This position has been underscored by the recent decision of *B v C*,[20] in which Brooks JA pointed out that applications for the appointment of a guardian are, in fact, an invocation of the courts inherent powers in wardship. The application will be heard in chambers, and the proceedings will be commenced by a fixed date claim form and supporting affidavits.

Applications for a Declaration of Paternity

Applications for a declaration of paternity can be made in the lower court, whether it be the Parish Court or the Family Court, or in the Supreme Court.[21] When such applications are heard in the Supreme Court, the proceedings will usually be commenced by fixed date claim form and supporting affidavits. The court will generally give a direction that tests be done as the most reliable means of ascertaining the parentage of the child. This is provided that the purported father is still alive. Where the application is being made after the death of the father, the court will consider other evidence and if proved 'to the satisfaction of the Court', the declaration will be made.

THE COURT OF APPEAL

Appeals from the lower courts, namely the Parish Court and in particular the Family Court, are made to the Court of Appeal. The procedure for appeal from the lower courts is far from straightforward and difficult to pursue without an attorney. Many people use the

19. Section 20.
20. *B v C and the Office of the Children's Advocate* [2016] JMCA Civ 48.
21. Section 10(4) Status of Children Act.

lower courts precisely because they cannot afford to retain the services of a lawyer so if the case is decided against them the matter will usually end at that point. The potential denial of a right of appeal because of a failure to comply with convoluted rules[22] and the injustice that flows from it has taken up a considerable amount of the court's time in numerous decisions,[23] and it would not be unreasonable to conclude that this is designed to restrict the number of cases with which the appellate court is faced. This is coupled with the legal restrictions on interfering with the decision of the judge at first instance. It has been stated that, for example, in maintenance cases, the Court of Appeal will not interfere with an order unless it is 'unreasonable, indiscreet or clearly wrong'.[24] This observation is applicable to all cases that could be the subject of an appeal from the summary courts to the Court of Appeal, whether civil, criminal, or familial. However, in family cases, the consequences of the restricted right of appeal can be far-reaching. Another unforeseen consequence of the restriction is that it can provide parish judges with the seeds of a sense of impunity because generally where the parties appear without a legal representative there is unlikely to be any call to account for the decisions that have been made.

Appeals from the Parish Courts are to be made in adherence to section 256 of the Judicature (Resident Magistrates) Act, that is, by filing in the lower court. After the parish judge has drawn up a statement of his reasons for the judgment, the papers will be lodged with the clerk of the Court of Appeal and the matter will proceed at the appellate level.

Appeal Court procedure is governed by the Court of Appeal Rules 2002.

By contrast, appeals from the Supreme Court are relatively straightforward. In divorce, appeals are rare because if the judge

---

22.   Subject to the falsely reassuring provisions of section 266 of the Judicature (Resident Magistrates) Act.
23.   See *Gordon v Russell* [2012] JMCA App 6 for a recent summary.
24.   *Valentine v Valentine* (1992) 29 JLR 35.

makes a ruling that does not find favour with the petitioner, it is usually easier and cheaper to comply with an unreasonable order and proceed than to challenge it on appeal. The same applies to decisions of the registrar that usually take the form of requisitions directing that the rules be complied with by way of supplying additional information or amending documents. The procedure for an appeal against these decisions is set out in part 62 of the CPR. In many instances, such issues can be settled informally by discussing the matter with the registrar, thereby side-stepping the time and expense of a formal application to a single judge. Sometimes the consequences of a disputed ruling will, in any event, have a contingent effect on other documents or, indeed, the status of the petition as a whole. In such instances, it may be easier for a petitioner to discontinue the action and recommence at a later date.[25]

From a substantive law perspective, the cases that are most likely to be appealed are division of property cases followed by cases concerning the custody of children, including cross-jurisdiction (kidnapping) cases.

THE COURT OF JUDICIAL REVIEW AND THE CONSTITUTIONAL COURT

Family cases like any other area of law may be the subject of judicial review proceedings. In such proceedings, the review court is looking at the way that the court exercised its powers, that is, whether or not a ruling is *ultra vires* or is in breach of the rules of natural justice. This can arise in the case of those courts where the power to act is derived from statute. In the lower courts, the power to act is given by statute and it can only act within the ambit of its statutory powers. If the court exceeds its powers then the order or judgment will be struck down as *ultra vires*. In these cases, the review court will be looking at administrative law principles in order to arrive at a decision as to whether or not the court acted properly.

---

25. For example, after a relevant child has attained the age of 18.

The procedure to apply to seek leave for judicial review is set out in the CPR under part 56, namely administrative law, and this section also includes applications to go before the Constitutional Court. The review court normally consists of a single judge of the Supreme Court, but where the matter concerns the liberty of the subject three judges will sit to hear the case. The court has wide powers and can make orders that fall within the scope of administrative law such as certiorari and mandamus but can also make orders in the place of the court whose orders are being overturned such as orders for damages. The court also has the power to remit to the originating court and notably, it is a court which is said to have a supervisory role in respect of the magistracy and therefore can issues guidelines and directions as required. In considering whether or not leave should be granted for judicial review the court will need to be persuaded that this is not a matter that could be adequately dealt with by way of an appeal, since the exercise of the court's powers of review are discretionary and such discretion is not to be too readily invoked. Since the review court and constitutional court are branches of the high court, such decisions may be the subject of an appeal to the Court of Appeal.

THE PRIVY COUNCIL

Family cases and, in particular, division of matrimonial property cases, will not generally be entertained by the Privy Council unless there is need to correct an egregious error or a substantial miscarriage of justice.[26] The cost of appeals to the Privy Council is, in most instances, a sufficient deterrent. This is a general rule that is as much applicable to family law as any other type of case. Family cases such as an appeal to the Judicial Board could completely exhaust the available resources of the family and would therefore be pointless. It is only cases where there are considerable assets (and a great deal of acrimony) that will reach the highest court. The cases

26. *Johnson v Johnson* (1992) 41 WIR 91.

of *Chin v Chin*[27] and *Stoeckert v Geddes*,[28] both property claims, are examples of the type of family case that has been decided by the final appellate court. More recently, cases which raise the issue of abandonment of joint tenancies[29] and adverse possession that were decided at the level of the Privy Council are also being seen as having implications on family property cases.

THE WAY FORWARD

The court structure for family law cases could be substantially improved by allocating the necessary resources to build, restore, and relocate suitably equipped family courts. The example set by Trinidad and Tobago in consolidating the family courts at the summary and high court levels and thereby concentrating high quality facilities in one building is a model worthy of consideration. There is little point in establishing new courts by way of enacted legislation, which is in statutes and regulations, when the infrastructure cannot be provided to allow these entities to operate as intended. It is clear that in some parishes there is a desperate need for additional court rooms given the amount of cases being initiated. The length of the court list for matters of maintenance is a clear indication that increased litigation is a consequence of greater awareness of rights. The inordinate delays or the cavalier rather than summary approach to dealing with these types of cases can only be alleviated by more court rooms and more persons appointed to sit and hear these matters speedily as was originally intended. In a sense, this does not represent progress, but merely an attempt to keep up with increasing demands on the system. One of the results of the consolidated approach in Trinidad and Tobago is that whether it was intended or not, the high court now has a dedicated family division. As family law matters become more complex, especially in the area of property division, it becomes necessary to have family specialists presiding in these matters so that time and expense is saved.

---

27.   [2001]UKPC 7; [2007]UKPC 5.
28.   [1999]UKPC 52; [2004]UKPC 54.
29.   *Wills v Wills* (2003) 64 WIR 176.

Questions for Discussion

CHAPTER 1: MARRIAGE

1. What are the reasons for a minimum age of marriage? Consider the advantages and disadvantages of the current minimum age of marriage.

2. Which is of greatest significance in the Marriage Act – Section 3 or the provisions creating criminal offences, and why?

3. How is a marriage proved?

4. What is the purpose of the prohibited degrees of consanguinity and affinity? Summarize the statutory exceptions and consider the changing attitude of the court in this area.

5. Why does the law make special provision for marriages in articulo mortis?

6. List the pre-ceremony requirements for marriage.

7. Why is Section 4 of the Marriage Act necessary?

8. What is the relevance of marriage in a modern Caribbean society?

9. How would you amend the Marriage Act? Give reasons and prepare a preliminary draft your amendments.

CHAPTER 2: NULLITY

1. List the grounds for obtaining a nullity decree in Jamaica, naming the statute and section of the statute in which each can be found.

2. What is the difference between a void marriage and a voidable marriage?

3. In what circumstances can previously voidable grounds for nullity still be relied upon in Jamaican matrimonial proceedings?

4. Does fraudulent behaviour nullify a marriage? Give reasons.

5. In what way does the procedure for obtaining a nullity decree differ from the procedure for dissolution of marriage?

6. In what circumstances can a third party institute nullity proceedings, and how would they do so?

7. What evidence would have to be provided to the court to have a marriage annulled on the grounds of bigamy?

8. Is knowledge relevant to the nullity ground concerning the failure to adhere to certain formalities under the Marriage Act? If so, in what way?

What is the difference between sex and gender, and how do they affect the law of nullity?

CHAPTER 3: DIVORCE

1. What are the advantages and disadvantages of a 'no fault' system of divorce?

2. Is fault really dead?

3. With reference to cases and statute, discuss the meaning of irretrievable breakdown.

4. Why and in what way is the relevant child given priority in divorce proceedings?

5. What is separation?

6. Consider the procedural methods of obtaining a maintenance order in the course of divorce proceedings.

7. What role can counselling play as a pre-requisite to instituting divorce proceedings?

8. In light of the case law, is there any room for contested divorces in our present system?

9. In what circumstances would you apply for the dissolution of a marriage on presumption of death, and what are the evidential requirements in such a case?

10. What is a relevant child, and how does a child become relevant by 'acceptance'?

CHAPTER 4: MAINTENANCE

1. What is a dependant, and where do we find statutory recognition of this term?

2. In what way, if any, does the entitlement to maintenance differ between unmarried and married spouses?

3. What are the time limits for the payment of child maintenance and what are the statutory provisions that set out these limitations?

4. In what circumstances does the Maintenance Act apply to grandparents?

5. Why is it important for the court to have the right to adjudicate on private maintenance agreements?

6. In what circumstances can maintenance applications be made in the High Court?

7. Under what statutory provisions can maintenance be granted other than under the Maintenance Act?

8. Consider the penalties for defaulting on maintenance orders which you think would be effective and appropriate for these times.

9. To what extent does the conduct of the parties affect the entitlement to spousal maintenance?

10. Consider in what circumstances you would apply for the different types of orders listed in section 15 of the Maintenance Act.

CHAPTER 5: MATRIMONIAL PROPERTY

1. Compare the definition of spouse in the Maintenance Act with the definition of spouse under the Property (Rights of Spouses) Act (PROSA).

2. What is the difference between the way the law treats the family home and the way the law treats other property under the act? Is there any justification for the distinction?

3. To what extent, if any, does PROSA impinge on inheritance and conveyance laws and practices?

4. Explain the difference between and application under s 11and an application under s 13 of PROSA.

5. Does PROSA have any powers in relation to trusts and settlements? Give reasons and examples for your views.

6. In what circumstances do you think a court is likely to make a lump sum order?

7. Considering the court's powers in relation to pensions, can it be said that the legal principle of privity of contract remains intact?

8. In what circumstances would you consider it advisable to draw up a pre-nuptial agreement, and why?

9. In what circumstances does the law allow an application under PROSA to be made in the Parish Court?

10. What is the significance of a contribution and in what way is it recognized under PROSA?

CHAPTER 6: DOMESTIC VIOLENCE

1. With reference to the Caribbean Domestic Violence Acts, how would you define sexual, financial, and psychological abuse?

2. With reference to the Domestic Violence Act, what is the difference between a protection order and an occupation order?

3. When would you use section 10 of the Matrimonial Causes Act to address an act of domestic violence?

4. What are the advantages of seeking relief under the Domestic Violence Act rather than section 10 of the Matrimonial Causes Act?

5. What is mental injury and how can it be proved?

6. Should a person who exposes a child to domestic violence be granted custody or access to that child, and if so what, if any, safeguards would you include in any order that could be made?

7. What new or additional penalties for domestic violence would you include in the legislation? Give reasons why you think such measures would be an effective deterrent to such behaviour?

CHAPTER 7: CUSTODY

1. Where is the welfare principle set out in statute? In what situations does it apply? Give practical examples.

2. What are the usual orders that a court will make in a custody dispute between the mother and father of a child?

3. Identify the criteria which comprise the welfare checklist and examine any three with the aid of decided case law.

4. Under what legislation and in which courts are custody orders made?

5. With reference to decided cases, summarize the approach of the court when dealing with cross-border custody disputes.

6. What is the difference between guardianship and adoption?

7. In what circumstances does the law state that guardianship orders may be made, and in what circumstances are guardianship orders frequently made in Jamaica? Is there any legal basis for such divergence?

8. Who can apply for custody of a child? What are the reasons for such a restriction and would you recommend any amendment to the law in this respect?

CHAPTER 8: STATUS OF CHILDREN AND PARENTAGE

1. Name two areas of law where questions of paternity frequently arise. Consider the terms and provisions which give rise to these issues.

2. In what situations described in the Status of Children Act, is there evidence of paternity, and to what standard?

3. Why is the declaration of paternity considered to be conclusive proof of paternity?

4. What scientific tests can be used in the process of establishing paternity? How are such tests admitted into evidence?

5. Consider the provisions of two statutes apart from the Status of Children Act that address the question of parentage.

6. Is it possible to ascertain paternity after the death of either the child or the 'father'? If so, what evidence would be used to support such a claim?

CHAPTER 9: CHILDREN AND THE STATE: CARE AND CRIME

1. With reference to the provisions of the Child Care and Protection Act, who is a 'fit person' and in what circumstances will the court make a 'fit person order'?

2. What is child trafficking?

3. What provisions, in addition to section 20 of the Child Care and Protection Act, would you consider to be useful in addressing the difficulties of children giving evidence in court proceedings?

4. What is meant in the Child Care and Protection Act when referring to the best interests of the child, and how is this principle to be applied according to section 65 of the Act?

Bibliography

Altink, Henrice. 'To Wed or Not to Wed? The Struggle to Define Afro-Jamaican Relationships, 1834–1838,' *Journal of Social History* 38, no. 1 (2004): 81.

Anderson, Nancy. 'Behind Closed Doors: Domestic Violence – Is the Law Strong Enough to Stop It?' *West Indian Law Journal* 21, no. 1 (1996): 25–40.

'The Argyll Charade.' *Journal (of the Law Society of Scotland)* (July 1, 1999). Acessed September 2014. http://www.journalonline.co.uk/Magazine/44-7/1001097.aspx.

Barrow, Christine. *Family in the Caribbean: Themes and Perspectives.* Kingston, Jamaica: Ian Randle Publishers, 1996.

Belle Antoine, Rose-Marie. *Commonwealth Caribbean Law and Legal Systems.* 2nd ed. Abingdon, Oxfordshire: Routledge-Cavendish, 2006.

Berry, David, and Tracy Robinson. *Transitions in Caribbean Law: Law-Making, Constitutionalism and the Convergence of National and International Law.* Kingston, Jamaica: The Caribbean Law Publishing Company, 2013.

Boxhill, Eileen. 'Developments in Family since Emancipation,' *West Indian Law Journal* 9, no. 2 (1985): 9–20.

———. 'The Reform of Family Law as it Affects Women.' In *Gender: A Caribbean Multi-Disciplinary Perspective,*' edited by Elsa Leo-Rhynie, Barbara Bailey, and Christine Barrow, 91–105. Kingston, Jamaica: Ian Randle Publishers, 1997.

———. 'Reforming the Law Relating to the Property Rights of Husband and Wife.' Family Law Committee Working paper on Matrimonial Property Reform. n.d.

Brathwaite, Joan A. *Women and the Law: A Bibliographical Survey of Legal and Quasi-Legal Materials.* Kingston, Jamaica: University of the West Indies Press, 1999.

Brown, Antonn. 'Sorry, but Adoption Severs the Legal Ties to Child's Biological Parents or Guardians.' *Daily Observer*, February 28, 2017. Accessed March 1, 2017, http://www.jamaicaobserver.com/news/Sorry--but-adoption-severs-the-legal-ties-to-child-s-biological-parents-or-guardians_90973.

Butler, Sara M. *The Language of Abuse: Marital Violence in Later Medieval England.* vol. 2. Leidon, Netherlands; Boston, MA: Brill, 2007.

Carter, Jediael. 'Marriages Down, Divorces Up – RGD, Statin.' *Sunday Observer*, January 24, 2016. Accessed January 2016. http://www.jamaicaobserver.com/news/Marriages-down--divorces-up-----RGD--STATIN-------_49547.

'Children's Advocate Calls for Lifting of Age of Consent to 18.' *Daily Observer*. November 14, 2014. Accessed February 2016. http://www.jamaicaobserver.com/news/Children-s-Advocate-calls-for-lifting-of-age-of-consent-to-18.

Clark, Anna. 'Project Muse – Domestic Violence, Past and Present.' *Journal of Women's History* 23, no. 3 (2011): 193–202.

Clarke, Edith. *My Mother Who Fathered Me: A Study of Families in Three Selected Communities of Jamaica*. London: Allen and Unwin, 1957.

Clarke, Roberta. 'An Evaluative Study of the Implementation of Domestic Violence Legislation: Antigua and Barbuda, St Kitts/Nevis, St Lucia, and St Vincent and the Grenadines.' Study conducted by The Economic Commission for Latin America and the Caribbean, https://www.cepal.org/mujer/noticias/noticias/4/10934/lccarg659.pdf.

Codlin, Raphael. *Historical Foundations of Jamaican Law*. Kingston, Jamaica: Canoe Press, 2003.

Coontz, Stephanie. *Marriage, A History*. New York, NY: Viking, 2005.

Cretney, Stephen M., Judith Masson and Rebecca Bailey-Harris. *Principles of Family Law*. 7th ed. London, England: Sweet and Maxwell, 2003.

Douglas, Lisa. *The Power of Sentiment: Love, Hierarchy, and the Jamaican Family Elite*. Boulder, CO: Westview Press, 1992.

Elisofon, Howard. 'A Historical and Comparative Study of Bastardy.' *Anglo American Law Review* 2, no. 3 (1973): 306.

Family Law Committee. 'Family Law Committee Report No. 1.' Kingston, Jamaica: Ministry of Justice, 1977.

———. 'Family Law Committee Report on Matrimonial Property Law Reform.' Kingston, Jamaica: Ministry of Justice,1978.

Field, Rachael, Belinda Carpenter and Susan Currie. 'Issues in the making of Ouster orders under the Domestic Violence (Family Protection) Act 1989 (Qld).' In *Family Law: Processes, Practices, and Pressures* edited by John Dewar and Stephen Parker, 99–116. West Sussex: Hart Publishing, 2003.

Finlay, H.A. 'Farewell to Affinity and the Calculus of Kinship.' *University of Tasmania Law Review* 5, no. 1 (1975): 16–32.

Forte, Margaret E. 'Matrimonial Property: The Existing Law in Jamaica.' *Caribbean Journal of Legal Information* 4, no. 1 (1987): 18–22.

———. 'Rights of Women in "Common Law" de facto Unions in Jamaica.' Kingston, Jamaica: Norman Manley Law School, 1982.

Freeman, Michael. 'Taking Child Rights Seriously.' *International Journal of Law and the Family* 6, no. 1 (1992): 52–71.

George, Robert. 'Some Observations on the Social Background: The Family Law in the Caribbean.' *West Indian Law Journal* 9, no. 2 (1985): 21–28.

The *Gleaner*. 'Don't Make Barrel Kids Become Victims – Children's Advocate.' June 11, 2008. Accessed August 2015. http://old.jamaica-gleaner.com/gleaner/20080611/news/news5.html.

Harris-Short, Sonia, and Joanna Miles. *Family Law: Text, Cases and Materials*. 2nd ed. Oxford: Oxford University Press, 2011.

Henriques, Fernando. *Family and Colour in Jamaica*. 2nd ed. London: MacGibbon and Kee, 1968.

Henriques, R.N.A. 'Inheritance Family Provisions.' *West Indian Law Journal* 1 (1978): 40–44

Human Rights Watch. *Nobody's Children': Jamaican Children in Police Detention and Government Institutions*. New York, NY: Human Rights Watch, 1999.

International Covenant on Civil and Political Rights. December 16, 1966. Article 16: Right of everyone to be recognized as a person before the law and Article 23: Right to Marry.

Jackson, Leighton Milton. 'Family Law and Domestic Violence in the Eastern Caribbean: Judicial and Legislative Reforms.' Summary of Research Reports, 2002.

———. 'Fi Wi Law.' In *Transitions in Caribbean Law: Law-Making, Constitutionalism and the Convergence of National and International Law*, edited by David Berry and Tracy Robinson, 3–32. Kingston, Jamaica: Ian Randle Publishers, 2013.

———. *The Law Relating to Children in Jamaica*. Kingston, Jamaica: Ministry of Justice, 1984.

———. 'The Procedure in Child Custody Cases.' *West Indian Law Journal* 8, no. 1 (1984): 64–82.

———. 'Some Difficulties with the Status of Children Acts'. Cave Hill, Barbados: Faculty of Law, University of the West indies, 1985.

Jamaica Bar Association. 'When Divorce Becomes Necessary.' *JAMBAR*, 1996.

James, Richard. 'Jamaican Migration Theory: Shift in Family Dynamics in Jamaican Families.' In *International Encyclopedia of Marriage and Families* edited by James J. Ponzetti, PAGE NUMBERS? New York, NY: Macmillan, 2003.

Jemmott, Jenny M. *Ties That Bind: The Black Family in Post-slavery Jamaica, 1834–1882*. Kingston: Jamaica: University of the West Indies Press, 2015.

Jones, Angela. 'Battered Women in the Jamaican Society.' In *Status of Women in the Caribbean: Report of Regional Seminar held* at *Wyndham Hotel, Kingston, Jamaica, 10–11 December 1987*. Kingston, Jamaica: Bustamante Institute of Public and International Affairs, 1988.

Kaime, Thoko. *The African Charter on the Rights and Welfare of the Child: A Socio-legal Perspective*. Pretoria, South Africa: Pretoria University Law Press, 2009.

Kodilinye, Lystra. 'Access: Is it the Right of the Parent or the Right of the Child? A Commonwealth View.' *International and Comparative Law Quarterly* 41, no. 1 (1992): 190–99.

———. 'The Judicial determination of Child Custody Issues in the Commonwealth Caribbean.' In Commonwealth Commonwealth Caribbean Legal Studies, edited by Gilbert Kodilinye and P.K. Menon, 219–50. London: Butterworth 1992.

LaFont, Suzanne. 'Baby-mothers and Baby-fathers: Conflict and Family Court Use in Kingston, Jamaica.' PhD dissertation, Yale University, 1992.

Law Commission. 'Reforming the Law Relating to the Property Rights of Husband and Wife.' Kingston, Jamaica: Law Commission, 1977.

Lazarus-Black, Mindie. 'Bastardy, Gender Hierarchy, and the State: The Politics of Family Law Reform in Antigua and Barbuda.' *Law and Society Review* 26, no. 4 (1992): 863–900.

———. *Legitimate Acts and Illegal Encounters: Law and Society in Antigua and Barbuda*. Washington, DC: Smithsonian Institution Press, 1994.

———. 'My Mother Never Fathered Me: Re-thinking Kinship and the Governing of Families, Should Paternity Really Be the Issue.' Paper presented at the Law and Society Association Annual Meeting, 1994.

Leo-Rhynie, E.A. 'Class, Race and Gender Issues in Child Rearing in the Caribbean.' In *Advances in Applied Developmental Psychology – Caribbean Families: Diversity among Ethnic Groups*, edited by J.L. Roopnarine and J. Brown, 25–55. Westport, CT: Ablex Publishing, 1997.

Mbiti, John S. *African Religions and Philosophy*. 2nd ed. Oxford: Heinemann, 1990.

McDowell, Zanifa. *Elements of Child Law in the Commonwealth Caribbean*. Kingston, Jamaica: The University of the West Indies Press, 2000.

McGregor, Sherry-Ann. 'Father by Fraud' – Laws of Eve. *Daily Gleaner*. June 19, 2017. Accessed June 2017. http://jamaica-gleaner.com/article/flair/20170619/laws-eve-father-fraud.

———. 'Paternity Fraud' – Laws of Eve. *Daily Gleaner*. January 18, 2010. Accessed November 2015. http://jamaica-gleaner.com/gleaner/20100118/flair/flair7.html.

———. 'Whose "Jacket" is it?' – Laws of Eve. *Daily Gleaner*. September 5, 2016. Accessed June 2017. http://www2.jamaica-gleaner.com/article/flair/20160905/laws-eve-whose-jcket-it.

Monahan, Geoff, and Lisa Young. *Family Law in Australia*. 6th ed. Chatswood, New South Wales: LexisNexis Butterworths, 2006.

Moore, Brian L., and Michele A. Johnson. *Neither Led Nor Driven: Contesting British Cultural Imperialism in Jamaica 1865–1920*. Kingston, Jamaica: University of the West Indies Press, 2010.

Mortimer, Ronnie. 'Spousal Maintenance: A "Meal Ticket" For Life.' *Solicitor's Journal* February 28, 2017.

Morrison, C. Dennis. 'Affiliation Proceedings: Aspects of Jamaican Law and Practice.' *West Indian Law Journal* 5, no. 1(1981): 17–26.

Moyne, Baron. *Jamaica Royal Commission Report* (The Moyne Report). London, England: The Royal Commission, 1938; reprinted with an Introduction by Denis Benn, Kingston, Jamaica: Ian Randle Publishers, 2011.

Nunez Tesheira, Karen. *Commonwealth Caribbean Family Law: Husband, Wife and Cohabitant*. New York, NY: Routledge, 2016.

O'Halloran, Kerry. 'Adoption-a Public or Private Legal Process? The Changing Social Functions of Adoption in Ireland and the Wider Implications for Coherence in Family Law.' In *Family Law: Processes, Practices, Pressures*, edited by John Dewar and Stephen Parker, 195–220. West Sussex: Hart Publishing, 2003.

Office of The Children's Advocate. *Recommendations to the Houses of Parliament Focusing on The Uncontrollable Child*. Kingston, Jamaica: Office of The Children's Advocate, 2013.

Patchett, Keith. 'English Law in the West Indies: A Conference Report.' *International and Comparative Law Quarterly* 12, no. 13 (1963): 922–66.

Pomeroy, Sarah B. *Wife Beating in Ancient Rome*. Cambridge, MA: Harvard University Press, 2007.

———. The Murder of Regilla – A Case of Domestic Violence in Antiquity.' Cambridge, MA: Harvard University Press, 2010.

Ramsaran, Dave. 'Globalization and Children's Rights in the English-speaking Caribbean.' In *Children's Rights: Caribbean Realities*, edited by Christine Barrow, 171–88. Kingston, Jamaica: Ian Randle Publishers, 2002.

Rayden, William, and J. Jackson. *Law and Practice in Divorce and Family Matters*. 15th ed. London: Butterworth & Co Publishers Ltd, 1988.

Reece, Helen. 'The Paramountcy Principle: Consensus or Construct.' *Current Legal Problems* 49, no.1 (January 1 1996): 267–304.

Rehman, Javaid. *International Human Rights Law: A Practical Approach*. 1st ed. Harlow, England; New York, NY: Pearson Longman, 2003.

Report of the Commission Appointed to Enquire into the System of Education in Jamaica (1898), The Lumb Report. Kingston, Jamaica 1898.

Risden-Foster, Suzanne. 'Flight or Right? Custody and Access in International Child Abduction Cases: Emerging Issues in Jamaica.' West Indian Law Journal 34, no. 2 (2009): 145–80.

Russell-Brown, Pauline A., Beverly Norville and Cheryl Griffiths. 'Child Shifting, a Survival Strategy for Teenage Mothers.' In Caribbean Families: Diversity Among Ethnic Groups, edited by Jaipaul L. Roopnarine and Janet Brown, 223–42. Greenwich, CT: Ablex Publishing Corporation,1997.

Roiphe, Katie. Uncommon Arrangements: Seven Portraits of Married Life in London Literary Circles 1910–1939. New York, NY: Dial Press, 2007.

Shepherd, Verene. Women in Caribbean History. Kingston, Jamaica: Ian Randle Publishers, 1998.

———. Working Slavery, Pricing Freedom: Perspectives from the Caribbean, Africa and African Diaspora. Kingston, Jamaica: Ian Randle Publishers, 1999.

Statistical Institute of Jamaica (STATIN). Demographic Statistics: Marriages and Divorces. Kingston, Jamaica: STATIN, 2015.

Stubbs-Gibson, Sheena. 'Bastards Are Still Around: PNP's Boast Incorrect.' Sunday Gleaner, September 20, 2015. Accessed September 2015. http://www2.jamaica-gleaner.com/article/news/20150920/bastards-are-still-around-pnps-boast-incorrect.

Thompson-Ahye, Hazel. 'Domestic Violence and Legal Protection in the Bahamas? A Reality or an Illusion.' West Indian Law Journal 29, no. 1 (2004): 73–85.

———. 'Women and Family and Related Issues: 229 Questions Answered.' St. Augustine, Trinidad: Hazel Thompson-Ahye, 2002.

Thorpe, Matthew, Phillip Waller, Mark Everall, Nigel Dyer, Rebecca J. Bailey-Harris, and Stephan Trowell. Rayden and Jackson on Divorce and Family Matters, 18th ed. London: LexisNexis Butterworths, 2016.

Tolstoy, D. 'Void and Voidable Marriages.' Modern Law Review 27, no. 4 (1964): 85–94.

United Nations. Convention on the Civil Aspects of International Child Abduction. 1980.

———. The Convention on the Elimination of All Forms of Discrimination against Women. December 18 1979. Article 16(a) and (b) the right to not be discriminated against in marriage.

———. The Convention on the Rights of Persons with Disabilities. 2006.

———. The Convention of the Rights of the Child. 1989.

———. *Universal Declaration of Human Rights.* Adopted by the General Assembly of the United Nations, December 10, 1948.

US Department of State. *Trafficking in Persons Report, Country Narrative: Jamaica.* Washington, DC: US Department of State, 2016.

Welstead, Mary, and Susan Edwards. *Family Law.* Oxford: Oxford University Press, 2006.

White, Dorcas. 'Patterns of Law Making in the West Indies.' Cave Hill, Barbados: University of the West Indies Law Library, n.d.

Wilson, Damian. 'Legal Aid for Children in Court for Being Uncontrollable.' Press release, The Ministry of Justice, August 15, 2013. http://moj.gov.jm/sites/default/files/Press%20Release%20 re%20Legal%20Representation%20of%20Children%20in%20 Court%20for%20being%20Uncontrollable.pdf.

Women Safe. 'Overview of Historical Laws that Supported Domestic Violence.' Womensafe.net. Accessed January 2017. http://www. womensafe.net/home/index.php/domesticviolence/29-overview- of-historical-laws-that-supported-domestic-violence.

Women's Aid Federation of England. *An Historical Perspective on Legal and Cultural Attitudes to Domestic Abuse.* The Woman's Aid Expect Respect Education Toolkit. http://www.womensaid.org.uk/ historicalperspective

World Health Organization (WHO). *Mental Health Aspects of Women's Reproductive Health: A Global Review of the Literature.* Geneva: WHO, 2009.

Index

of care and protection, 356; property of, 264; warrants for search and detention of, 358–59

Children (Adoption of) Act, 306–11

Children (Guardianship and Custody) Act: application for maintenance orders under the, 159; and child maintenance, 60, 110, 154–56; and custody, 258, 260–301, 322–23; inherent jurisdiction under the, 283; and minimum age, 43; and powers of the Supreme Court, 383; the welfare principle in the, 263–68

Children's advocate: responsibilities of the, 353–54, 368, 374

Children's Court: powers of the, 359–65, 377

Children's Register: responsibilities of the, 354–56

Chin v Chin: and fairness in division of property, 186–88

Church: and divorce, 35; and marriage, 1; and nullity, 32–33

Civil law: and domestic violence, 235–37

Civil Procedure Rules (CPR): and custody applications, 290; divorce and Part 76 of the, 91; and domestic violence, 251–52; and the Marriage Act, 28

Cohabit: right to, 25

Cohabitation: definition of, 125; application for property division and termination of, 217–18; division of property and duration of, 209; presumption of, 82–83; and spousal maintenance, 60; and the spousal relationship, 191; and social norms, 29

Colonial law: influence on the independent state, 46

Common law: custody and the, 279; and division of property, 188, 212, 213–14, 221; and marriages, 7, 10–18; and parental status, 263; and paternity, 318

Common law marriages, 7; and division of property, 209

Commonwealth Caribbean Jurisprudence, xviii, xix, 46. *See also* Antigua and Barbuda, Anguilla, Barbados, Belize, St Kitts and Nevis.

Conjugal rights: courts powers and, 112

Consanguinity: legal concept of, 15; prohibited degrees of, 43–47, 63

Consent: age of, 63

Consortium: concept of, 23–24

Constructive trusts: and division of matrimonial property, 181–82; and unjust enrichment, 182–83

Consummation: in marriage, 25

Constitutional Court: and family law, 386–87

Continuity: of separation, 81–82

Convention on the Elimination of All Forms of Discrimination Against Women (CEDAW): and the right to marry, 53

Convention on the Rights of Persons with Disabilities: and right to marry, 53

Corbett v Corbett: and sex v gender, 54

Costs: and family property, 229–31

Courts: family law and the, 376–89; and guidelines for spousal maintenance orders, 132–37; Maintenance Act and powers of the, 122–25, 153–54; maintenance orders and jurisdiction of, 158–60; MCA and the powers of the, 153–54; MWPA: and powers of the, 207–208

Court of Appeal: case citations, xxiii; and family law, 384–86

Court of Judicial Review: and family law, 386–87

Cowley v Cowley: and right to married name, 114

Creditors: matrimonial property and protection of, 225–26

Criminal law: and children, 370–373; and domestic violence, 234–35

Criminal offences: under the Marriage Act, 21

Custody, 256–312; and access, 284–289; agreements, 280–281; applications, 290–93, 322–23, 379, 383–84; care and control and, 273–74; hearings, 292–94; legislation, 260–300; Minors Act (Anguilla) and, 260; orders, 269–70, 278–80, 294–96; parental status and, 269; proceedings, 252, 289–98; Supreme Court and, 383; and the welfare principle, 259–60,264

Custodial responsibility, 340

Darby v Darby: and the right to spousal maintenance, 127–28

DaSilva v DaSilva: and non-compliance with the Marriage Act, 11

Death: divorce on presumption of, 83–84; and division of property, 212; and the family home, 196;

Declaration of property ownership, 221–22, 380

Declaration of paternity, 315, 317, 333–34, 380, 384

Decree absolute: filing for the, 98–99, 102; rescission of the,

105–107; restrictions to granting the, 102–105; and spousal maintenance, 114; v divorce order, 107–108

Decree of dissolution: and application for property division, 217

Decree nisi: filing for the, 58, 98–99, 100–101, rescission of the, 101; and spousal maintenance, 114

Default proceedings: and nullity, 58–59

Defended divorce, 97–98

Deniz: and fraud, 49

Dependants: definition of, 141–42, 160

Discipline: children and, 349

Dissenters' Marriage Act, 4

Divorce, 5, 65–116; affidavit of service in, 95–97; defended and undefended, 97–98; and division of the family home, 195–96; legal effects of, 113–16; and matrimonial property, 115–16; and nullity, 32–33; parties to a, 73–74; petition, 91–94; proceedings, 89–98; restriction in, 94; and right to inherit, 115; Supreme Court and, 381

Divorce Act: in the Caribbean, 55; and nullity, 35–36,

Divorce Law (1879): historical overview of the, 67–68

Divorce petition: proof of marriage and, 92; relevant children and, 93

DNA evidence: and proof of paternity, 326, 336–38, 343

Domestic violence: applications for protection from, 379; civil law and, 235–36; criminal law and, 234–35; definition of, 238–39; help lines, 255; legislation,

www.ingramcontent.com/pod-product-compliance
Lightning Source LLC
Chambersburg PA
CBHW052102230326
41599CB00054B/3590